The Philosophy of
Death Reader

D1522883

The Philosophy of Death Reader

Cross-cultural readings on immortality and the afterlife

Edited and Annotated by Markar Melkonian

Epicurus*

---

*Line drawing from post-Hellenistic sculpture, 1972 by Markar Melkonian.

BLOOMSBURY ACADEMIC
LONDON · NEW YORK · OXFORD · NEW DELHI · SYDNEY

BLOOMSBURY ACADEMIC
Bloomsbury Publishing Plc
50 Bedford Square, London, WC1B 3DP, UK
1385 Broadway, New York, NY 10018, USA

BLOOMSBURY, BLOOMSBURY ACADEMIC and the Diana logo are trademarks of
Bloomsbury Publishing Plc

First published in Great Britain 2019

Cover design by Eleanor Rose
Cover image: The Last Judgement (oil on panel), Hieronymus Bosch (c.1450–1516) /
Akademie der Bildenden Kunste, Vienna, Austria / Bridgeman Images

A catalogue record for this book is available from the British Library.

A catalog record for this book is available from the Library of Congress.

ISBN: HB: 978-1-3500-6934-3
PB: 978-1-3500-6933-6
ePDF: 978-1-3500-6935-0
eBook: 978-1-3500-6937-4

Typeset by Deanta Global Publishing Services, Chennai, India
Printed and bound in Great Britain

To find out more about our authors and books visit www.bloomsbury.com
and sign up for our newsletters.

Contents

Part IV Problems with Immortality

Part V Living with Mortality

Preface:
What This Book Is (Not) About

This book is more sharply focused than other philosophy of death readers. For one thing, it is not a book of applied ethics: in these pages you will not find out about the rightness or wrongness of suicide, abortion, euthanasia, the death penalty, killing in war, or killing nonhuman animals for food. Nor is this book concerned much about the strange and wondrous things that people have believed about death: it does not focus on anthropological, sociological, or psychological topics relating to death, and it does not delve into the funerary rites of cultures in different times and climes, nor attitudes and institutions of dying, bereavement, mourning, and acceptance. A recent Google search for the keyword *death* turned up 1.8 billion hits. It would be a safe bet that the larger part of this material does not concern itself with death at all, properly speaking, but rather with *dying*. Dying, though, is a process that only a living thing can undergo. As such, bereavement, mourning, and even fear of dying should not be the chief concerns of a book on the philosophy of death.

What then is this book about? It is about the nature of death, what it is, and perhaps more revealingly, what it is *not*. In this book we will consider such questions as: Does the mind or soul share the same fate as the body? If not, then what sort of thing is it? What sense can we make of the claim that *persons*, or at least some of them, survive after the death of the body? If persons somehow do survive, then where do they go, how do they get there, and in what form? If the belief in a personal afterlife is the belief that a given consciousness does not end with bodily death, then are there good reasons, scientific, experiential, or supernatural, to believe in it? If there is a soul, is it immortal? Can anything at all *experience* death? If so, then what sort of thing? Is there anything that it is *like* to be dead? If so, then what is it like? What in heaven's name could it mean to claim, as some philosophers and religious thinkers have, that "impersonal survival" follows a person's death? Questions as broad as these, about the nature of things such as immortality, personal identity, and the soul and its fate are sometimes called *metaphysical* questions.[1]

In later readings, we will also explore questions such as: Is death a misfortune? If so, then for whom? Or for what? Is the fear of it rational? If it turns out that death can be a bad thing, would immortality be better? And in view of these considerations, is it prudent or even possible to live from day to day with death in mind? These sorts of general questions having to do with *values* like desirability and misfortune, goodness and badness, importance and unimportance are called *axiological* questions.

Although the scope of this book is narrower than that of other philosophy of death textbooks, the readings range widely across the centuries and the continents. A glance at the table of contents will reveal several titles from religious traditions—Vedanta, Buddhist doctrines, and Christian apologetics. Be not afraid: this is first and foremost a *philosophy* book, not a book on comparative religions. It is dedicated to the *philosophical* examination of death and the afterlife. We are here concerned with analyzing and critically evaluating *arguments* that people have given for and against beliefs about what, if anything, will happen to you after you die.

As we will see, though, not all of the readings contain *compelling* arguments; indeed, several of them appear to fall short at pivotal points when it comes to evidential or logical support for the doctrines that are defended. More than one of the readings might contain arguments that are shaky and appear to rely for their believability on the authority of divine revelation. Here we encounter the well-known theme of the conflict of faith and reason. Perhaps faith should or must override reason in many contexts. In any case, there is something to learn from a weak argument, so we will be examining several of these, too. Once we do this, readers are free to evaluate alternative arguments for themselves.

Even with our sharp focus, then, it would seem that we have a lot of interesting ground to cover.

Our readings fall into five parts, each dealing with a particular problem in the philosophy of death. There are problems having to do with the immortality of the disembodied soul (Part I) and personal survival of the

---

[1]The word *metaphysics* is notoriously hard to define. It has been described as the study of "things that do not change," "being as such," and "first causes," or as the examination of such tricky topics as substance, space and time, causation, and modality. Metaphysics, in the modern usage of the word, is comprised of a number of topics that might or might not be closely related, including the relation of mind and body, freedom of will, and personal identity across time.

embodied soul by rebirth (Part II) and by bodily resurrection (Part III). In Part IV we consider some of the challenges that the doctrine of immortality of the soul faces, including the question whether immortality is at all a state to be wished for, and then speculations about mortality and circular time. Finally, in Part V, we turn to the question of how to live with mortality, including thoughts about how to valorize mortal lives within the much larger context of an ongoing collective life. Although the problems are distinct, they are interrelated in ways that should become clear.

The readings in Parts I, II, and III address the question whether the body and the soul share the same fate. We will see that, in the course of trying to answer this question, thinkers since before Plato have committed themselves to one or another particular conception of what sort of thing a soul is. Philosophers inform us that, as one of their representatives put it, "It is the mind that sees and hears and feels and thinks and chooses—in a word, is conscious."[2] The mind, we are told, is the *person*, or the *self*. As we will see in the General Introduction, many contemporary biologists and neuroscientists believe that the mind just is part of the brain, or one of the things that the brain does, and that when the higher functions of the brain cease, the mind, person, and self go the way of all passing things. But what if there is something more to the mind, self, or soul than contemporary biologists and neuroscientists have described, and what if this "something more" does not cease to exist when a body dies? This is certainly Plato's view, in our reading in Part I.

In Part II, we will consider traditional views that hold that after we die our souls, or at any rate something important *about us*, is sooner or later taken up in another body, whether human or otherwise. This is the doctrine of reincarnation, or *rebirth*. We will encounter two versions of this doctrine, one from the *Katha Upanishad*, an Indian text from the fifth century BC, and the other from the *Milinda Pañha*, or *The Questions of King Milinda*. According to the *Katha Upanishad*, after you have been reborn many times, you will cease to exist as a distinct person or soul, but "your" consciousness *itself* will not disappear; rather, it will meld into a larger cosmic consciousness or Absolute, and somehow "merge with the One." These claims are characteristic of a view that is sometimes called *impersonal survival*. By contrast, Walpola Rahula's account of Nirvana and the cessation of rebirth comes close to the doctrine of *non-survival*, the view that after a person dies

---

[2]Peter Geach, *God and the Soul* (New York: Schocken Books, 1969), 18–19.

that person and its "consciousness," too, no longer exist. To round out the discussion, we will consider objections to the doctrine of rebirth from the ancient Indian school of Charvaka, the "World Outlook of the People."

The readings in Part III address another widespread picture of the afterlife, but one that is very different from the picture of rebirth. Traditional Jewish, Christian, and Muslim doctrines of Judgment Day, Resurrection, Heaven, and Hell describe a soul that differs greatly from the deathless soul that Plato's Socrates describes. It is a central tenet of Judaism, Christianity, and Islam, at least in their orthodox interpretations, that the human person consists of a body and a soul united, and that bodily death puts an end to a *person*, at least temporarily, in the same way that a divorce puts an end to a marriage. Orthodox believers claim that the human person, like the body, is not immortal by nature, but that the Almighty is well capable of reconstituting the body, reuniting it with the soul, and bringing a complete person back to life. On a promised Day of Judgment, everyone who has ever died will be resurrected, body and soul. By granting some of us life everlasting, God rewards obedience, faith, and perhaps good works too, and punishes evil. In this way the Creator steps in to set things right, to ensure that justice, so obviously outraged here on Earth, will win out in the end. In our first reading in Part III, we will encounter an influential presentation of this orthodox view, from the pen of none other than Thomas Aquinas, the great systematic thinker of the late Middle Ages. Then, the Scottish Enlightenment thinker David Hume will argue that this view cannot stand up to rational scrutiny. After that, we will consider two recent philosophical defenses of the doctrine of resurrection, presenting two very different views of what it is that survives bodily death, and how it survives.

Readings in Parts IV and V explore conflicting views of personal survival and non-survival, when it comes to prospects for happiness in this life. Part IV begins with Lucretius' sweeping picture of mortal humans struggling under the sun, but unconcerned about the prospect of death. By contrast, the Spanish-Basque philosopher Miguel de Unamuno insists that even "the tortures of hell" are preferable to the "nothingness" of death: "It is better to live in pain," he writes, "than to cease to be in peace." Bernard Williams' influential paper, "The Makropulos Case," appears next, as a comeback to Unamuno's powerful paper, and then Lisa Bortolotti and Yujin Nagasawa present what they believe is a corrective to Williams. In our last reading in Part IV, we turn to the strange hypothesis of *eternal return*, the doctrine that the same events occurring in the same sequence have occurred infinitely many times in the past and will occur infinitely many times in the future.

The idea of eternal return rejects the notion of an immortal soul, and it does not require any notion of rebirth or resurrection, either. Nevertheless, it could in a sense countenance something like an "after"-life.

In Part V we will consider how to live with mortality. In an influential paper, the philosopher Thomas Nagel will argue that death is bad because of what it deprives us of. The next reading, by Samuel Scheffler, provides a startlingly fresh insight on the topic of our "lived relation to death." Susan Wolf then offers her critical insights on Scheffler's version of the afterlife. In our last reading Beverley Clack shifts the perspective to the social and ideological context of prevailing assumptions about death. Far from comprising timeless reflections on a universal theme, these assumptions have only achieved the status of unchallenged truth in recent decades, within the context of frenetic capital accumulation, the near-total subordination of labor to capital, and the resulting monopoly of a set of economic articles of faith associated with the term *neoliberalism*.

In broad contours, then, this is the road that lies ahead. But first things first: let us consider the facts of life.

Acknowledgments

The form that this book has taken has much to do with classroom discussions, written work, and conversations with students in my upper division and lower division Philosophy of Death courses at the large public university where I have taught for years. These students, like the students in my other classes, have come from a wide range of backgrounds, with a wide range of academic preparation, English language abilities, and life experiences. More than one of them has thanked me for a life-changing semester. But it might not have been apparent to my students how much I have learned from them. Thank you, dear students, for teaching me so much.

This book is in much better shape thanks to the hard work of Colleen Coalter, my editor at Bloomsbury Academic. Preparing a textbook for publication is a tedious process, and Colleen met the challenges with good sense and patience. Flaws in this work are due to my intransigence in the face of her their better advice.

I am grateful, too, for the criticisms and suggestions of Bloomsbury Academic's anonymous reviewers. Thanks are due to my long-time collaborator, Levon Chorbajian of the University of Massachusetts, Lowell, for his readiness at all times to give good counsel. Thanks are also due to Tamar Cienfuegos Melkonian for her digital graphics prowess.

Finally, I want to thank Suzy Melkonian, as always, for her patience, her ideas, and her constant support. This book is dedicated to her, and to our three muses, Sureya, Tamar, and Narineh, who could hardly care less about the topic. Such people do exist.

Great efforts have been made to obtain permission to reproduce copyrighted material. If any proper acknowledgment has not been made, or permission not received, I invite copyright holders to inform me of the oversight.

General Introduction:
What Is the Meaning of "Life"?

If one does not yet know life, how should he know death?

—Attributed to Confucius

... to say that life does not consist of chemical processes is to my mind as futile and untrue as to say that poetry does not consist of words.

—J.B.S. Haldane[1]

In this introduction, we will try to settle on a baseline definition of death. First we will consider in broad terms what contemporary biology has to say about the matter. In the second section we will say a few words about the relationship between the "higher functions" of the brain and the mind or consciousness. We will then be in a position to distinguish between two contemporary science-based conceptions of death: *biological death* and *brain death*. These two conceptions are closely related in ways that can be described in the vocabulary of contemporary forensic pathology. In the third and final sections of this introduction we will draw on these insights to examine some important logical and conceptual relationships between life and our biologically informed conceptions of death.

Of course, this will not definitively resolve the question whether the body and the soul share the same fate. Nevertheless, by the end of this introduction we should be in a better position to understand and evaluate the readings that follow, starting with Part I. Before that, though, let us get our bearings when it comes to popular beliefs about death and the afterlife.

Most adults these days believe that after they die they will continue to exist somewhere, in one form or another. According to a recent report by the Pew Research Center, seven in ten Americans (72 percent of them) say they believe in heaven, defined as a place "where people who have led good lives

---

[1] *What Is Life?* (London: Acuin Press, 1949), 62.

are eternally rewarded," and 58 percent of U.S. adults also believe in hell—a place "where people who have led bad lives and die without being sorry are eternally punished."[2] According to a 2003 Harris Poll, 84 percent of American adults believe that they possess a soul that will survive after the death of their bodies.[3] Another poll conducted the same year by a religiously oriented research group corroborates these findings: according to the California-based Barna Group poll, eight out of ten adult Americans (81 percent) believe in an afterlife of some sort, while another 9 percent agreed that life after death may exist, but were not certain. Moreover, a large majority of Americans (79 percent) agreed with the statement, "every person has a soul that will live forever, either in God's presence or absence." Only 10 percent of the respondents agreed that after dying on Earth, one's life ceases. (Surprisingly, the same poll also found that "Half of all atheists and agnostics say that every person has a soul, that Heaven and Hell exist, and that there is life after death.")[4]

To internationalize the picture, let us consider the results of a 2011 poll conducted by a global research company. The Ipsos Social Research Institute polled 18,000 people in twenty-three countries and found that 51 percent believe that there is an afterlife, while only 23 percent believe they will just "cease to exist." The remainder, about one-quarter of the people polled, indicated that they simply do not know what, if anything, will happen to them after they die.[5]

If the polling results are to be believed, then, it seems that large majorities of respondents believe that after they die, they—or something very important about them, something that we could call consciousness, selfhood, personhood, or a soul—continue to exist. In poll after poll a majority of respondents claim to believe in what we might call the *survival*

[2]Carlye Murphy, "Most Americans Believe in Heaven . . . and Hell," *2014 Religious Landscape Study* (Pew Research Center, Religion and Public Life, November 10, 2015).
[3]Humphrey Taylor, "The Religious and Other Beliefs of Americans," *The Harris Poll* no. 11 (February 26, 2003), http://www.harrisinteractive.com/vault/Harris-Interactive-Poll-Research-The-Religious-and-Other-Beliefs-of-Americans-2003-2003-02.pdf (accessed September 27, 2013).
[4]Barna Group, "Americans Describe Their Views about Life after Death" (Ventura, CA: Barna Group, 2003), https://www.barna.org/barna-update/article/5-barna-update/128-americans-describe-their-views-about-life-after-death#.UkXDBiihCFI (accessed September 27, 2013).
[5]Ariel R. Rey, *Christian Post Reporter* (April 26, 2011), http://www.christianpost.com/news/global-poll-most-believe-in-god-afterlife-49994/ (accessed September 27, 2013). The countries polled were Argentina, Australia, Belgium, Brazil, Canada, China, France, Germany, Great Britain, Hungary, India, Indonesia, Italy, Japan, Mexico, Poland, Russia, Saudi Arabia, South Africa, South Korea, Spain, Sweden, Turkey, and the United States.

hypothesis: the claim that, with respect to some living entities, notably humans, *there is a seat of consciousness, or perhaps just consciousness itself, that continues to exist after bodily death.*

This observation might come as a surprise, since it seems to fly in the face of everyday experience. It is safe to say that hundreds of generations in far-flung societies have noticed what we ourselves have observed, namely, that after an animal dies it no longer moves itself, eats, or reproduces, and it decomposes, usually in short order. Since the body clearly does not last long after dying, what exactly is this thing that is supposed to survive after a human has died?

Well, the atoms that comprise you as a living thing will remain after your bones or ashes have decomposed. But the remains of a once-living thing, whether atoms, ashes, or a cadaver, are only one kind of many enduring consequences of a life that has ceased. Those other consequences, myriads of them, continue to reverberate across an organism's larger environment after it has died, the way a voice continues to echo after the vocal chords are stilled. Every footprint left in the sand, every paper cup crumpled and tossed, every bit of good or bad advice given, every photon of light the skin has reflected, every change that a life has wrought has made a difference that in turn has made a difference, however infinitesimally slight, on the passing scene. Beyond the most immediate effects of a life, of course, it is hard to say what those consequences are, across the unimaginably vast and finely interlaced fabric of interactions that constitutes our *environment*, in the broadest sense of the word. But these overlapping and ever-dilating consequences clearly do not count as the *afterlife* of the thing that has died—not *literally* in any case—any more than the shockwave of a supernova counts as the afterlife of the star that has exploded.

Poets have depicted death as a sort of entity, a dark cloud perhaps, or a shadow, or a figure standing in the gloom just beyond our circle of light. As we will see, though, philosophers have provided reasons to doubt these pictures. Whatever else death may be, one does not often hear objections to the view that, at least in one common understanding, it is a *property* or *state* of something—or a property or state of *the remains* of something—that had once been alive. One may speak of the "death" of a star or of the theater, but one speaks of these things only *metaphorically*, as having once lived or been alive. As long as the force of helium fusion in the core of a low-mass star balances the force of gravity, or as long as the theatre is a vibrant institution, we may say that they are *alive*—in a metaphorical sense. Neither stars nor theatres have nervous systems of course, nor do they have respiratory systems, chloroplasts, or anything functionally equivalent to these things, as far as we know. When it comes to talk about dead stars and institutions, we assume that the case at hand is similar—in one or several ways, but not in *many* ways—to exemplary comparison cases, in this case, perhaps, an organism or the remains of an organism.

A biological definition of *life* and a related definition of *death*

Here is a common and rather flat definition: *death is the irreversible cessation of life*.[6] Or consider the slightly more informative *Wikipedia* one-liner: *death is the permanent cessation of all biological functions that sustain a living organism*. If death is the permanent cessation of life,[7] then the question immediately arises, *what is life?* In this section we will take a closer look at this question.

First, though, let us notice that the formulation *death is the cessation of life* is not altogether uninformative. If it does nothing else, at least it identifies a logical relationship between life and death, namely, that they are predicates of contraries: one and the same thing cannot be both alive and dead at one and the same time. (Of course this is not to say that something *alive* cannot be *dying*, and vice versa. Indeed, something dying *must* be alive. But more about this later.) It would seem, then, that *life and death are perfectly exclusive states*; moreover, if death is the *irreversible* cessation of life, then of course the phrase *life after death*, applied to an entity that is no longer alive, is an oxymoron, like the term *square circle*.

As it turns out, the question *what is life?* is not easy to answer. Peter H. Raven and George B. Johnson, authors of a widely used college biology textbook, tell a story about two astronauts exploring a planet who encounter

---

[6]*Dorland's Illustrated Medical Dictionary* (Philadelphia: W.B. Sanders Company, 1985) defines death "for legal and medical purposes" as "the irreversible cessation of all of the following: (1) total cerebral function, (2) spontaneous function of the respiratory system, and (3) spontaneous function of the circulatory system." Notice that, according to this "definition," an orchid, a virus, and the mushroom in your soup cannot be dead, either. For one thing, they have no cerebrums, let alone cerebral functions. So however useful the "definition" may be for medical and legal purposes, it is not very useful for biologists.
[7]By defining death as the *irreversible* cessation of life, though, we prejudge such doctrines as rebirth and resurrection, discussed in readings starting with Part II.

a blob. Naturally, they want to know if it is alive. How might they go about trying to determine this? First, they might observe the blob, to see if it moves. Self-movement, or "motility," has long been seen as a hallmark of animal life. Then perhaps they might poke it with a stick, to try to detect sensitivity or responsiveness. After that, as good Americans, they will try to kill it. If it can die, then presumably it is—or *was*—alive. But again the question arises: how would they know that it is *dead* if they cannot first know that it is *alive*? Raven and Johnson conclude that the ability to die is a "terribly inadequate criterion" of life, because unless one can detect life in the first place, "death is a meaningless concept."[8]

Actually, the ability to die is an even worse criterion of life than Raven and Johnson thought it was when they wrote:

> All living things die, whereas no inanimate objects do. Death is not easily discriminated from disorder, however; a car that breaks down does not die— it was never alive. Death is simply the absence of life.[9]

Dying, as we've noted, is a process that only a living thing can undergo; however, it is not true that "all living things die." Unknown trillions of organisms alive today will never die: their vital functions will never cease due to aging, predation, starvation, disease, dehydration, or trauma resulting in terminal injury. An amoeba, for instance, need not die: more often, at some point its nucleus divides by pinching into two equal halves, and then the entire organism divides, resulting in two organisms where before there had been but one. In the process, the original amoeba never loses the attributes that we commonly associate with a living thing: it never loses its ability to move itself, to absorb food, to excrete, to diffuse carbon dioxide, or of course to reproduce. Thus, the individual organism has ceased to exist without dying. Many single-celled organisms reproduce this way, by simple division, or *fission*, and so do some multicell organisms, such as sea anemones. But simple fission is only one of several forms of reproduction in which an organism may cease to exist without dying, and as it turns out, much of Earth's total volume of living matter, its *biomass*, comprises organisms that never die.[10]

---

[8]Peter H. Raven and George B. Johnson, *Biology* (St. Louis: Times Mirror/Mosby College Publishing, 1986), 42.
[9]Raven and Johnson, *Biology*, 42.
[10]Archaea, for example, are single-celled microorganisms that we now believe make up a large part of Earth's biosphere. Archaea thrive in diverse environments, from your mouth to the ocean floor and

Moreover, some organisms may survive successive life cycles in ways that do not directly depend on the way they reproduce. Consider, for example, the immortal jellyfish (*Turritopsis nutricula*), a hydrozoan whose mature medusa form can revert to the sexually immature polyp stage. An immortal jellyfish may be eaten by a predator, of course, or succumb to a bacterial infection or a fatal accident. Nevertheless, we are told that this particular jellyfish never dies of biological aging (*senescence*).

In view of these considerations, perhaps we should abandon the attempt to define *life* as the condition that can revert to being dead. But if we are to circle back to a conception of *death* as the cessation of life, then our definition of death will depend on a definition of life. So we return to the question *what is life?*

Let us rejoin Raven and Johnson's inquisitive astronauts. They have decided to examine the structure of the blob, and in the course of this examination perhaps they discover *complexity*. Not all complexity, of course, is a hallmark of life. As far as we can guess so far, some of the largest and most massive objects are also among the most complex. The intricate and unimaginably vast superstructures of galaxies that astronomers call galaxy filaments or Great Walls[11] are not alive, nor are cities or computer programs. But perhaps we could say that a *certain sort* of complexity characterizes life, namely *cellular* complexity. Cellular complexity involves a unique sort of structure with the kind of "inside" that is characteristic of *syntropy*,[12] and with certain characteristic processes, including nutrition, elimination, and reproduction. Cellular complexity has to do with another characteristic of life on Earth, namely *acclimation* or *adaptability*—the ability of an organism to respond to changes in its

---

miles beneath the surface of dry land. Eventually, of course, all life on Earth, presumably including archaea, will come to an end: astronomers assure us that within the next five billion years or so, our Sun will expand into a Red Giant, swallow up the planet Mercury, and singe all life from our planet. But of course this will not change the fact that trillions of microorganisms existed yesterday that no longer exist today, but that never died.

[11]The Hercules–Corona Borealis Great Wall is the largest and most massive object that we have managed to detect so far (but stay tuned!). It is perhaps ten billion light years across, and at its nearest point it is ten billion light years from Earth.

[12]The late American philosopher Jay F. Rosenberg observed that a physical thing, in the course of its transactions with its environment, might exhibit one of two possible tendencies: it might change in the direction of less structure and organization, or "it might preserve its initial organization and structure or even tend in the direction of greater and more intricate arrangements of constituent elements." With reference to the latter state, Rosenberg followed earlier writers in calling it *syntropy*. (The passage quoted is from page 162 of Rosenberg's book, *Thinking Clearly about Death*, cited in the Further Readings section at the end of this introduction.)

environment by adjusting its insides to maintain growth and other functions. These, as well as the transmission of genetic material such as RNA or DNA, are all hallmarks of life on Earth.

Combining these observations, Raven and Johnson identify certain general properties that all living things that we know about share: "All living things on earth are characterized by cellular organization, growth, reproduction, and heredity. These characteristics may serve to define the term *life*."[13] In the light of these characteristics, and perhaps with the addition of the characteristic of *acclimation* as well, we can come up with a rough definition that will serve our purposes. Perhaps a definition along the lines of the following:

> *Life is the characteristic state of things with cellular organization that grow, reproduce, pass on genetic material, and adapt to their environments.*

Let us call this our *biological definition of life*, and let us call growth, respiration, nutrition, excretion, cellular regeneration, reproduction, heredity, and responsiveness to the environment *vital processes*. If Raven and Johnson's astronauts determine that the mysterious blob has at least some of these characteristics, then they have determined that it is a living thing.

At this point, a cautionary note is in order: the presence in a structure of one or more of these general properties does not *guarantee* that it is a living thing. For instance, the properties of growth and reproduction (or replication) alone are not enough to distinguish life from nonlife. Plasma crystals or synthetic DNA strands may grow, split in half, and then grow more; nevertheless, biologists have not characterized these structures as living things. It seems, at least at present, that an object needs to exhibit *all or almost all* of the properties mentioned, including cellular organization, in order to count as a living thing. This observation, together with the recognition that research has a long way to go, may help explain why some biologists do not even try to come up with a definition of life.

---

[13]Raven and Johnson, *Biology*, 44. Compare this to Kim Sterelny and Paul E. Griffiths, *Sex and Death: An Introduction to Philosophy of Biology* (Chicago: University of Chicago Press, 1999), 357–77. Sterelny and Griffiths, two leading philosophers of biology, doubt that definitions of *life* are very helpful for biologists, and they caution that such definitions run the risk of being Earth-specific and not generalizable to possible life forms on other planets. They suggest abandoning the attempt to define "life," pointing out that biologists have gone about their business quite well so far without agreeing on a definition of the word. When it comes to terrestrial life, though, they identify such defining characteristics as cellular organization and the operation of such processes as reproduction, adaptation, and natural selection (*Sex and Death*, 358).

We might make two additional observations. First, let us note that our biological definition of life is not something that our ancestors two centuries ago would have understood, because the notion of cellular organization can only be understood within the larger context of modern biology. Nevertheless, cultures of distant times and places have associated life with heartbeat, breathing, self-movement, growth, and reproduction, and they have associated death with the onset of unresponsiveness and coldness of the body. So our biological definition of life, though distinctively modern, validates age-old observations.

Second, let us clear up a possible confusion. New Age personalities like to upbraid "western science" for supposedly viewing Mother Earth as "dead."[14] Several of the more thoughtful proponents of this view offer the important insight that private ownership in land is a relatively recent institution that has had huge repercussions when it comes to the ways we ruin our planet.[15] But this is a different discussion for a different time, and it does not change the fact that, if contemporary biology has any say in the matter, then clearly *most things are neither dead nor alive*: as far as we can tell, electrons, galaxies, rivers, and mountains do not have cellular structures; they do not contain genetic material or reproduce; they do not have respiratory systems or chloroplasts, and they do not have anything functionally equivalent. There is no good reason to believe, then, that they have ever been *alive*, at least according to our biological definition. And precisely because of this, there is no good reason to believe that they could be dead. Strictly speaking, not being alive is a necessary but insufficient condition for being dead. Most things, it would seem, are neither dead nor alive; they just *are*.

From these considerations, we return to a definition of death as the privation of life, but we do so with a provisional but properly *biological* definition of *life* in hand. Accordingly, we might define *death* as *the absence of vital processes in the (recognizable) remains of something that until recently had been characterized by these processes*.[16] Or more colloquially, *death is the absence of life where before there had been life.*

---

[14]Inventor and environmentalist James Lovelock (b. 1919) has drawn insightful analogies between Earth and a living organism. See James Lovelock, *Gaia: A New Look at Life on Earth* (Oxford: Oxford University Press, 2000 [1979]), 30–43. For an alternative view, see James W. Kirchner, "The Gaia Hypothesis: Fact, Theory, and Wishful Thinking," *Climatic Change* 52, no. 4 (2002): 391–408.
[15]See, for example, Carolyn Merchant, "Science and Worldviews," in *Radical Ecology: The Search for a Livable World* (New York: Routledge, 1992), 41–60.
[16]This definition of death, or something close to it, is what the philosopher Fred Feldman and others have called *the biological definition of death*. See Fred Feldman, "Death and the Disintegration

Let us now consider whether this biologically informed definition of death gives us any insights when it comes to the survival hypothesis.

Mind and brain

In recent decades neuroscientists have confirmed the very persistent view— going back a long time and impressed upon each of us daily—that our mental states depend on internal states of our bodies, as well as what we refer to very broadly as "the environment," including sensory input, diet, health, and other predominantly nonmental factors, notably the historically variant social environment.[17] In light of the daily confirmed obviousness of it all, it should not come as a surprise that, despite persecution, worldly thinkers since ancient times have taught that consciousness is a product of the observable stuff around us. This was, for instance, a pivotal belief among the Charvaka thinkers of ancient India.[18] We will encounter this school of thought in the Madhava Acharya reading in Part II. In Part IV we will meet the Greek-Roman poet Lucretius, who more than two thousand years ago described the effects of aging, disease, wine, and epilepsy on the mind. The close connection between feeling and thinking, on the one hand, and the body and its environment, on the other, is as unavoidable as the recognition that, as the body undergoes change, so do our feelings, memories, thoughts, and behaviors.

Indeed, perceptive people have for a long time suspected that thinking, feeling, consciousness, and emotions depend on the structure and stuff of a particular organ, namely the brain. The Greek physician Hippocrates of Cos (c. 460–370 BC), for example, is said to have believed that the brain is involved with sensation and is the seat of intelligence.[19] Although much

---

of Personality," in *The Oxford Handbook of Philosophy of Death*, ed. Ben Bradley, Fred Feldman, and Jens Johansson (Oxford and New York: Oxford University Press, 2013), 60–79.
[17]David Eagleman, *Incognito: The Secret Lives of the Brain* (New York: Pantheon Books, 2011), 215–16.
[18]See Pradeep P. Gokhale, "The Value Perspective/s of Carvakas," in *Studies in Indian Moral Philosophy Problems: Concepts and Perspectives*, ed. S.E. Bhelke and P.P. Gokhale (2002), 185– 205, and Debiprasad Chattopadhyaya, *Indian Philosophy: A Popular Introduction* (Delhi: People's Publishing House, 1976). The Chattopadhyaya survey, written decades ago, is still a great, accessible introduction to the ancient philosophical traditions of India, one that casts doubt on the exotic stereotype of India as a land of mysticism.
[19]According to a quote attributed to Hippocrates, "from nothing else but [the brain] come joys, delights, laughter, and sports, and sorrows, grief, despondency, and lamentations" (*The Genuine Works of Hippocrates*, trans. Francis Adams (London: The Sydenham Society, 1886), vol. 2, 344–45).

remains to be explained, there is today a consensus among brain scientists that, if the words *consciousness, feeling, memory, reasoning,* or *self-awareness* refer to anything at all, then they refer to electrochemical processes that take place in the brains of some vertebrates, notably our own species. So far at least, researchers are aware of no "consciousness" without electrical activity in the neocortex, the outer layer of the brain in mammals, which in humans is involved in such "higher functions" as conscious thought and language. Recent research has provided an ever-more-detailed account of how thinking (or cognition) depends on the body's structures and substances, such as neurons (the cells that process and transmit information through electrical and chemical signals), neurotransmitters (the chemicals, such as serotonin, that transmit signals from neurons to other cells), and hormones (such as testosterone, estrogen, and progesterone). Cognition is affected by substances introduced into the body from the environment, including nicotine, alcohol, hallucinogens, antidepressants, and opiates. Pathogens within the body, notably certain bacteria and viruses, influence "consciousness," too: someone with the flu, for example, *feels* bad. Strokes, tumors, and multiple varieties of brain injury also affect the way we feel, what we think, our moods, and our personalities. Moreover, personality and mood is also partially a result of genetic inheritance: the structure of your DNA accounts in part for the way you think and how you behave. Accordingly, random mutations also play a role in personality: to take an especially clear example, Huntington's disease, with its drastic behavioral symptoms, appears to be caused by a mutation in a single gene.

To fill out the picture a bit more completely, consider *memory,* an indispensable component of personality and self-identity. If neuroscientists are right, then memories take the form of neural patterns in the brain, and cognition depends on precisely timed interactions among neurons forming networks that support cognitive processes. Various sorts of patterns and interactions take place in certain parts of the brain (see Figure 1 below). Short-term memory, for example, appears to depend on activity in the pre-frontal lobe; long-term declarative memory (or memory of facts) depends in large part on the hippocampus; emotional memory depends largely on the brain structure called the amygdala, and procedural memory (memory of how to do things) appears to depend on the cerebellum, basal ganglia, and motor cortex. The neurological basis of memory in humans is amply confirmed in many ways, including the study of stroke, epilepsy, brain lesions, and neurodegenerative diseases such as dementia, schizophrenia, Parkinson's disease, and Huntington's disease. Alzheimer's disease, to take another example, involves an uncontrolled inflammatory response brought on by extensive deposits in the brain of a fibrous protein-like substance called amyloids. This leads to cell death in the brain, which eventually leads to loss of memory and cognitive decline. In these diseases, memory loss is an effect of generalized deterioration of neurons, the characteristic stuff of the brain.

Much about memory and other cognitive processes remains mysterious to us today. Nevertheless, a wide range of mounting evidence bolsters the long-standing suspicion that memory and cognition as a whole are part of what the brain does. Researchers today agree that the best hope for greater insight into thought, language, and other cognitive processes lies in the study of the structures and stuff of the brain—not the study of an immaterial soul. Indeed, there is a question how one would even go about studying an immaterial soul, and this might have to do with the difficulty or impossibility of describing it in a coherent way. These are considerations that we will take up in the readings below.

In any case, if contemporary neuroscience is even roughly accurate, then cognition is a function of biological brains, which respond in organized ways to the states of the organism as it acts on its environment. Brains do

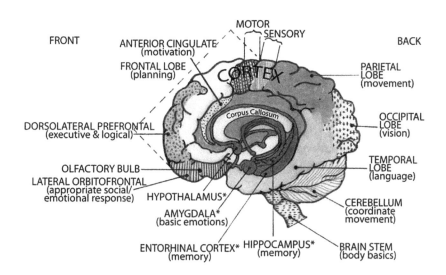

Figure 1 Diagram showing main structures of the brain & their functions (side view).

much more than think, but as far as we know at present, nothing thinks but brains. If there were such a thing as a seat of thought, consciousness, or self-awareness, then it would appear to be the brain. And if there is anything like a mind or soul, then it would seem that it is either identical to the brain, or it is what the brain does, or it is in some other way dependent for its continued existence on a functioning brain.

So if contemporary neuroscience is even roughly right, then after a person's brain ceases to function, that person no longer exists. When circulation ceases in an animal with a relatively complex nervous system, oxygenation of brain tissue ceases, and the enzymes within the brain destroy its neurons in a process called *autolysis*. In short order the brain ceases to function, including the "higher functions" of the cerebral cortex. As a result, sensation, memory, and consciousness or awareness come to an end, and when that happens it would appear—at least to brain scientists during business hours—that personhood comes to an end, too.

Neuroscientists and medical professionals distinguish between *biological death* and *brain death*.[20] In the case of humans and other animals with relatively complex brains, biological death and brain death usually occur at about the same time; nevertheless, the two are not the same thing: brain death can precede biological death by years. This leads physiologists to conclude that, at least in the case of adult humans, brain death is the end of a mind or a person.[21]

Many other people, however, believe that contemporary neuroscience leaves out something very important when it comes to its description of the mind. The mind and the brain appear to be very different sorts of things. Consider, for instance, the difference between reports about brain events and reports about mental events: you can make an honest mistake when it comes to describing events inside your brain (you might erroneously believe that a certain mental event, a particular memory perhaps, is caused by activities in a certain part of the brain); but it is hard to imagine that you could be wrong when you honestly report feeling a pain or thinking of a red

---

[20]An important document in this regard is the 1980 *Uniform Determination of Death Act* (included in the President's Commission report, cited in the Further Readings section below).

[21]There is broad agreement among qualified experts on this point (Eagleman, *Incognito: The Secret Lives*, 203–04). Biologist David Buller was expressing a common view among his colleagues when he wrote that, "the overwhelming majority of cognitive scientists [identify] the mind with the functional, information-processing design of the brain" (David J. Buller, *Adapting Minds: Evolutionary Psychology and the Persistent Quest for Human Nature* (Cambridge, MA: MIT Press, 2005), 54).

circle. There is a difference between describing a brain event, on the one hand, and describing a "mental event" such as a feeling, on the other hand. This appears, at least to some philosophers, to point up a fundamental difference between *brain events* and *mental events*. If these really are two fundamentally different types of events, then perhaps brains and minds are fundamentally different, too—and perhaps they have different fates.

Survival?

In the philosophy of death, *survival* refers to the continued existence of a person, a self, a consciousness, a soul, or an experiencing subject after an organism's death. If we accept this usage, and if the biological definitions of life and death are at least roughly right, then one and the same thing cannot be *dead* and yet *survive* at the same time. As we will see in our reading in Part I, the Greek philosopher Epicurus expressed this exclusionary relation with his famous twin claims: "when we are, death is not come, and when death is come, we are not." Epicurus' view is, of course, compatible with our everyday good-sense view that death is the permanent cessation of life, but it is more than that. What Epicurus is saying is that the death of a human, a type of animal, is incompatible with the continued existence of a particular common consequence of *being a human*, namely, *being a person*.

Let us recall our biological definition of life. This definition has an interesting implication that we have already noted in passing: if it is right, then dying is something that only a living thing can do, and it can do it only while it is alive. Dying is part of life, while death is not,[22] and just as surely as death marks the end of life, it also puts an end to dying. Much confusion arises when we forget this simple point.

Combining this insight with what we have said about survival, it is hard to avoid the following conclusion: the profuse literature on "near-death experiences" provides little if any insight about death or evidence for life

---

[22]The Austrian philosopher Ludwig Wittgenstein famously wrote that, "Death is not an event of life. Death is not lived through" (Wittgenstein, *Tractatus Logico-Philosophicus* [1921] (Create Space Independent Publishing Platform, 2013), 153. What Wittgenstein was saying, perhaps, is that the final moment of *dying*, though it is "in" life, nevertheless does not count as an *event* in the life of the one dying, because for something to count as an event requires that it be followed by another lived moment.

thereafter.[23] For this reason, as some readers will be disappointed to find out, we will not have much to say in the following pages about near-death experiences.

It may be objected, however, that as the philosopher H.H. Price has pointed out, the real issue of the afterlife is not *life* after death, but rather *experience* after death. Perhaps an experiencing subject could somehow survive even after the corresponding man or woman has died, and even after the corresponding person has ceased to exist. By our biological definitions of life and death, though, it is surely a contradiction to claim that after "you" die "you" are not dead. But perhaps we are not referring here to the same "you's." According to Price at least, there is no contradiction in the notion of having experiences after the death of the body.[24]

* * *

Let us recap. It makes little sense to try to base a definition of *life* on death: the terms are exclusionary, and the latter is a term that, at least for biologists, has meaning only as a privation of the former. Of course, we can define *death* in terms of life, as the absence of vital processes where previously there had been these processes. As long as we can come up with a substantive description of *vital processes,* this negative definition of "death" may not be as trivial as it may seem at first. If biologists today are even roughly accurate, then life, or at least *terrestrial* life, is a state of something with cellular organization, growth, and heredity, and with functions that maintain syntropy and that transmit genetic material. With this biological definition of life in hand, we can define *death,* straightforwardly, as *the absence of these properties in something that had previously displayed them.* Death is a state of the remains of something after vital functions have ceased.

This negative, biologically informed definition of death might count as a starting point for our philosophical purposes, but it is not much more than

---

[23]The term *near-death experience* was popularized by psychologist and medical doctor Raymond Moody, in his 1975 book, *Life after Life.* The book has sold over thirteen million copies worldwide. In it, Moody reported results of interviews with roughly fifty people who had come very close to death, some revived after being pronounced "clinically dead." Although their reports differed in details, he found them to be remarkably similar. Many, for example, had the experience of appearing to be calmly looking down on their own bodies, perhaps watching physicians working to revive them, and many others had a sense of moving down a dark tunnel toward a light and then entering a place of incredible brightness and beauty. Moody believed that his research provided strong evidence for life after death. Several later researchers report that they have corroborated his original findings.
[24]Price's paper "The Soul Survives and Functions after Death" appears in Part III. Also refer to the reading from Lynne Rudder Baker, in Part III.

that. Since we are concerned with the fate of the person, soul, mind, or some other supposed "seat of consciousness," and since it is difficult to make sense of consciousness without connecting it with physical processes, we appear to face a big philosophical obstacle to the notion that the human body and the human soul have different fates. On the other hand, daily experience, as well as the arguments of some philosophers, point to the fundamental difference between brain events and mental events.

The stakes are high—or at least this is what some of our authors assure us. We should take a closer look at arguments for and against the survival hypothesis. In Part I we will ask ourselves what this thing is that is supposed to survive after physical death, and whether it survives forever. Our search for an answer to this question will raise further questions, which we will consider in subsequent readings.

For Discussion or Essays

- If a human is a certain sort of animal, then surely there is such a thing as a dead *human*. But what are we to make of the contention that, strictly speaking, there is no such thing as a dead *person*? Do you agree with this contention? Why or why not?

- According to the influential President's Commission study entitled *Defining Death: A Report on the Medical, Legal and Ethical Issues in the Determination of Death* (1981), an individual is dead "who has sustained either (1) irreversible cessation of circulatory and respiratory functions, or (2) irreversible cessation of all functions of the entire brain, including the brain stem." This formulation was intended to describe death "for legal and medical purposes." Why is this not a proper *definition* of death?

- In the context of philosophy of death, the word *survival* means "continued existence after one's biological death."[25] But continued existence of what? *Personal survival*, presumably, would require the continued existence of an experiencing subject, consciousness, or self—the continued existence of the same *person*, in the sense of something that is not only conscious or aware, but than can be conscious of itself. But what might *impersonal* survival consist of? Here are some related questions:

- Should the transmission of genetic material count as impersonal survival? Explain.

- A student in a philosophy of death course wrote: "A person who dies and donates her organs to another person has achieved a measure of impersonal survival." Do you agree? Why or why not?

- The carbon atoms that make up a large part of your body are the result of nuclear processes that took place billions of years ago in the cores of massive stars. Should this fact make a difference when it comes to thoughts of personal mortality?

[25]*The Cambridge Dictionary of Philosophy*, ed. Robert Audi, 2nd ed. (New York: Cambridge University Press, 2015), 892.

Further Readings on Brains, Death, and "Consciousness"

Dehaene, Stanislas. *The Cognitive Neuroscience of Consciousness.* Cambridge, MA: MIT Press, 2002. This book investigates the philosophical, empirical, and theoretical bases on which a cognitive neuroscience of consciousness might be founded.

Edwards, Paul. "The Dependence of Consciousness on the Brain." Chapter 17 of *Reincarnation: A Critical Examination*, 279–300. Amherst, NY: Prometheus Books, 1996. Neuroscience has made strides in the years since Edwards wrote this survey; nevertheless, it remains an excellent run-down of some basic arguments against pictures of survival that rely on the notion of a disembodied mind.

Klarsfeld, Andre, and Frederic Revah. *The Biology of Death: Origins of Mortality*, translated by Lydia Brady. Ithaca, NY: Comstock Publishing, 2003. The authors, both neuroscientists, survey the modern history of aging and death, including discussions of demography, biochemistry, evolutionary theories of aging, and medical advances that are extending our active life spans.

Martin, Michael and Keith Augustine, eds. *The Myth of an Afterlife: The Case against Life after Death*. Lanham, MD: Rowman & Littlefield, 2015. Part I, entitled "Empirical Arguments for Annihilation," includes papers by researchers and practitioners in the fields of behavioral genetics, cognitive neuroscience, psychology, forensic and neurodevelopmental science, and pharmacology. According to the editors, these readings provide "empirical evidence of a very tight correlation between mental states and the corruptible brain states that underlie them" (p. xxix). Part II, entitled "Conceptual and Empirical Difficulties with Survival," consists of nine papers, mostly by philosophers, who focus on the incoherence or unfeasibility of survival of a nonphysical soul, an "ethereal body," or the same person in a new body after the old body is destroyed.

President's Commission for the Study of Ethical Problems in Medicine and Biomedical and Behavioral Research, The. *Defining Death: A Report on the Medical, Legal and Ethical Issues in the Determination of Death*. Washington, D.C.: U.S. Government Printing Office, July 1981. This document contains the influential *Uniform Determination of Death Act* (1980).

Rosenberg, Jay F. *Thinking Clearly about Death*, 2nd ed. Indianapolis: Hackett, 1998.

Part I

Our Immortal Souls

Introduction to Part I:
Personal Survival and Immortality

Forever is composed of nows.

—Emily Dickinson, 1830–1886

Many of us appear to be invested in the notion that *after you die you still exist*. Here is a little report for your consideration:

> St. Columba is said to have called for a volunteer from among his followers to be buried as part of the consecration ceremony on the island of Iona (one version of the story says that this sacrifice was to placate a devil who spent each night undoing the good that Columba had done during the day). One, named Oran, volunteered and was duly buried; after three days they dug up the grave and found him alive. He immediately began to tell them there was no heaven or hell, neither was there God nor devil, but Columba would not countenance such blasphemy and had him buried again.[1]

Oran, the hapless volunteer in this story, literally returned from the grave, though briefly. But can we make sense of the claim that he *died* and then *returned from death*? If he did, then he has demonstrated that after you die you are not necessarily dead. If on the other hand he did not die the first time he was buried, then setting aside the question of the existence of God, what credence should we give to his report about the afterlife, or the lack thereof? After all, if he had not "crossed over" and then returned from the dead, then how could his ordeal, however unusual, count as evidence for an afterlife?

---

[1] The quoted passage and the account are from Ronald Holmes, *Witchcraft in History* (Secaucus, NJ: The Citadel Press, 1977), 207. The Isle of Iona is a small pretty island off the western coast of Scotland. St. Columba and twelve followers are said to have settled there in AD 563, establishing it as a center of monasticism. According to another version of the story, the volunteer who survived burial reported that he had seen hell, and it was not all that bad.

Oran, of course, is not the only person to claim to have returned from "the other side." Stories abound: patients pronounced clinically dead rise above their deathbeds; others envision tunnels, green pastures, blue skies, and bright lights. They hear crescendos, review their lives in a flash, feel euphoria, or greet angels and long-lost loved ones. But then pathologists arrive on the scene to spoil all the fun, raising doubts as to whether the reporters are bona fide returnees from the Hereafter.[2] Oran's report might well fall under this doubt. He seems to have undergone what we today call a "near-death experience," but such experiences are no more experiences of *death* than near-pregnancy experiences are experiences of pregnancy.[3] If near-death experiences are taken to be reports about *dying*, then there is no good reason to believe that they tell us much at all about *death*. Dying, after all, is something that only a living thing can do, and it can only do it while it is alive.

"Death is nothing to us"

Long before St. Columba, the Greek philosopher Epicurus drew far-reaching conclusions from the simple observation that if something is dead it is not alive. "Accustom yourself to believe that death is nothing to us," Epicurus wrote in a letter to his young friend Menoeceus, "for good and evil imply awareness, and death is the privation of all awareness." Epicurus explains that death is *nothing to us* because after we die we no longer exist, and that which does not exist cannot feel anything or be aware of anything: neither pain nor misfortune can befall that which does not exist. If this is the case, then it is foolish to dread death, which can bring neither pain nor injury of any sort to that which has died.

---

[2]Much has been published in this regard in recent years. In the article "The Case against Immortality," for example, philosopher Keith Augustine reviews the evidence for life after death and concludes that it does not stand up to scientific scrutiny (*Skeptic Magazine* 5, no. 2 (1997): 81–87). For a fun though somewhat unfocused introduction to the debate, see "The Great Afterlife," an exchange between Michael Shermer, editor of *Skeptic Magazine*, and Deepak Chopra, author of many popular books, including *Life after Death: The Burden of Proof* (New York: Three Rivers Press, 2006). The exchange, first published in *Skeptic Magazine* 13, no. 4 (Winter 2008), appears at: http://www.skeptic.com/reading_room/the-great-afterlife-debate (accessed December 30, 2013).
[3]This analogy, however, collapses quickly. Billions of women assuredly have had pregnancy experiences, but if Epicurus (whom we will soon meet in Part I) is right, *no one* could have a death experience.

One may, of course, dread the pain of *dying*, and one may worry about the fate of one's dependents, friends, and reputation after one has died. One may dread much more, too, such as the fate of one's ideals, descendants, or planet. But it is foolish to dread death per se—or rather to convince oneself that one does so. Or perhaps, as we will see when we meet the Roman poet Lucretius in Part IV, it is *impossible*, properly speaking, to dread death—in which case what we dread is not really death at all but something else. Or perhaps the dread is not *of* anything in particular: perhaps it is just a vague anxiety, without a definite object.

Some readers of Epicurus have, boldly or rashly, relinquished "fear of death," while others have not. But if Epicurus and his followers are right, then what is there left to say about death per se? The late American philosopher Mary Mothersill, in a similar vein, wrote that,

> death, about which philosophers have written a great deal, is an unrewarding, virtually sterile concept. There is nothing to be said: talk of death, though it may have poetic power, is embarrassingly trivial and ends, sooner rather than later, in a blind alley, in a dead end.[4]

In the course of our readings, you might come to agree with Mothersill that when it comes to death as a personal fate, there is little at all to be said. Or at least little to be said that is descriptively useful or interesting. But even if Mothersill turns out to be right about this, it might still be worth the effort to sort through the trivial material and the nonsense, in order to establish to our own satisfaction that there really is nothing much to be said about death. And whether or not she is right, there is much to be learned from casting a critical eye at *what people have said about death*. In the course of doing this, we might find out a lot about philosophy, life, and ourselves.

In the following pages we will hear from Epicurus and from several of his followers, too, including Lucretius, David Hume, Thomas W. Clark, and Samuel Scheffler. We will also hear from others, including thinkers who in various ways reject Epicurus' claim that "when death is come, we are not." In the remainder of this Introduction, though, let us consider our options when it comes to what might happen after we die.

---

[4]Mary Mothersill, "Old Age," *Proceedings and Addresses of the American Philosophical Association* 73, no. 2 (November 1999): 9–23. The cited passage appears on page 9.

Naturalism and the problem of mental states

First a brief recap of the General Introduction: In our discussion of the meaning of "life," we saw that contemporary biologists and brain researchers confirm much older views of dying as the ebbing of life, and of death as simply the absence of life where there had previously been life. The sort of thing that dies is an organism, such as an orchid or a human. If biologists today are even approximately right, then we may define life in terms of cellular organization and vital processes, including the transmission of genetic material. With this sort of biological definition in hand, we may then define death in a straightforward manner as *the absence of life in the (recognizable) remains of something that had been alive.*

This is a conclusion in keeping with a very broad perspective that sometimes goes by the name of *naturalism*. One way to define naturalism is to say that it is the very general view that "nature" is just another name for *whatever there is.*[5] Naturalism rejects religious pictures of the world as God's creation, and it rejects pictures of gods, men, or anything else standing above nature or outside of it. Indeed, it denies the existence of any gods, or at least any gods distinct from nature. Thus, naturalism sets itself against *supernaturalism*, which is the doctrine that nature is *not* the whole of reality and that part of reality transcends, or is beyond, nature.[6] Naturalists deny the existence of disembodied minds, ghosts, spirits, and occult agencies that are said to be inexplicable in principle. Not only does naturalism reject the idea of an immortal soul, it rejects the picture of a soul as distinct from a body. Naturally, it rejects miracles, too, as well as the idea of divine intervention in human affairs.

---

[5]The technical term for this position is *ontological naturalism*, which has also been described as the view that *everything is composed of entities that could in principle be studied in the sciences, present and future*—entities whose properties determine all the properties of things, including humans (*The Cambridge Dictionary of Philosophy*, 596). The Latin word *natura* comes from the verb *to be born*. The natural is that which comes forth or passes away spontaneously, on its own accord. *Nature* happens "by itself," or "of its own accord," without the assistance of supernatural forces or occult agencies.

[6]According to American philosopher Barry Stroud, naturalists are simply "those who agree that no supernatural agents are at work in the world" (Barry Stroud, "The Charm of Naturalism," *Proceedings and Addresses of the American Philosophical Association* 70, no. 2 (November 1996): 43–55. The citation is from page 54).

But again, what if biologists are wrong about this? In the General Introduction we encountered the view that, from the first-person perspective, mental states like thinking, experiencing, and consciousness appear to be very different phenomena from brain processes, as described naturalistically by contemporary neuroscience. If thinking, experiencing, and consciousness are what the mind does, then perhaps the mind cannot be explained naturalistically, at least not yet. So what if a naturalistic view of things is not the end of the story? What if the seat of consciousness is not the brain after all, but rather something that today's neurology, biology, and physics cannot account for? Or what if our negative definition of death, based as it is on a biological definition of life, accounts for only the death of the *body*, and not the death of something else, something non-bodily that is the real person or the soul? These are questions we will examine in the readings to come. First, though, let us consider the array of possible afterlife states.

Candidates for survival and persons

As we have seen, the question of survival is inseparable from the question *What is it that survives or does not survive?* What sort of thing is it? Common answers to these questions are: the soul (physical or non-physical); the person or personality, the self, or the spirit. Some philosophers categorize three sorts of candidates for survival, corresponding to three conceptions of what it means for us to persist in existence:

- *animalism*, which says that, at the end of the day, we are human beings (Snowdon 1990, Olson 1997, 2007), and so our posthumous fate is the fate of our body, notably loss of syntropy and organic functionality, and disintegration, decomposition.
- *personism*, which says that we are creatures with the capacity for self-awareness. Some personists claim that this awareness or consciousness differs from the body to which it is connected, and so we do not necessarily share the same fate as the body.
- *mindism*, which says that we are minds (which may or may not have the capacity for self-awareness) (McMahan 2002). The mind is often taken to be either immaterial (Plato) or subtly material; in either case, it is distinct from the body and separable from it, and so minds do not necessarily share the same fate as the body.

Animalism suggests that we persist over time just in case we remain the same animal. This is a view that is consistent with the biological definition of life that we have discussed. Our biological definition of death conforms to *animalism*, as a way of answering the question What is it about a human that can be dead?

Mindism suggests that we persist just when we remain the same mind. This is a view that is not necessarily inconsistent with the biological view, but it is clearly consistent with dualism.

Personism is the view that what survives is your *personhood* or your selfhood, or your soul, spirit, or consciousness—whatever it is that makes you a person rather than just a point-mass. Personism is usually paired with the view that our persistence is determined by our psychological features and the relations among them.

Notice that an animalist could very well believe that we are both animals and persons, and a mindist need not deny that we are, among other things, animals or persons.

What, then, is a *person*? Various answers have been offered, including the view that *a person is something that possesses a rational essence*, and the view that *a person is something that possesses a free will*. Questions of essences and free will are notoriously controversial, though, and if we can come up with a less controversial and vague definition of *personhood*, then we will save ourselves much trouble.

For well-known modern European philosophers, including Rene Descartes and David Hume, a *person* is a *conscious agent*: it is a kind of thing that acts in and on an environment in a deliberative way. A conscious agent possesses consciousness and is therefore capable of framing representations about the world, formulating plans and acting on them. As a deliberative or conscious agent, a person is said to be a subject of experience—something that can experience the passing scene.

By this definition, personhood ceases when a human becomes brain dead because a brain-dead human is not a subject of experience. The human may continue to live—vital processes may continue—but personhood (or personality or subjectivity) has already come to an end. When this happens, we don't typically say that a person or personality has died, and when we do, it is usually clear, at least upon reflection, that the verb *has died* is being used metaphorically, to mean something like "has ceased to exist."

We will return to the problem of personhood in some of the readings below. In our reading in Part III, for example, Lynne Rudder Baker will argue that the defining characteristic of a person is not just consciousness, but rather a kind of *self*-consciousness, or a "first-person perspective."

Posthumous scenarios

The seventeenth-century French thinker Rene Descartes famously believed that in essence a person is a *thing that thinks*, and that this in turn must be a non-material soul. Since a soul is non-material and has no parts, Descartes argued, it cannot fall apart and so it is deathless. This is how he answered his urgent question, whether "in death there is an end of me?"

A conjecture about what, if anything, happens to a person after dying is what we will call a *posthumous scenario*. The word *posthumous* means "after dying," and a *scenario* is a little story about a possible course of events. When it comes to posthumous scenarios, there are at least two main versions to consider: *survival* and *non-survival*. The survival scenario entails the belief that, in one form or another, a mind, soul, person, or self survives the death of a body. Readers will recognize this as the survival hypothesis that we encountered in the General Introduction. *Non-survival*, by contrast, is the denial of survival, whether personal or impersonal. More bluntly, it is the view that after you die you are no more; there is nothing left *of you* or *about you* but your physical remains and the physical consequences of having lived. According to the non-survival scenario, we have no soul, or no soul that is detachable from the body, and when vital processes cease the person ceases to exist.

The non-survival scenario could of course easily embrace the idea that, besides a corpse or ashes, the deceased does "survive" in a *metaphorical* sense, simply because the consequences of her life endure, the way the ripples of a stone-toss continue to expand across the surface of a pond long after the stone has sunk to the bottom. All the difference that a life has made continues to make a difference, however faint. Of course, this observation need not be limited to humans, nor even to living things: an avalanche into a ravine might well have more consequences than a human life. It is consistent with the non-survival scenario, then, that each of us "survives" metaphorically, not as persons, but as the consequences of "our" now-extinguished life.

As it turns out, though, there is a version of non-survival that asserts that after I die I am *totally* annihilated, leaving neither a consciousness nor physical remains nor any other consequences of my life. But this conflicts with our good-sense conviction that "life goes on" after we die, and that the repercussions of each life continue to reverberate, however faintly. The "total annihilation" scenario, taken to its logical extreme, would amount to the view that after I die *everything* (or, as some Californians are fond of saying, "my world") ceases to exist. In this case, "total annihilation" would amount to an extreme version of what has been called ontological *solipsism*—the ultra-subjectivist view that the only things that can justifiably be said to exist are my mental states and myself. This leads to another philosophical discussion for another time, but let us note here that the solipsist's view of death precludes any form of survival, personal or otherwise, and so it amounts to a version of the non-survival view.

As an aside, we might note that some religious traditions have integrated elements of both scenarios, survival and non-survival, into their respective stories of posthumous existence. For example, in some versions of Judaism and Christianity, non-survival, or something close to it ("soul death"), is followed on Judgment Day by personal survival. In other forms of Christianity and Islam, you survive as a disembodied soul after you die, until you are physically resurrected on Judgment Day, when the soul and the body are united. Other religious doctrines reserve personal survival for those who are saved, and non-survival for the rest.

So far, we have identified two main posthumous scenarios: survival and non-survival. Are these two scenarios *exhaustive*? Do they cover all imaginable posthumous scenarios, or are we missing something here? It is difficult to imagine a third option; nevertheless, some authors have claimed to do just that. As the reader might recall from the General Introduction, some authors have distinguished between two types of survival: *personal survival*, which emphasizes the discrete, individual character of the soul, mind, person, or self that is said to survive, and *impersonal survival*, which holds that after an individual dies, the individual soul merges into a larger universal soul or cosmic consciousness.[7] If we could make sense of this view, then it might count as a third sort of posthumous survival. It is not easy to

---

[7]In an article entitled "The Over-Soul" (published in 1841), the American writer Ralph Waldo Emerson (1803–82) attempted to explicate a version of impersonal survival. Emerson, who was influenced by Advaita Vedanta, the Indian "philosophy of unity," wrote that, "There is one mind common to all individual men. Every man is an inlet to the same and to all the same. He that is once admitted to the right of reason is made a freeman of the whole estate" (quoted by Swami Paramananda, in *Emerson and Vedanta*, 2nd ed. (Boston: The Vedanta Society, 1918), 14–15).

imagine how the *experience* of impersonal awareness or consciousness could differ from the personal variety of experience, though, and so far at least, attempts to force the distinction between personal and impersonal survival seem to have produced little more than avoidable confusion. For that reason we will not have much to say about impersonal survival.

Unless we can come up with a plausible third scenario, then, it would seem that we are stuck with *personal survival* and *non-survival*, in their various permutations, as the only basic posthumous scenarios. Taken together, these two scenarios appear to be exhaustive: no other option, whether expressed in philosophical or religious terms, is in the offing.

The readings in Parts I through IV of this book constitute a critical examination of these two basic posthumous scenarios, personal survival or the lack thereof. The question of survival, however, is different from the question of deathlessness, or immortality, which we will take up in Part I. Our first reading is from Plato's dialogue *Phaedo*, but in a later passage from that dialogue, a part not included in our excerpted reading, one of the discussants points out that even if you can establish that the soul does not perish with the body, you have not thereby established that the soul will never ever perish: survival after this life might be merely temporary, and our ultimate fate, some time after this life, might be sealed. Many authors, notably Miguel de Unamuno, whom we will meet in Part IV, insist that it is the question of *immortality*, not merely survival after this life, that truly concerns us.

1

The Soul Will Not Fade Away

Plato

Translated by Hugh Tredennick[1]

Phaedo is a philosophical exchange, or *dialogue*, that purportedly took place in 399 BC between the old philosopher Socrates and a group of close friends in a jail cell where Socrates was being held pending his execution. A jury of Socrates' fellow Athenians has found him guilty of "refusing to recognize the gods recognized by the state" and "corrupting the youth." The dialogue begins on the morning of the day that Socrates has been condemned to die. His friends met at the jail, and when they are led into Socrates' cell, the warders have just released Socrates from his chains. The ensuing dialogue continues until sunset, when Socrates drinks the lethal poison hemlock in the presence of his friends. Appropriately enough, the topic of discussion is the fate of the soul.

Phaedo was written in 360 BC by Socrates' most brilliant student, Plato. It is important to note that the figure of Socrates in this dialogue is, at least to some extent, Plato's invention. Scholars are not entirely sure which of the views that Plato puts into Socrates' mouth were in fact those of the historical Socrates, but according to many experts the views on the nature and the fate of the soul are largely Plato's own views.

The dialogue is narrated in the voice of Phaedo, an out-of-town follower of Socrates who was present on Socrates' final day. On his way back to Elis, a city-state on the west of the Peloponnesian Peninsula of Greece, Phaedo encounters Echecrates, who asks him to

---

[1]The section headings have been added by your editor (MM).

give a full report of the discussion that took place on Socrates' last day. The main characters in the dialogue are

Socrates: The protagonist of the *Phaedo*, and most of Plato's dialogues. In this dialogue Socrates is a seventy-year-old "lover of wisdom" who is calm and confident that something good awaits him after death.

Simmias: One of Socrates' two main interlocutors in this dialogue, along with Cebes. Simmias is from the Greek city-state of Thebes, and like Echecrates, he is a young follower of the philosopher Pythagoras.

Cebes: The other main interlocutor, along with Simmias. Cebes, too, is a follower of Pythagoras.

Phaedo: The narrator and namesake of the dialogue. He is a handsome young man from Elis who has become enamored of Socrates and his teachings.

Echecrates: A Pythagorean philosopher from the Peloponnesian city-state of Phlius, where he encounters Phaedo and asks him to tell the story of Socrates' final hours. On a couple of occasions in the complete dialogue, the narrative is interrupted by a brief conversation between Echecrates and Phaedo, but in our abridged reading we do not encounter Echecrates.

Crito: An old friend of Socrates, of about Socrates' age. We do not hear mention of Crito until the very end of our excerpted reading.

Phaedo contains several arguments for the survival of the soul and its immortality. After the first section below, our abridged reading includes the following four main arguments:

I) Opposites from Opposites (Stephanus numbers 70a-72d).[2]
   Coming-to-life follows dying.
II) Knowledge as Recollection (72e-75e).
   The soul pre-exists the body.
III) The Affinity Argument (78d-81a).
   The soul resembles the changeless forms.
IV) The Soul Does Not Admit Death (104e-105e).
   The soul is immortal.

---

[2]Stephanus numbers are a standardized reference system intended to make it easier to cite passages in Plato's dialogues.

The soul can best pursue truth when free of sensual distractions (Stephanus numbers 64c–68b)

Socrates: Do we believe that there is such a thing as death?

Most certainly, said Simmias, taking up the role of answering.

Is it simply the release of the soul from the body? Is death nothing more or less than this, the separate condition of the body by itself when it is released from the soul, and the separate condition by itself of the soul when released from the body? Is death anything else than this?

No, just that.

Well then, my boy, see whether you agree with me. I fancy that this will help us to find out the answer to our problem. Do you think that it is right for a philosopher to concern himself with the so-called pleasures connected with food and drink?

Certainly not, Socrates, said Simmias.

What about sexual pleasures?

No, not at all.

And what about the other attentions that we pay to our bodies? Do you think that a philosopher attaches any importance to them? I mean things like providing himself with smart clothes and shoes and other bodily ornaments; do you think that he values them or despises them—in so far as there is no real necessity for him to go in for that sort of thing?

I think the true philosopher despises them, he said.

Then it is your opinion in general that a man of this kind is not concerned with the body, but keeps his attention directed as much as he can away from it and toward the soul?

Yes, it is.

So it is clear first of all in the case of physical pleasures that the philosopher frees his soul from association with the body, so far as is possible, to a greater extent than other men?

It seems so.

And most people think, do they not, Simmias, that a man who finds no pleasure and takes no part in these things does not deserve to live, and that anyone who thinks nothing of physical pleasures has one foot in the grave?

That is perfectly true.

Now take the acquisition of knowledge. Is the body a hindrance or not, if one takes it into partnership to share an investigation? What I mean is this. Is there any certainty in human sight and hearing, or is it true, as the poets are always dinning into our ears, that we neither hear nor see anything accurately? Yet if these senses are not clear and accurate, the rest can hardly be so, because they are all inferior to the first two. Don't you agree?

Certainly.

Then when is it that the soul attains to truth? When it tries to investigate anything with the help of the body, it is obviously led astray.

Quite so.

Is it not in the course of reflection, if at all, that the soul gets a clear view of facts?

Yes.

Surely the soul can best reflect when it is free of all distractions such as hearing or sight or pain or pleasure of any kind—that is, when it ignores the body and becomes as far as possible independent, avoiding all physical contacts and associations as much as it can, in its search for reality.

That is so.

Then here too—in despising the body and avoiding it, and endeavoring to become independent—the philosopher's soul is ahead of all the rest.

It seems so.

Here are some more questions, Simmias. Do we recognize such a thing as absolute uprightness?

Indeed we do.

And absolute beauty and goodness too?

Of course.

Have you ever seen any of these things with your eyes?

Certainly not, said he.

Well, have you ever apprehended them with any other bodily sense? By "them" I mean not only absolute tallness or health or strength, but the real nature of any given thing—what it actually is. Is it through the body that we get the truest perception of them? Isn't it true that in any inquiry you are likely to attain more nearly to knowledge of your object in proportion to the care and accuracy with which you have prepared yourself to understand that object in itself?

Certainly.

Don't you think that the person who is likely to succeed in this attempt most perfectly is the one who approaches each object, as far as possible, with the unaided intellect, without taking account of any sense of sight in his thinking, or dragging any other sense into his reckoning—the man who pursues the truth by applying his pure and unadulterated thought to the pure and unadulterated object, cutting himself off as much as possible from his eyes and ears and virtually all the rest of his body, as an impediment which by its presence prevents the soul from attaining to truth and clear thinking? Is not this the person, Simmias, who will reach the goal of reality, if anybody can?

What you say is absolutely true, Socrates, said Simmias.

All these considerations, said Socrates, must surely prompt serious philosophers to review the position in some such way as this. It looks as though this were a bypath leading to the right track. So long as we keep to the body and our soul is contaminated with this imperfection, there is no chance of our ever attaining satisfactorily to our object, which we assert to be truth. In the first place, the body provides us with innumerable distractions in the pursuit of our necessary sustenance, and any diseases that attack us hinder our quest for reality. Besides, the body fills us with loves and desires and fears and all sorts of fancies and a great deal of nonsense, with the result that we literally never get an opportunity to think at all about anything. Wars and revolutions and battles are due simply and solely to the body and its desires. All wars are undertaken for the acquisition of wealth, and the reason why we have to acquire wealth is the body, because we are slaves in its service. That is why, on all these accounts, we have so little time for philosophy. Worst of all, if we do obtain any leisure from the body's claims and turn to some line of inquiry, the body intrudes once more into our investigations, interrupting, disturbing, distracting, and preventing us from getting a glimpse of the truth. We are in fact convinced that if we are ever to have pure knowledge of anything, we must get rid of the body and contemplate things by themselves with the soul by itself. It seems, to judge from the argument, that the wisdom which we desire and upon which we profess to have set our hearts will be attainable only when we are dead, and not in our lifetime. If no pure knowledge is possible in the company of the body, then either it is totally impossible to acquire knowledge, or it is only possible after death, because it is only then that the soul will be separate and independent of the body. It seems that so long as we are alive, we shall continue closest to knowledge if we avoid as much as we can all contact and association with the body, except when they are absolutely necessary, and instead of allowing ourselves to become infected with its nature, purify ourselves from it until God himself gives us deliverance. In this way, by keeping ourselves uncontaminated by the follies of the body, we shall probably reach the company of others like ourselves and gain direct knowledge of all that is pure and uncontaminated—that is, presumably, of truth. For one who is not pure himself to attain to the realm of purity would no doubt be a breach of universal justice. Something to this effect, Simmias, is what I imagine all real lovers of learning must think themselves and say to one another. Don't you agree with me?

Most emphatically, Socrates.

Very well, then, said Socrates, if this is true, there is good reason for anyone who reaches the end of this journey which lies before me to hope that there, if anywhere, he will attain the object to which all our efforts have been directed during my past life. So this journey which is now ordained for me carries a happy prospect for any other man also who believes that his mind has been prepared by purification.

It does indeed, said Simmias.

And purification, as we saw some time ago in our discussion, consists in separating the soul as much as possible from the body, and accustoming it to withdraw from all contact with the body and concentrate itself by itself, and to have its dwelling, so far as it can, both now and in the future, alone by itself, freed from the shackles of the body. Does not that follow?

Yes, it does, said Simmias.

Is not what we call death a freeing and separation of soul from body?

Certainly, he said.

And the desire to free the soul is found chiefly, or rather only, in the true philosopher. In fact the philosopher's occupation consists precisely in the freeing and separation of soul from body. Isn't that so?

Apparently.

Well then, as I said at the beginning, if a man has trained himself throughout his life to live in a state as close as possible to death, would it not be ridiculous for him to be distressed when death comes to him?

It would, of course.

Then it is a fact, Simmias, that true philosophers make dying their profession, and that to them of all men death is least alarming. Look at it in this way. If they are thoroughly dissatisfied with the body, and long to have their souls independent of it, when this happens would it not be entirely unreasonable to be frightened and distressed? Would they not naturally be glad to set out for the place where there is a prospect of attaining the object of their lifelong desire—which is wisdom—and of escaping from an unwelcome association? Surely there are many who have chosen of their own free will to follow dead lovers and wives and sons to the next world, in the hope of seeing and meeting there the persons whom they loved. If this is so, will a true lover of wisdom who has firmly grasped this same conviction—that he will never attain to wisdom worthy of the name elsewhere than in the next world—will he be grieved at dying? Will he not be glad to make that journey? We must suppose so, my dear boy, that is, if he is a real philosopher, because then he will be of the firm belief that he will never find wisdom in all its purity in any other place. If this is so, would it not be quite unreasonable, as I said just now, for such a man to be afraid of death?

It would, indeed.

[…]

Opposites from opposites (70a–72d)

When Socrates had finished, Cebes made his reply. The rest of your statement, Socrates, he said, seems excellent to me, but what you said about the soul leaves the average person with grave misgivings that when it is released from the body it may no longer exist anywhere, but may be dispersed and destroyed on the very day that the man himself dies, as soon as it is freed from the body, that as it emerges it may be dissipated like breath or smoke, and vanish away, so that nothing is left of it anywhere. Of course if it still existed as an independent unity, released from all the evils which you have just described, there would be a strong and glorious hope, Socrates, that what you say is true. But I fancy that it requires no little faith and assurance to believe that the soul exists after death and retains some active force and intelligence.

Quite true, Cebes, said Socrates. But what are we to do about it? Is it your wish that we should go on speculating about the subject, to see whether this view is likely to be true or not?

For my part, said Cebes, I should be very glad to hear what you think about it.

At any rate, said Socrates, I hardly think that anyone who heard us now—even a comic poet—would say that I am wasting time and discoursing on subjects which do not concern me. So if that is how you feel, we had better continue our inquiry. Let us approach it from this point of view. Do the souls of the departed exist in another world or not? There is an old legend, which we still remember, to the effect that they do exist there, after leaving here, and that they return again to this world and come into being from the dead. If this is so—that the living come into being again from the dead—does it not follow that our souls exist in the other world? They could not come into being again if they did not exist, and it will be sufficient proof that my contention is true if it really becomes apparent that the living come from the dead, and from nowhere else. But if this is not so, we shall need some other argument.

Quite so, said Cebes.

If you want to understand the question more readily, said Socrates, consider it with reference not only to human beings but to all animals and plants. Let us see whether in general everything that admits of generation is generated in this way and no other—opposites from opposites, wherever there is an opposite—as for instance beauty is opposite to ugliness and right to wrong, and there are countless other examples. Let us consider whether it is a necessary law that everything which has an opposite is generated from that opposite and from no other source. For example, when a thing becomes bigger, it must, I suppose, have been smaller first before it became bigger?

Yes.

And similarly if it becomes smaller, it must be bigger first, and become smaller afterward?

That is so, said Cebes.

And the weaker comes from the stronger, and the faster from the slower?

Certainly.

One more instance. If a thing becomes worse, is it not from being better? And if more just, from being more unjust?

Of course.

Are we satisfied, then, said Socrates, that everything is generated in this way—opposites from opposites?

Perfectly.

Here is another question. Do not these examples present another feature, that between each pair of opposites there are two processes of generation, one from the first to the second, and another from the second to the first? Between a larger and a smaller object are there not the processes of increase and decrease, and do we not describe them in this way as increasing and decreasing?

Yes, said Cebes.

Is it not the same with separating and combining, cooling and heating, and all the rest of them? Even if we sometimes do not use the actual terms, must it not in fact hold good universally that they come one from the other, and that there is a process of generation from each to the other?

Certainly, said Cebes.

Well then, said Socrates, is there an opposite to living, as sleeping is opposite to waking?

Certainly.

What?

Being dead.

So if they are opposites, they come from one another, and have their two processes of generation between the two of them?

Of course.

Very well, then, said Socrates, I will state one pair of opposites that I mentioned just now—the opposites themselves and the processes between them—and you shall state the other. My opposites are sleeping and waking, and I say that waking comes from sleeping and sleeping from waking, and that the processes between them are going to sleep and waking up. Does that satisfy you, he asked, or not?

Perfectly.

Now you tell me in the same way, he went on, about life and death. Do you not admit that death is the opposite of life?

I do.

And that they come from one another?

Yes.

Then what comes from the living?

The dead.

And what, asked Socrates, comes from the dead?

I must admit, he said, that it is the living.

So it is from the dead, Cebes, that living things and people come?

Evidently.

Then our souls do exist in the next world.

So it seems.

And one of the two processes in this case is really quite certain—dying is certain enough, isn't it?

Yes, it is, said Cebes.

What shall we do, then? Shall we omit the complementary process, and leave a defect here in the law of nature? Or must we supply an opposite process to that of dying?

Surely we must supply it, he said.

And what is it?

Coming to life again.

Then if there is such a thing as coming to life again, said Socrates, it must be a process from death to life?

Quite so.

So we agree upon this too—that the living have come from the dead no less than the dead from the living. But I think we decided that if this was so, it was a sufficient proof that the souls of the dead must exist in some place from which they are reborn. It seems to me, Socrates, he said, that this follows necessarily from our agreement. I think there is another way too, Cebes, in which you can see that we were not wrong in our agreement. If there were not a constant correspondence in the process of generation between the two sets of opposites, going round in a sort of cycle, if generation were a straight path to the opposite extreme without any return to the starting point or any deflection, do you realize that in the end everything would have the same quality and reach the same state, and change would cease altogether?

What do you mean?

Nothing difficult to understand, replied Socrates. For example, if "falling asleep" existed, and "waking up" did not balance it by making something come out of sleep, you must realize that in the end everything would make Endymion[3] look foolish. He would be nowhere, because the whole world would be in the same state—asleep. And if everything were combined and nothing separated, we should soon have Anaxagoras' "all things together." In just the same way, my dear Cebes, if everything that has some share of life were to die, and if after death the dead remained in that form and did not come to life again, would it not be quite inevitable that in the end everything should be dead and nothing alive? If living things came from other living things, and the living things died, what possible means could prevent their number from being exhausted by death?

None that I can see, Socrates, said Cebes. What you say seems to be perfectly true.

Yes, Cebes, he said, if anything is true, I believe that this is, and we were not mistaken in our agreement upon it. Coming to life again is a fact, and it is a fact that the living come from the dead, and a fact that the souls of the dead exist.

---

[3]According to the myth, Selene, the Titan goddess of the moon, fell in love with the handsome youth Endymion and asked Zeus to grant him everlasting youth. In response, Zeus put Endymion into an eternal sleep. —MM

Knowledge as recollection (72e–75e)

Besides, Socrates, rejoined Cebes, there is that theory which you have often described to us—that what we call learning is really just recollection. If that is true, then surely what we recollect now we must have learned at some time before, which is impossible unless our souls existed somewhere before they entered this human shape. So in that way too it seems likely that the soul is immortal.

How did the proofs of that theory go, Cebes? broke in Simmias. Remind me, because at the moment I can't quite remember.

One very good argument, said Cebes, is that when people are asked questions, if the question is put in the right way they can give a perfectly correct answer, which they could not possibly do unless they had some knowledge and a proper grasp of the subject. And then if you confront people with a diagram or anything like that, the way in which they react is an unmistakable proof that the theory is correct.[4]

And if you don't find that convincing, Simmias, said Socrates, see whether this appeals to you. I suppose that you find it hard to understand how what we call learning can be recollection?

Not at all, said Simmias. All that I want is to be helped to do what we are talking about—to recollect. I can practically remember enough to satisfy me already, from Cebes' approach to the subject, but I should be nonetheless glad to hear how you meant to approach it.

I look at it in this way, said Socrates. We are agreed, I suppose, that if a person is to be reminded of anything, he must first know it at some time or other?

Quite so.

Are we also agreed in calling it recollection when knowledge comes in a particular way? I will explain what I mean. Suppose that a person on seeing or hearing or otherwise noticing one thing not only becomes conscious of that thing but also thinks of a something else which is an object of a different sort of knowledge. Are we not justified in saying that he was reminded of the object which he thought of?

What do you mean?

---

[4]In Plato's dialogue *Meno*, Socrates uses a drawing to help a servant boy to "recall" consequences of the Pythagorean theorem. —MM

Let me give you an example. A human being and a musical instrument, I suppose you will agree, are different objects of knowledge.

Yes, certainly.

Well, you know what happens to lovers when they see a musical instrument or a piece of clothing or any other private property of the person whom they love. When they recognize the thing, their minds conjure up a picture of its owner. That is recollection. In the same way the sight of Simmias often reminds one of Cebes, and of course there are thousands of other examples.

Yes, of course there are, said Simmias.

So by recollection we mean the sort of experience which I have just described, especially when it happens with reference to things which we had not seen for such a long time that we had forgotten them.

Quite so.

Well, then, is it possible for a person who sees a picture of a horse or a musical instrument to be reminded of a person, or for someone who sees a picture of Simmias to be reminded of Cebes?

Perfectly.

And is it possible for someone who sees a portrait of Simmias to be reminded of Simmias himself?

Yes, it is.

Does it not follow from all this that recollection may be caused either by similar or by dissimilar objects?

Yes, it does.

When you are reminded by similarity, surely you must also be conscious whether the similarity is perfect or only partial.

Yes, you must.

Here is a further step, said Socrates. We admit, I suppose, that there is such a thing as equality—not the equality of stick to stick and stone to stone, and so on, but something beyond all that and distinct from it—absolute equality. Are we to admit this or not?

Yes indeed, said Simmias, most emphatically.

And do we know what it is?

Certainly.

Where did we get our knowledge? Was it not from the particular examples that we mentioned just now? Was it not from seeing equal sticks or stones or other equal objects that we got the notion of equality, although it is something quite distinct from them? Look at it in this way. Is it not true that equal stones and sticks sometimes, without changing in themselves, appear equal to one person and unequal to another?

Certainly.

Well, now, have you ever thought that things which were absolutely equal were unequal, or that equality was inequality?

No, never, Socrates.

Then these equal things are not the same as absolute equality.

Not in the least, as I see it, Socrates.

And yet it is these equal things that have suggested and conveyed to you your knowledge of absolute equality, although they are distinct from it?

Perfectly true.

Whether it is similar to them or dissimilar?

Certainly.

It makes no difference, said Socrates. So long as the sight of one thing suggests another to you, it must be a cause of recollection, whether the two things are alike or not.

Quite so.

Well, now, he said, what do we find in the case of the equal sticks and other things of which we were speaking just now? Do they seem to us to be equal in the sense of absolute equality, or do they fall short of it in so far as they only approximate to equality? Or don't they fall short at all?

They do, said Simmias, a long way.

Suppose that when you see something you say to yourself, This thing which I can see has a tendency to be like something else, but it falls short and cannot be really like it, only a poor imitation. Don't you agree with me that anyone who receives that impression must in fact have previous knowledge of that thing which he says that the other resembles, but inadequately?

Certainly he must.

Very well, then, is that our position with regard to equal things and absolute equality?

Exactly.

Then we must have had some previous knowledge of equality before the time when we first saw equal things and realized that they were striving after equality, but fell short of it.

That is so.

And at the same time we are agreed also upon this point, that we have not and could not have acquired this notion of equality except by sight or touch or one of the other senses. I am treating them as being all the same.

They are the same, Socrates, for the purpose of our argument.

So it must be through the senses that we obtained the notion that all sensible equals are striving after absolute equality but falling short of it. Is that correct?

Yes, it is.

So before we began to see and hear and use our other senses we must somewhere have acquired the knowledge that there is such a thing as absolute equality. Otherwise we could never have realized, by using it as a standard for comparison, that all equal objects of sense are desirous of being like it, but are only imperfect copies.

That is the logical conclusion, Socrates.

Did we not begin to see and hear and possess our other senses from the moment of birth?

Certainly.

But we admitted that we must have obtained our knowledge of equality before we obtained them.

Yes.

So we must have obtained it before birth.

So it seems.

Then if we obtained it before our birth, and possessed it when we were born, we had knowledge, both before and at the moment of birth, not only of equality and relative magnitudes, but of all absolute standards. Our present argument applies no more to equality than it does to absolute beauty, goodness, uprightness, holiness, and, as I maintain, all those characteristics which we designate in our discussions by the term *absolute*. So we must have obtained knowledge of all these characteristics before our birth.

That is so.

And unless we invariably forget it after obtaining it we must always be born knowing and continue to know all through our lives, because "to know" means simply to retain the knowledge which one has acquired, and not to lose it. Is not what we call "forgetting" simply the loss of knowledge, Simmias?

Most certainly, Socrates.

And if it is true that we acquired our knowledge before our birth, and lost it at the moment of birth, but afterward, by the exercise of our senses upon sensible objects, recover the knowledge which we had once before, I suppose that what we call learning will be the recovery of our own knowledge, and surely we should be right in calling this recollection.

Quite so.

[…]

The affinity argument (78d–81a)

Socrates: Then let us return to the same examples which we were discussing before. Does that absolute reality which we define in our discussions remain always constant and invariable, or not? Does absolute equality or beauty or any other independent entity which really exists ever admit change of any kind? Or does each one of these uniform and independent entities remain always constant and invariable, never admitting any alteration in any respect or in any sense?

They must be constant and invariable, Socrates, said Cebes.

Well, what about the concrete instances of beauty—such as men, horses, clothes, and so on—or of equality, or any other members of a class corresponding to an absolute entity? Are they constant, or are they, on the contrary, scarcely ever in the same relation in any sense either to themselves or to one another?

With them, Socrates, it is just the opposite; they are never free from variation.

And these concrete objects you can touch and see and perceive by your other senses, but those constant entities you cannot possibly apprehend except by thinking; they are invisible to our sight.

That is perfectly true, said Cebes.

So you think that we should assume two classes of things, one visible and the other invisible?

Yes, we should.

The invisible being invariable, and the visible never being the same?

Yes, we should assume that too.

Well, now, said Socrates, are we not part body, part soul?

Certainly.

Then to which class do we say that the body would have the closer resemblance and relation?

Quite obviously to the visible.

And the soul, is it visible or invisible?

Invisible to men, at any rate, Socrates, he said.

But surely we have been speaking of things visible or invisible to our human nature. Do you think that we had some other nature in view?

No, human nature.

What do we say about the soul, then? Is it visible or invisible?

Not visible.

Invisible, then?

Yes.

So soul is more like the invisible, and body more like the visible?

That follows inevitably, Socrates.

Did we not say some time ago that when the soul uses the instrumentality of the body for any inquiry, whether through sight or hearing or any other sense—because using the body implies using the senses—it is drawn away by the body into the realm of the variable, and loses its way and becomes confused and dizzy, as though it were fuddled, through contact with things of a similar nature?

Certainly.

But when it investigates by itself, it passes into the realm of the pure and everlasting and immortal and changeless, and being of a kindred nature, when it is once independent and free from interference, consorts with it always and strays no longer, but remains, in that realm of the absolute, constant and invariable, through contact with beings of a similar nature. And this condition of the soul we call wisdom.

An excellent description, and perfectly true, Socrates.

Very well, then, in the light of all that we have said, both now and before, to which class do you think that the soul bears the closer resemblance and relation?

I think, Socrates, said Cebes, that even the dullest person would agree, from this line of reasoning, that the soul is in every possible way more like the invariable than the variable.

And the body?

To the other.

Look at it in this way too. When soul and body are both in the same place, nature teaches the one to serve and be subject, the other to rule and govern. In this relation which do you think resembles the divine and which the mortal part? Don't you think that it is the nature of the divine to rule and direct, and that of the mortal to be subject and serve?

I do.

Then which does the soul resemble?

Obviously, Socrates, soul resembles the divine, and body the mortal.

Now, Cebes, he said, see whether this is our conclusion from all that we have said. The soul is most like that which is divine, immortal, intelligible, uniform, indissoluble, and ever self-consistent and invariable, whereas body is most like that which is human, mortal, multiform, unintelligible, dissoluble, and never self-consistent. Can we adduce any conflicting argument, my dear Cebes, to show that this is not so?

No, we cannot.

Very well, then, in that case is it not natural for body to disintegrate rapidly, but for soul to be quite or very nearly indissoluble?

Certainly.

Of course you know that when a person dies, although it is natural for the visible and physical part of him, which lies here in the visible world and which we call his corpse, to decay and fall to pieces and be dissipated, none of this happens to it immediately. It remains as it was for quite a long time, even if death takes place when the body is well nourished and in the warm season. Indeed, when the body is dried and embalmed, as in Egypt, it remains almost intact for an incredible time, and even if the rest of the body decays, some parts of it—the bones and sinews and anything else like them—are practically everlasting. That is so, is it not?

Yes.

Bu the soul, the invisible part, which goes away to a place that is, like itself, glorious, pure, and invisible—the true Hades or unseen world—into the presence of the good and wise God, where, if God so wills, my soul must shortly go—will it, if its very nature is such as I have described, be dispersed and destroyed at the moment of its release from the body, as is the popular view? Far from it, my dear Simmias and Cebes. The truth is much more like this. If at its release the soul is pure and carries with it no contamination of the body, because it has never willingly associated with it in life, but has shunned it and kept itself separate as its regular practice—in other words, if it has pursued philosophy in the right way and really practiced how to face death easily—this is what "practicing death" means isn't it?

Most decidedly.

[...]

The soul does not admit death (104e–105e)

Socrates: I proposed just now to define what sort of things they are which, although they are not themselves directly opposed to a given opposite, nevertheless do not admit it, as in the present example, three, although not the opposite of even, nevertheless does not admit it, because three is always accompanied by the opposite of even—and similarly with two and odd, or fire and cold, and hosts of others. Well, see whether you accept this definition. Not only does an opposite not admit its opposite, but if anything is accompanied by a form which has an opposite, and meets that opposite, then the thing which is accompanied never admits the opposite of the form by which it is accompanied. Let me refresh your memory; there is no harm in hearing a thing several times. Five will not admit the form of even, nor will ten, which is double five, admit the form of odd. Double has an opposite of its own, but at the same time it will not admit the form of odd. Nor will one and a half, or other fractions such as one half or three quarters and so on, admit the form of whole. I assume that you follow me and agree.

I follow and agree perfectly, said Cebes.

Then run over the same ground with me from the beginning, and don't answer in the exact terms of the question, but follow my example. I say this because besides the "safe answer" that I described at first, as the result of this discussion I now see another means of safety. Suppose, for instance, that you ask me what must be present in body to make it hot. I shall not return the safe but ingenuous answer that it is heat, but a more sophisticated one, based on the results of our discussion—namely that it is fire. And if you ask what must be present in a body to make it diseased, I shall say not disease but fever. Similarly if you ask what must be present in a number to make it odd, I shall say not oddness, but unity, and so on. See whether you have a sufficient grasp now of what I want from you.

Quite sufficient.

Then tell me, what must be present in a body to make it alive?

Soul.

Is this always so?

Of course.

So whenever soul takes possession of a body, it always brings life with it?

Yes, it does.

Is there an opposite to life, or not?

Yes, there is.

What?

Death.

Does it follow, then, from our earlier agreement, that soul will never admit the opposite of that which accompanies it?

Most definitely, said Cebes.

Well, now, what name did we apply just now to that which does not admit the form of even?

Uneven.

And what do we call that which does not admit justice, or culture?

Uncultured, and the other unjust.

Very good. And what do we call that which does not admit death?

Immortal.

And soul does not admit death?

No.

So soul is immortal.

Yes, it is immortal.

Well, said Socrates, can we say that that has been proved? What do you think?

Most completely, Socrates.

[...]

* * *

Our excerpt does not include the final passage of the *Phaedo*, but it is so famous and so moving that we would be remiss not to mention it here. As Socrates feels the effects of the hemlock that he has just drunk, he suddenly lifts his head and tells his old friend Crito, "we ought to offer a cock to Asclepius." It was the Greek custom after recovery from an illness to make an offering to the divine healer, Asclepius. In those final moments, it seems, Socrates felt himself to be recovering from a long state of debilitating captivity—the captivity of the soul imprisoned in the body.

The dialogue ends with the following words: "Such was the end of our comrade, Echecrates, a man who, we would say, was of all those we have known the best, and also the wisest and the most upright."

2

Letter to Menoeceus

Epicurus

Translated by Robert Drew Hicks

We know little of Epicurus' life, but according to the ancient writer Diogenes Laertius, in his *Lives and Opinions of Eminent Philosophers* (Vol. II, Book X), he was born on the island of Samos in 341 BC. After some years of travel, he opened a school outside of Athens in about 306 BC. The property included a garden, and soon his followers were called "philosophers of the Garden." Members of the school included women and at least one slave. This exposed Epicurus and his followers to ridicule, although the scoffers grudgingly admired the philosophers of the Garden for their close friendship and mutual support. Epicurus wrote prolifically, but only scattered fragments of his works have come down to us. Among these fragments are several letters, including our reading below, which summarizes Epicurus' views and sets down his advice to followers. His most famous follower, Titus Lucretius Carus, wrote two centuries after the master's death. We will encounter Lucretius in Part IV.

Greetings,

Let no one be slow to seek wisdom when he is young nor weary in the search when he is grown old. For no age is too early or too late for the health of the soul. And to say that the season for studying philosophy has not yet come, or that it is past and gone, is like saying that the season for happiness is not yet or that it is now no more. Therefore, both old and young ought to seek wisdom, the former in order that, as age comes over him, he may be young in good things because of the grace of what has been, and the latter in order that, while he is young, he may at the same time be old, because he has no fear of the things which are to come. So we must exercise ourselves in the things that bring happiness, since, if that be present, we have everything, and, if that be absent, all our actions are directed toward attaining it.

Those things which I have always declared to you, do them and exercise yourself in them, holding them to be the elements of right life. First believe that God is a living being immortal and happy, according to the notion of a god indicated by the common sense of humankind; and so of him do not affirm anything that is foreign to his immortality or that is repugnant to his blessedness. Believe about him whatever may uphold both his happiness and his immortality. For truly there are gods, and knowledge of them is evident; but they are not such as the multitude believe, seeing that people do not steadfastly maintain the notions they form respecting them. Not the person who denies the gods worshipped by the multitude, but he who affirms of the gods what the multitude believes about them is truly impious. For the utterances of the multitude about the gods are not true preconceptions but false assumptions; hence it is that the greatest evils happen to the wicked and the greatest blessings happen to the good from the hand of the gods, seeing that they are always favorable to their own good qualities and take pleasure in people like to themselves, but reject as alien whatever is not of their kind.

Accustom yourself to believe that death is nothing to us, for good and evil imply awareness, and death is the privation of all awareness; therefore a right understanding that death is nothing to us makes the mortality of life enjoyable, not by adding to life an unlimited time, but by taking away the yearning after immortality. For life has no terror for those who thoroughly apprehend that there are no terrors for them in ceasing to live. Foolish, therefore, is the person who says that he fears death, not because it will pain when it comes, but because it pains in the prospect. Whatever causes no annoyance when it is present causes only a groundless pain in the expectation. Death, therefore, the most awful of evils, is nothing to us, seeing that, when we are, death is not come, and, when death is come, we are not. It is nothing, then, either to the living or to the dead, for with the living it is not and the dead exist no longer.

But in the world, at one time people shun death as the greatest of all evils, and at another time choose it as a respite from the evils in life. The wise person does not deprecate life nor does he fear the cessation of life. The thought of life is no offense to him, nor is the cessation of life regarded as an evil. And even as people choose of food not merely and simply the larger portion, but the more pleasant, so the wise seek to enjoy the time which is most pleasant and not merely that which is longest. And he who admonishes the young to live well and the old to make a good end speaks foolishly, not merely because of the desirability of life, but because the same exercise at once teaches to live well and to die well. Much worse is he who says that it were good not to be born, but when once one is born to pass with all speed through the gates of Hades. For if he truly believes this, why does he not depart from life? It were easy for him to do so, if once he were firmly convinced. Even if he speaks only in jest his words are foolishness, for those who hear him do not believe it.

We must remember that the future is neither wholly ours nor wholly not ours, so that neither must we count upon it as quite certain to come nor despair of it as quite certain not to come.

We must also reflect that of desires some are natural, others are groundless; and that of the natural some are necessary as well as natural, and some natural only. And of the necessary desires some are necessary if we are to be happy, some if the body is to be rid of uneasiness, some if we are even to live. He who has a clear and certain understanding of these things will direct every preference and aversion toward securing health of body and tranquility of mind, seeing that this is the sum and end of a happy life. For the end of all our actions is to be free from pain and fear, and, when once we have attained all this, the tempest of the soul is calmed; seeing that the living creature has no need to go in search of something that is lacking, nor to look for anything else by which the good of the soul and of the body will be fulfilled. When we are pained because of the absence of pleasure, then and only then do we feel the need of pleasure. For this reason we call pleasure the alpha and omega of a happy life. Pleasure is our first and kindred good. It is the starting-point of every choice and of every aversion, and to it we come back, inasmuch as we make feeling the rule by which to judge of every good thing.

And since pleasure is our first and native good, for that reason we do not choose every pleasure whatever, but often pass over many pleasures when a greater annoyance ensues from them. And often we consider pains superior to pleasures when submission to the pains for a long time brings us as a consequence a greater pleasure. While therefore all pleasure because it is naturally akin to us is good, not all pleasure is worthy of choice, just as all pain is an evil and yet not all pain is to be shunned. It is, however, by measuring one against another, and by looking at the conveniences and inconveniences, that all these matters must be judged. Sometimes we treat the good as an evil, and the evil, on the contrary, as a good.

Again, we regard independence of outward things as a great good, not so as in all cases to use little, but so as to be contented with little if we have not much, being honestly persuaded that they have the sweetest enjoyment of luxury who stand least in need of it, and that whatever is natural is easily procured and only the vain and worthless hard to win. Plain fare gives as much pleasure as a costly diet, when once the pain of want has been removed, while bread and water confer the highest possible pleasure when they are brought to hungry lips. To habituate one's self therefore, to simple and inexpensive diet supplies all that is needful for health, and enables a person to meet the necessary requirements of life without shrinking and it places us in a better condition when we approach at intervals a costly fare and renders us fearless of fortune.

When we say, then, that pleasure is the end and aim, we do not mean the pleasures of the prodigal or the pleasures of sensuality, as we are understood to do by some through ignorance, prejudice, or willful misrepresentation. By pleasure we mean the absence of pain in the body and of trouble in the soul. It is not an unbroken succession of drinking-bouts and of merrymaking, not sexual love, not the enjoyment of the fish and other delicacies of a luxurious table, which produce a pleasant life; it is sober reasoning, searching out the grounds of every choice and avoidance, and banishing those beliefs through which the greatest disturbances take possession of the soul. Of all this, the beginning and the greatest good is prudence. For this reason prudence is a more precious thing even than the other virtues, teaching us that it is not possible to lead a life of pleasure which is not also a life of prudence, honor, and justice; nor lead a life of prudence, honor, and justice, which is not also a life of pleasure. For the virtues have grown into one with a pleasant life, and a pleasant life is inseparable from them.

Who, then, is superior in your judgment to such a person? He holds a holy belief concerning the gods, and is altogether free from the fear of death. He has diligently considered the end fixed by nature, and understands how easily the limit of good things can be reached and attained, and how either the duration or the intensity of evils is but slight. Destiny which some introduce as sovereign over all things, he laughs to scorn, affirming rather that some things happen of necessity, others by chance, others through our own agency. For he sees that necessity destroys responsibility and that chance or fortune is inconstant; whereas our own actions are free, and it is to them that praise and blame naturally attach. It were better, indeed, to accept the legends of the gods than to bow beneath destiny which the natural philosophers have imposed. The one holds out some faint hope that we may escape if we honor the gods, while the necessity of the naturalists is deaf to all entreaties. Nor does he hold chance to be a god, as the world in general does, for in the acts of a god there is no disorder; nor to be a cause, though an uncertain one, for he believes that no good or evil is dispensed by chance to people so as to make life happy, though it supplies the starting-point of great good and great evil. He believes that the misfortune of the wise is better than the prosperity of the fool. It is better, in short, that what is well judged in action should not owe its successful issue to the aid of chance.

Exercise yourself in these and kindred precepts day and night, both by yourself and with one who is like-minded; then never, either in waking or in dream, will you be disturbed, but will live as a god among people. For people lose all appearance of mortality by living in the midst of immortal blessings.

3

Ten Reasons for Believing in Immortality

John Haynes Holmes

The author of the next reading claims, rather eagerly, that the idea of immortality "has appeared in all ages and among all People"—and for good reasons, which he proceeds to describe. The reading contains "ten of the many reasons for the most persistent faith which has ever beset the heart of man," namely, that the death of the body is not extinction of the personality, and that the latter never dies.

The reader will notice that Holmes' views of immortality, and some of his arguments, too, are familiar from *Phaedo*. Like Plato, the Reverend Holmes assures us that his authority is *reason*, not religious tradition: "I see no reason for believing in immortality of the soul," he writes, "[just] because Jesus is reputed to have risen from the dead." This is not the usual Christian view, but it does point up the fact that, with reference to the afterlife, believers of various stripes subscribe to a variety of arguments.

Another authority whom Holmes invokes—at least in phraseology, if not in actual ideas—is Charles Darwin. This is evident in his second Reason, and in his fourth to seventh Reasons. He was writing at a time when Darwin's reputation held sway among educated, upper-class urban adults, and "especially to the members of our younger generation," as we read in the second paragraph of his paper. Since then things have changed in America, and the popular reception of Darwin's ideas has cooled.[1]

[1]See, for example, Francis Wheen, "When Reason Sleeps Mumbo-Jumbo Frolics," *Los Angeles Times* (May 24, 2004), B-11. Wheen writes: "In 1922, just after his second term as president, Woodrow Wilson

John Haynes Holmes (1879–1964) was a Unitarian minister, one of the founders of the National Association for the Advancement of Colored People (NAACP) and the American Civil Liberties Union (ACLU), and an opponent of U.S. participation in both world wars. Our reading was first delivered as a sermon in 1929 and was published in a book about one year later. It is reprinted here with the kind permission of the Community Church of New York.

Nobody can speak on the immortality of the soul at this late date without being acutely conscious of the fact that there is nothing new that can be said. Since the time of Plato, at least, five hundred years before the birth of Jesus, the discussion of immortality has been conducted by the greatest minds upon the highest levels of human thought. Theology, philosophy, psychology and science have all been called upon to make their contributions to the theme. Poetry has offered its voice and religion its faith, with the result that every corner of knowledge has been explored, every depth of truth uncovered and revealed! There is always the possibility, of course, that the veil which hangs over every grave to divide this life from the mystery that lies beyond, may some day be lifted to our gaze. There are those who claim—not without some reason, it seems to me—that they have penetrated this veil, and thus have looked upon the reality of survival after death. But short of some such remarkable discovery as this, there is nothing new to be anticipated in this field. Everything has been said that can be said. The case for immortality is in!

Now it is this case which I want to present to you this morning. Since I cannot hope to say anything that is new, I want to see what I can do in the way of saying something that is old. I cannot say much, to be sure, for no discourse however merciless in length, can compass the range and beauty of the argument for immortality. But since ten is a goodly number, I take ten of the reasons which have brought conviction to the minds of men and offer

---

was asked for his thoughts on Darwinian theory. 'Of course, like every other man of intelligence and education, I do believe in organic evolution,' he replied. 'It surprises me that at this late date such questions should be raised.' Now imagine Wilson's downright astonishment had he been informed that in 2004, more than eight decades later, the state schools superintendent in Georgia would propose excising the word *evolution* from the biology curriculum." Also see Pew Research Center, *Religious Landscape Study*, 2014, http://www.pewforum.org/2015/11/03/chapter-4-social-and-political-attitudes, accessed January 15, 2018. According to the Pew study, 34 percent of respondents claimed to believe that humans have always existed in their present form.

these as the case for immortality today. I trust that it may be interesting, and also persuasive, especially to the members of our younger generation, to be reminded of what has been thought upon this question for many years.

By way of introduction, may I make mention of some two or three reasons for believing in immortality which do not concern me. I speak of these not because they are important, but because some of you may wonder, if I am silent, why they do not appear in my list of ten.

Thus I do not see any reason for believing in immortality because Jesus is reputed to have risen from the dead. In the first place, I do not believe that he rose from the dead. There is no evidence to substantiate this miracle. In the second place, even if he did break the barriers of the tomb, I fail to see what the resurrection of the body has to do with the immortality of the soul. The two things are irrelevant, the one to the other. What we have here is one of the myths of Christianity which, even if it were true, would have nothing seriously to do with our question.

Again, I find no argument for immortality in the succession of the seasons, the revival of nature in the spring, the blossoming of the flowers after the winter's cold. Poets are fond of this idea, as Shelley, for example, when he wrote his famous line,

If winter comes, can spring be far behind?

I think we may see in it a pretty parable, a rather beautiful poetic concept. But as an argument for immortality, it is what Ruskin called an instance of the "pathetic fallacy." The flowers that blossom in the spring are not the flowers that died the preceding autumn. The tide of life that flows on through nature, season after season, is the same tide that flows on through humanity, generation after generation, and it touches as little in the one case as in the other the survival of the individual. Like most parables, this does not hold when applied rigorously to the issue that is involved.

Again, I must confess that I am not convinced by the argument that men must be immortal because the heart demands it. It is natural that we should cling to those we love. It is inevitable that we should believe that providence, if it be beneficent, must give answer to our plea that we have not permanently separated from our friends and kindred. Whittier was yielding to the deepest impulses of the soul when he suggested in his "Snow Bound" that "Life is ever Lord of Death," because "Love can never lose its own." This is the cry of the human heart, and I personally believe that it is not destined to go unanswered. But a longing is one thing, and a reason is another. I see no evidence, in the scheme of things, that what we want we are therefore going to have. On the contrary, Felix Adler has taught us that frustration is the basic principle of life, that experience is "permeated with the sense of incompleteness," and that this "sense of incompleteness" is a perpetual doom that is laid upon us as "a necessary instrument of spiritual development." Whether this be true or not I do not know, but in either case I still believe that love gives no guarantee of its own survival.

But there are arguments for immortality which seem to suggest that it is true. Surveying all the field, I find myself agreeing with William James that, while we are under no compulsion to believe in immortality, as we are under a compulsion, for example, to believe that "things equal to the same thing are equal to each other," yet we are free to believe, if we so desire, without being guilty of superstition. "You may believe henceforward," said Professor James, "whether you care to profit by the permission or not." There are perfectly good and sufficient reasons, in other words, why an intelligent man may intelligently believe in immortality. Ten of these reasons I propose to submit to you this morning, beginning with those which open up the question, so to speak, and ending with those which close it as a conviction of the soul.

(1) First of all, may I offer the suggestion, not important in itself and yet of real significance to the thinking mind, that we may believe in immortality because there is no reason for *not* believing in it. In discussions of this question we are constantly reminded that immortality has never been proved. To which there is the immediate and inevitable reply that immortality has never been disproved! As there is no positive testimony to prove it true, so is there no negative testimony to prove it untrue. What we have here is an absence of testimony, and such "absence of testimony," says John Fiske, "does not even raise a negative presumption, except in cases where testimony is accessible." In this case, testimony is not accessible. Therefore the question is open "for those general considerations of philosophic analogy and moral probability which are the grounds upon which we can call for help in this arduous inquiry." As the question is open, so must our minds be open. My first reason, therefore, for believing in immortality or for being ready to believe in immortality, is the primarily interesting fact that there is no reason for not believing in immortality. My mind is absolutely at one with that of John Stuart Mill when he said upon his question, "To anyone who feels it conducive either to his satisfaction or to his usefulness to hope for a future state, . . . there is no hindrance to his indulging that hope."

(2) My second reason for believing in immortality is to be found in the universality of the idea. In saying this, I am not seeking to substantiate my

position by taking a majority vote upon the question. I am not arguing that a proposition is necessarily true because most persons have believed it. All too many beliefs have clung pertinaciously to the human mind, only in the end to be revealed as superstitions, and it may very well be that this concept of immortality is one of them.

What I have in mind here is the very different consideration that immortality is not merely a belief to be accepted but an idea to be explained. "Here is this wonderful thought," says Emerson, "Wherever man ripens, this audacious belief presently appears. . . . As soon as thought is exercised, this belief is inevitable . . . Whence came it? Who put it in the mind?" In itself it is remarkable, this idea that the death of the body is not the extinction of personality. Who has ever looked upon a dead body without marveling that man has ever thought of survival beyond the grave? Emerson could not explain the fact, as it has appeared in all ages and among all peoples, except upon the supposition that the thought of immortality is "not sentimental" but "elemental"—elemental in the sense that it is "grounded in the necessities and forces we possess."

That this idea is something more than idle speculation is shown by the whole philosophy of evolution, which has given to us that fundamental interpretation of life as "the continuous adjustment of inner relations to outer relations." An organism lives by successfully adjusting itself to the conditions of its environment, by developing itself inwardly in such a way as to meet the conditions of reality. When we find in plant or animal some inner faculty or attitude which is universally present, and which persists from generation to generation, we may be perfectly sure that it represents some correspondence with reality which has made survival possible. Life, in other words, is so definitely a matter of the successful coordination of inner relations with outer relations, that it is altogether impossible to conceive that in any specific relation the subjective term is real and the objective term is non-existent. What exists within is the sign and symbol, and guarantee, of what exists without.

Now man has never existed without the thought of immortality. From the earliest period of his life upon the earth, he has been profoundly concerned with this idea. He has never been able to live without it; even when he has tried to deny it, he has not been able to get rid of it. The immortal life is part of his being, as a line on the surface of a coin is a part of the pattern of its design. And as the line upon the coin could not have been set there except as the impression of the die which stamped its mark upon the metal, so the idea of immortality could not have appeared within the consciousness of man, except as the impression of the reality which made it what it is. Our faculties, our attributes, our ideas, as we have seen, are the reflection of the environment to which we adapt ourselves as the condition of survival. What we feel within is the reaction upon what exists without. As the eye proves the existence of light, and the ear the existence of sound, so the immortal hope may not unfairly be said to prove the existence of the immortal life. It is this that we mean when we say that the universality of the idea is an argument for the acceptance of the idea. In his great essay on "Immortality," Emerson tells us of two men who early in life spent much of their time together in earnest search for some proof of immortality. An accident separated them, and they did not meet again for a quarter of a century. They said nothing, "but shook hands long and cordially. At last his friend said, 'Any light, Albert?' 'None,' replied Albert. 'Any light, Lewis?' 'None,' he replied." And Emerson comments "that the impulse which drew these two minds to this inquiry through so many years was a better affirmative evidence for immortality than their failure to find a confirmation was a negative."

(3) This universal diffusion of the idea of immortality takes on an added significance when I come to my third reason for believing in immortality. I refer to the fact so memorably stated by Cicero. "There is in the minds of men," he says, "I know not how, a certain presage, as it were, of a future existence; and this takes deepest root in the greatest geniuses and the most exalted souls." The leaders of the race, in other words, have always believed in immortality. They are not separated in this case, as in so many cases, from the masses of ignorant and superstitious men by doctrines of dissent. On the contrary, in this case the ideas of the highest are at one with the hopes of the humblest among mankind.

In referring thus to the great names that are attached to the idea of immortality, I would not have you believe that I am making any blind appeal to the concept of authority. I have never seen any reason for arbitrarily separating our minds from the companionship of other minds. There is such a thing, even for the independent thinker, as a consensus of best opinion which can not be defied without the weightiest of reasons. And in this matter of immortality there is a consensus of best opinion which constitutes, to my mind, one of the most remarkable phenomena in the whole history of human thinking. I have no time this morning to list the names of those who have believed in the immortality of the soul. If I did so, I should have to include the names of scientists from Aristotle to Darwin and Eddington, of philosophers from Plato to Kant and Bergson, of poets from Sophocles to

Goethe and Robert Browning, of ethical teachers and public leaders from Socrates to Tolstoi and Mahatma Gandhi. There are dissenters from the doctrine, like Epictetus yesterday and Bernard Shaw today, but the consensus of opinion the other way is remarkable. Even the famous heretics stand in awe before this conception of eternity. Thus, Voltaire declared that "reason agrees with revelation . . . that the soul is immortal." Thomas Paine affirmed that he did not "trouble (himself) about the manner of future existence," so sure he was that "the Power which gave existence is able to continue it in any form." Even Robert G. Ingersoll confessed, as he stood by his brother's grave, that love could "hear the rustle of an angel's wing." In the light of such testimony as this, are we not justified in believing that there is reason for believing in immortality? If not, then we know, with James Martineau, "who are those who are mistaken. Not the mean and groveling souls who never reached to so great a thought. . . . No, the deceived are the great and holy, whom all men revere; the men who have lived for something better than their happiness and spent themselves on the altar of human good. Whom are we to reverence, and what can we believe, if the inspirations of the highest nature are but cunningly devised fables?"

(4) This conviction of immortality as rooted in the minds of men, and the greatest men, brings us immediately to the consideration of human nature itself as evidence for its own survival. Thus, my fourth reason this morning for believing in immortality is found in what I would call man's over-endowment as a creature of this earth, his surplus equipment for the adventure of his present life. If we want to know what is needed for successful existence upon this planet, we have only to look at any animal. His equipment of physical attributes and powers seems perfectly adapted to the necessities of his natural environment. The outfit of man, on the contrary, seems to constitute something like "a vast over-provision" for his necessities. If this life is all, in other words, what need has man for all these mental faculties, moral aspirations, spiritual ideals, which make him to be distinctly a man as contrasted with the animal? If existence upon the earth is his only destiny, why should man not prefer the swiftness of the deer, the strength of the lion, the vision of the eagle, to any endowment of mind and heart, as more adequate provision for the purely physical task of physical survival in a physical world? What we have here is a fundamental discrepancy between the endowment of man and the life he has to live; and this constitutes, if this life be all, an unparalleled violation of the creative economy of the universe. In every other form of life, an organism is equipped to meet the exactions of

its immediate environment. Man is equipped for this environment, and also for something more. Why is this not proof that he is destined for something more? As we estimate the length of the voyage of a ship by the character of its equipment, never confusing a little coasting vessel with a transatlantic liner or an arctic exploration steamer, why should we not estimate the length of man's voyage upon the seas of life in exactly the same way? What man bears within himself is evidence that he is destined for some farther port than any *upon* these *shores*. What he is in mind and heart and spirit, in the range of his interests and the lift of his soul, can only be explained on the supposition that he is preparing for another and a vaster life. I believe that man is immortal because already the signs of immortality are upon him.

(5) This consideration is basic, and sums up our whole case for immortality as rooted in human nature. But it opens out into other considerations which may well be taken as other reasons for believing in immortality. Thus, I would specify as my fifth reason for believing in immortality the lack of coordination, or proportion, between a man's body and a man's mind. If these two are to be regarded as aspects of a single organism, adapted only to the conditions of this present life, why do they so early begin to pull apart, and the weakness of the one to retard and at last to defeat the other? For a while, to be sure, there seems to be a real coordination between *soul* and body, between the personality, on the one hand, and the physical frame which it inhabits, on the other. Thus the child is in nothing so delightful as in the fact that it is a perfect animal. Then, as maturity approaches, two exactly opposite processes begin to take place within the life of the human being. On the one hand, the body begins to lose its resiliency and harden, to stop its growth and become static, then to decay and at last to dissolve. There is a definite cycle, in other words, in the physical life of the individual. There is a beginning, then a pause, and then an end. It is from first to last a process of completion. But there is no completion in the life of the soul. "Who dares speak the word 'completed,'" says Professor Munsterberg, the great psychologist. "Do not our purposes grow? Does not every newly created value give us the desire for further achievement? Is our life ever so completely done that no desire has still a meaning?" The personality of man is an enduring thing. As the body weakens through the years, so the soul only grows the stronger and more wonderful. As the body approaches irrevocably to its end, so the soul only mounts to what seems to be a new beginning. We come to death, in other words, only to discover within ourselves exhaustless possibilities. The aged have testified again and again to this amazing truth

that as the body turns to ashes, the spirit mounts as to a flame. Victor Hugo, protesting against the waning of his powers, said, "For half a century I have been writing my thoughts in prose and verse . . . but I feel that I have not said a thousandth part of what is in me." "How small a part of my plans have I been able to carry out! Nothing is so plain as that life at its fullest on earth is but a fragment." Robert Browning catches this thought in his poem, "Cleon," where he makes his hero say,

> . . . Every day my sense of joy
> Grows more acute, my soul . . . enlarged, more keen,
> While ever day my hairs fall more and more,
> My hand shakes, and the heavy years increase
> The horror quickening still from year to year,
> When I shall know most, and yet least enjoy.

What to do, in such emergency, except what Cleon did,

> . . . imagine to (our) need
> Some future state . . .

(6) But there is a lack of coordination not only between our personalities and our physical bodies, but also between our personalities and the physical world. This is my sixth reason for believing in immortality—that our souls have potentialities and promises which should not, as indeed they cannot, be subject to the chance vicissitudes of earthly fortune. What are we going to say, for example, when we see some life of eminent utility, of great achievement, of character and beauty and noble dedication to mankind, not merely borne down by the body, but cut off sharply before its time by an automobile accident, a disease germ, a bit of poisoned food? What shall we think when we see a Shelley drowned in his thirtieth year by the heedless sea, a Phillips Brooks stricken in the prime of his manhood by a diphtheric sore throat, a Captain Scott frozen in mid-career by an accident of weather? Is it possible that these lives of ours are dependent upon a fall of snow, a grain of dust, a passing breeze upon the sea? Is it conceivable that our personalities, with all their potencies of spirit, can be destroyed, as our bodies can be broken, by the material forces of the world? Are we to believe that eternal powers can be annihilated by transient accidents? I cannot think so! Rather must I think, as Professor George Herbert Palmer thought, as he looked upon the dead body of his wife, one of the greatest and most beautiful women of her time, stricken ere her years were ripe. "Though no regrets are proper for the manner of her death," said this noble husband, "yet who can contemplate the

fact of it and not call the world irrational if, out of deference to a few particles of disordered matter, it excludes so fair a spirit?"

(7) But this question of the irrationality of a world which would allow death to exercise mastery over a radiant spirit, has application not merely to the individual but also to the race. This brings me to my seventh reason for believing in immortality—a reason drawn from the logic of evolution. There is nothing more familiar, of course, than the fact that this world is the result of a natural process of development which has been going on for unnumbered millions of years. If this process is rational, as man's processes are rational, it must have been working all these eons of time to the achievement of some permanent and worthy end. What is this end? It is not the physical world itself, for the day must come when this earth will be swallowed up by the sun, and all the universe be merged again into the original fire-mist from which it sprang. It is not the works of man, for these perish even as man lives, and must vanish utterly in the last cataclysm of ruin. It is not man himself, for man, like the earth on which he lives, must finally disappear. Is there nothing that will remain as the evidence and vindication of this cosmic process? Or must we believe that, from the beginning, it has been like a child's tower of blocks built up only to be thrown down?

It was the challenge of this contingency, of evolution coming in the end to naught that moved no less a man than Charles Darwin, agnostic though he was, to proclaim the conviction that "it is an intolerable thought that (man) and all other sentient beings are doomed to complete annihilation after such long-continued slow process." Unless the universe is crazy, something must remain. The process must justify itself by producing something that endures. And what can this thing be but the spiritual essence of man's nature—the soul which is immortal? "The more thoroughly we comprehend the process of evolution," says John Fiske, in an unforgettable statement, "the more we are likely to feel that to deny the everlasting persistence of the spiritual element in man is to rob the whole process of its meaning. It goes far toward putting us to permanent intellectual confusion." Which led him to his famous verdict upon all the evidence: "I believe in the immortality of the soul as a supreme act of faith in the reasonableness of God's work."

(8) This leads us deep into the realm of science—to a fundamental principle that provides my eighth reason for believing in immortality. I refer to the principle of persistence or conservation. The gist of this doctrine is that nothing in the universe is ever lost. All energy is conserved. No matter what changes take place in any particular form of energy, that energy persists,

if not in the *old* form then in a new, and the sum total of energy in the universe remains the same. "Whatever is," says Sir Oliver Lodge, speaking of forms of energy in the physical universe, "whatever is, both was and shall be." And he quotes the famous statement of Professor Tait, that "persistence, or conservation, is the test or criterion of real existence."

Now if this principle applies to the "real existence" of the material world, why not to the "real existence" of the spiritual world as well? If it is impossible to think of physical energy as appearing and disappearing, coming into and going out of existence, why is it not equally impossible to think of intellectual or moral or spiritual energy as acting in this same haphazard fashion? We would laugh at a man who contended that the heat in molten metal, which disappears under the cooling action of air or water, had thereby been destroyed. Why should we not similarly laugh at a man who argues that the personality of a human being, which disappears under the chilling influence of death, has thereby been annihilated? What the personality may be, I do not know. Whether it is a form of energy itself, as some scientists assert, or "belongs to a separate order of existence," as Sir Oliver Lodge, for example, argues, I cannot say. But of this thing I am sure—that the soul of man is just as much a force in the world as magnetism or steam, or electricity, and that if the cosmic law of conservation forbids the destruction of the latter, it must as well forbid the destruction of the former. Anything else is inconceivable. The universe cannot be so thrifty of its physical, and so wasteful of its spiritual, resources. It is madness to conceive that the heat of an engine must be preserved, while the love of a heart may be thrown away. What prevails in the great realm of matter can be only an anticipation of what must equally prevail in the greater realm of spirit. For the universe is one. Its laws are everywhere the same. What science has discovered about the conservation of energy is only the physical equivalent of what religion has discovered about the immortality of the soul.

(9) We are coming now to ultimate things—to those first and last questions of origins and meanings. This brings me to my ninth reason for believing in immortality—the fact, namely, that all the values of life exist in man, and in man alone. For the world as we know it and love it is not the world as we receive it, but the world as we make it by the creative genius of the inward spirit. Consider this earthly scene with man eliminated! The sun would be here, and the stars. Mountains would still lift themselves to the skies, and oceans spread afar to vast horizons. Birds would sing, and leaves rustle, and sunsets glow. But what would it all mean without man to see and hear, to interpret? What do the stars mean to the eagle, or the sea to the porpoise,

or the mountain to the goat? It is man's ear which has heard the cuckoo as a "wandering voice," his eye which has seen "the floor of heaven thick inlaid with patinas of bright gold," his mind which has found "sermons in stone, books in the running brooks, and good in everything." All that is precious in the world—all its beauty, its wonder, its meaning—exists in man, and by man, and for man. The world is what man has done with it in the far reaches of his soul. And we are asked to believe that the being who sees and glorifies shall perish, while the world which he has seen and glorified endures! Such a conclusion is irrational. The being who created the world must himself be greater than the world. The soul which conceives Truth, Goodness and Beauty, must itself be as eternal as the Truth, Goodness, and Beauty which it conceives. Nothing has any value without man. Man, therefore, is the supreme value. Which is the essence of the Platonic philosophy of eternal life for man!

> "Tell me, then," says Socrates in the *Phaedo*, "what is that the inherence of which renders the body alive?"
> "The soul, Cebes replied . . ."
> "Then whatever the soul possesses, to that she comes bearing life?"
> "Yes, certainly."
> "And is there any opposite to life?"
> "There is . . . Death."
> "And will the soul . . . ever receive the opposite of what she brings?"
> "Impossible, replied Cebes."
> "Then, said Socrates, the soul is immortal!"

(10) These, now, are my main reasons for believing in immortality. I have but one more, the tenth to add. It is the pragmatic argument that faith in an eternal life beyond the grave justifies itself in terms of the life that we are now living upon this side of the grave. For immortality does not concern the future alone; it concerns, also, the present. We are immortal today, if we are ever going to be immortal tomorrow. And this means that we have the chance to put to the test, even now and here, the belief to which we hold. It is the essence of the pragmatic philosophy that what is true will conduce to life, as food conduces to health, and that what is false will destroy life, as poison the body. Whatever is true enlarges and lifts and strengthens the life of man; whatever is false represses and weakens and disintegrates his life. Now what does immortality do when we put its affirmation to this test? What are the consequences which follow if we live as though we were eternal spirits? Can there be any doubt as to the answer?

We see a universe where spiritual values, not material forces, prevail; where personality, whether in ourselves or in others, is precious, and therefore to be conserved; where principles, not possessions, are the supreme concern of life; where man is equal to his task, and labors not in vain for the high causes of humanity; where sacrifice is not foolish but wise, and love "the greatest thing in the world." The man who lives an immortal life takes on immortal qualities. His character assumes the proportions of his faith, and his work the range of his high destiny. "Immortality makes great living," says Dr. Fosdick. Therefore I believe in immortality.

Ten reasons! Are these all? No, they are not all! They are simply ten of the many reasons for the most persistent faith which has ever beset the heart of man. In choosing these ten, I have sought to gather reasons which were reasons, and not mere superstitions—arguments which appeal to intellect rather than emotion, and which are based upon experience rather than credulity. That these reasons prove the idea of immortality to be true, I cannot claim. But there is many an idea which we accept for good reasons, even though it be not proved, as there is many a verdict in court which is returned for good reasons, even though it be not proved, and immortality is one of them. What impresses me, as I follow the course of this great argument through the ages, is what impressed the mind of James Martineau when he said, "We do not believe immortality because we have proved it, but we forever try to prove it because we believe it." Hence the judgment of the poet, Tennyson—

> O, yet we trust that somehow good
> Will be the final goal of ill,
> To pangs of nature, sins of will,
> Defects of doubt, and taints of blood.
>
> That nothing walks with aimless feet;
> That not one life shall be destroyed,
> Or cast as rubbish to the void,
> When God hath made the pile complete . . .
>
> I stretch lame hands of faith, and grope
> And gather dust and chaff, and call
> To what I feel is Lord of all,
> And faintly trust the larger hope.

4

Next Stop Goofville

Clarence Darrow

Clarence Darrow (1857–1938) was an American lawyer—one of the most famous of them all—and, like John Haynes Holmes, a leading member of the American Civil Liberties Union. As we will see, though, the two men held very different views on religion: Darrow, after all, defended high school teacher John T. Scopes against Bible literalists, in *The State of Tennessee v. Scopes* "Monkey Trial" in 1925. Our reading is from Darrow's piece, "The Myth of the Soul: Is the Belief in Immortality Necessary or Even Desirable?" (1929).

In our previous reading, John Haynes Holms defended a dualistic interpretation of survival and immortality of the soul—an interpretation that owes much to Plato. Darrow's article is in part a rebuttal of Holmes. His case against the survival hypothesis takes the form of a series of objections to the consequences of the doctrine. Some of these objections are of a scientific character, and some are based on what Darrow called "the common experience of all men." Among other targets of Darrow's attack is the doctrine of bodily resurrection, a doctrine that Holmes explicitly rejects. We will return to this doctrine in Part III, where more than one of its defenders will present their cases.

In the decades since Darrow's article was first published, the sciences of biology and astronomy have advanced greatly—but they have advanced in a direction that would tend to bolster Darrow's case. Consider, for example, Darrow's remarks, toward the middle of his article, about "celestial geography": seven years after the article appeared, the great astronomer Edwin Hubble published his book *The Realm of the Nebulae* (1936), in which he argued that our galaxy is but one "island universe" among many. Today we believe that our solar system is located in the outer third of one of four spiral arms of a galaxy some 100,000 light years in diameter, a galaxy that includes more than 200 billion stars. The Milky Way, in turn, is but one of more than 100 billion galaxies in the observable part of what we call the universe. If the Inflationary Hypothesis[1] of cosmology is correct, the observable universe is but a tiny part of the universe. Moreover, according to some current cosmological models, "the" universe is but one of indefinitely many universes that make up "the" multiverse.

Thus, confining ourselves to only a few claims of modern astronomy, it is clear enough that the passing scene, as the sciences describe it, bears little resemblance to the cosmoses of the ancient creation stories that are part of religious traditions familiar to us today. And yet the belief is as widespread as ever that our tiny, fleeting species is so special that God, the presumed Creator of all of this, preserves the consciousness of individual *Homo sapiens* after bodily death, perhaps forever.

For many religious believers, though, the best-established claims of astronomy and physics all go to show that God is indeed awesome.

―――――――――

There is, perhaps, no more striking example of the credulity of man than the widespread belief in immortality. This idea includes not only the belief that death is not the end of what we call life, but that personal identity involving memory persists beyond the grave. So determined is the ordinary individual to hold fast to this belief that, as a rule, he refuses to read or think upon the subject lest it cast doubt upon his cherished dream. Of those who may chance to look at this contribution, many will do so with the determination not to be convinced, and will refuse to even consider the manifold reasons that might weaken their faith. I know that this is true, for I know the reluctance with which I long approached the subject and my firm determination not to give up my hope. Thus the myth will stand in the way of a sensible adjustment to facts.

Even many of those who claim to believe in immortality still tell themselves and others that neither side of the question is susceptible to proof. Just what

―――

[1]The view, widely accepted as of this writing, that moments after the Big Bang space expanded exponentially.

can these hopeful ones believe that the word *proof* involves? The evidence against the persistence of personal consciousness is as strong as the evidence of gravitation, and much more obvious. It is as convincing and unassailable as the proof of the destruction of wood or coal by fire. If it is not certain that death ends personal identity and memory, then almost nothing that man accepts as true is susceptible to proof.

The beliefs of the race and its individuals are relics of the past. Without careful examination no one can begin to understand how many of man's cherished opinions have no foundation in fact. The common experience of all men should teach them how easy it is to believe what they wish to accept. Experienced psychologists know perfectly well that if they desire to convince a man of some idea, they must first make him *want* to believe it. There are so many hopes, so many strong yearnings and desires attached to the doctrine of immortality that it is practically impossible to create in any mind the wish to be mortal. Still, in spite of strong desires, millions of people are filled with doubts and fears that will not die down. After all, is it not better to look the question squarely in the face and find out whether we are harboring a delusion?

It is customary to speak of a "belief in immortality." First, then, let us see what is meant by the word *belief*. If I take a train in Chicago at noon, bound for New York, I believe I will reach that city the next morning. I believe it because I have been to New York, I have read about the city, I have known many other people who have been there, and their stories are not inconsistent with any known facts in my own experience. I have even examined the timetables and I know just how I will go and how long the trip will take. In other words, when I board the train for New York, I believe I will reach that city because I have *reason* to believe it.

If, instead, I wanted to see Timbuktu or some other point on the globe where I had never been, or of which I had only heard, I still know something about geography, and if I did not I could find out about the place I wished to visit. Through the encyclopedia and other means of information, I could get a fair idea of the location and character of the country or city, the kind of people who lived there and almost anything I wished to know, including the means of transportation and the time it would take to go and return. I already am satisfied that the earth is round, and I know about its size. I know the extent of its land and water. I know the names of its countries. I know perfectly well that there are many places on its surface that I have never seen. I can easily satisfy myself as to whether there is any such place and how to get there, and what I shall do when I arrive.

But if I am told that next week I shall start on a trip to Goofville; that I shall not take my body with me; that I shall stay for all eternity: can I find a single fact connected with my journey—the way I shall go, the time of the journey, the country I shall reach, its location in space, the way I shall live there—or anything that would lead to a rational belief that I shall really make the trip? Have I ever known anyone who has made the journey and returned? If I am really to believe, I must try to get some information about all these important facts.

But people hesitate to ask questions about life after death. They do not ask, for they know that only silence comes out of the eternal darkness of endless space. If people really believed in a beautiful, happy, glorious land waiting to receive them when they died; if they believed that their friends would be waiting to meet them; if they believed that all pain and suffering would be left behind: why should they live through weeks, months, and even years of pain and torture while a cancer eats its way to the vital parts of the body? Why should one fight off death? Because he does *not* believe in any real sense; he only hopes. Everyone knows that there is no real evidence of any such state of bliss; so we are told not to search for proof. We are to accept through faith alone. But every thinking person knows that faith can only come through belief. Belief implies a condition of mind that accepts a certain idea. This condition can be brought about only by evidence. True, the evidence may be simply the unsupported statement of your grandmother; it may be wholly insufficient for reasoning men; but, good or bad, it must be enough for the believer or he could not believe.

Upon what evidence, then, are we asked to believe in immortality? There is no evidence. One is told to rely on faith, and no doubt this serves the purpose so long as one can believe blindly whatever he is told. But if there is no evidence upon which to build a positive belief in immortality, let us examine the other side of the question. Perhaps evidence can be found to support a positive conviction that immortality is a delusion.

The belief in immortality expresses itself in two different forms. On the one hand, there is a belief in the immortality of the "soul." This is sometimes interpreted to mean simply that the identity, the consciousness, the memory of the individual persists after death. On the other hand, many religious creeds formulated a belief in "the resurrection of the body"—which is something else again. It will be necessary to examine both forms of this belief in turn.

The idea of continued life after death is very old. It doubtless had its roots back in the childhood of the race. In view of the limited knowledge of primitive man, it was not unreasonable. His dead friends and relatives visited him in dreams and visions and were present in his feeling and imagination until they were forgotten. Therefore, the lifeless body did not raise the question of dissolution, but rather of duality. It was thought that man was a dual being possessing a body and a soul as separate entities, and that when a man died, his soul was released from his body to continue its life apart. Consequently, food and drink were placed upon the graves of the dead to be used in the long journey into the unknown. In modified forms, this belief in the duality of man persists to the present day. But primitive man had no conception of life as having a beginning and an end. In this he was like the rest of the animals. Today, everyone of ordinary intelligence knows how life begins, and to examine the beginnings of life leads to inevitable conclusions about the way life ends. If man has a soul, it must creep in somewhere during the period of gestation and growth.

All the higher forms of animal life grow from a single cell. Before the individual life can begin its development, it must be fertilized by union with another cell; then the cell divides and multiplies until it takes the form and pattern of its kind. At a certain regular time the being emerges into the world. During its term of life millions of cells in its body are born, die, and are replaced until, through age, disease, or some catastrophe, the cells fall apart and the individual life is ended.

It is obvious that but for the fertilization of the cell under right conditions, the being would not have lived. It is idle to say that the initial cell has a soul. In one sense it has life; but even that is precarious and depends for its continued life upon union with another cell of the proper kind. The human mother is the bearer of probably ten thousand of one kind of cell, and the human father of countless billions of the other kind. Only a very small fraction of these result in human life. If the unfertilized cells of the female and the unused cells of the male are human beings possessed of souls, then the population of the world is infinitely greater than has ever been dreamed. Of course no such idea as belief in the immortality of germ cells could satisfy the yearnings of the individual for a survival of life after death.

If that which is called a "soul" is a separate entity apart from the body, when, then, and where and how was this soul placed in the human structure? The individual began with the union of two cells, neither of which had a soul. How could these two soulless cells produce a soul? I must leave this search to the metaphysicians. When they have found the answer, I hope they will tell me, for I should really like to know.

We know that a baby may live and fully develop in its mother's womb and then, through some shock at birth, may be born without life. In the past, these babies were promptly buried. But now we know that in many such cases, where the bodily structure is complete, the machine may be set to work by artificial respiration or electricity. Then it will run like any other human body through its allotted term of years. We also know that in many cases of drowning, or when some mishap virtually destroys life without hopelessly impairing the body, artificial means may set it in motion once more, so that it will complete its term of existence until the final catastrophe comes. Are we to believe that somewhere around the stillborn child and somewhere in the vicinity of the drowned man there hovers a detached soul waiting to be summoned back into the body by a pulmotor? This, too, must be left to the metaphysicians.

The beginnings of life yield no evidence of the beginnings of a soul. It is idle to say that something in the human being which we call "life" is the soul itself, for the soul is generally taken to distinguish human beings from other forms of life. There is life in all animals and plants, and at least potential life in inorganic matter. This potential life is simply unreleased force and matter—the greatest storehouse from which all forms of life emerge and are constantly replenished. It is impossible to draw the line between inorganic matter and the simpler forms of plant life, and equally impossible to draw the line between plant life and animal life, or between other forms of animal life and what we human beings are pleased to call the highest form. If the thing which we call "life" is itself the soul, then cows have souls; and, in the very nature of things, we must allow souls to all forms of life and to inorganic matter as well.

Life itself is something very real, as distinguished from the soul. Every man knows that his life had a beginning. Can one imagine an organism that has a beginning and no end? If I did not exist in the infinite past, why should I, or could I, exist in the infinite future? "But," say some, "your consciousness, your memory may exist even after you are dead. This is what we mean by the soul." Let us examine this point a little.

I have no remembrance of the months I lay in my mother's womb. I cannot recall the day of my birth nor the time when I first opened my eyes to the light of the sun. I cannot remember when I was an infant, or when I began to creep on the floor, or when I was taught to walk, or anything before I was five of six years old. Still, all of these events were important, wonderful, and strange in a new life. What I call my "consciousness," for lack of a better word and a better understanding, developed with my growth and the crowding experiences I met at every turn. I have a hazy recollection of the burial of a boy soldier who was shot toward the end of the Civil War. He was buried near the schoolhouse when I was seven years old. But I have no remembrance of the assassination of Abraham Lincoln, although I must then have been eight years old. I must have known about it at the time, for my family and my community idolized Lincoln, and all America was in mourning at his death. Why do I remember the dead boy soldier who was buried a year before? Perhaps because I knew him well. Perhaps because his family was close to my childish life. Possibly because it came to me as my first knowledge of death. At all events, it made so deep an impression that I recall it now.

"Ah, yes," say the believers in the soul, "What you say confirms our own belief. You certainly existed when these early experiences took place. You were conscious of them at the time, even though you are not aware of it now. In the same way, may not your consciousness persist after you die, even though you are not aware of that fact?

On the contrary, my fading memory of the events that filled the early years of my life leads me to the opposite conclusion. So far as these incidents are concerned, the mind and consciousness of the boy are already dead. Even now, am I fully alive? I am seventy-one years old. I often fail to recollect the names of some of those I knew full well. Many events do not make the lasting impression that they once did. I know that it will be only a few years, even if my body still survives decay, when few important matters will even register in my mind. I know how it is with the old. I know that physical life can persist beyond the time when the mind can fully function. I know that if I live to an extreme old age, my mind will fail. I shall eat and drink and go to my bed in an automatic way. Memory—which is all that binds me to the past—will already be dead. All that will remain will be a vegetative existence; I shall sit and doze in the chimney corner, and my body will function in a measure even though the ego will already be practically dead. I am sure that if I die of what is called "old age," my consciousness will gradually slip away with my failing emotions! I shall no more be aware of the near approach of final dissolution than is the dying tree.

I am aware that now and then at long intervals there is a man who preserves his faculties until a late period of his life. I know that these cases are very, very rare. No superstition needs to be called into service to account for the unusual things that are incident to life. There may be those who retain, in a measurable degree, consciousness and mental activity beyond the time of the ordinary mortal. Still, everyone with the least information knows that it is almost a universal rule that the body declines with age, and that those who live a long life gradually yield their intellectual activity until they reach the period of senility and unconsciousness.

In primitive times, before men knew anything about the human body or the universe of which it is a part, it was not unreasonable to believe in spirits, ghosts, and the duality of man. For one thing, celestial geography was much simpler then. Just above the earth was a firmament in which the stars were set, and above the firmament was heaven. The place was easy of access and in dreams the angels were seen going up and coming down on a ladder. But now we have a slightly more adequate conception of space and the infinite universe of which we are so small a part. Our great telescopes reveal countless worlds and planetary systems which make our own sink into utter insignificance in comparison. We have every reason to think that beyond our sight there is endless space filled with still more planets, so infinite in size and number that no brain has the smallest conception of their extent. Is there any reason to think that in this universe, with its myriads of worlds, there is no other life so important as our own? Is it possible that the inhabitants of the earth have been singled out for special favor and endowed with souls and immortal life? Is it at all reasonable to suppose that any special account is taken of the human atoms that forever come and go upon this planet?

If man has a soul that persists after death, that goes to a heaven of the blessed or to a hell of the damned, where are these places? It is not so easily imagined as it once was. How does the soul make its journey? What does immortal man find when he gets there, and how will he live after he reaches the end of endless space? We know that the atmosphere will be absent; that there will be no light, no heat—only the infinite reaches of darkness and frigidity.

If there is a future place for the abode of the spirits of the dead, where is this place? Trusting people have made pictures and mental images of this abode of the dead. The revelation of St. John treats rather specifically of this far-off land, but it is evident that St. John was a psychopath and his case would be plainly recognized today. True, this picture of St. John's is not very alluring to intelligent men. Still, trusting and confiding mortals have envisioned, in words at least, a land where families would be reunited and neighbors and friends come together once more. In this smug little place, fashioned upon experiences of life upon this mundane sphere, husbands and wives, long parted, will be united. Parents and children, and grandparents and grandchildren, too, will assemble in families in that land of the blessed and the dead.

These conceptions were formed early in the history of man;[2] in fact, it has only been in recent years that we have had any knowledge or vision of the immensity of space and the impossibility of any such place as is envisioned by the credulous and trusting. We know now that the earth revolves upon its axis at a terrific speed. This motion makes a complete revolution in twenty-four hours. We know down to the second of time that no spot bears the same relation to space as it did before. If one who dies at midnight has a soul and starts on his trip to Heaven, he goes in an opposite direction from one who dies at noon, and chances to meet under any circumstances which can be conceived would grow less as they traveled on. Besides this revolution on its axis, the earth is traveling at an inconceivable speed around the sun, which, at times, is about ninety-three million miles away. This complete journey is made once a year. In its orbit around the sun it travels more than a thousand miles a minute. This constant appalling speed would evidently add to the confusion of two mortals locating themselves in the same spot in space, even though they had souls. The atmosphere, even in its most attenuated form, does not reach over five hundred miles away from the earth, and for only a small fraction of that space could life as we conceive it exist. And when the earth leaves a given spot in space the atmosphere is carried along with it. In addition to the motion of the earth on its axis and its unthinkable speed in its circuit around the sun, the whole solar system is traveling around the pole star, accompanied no doubt by many other systems like our own; no one can tell how fast it goes or how far it goes, in what seems endless space. And these systems travel in turn around some other central point in the far-off Milky Way, and no one knows how many other apparently central points somewhere off amongst the stars and worlds and suns furnish foci around which the earth and all the systems constantly revolve. What possible means of locomotion could be furnished for mortals to find a place of rest, and what possible unimaginable guide could pilot individuals going in different directions at all times of the day and night and all portions of the year and century, and other greater periods of time, to this haven

[2]Colleen McDannell and Bernhard Lang contend that the human-centered depictions of heaven as a place of reunion with loved ones, or at least those depictions that decorate the popular imagination these days, were not "formed early in the history of man." Rather, they are post-renaissance and modern notions, which gained widespread popularity in the late 18th and 19th centuries in parts of Europe and America. (Colleen McDannell and Bernhard Lang, *Heaven: A History*, second ed. (New Haven and London: Yale University Press, 2001), Chapters 7, 8, and 9.) —MM

of the blessed? All of these conceptions beggar any sort of imagination and make one substitute the wildest unthinkable dreams in place of real beliefs.

There are those who base their hope of a future life upon the resurrection of the body. This is a purely religious doctrine. It is safe to say that few intelligent men who are willing to look obvious facts in the face hold any such belief. Yet we are seriously told that Elijah was carried bodily to heaven in a chariot of fire, and that Jesus arose from the dead and ascended into heaven. The New Testament abounds in passages that support this doctrine. St. Paul states the tenet over and over again. In the fifteenth chapter of *I Corinthians* he says: "If Christ be preached that he rose from the dead, how say some among you that there is no resurrection of the dead? ... and if Christ be not risen, then is our preaching vain ... For if the dead rise not, then is not Christ raised." The Apostles' Creed says: "I believe in the resurrection of the body." This has been carried into substantially all the orthodox creeds; and while it is more or less minimized by neglect and omission, it is still a cardinal doctrine of the orthodox churches.

Two thousand years ago, in Palestine, little was known of man, of the earth, or of the universe. It was then currently believed that the earth was only four thousand years old, that life had begun anew after the deluge about two thousand years before, and that the entire earth was soon to be destroyed. Today it is fairly well established that man has been upon the earth for a million years. During that long stretch of time the world has changed many times; it is changing every moment. At least three or four ice ages have swept across continents, driving death before them, carrying human beings into the sea or burying them deep in the earth. Animals have fed on man and on each other. Every dead body, no matter whether consumed by fire or buried in the earth, has been resolved into its elements, so that the matter and energy that once formed human beings has fed animals and plants and other men. As the great naturalist, Fabre, has said: "At the banquet of life each is in turn a guest and a dish." Thus the body of every man now living is in part made from the bodies of those who have been dead for ages.

Yet we are still asked to believe in the resurrection of the body. By what alchemy, then, are the individual bodies that have successfully fed the generations of men to be separated and restored to their former identities? And if I am to be resurrected, what particular *I* shall be called from the grave, from the animals and plants and the bodies of other men who shall inherit this body I now call my own? My body has been made over and over, piece by piece, as the days went by, and will continue to be so made until the end. It has changed so slowly that each new cell is fitted into the living part, and will go on changing until the final crisis comes. Is it the child in the mother's womb or the tottering frame of the old man that shall be brought back? The mere thought of such a resurrection beggars reason, ignores facts, and enthrones blind faith, wild dreams, hopeless hopes, and cowardly fears as sovereign of the human mind.

Some of those who profess to believe in the immortality of man—whether it be of his soul or body—have drawn what comfort they could from the modern scientific doctrine of the indestructibility of matter and force. This doctrine, they say, only confirms in scientific language what they have always believed. This, however, is pure sophistry. It is probably true that no matter or force has ever been or ever can be destroyed. But it is likewise true that there is no connection whatever between the notion that personal consciousness and memory persist after death and the scientific theory that matter and force are indestructible. For the scientific theory carries with it a corollary, that the forms of matter and energy are constantly changing through an endless cycle of new combinations. Of what possible use would it be, then, to have a consciousness that was immortal, but which, from the moment of death, was dispersed into new combinations, so that no two parts of the original identity could ever be reunited again?

These natural processes of change, which in the human being take the forms of growth, disease, senility, death, and decay, are essentially the same as the processes by which a lump of coal is disintegrated in burning. One may watch the lump of coal burning in the grate until nothing but ashes remains. Part of the coal goes up the chimney in the form of smoke; part of it radiates through the house as heat; the residue lies in the ashes on the hearth. So it is within human life. In all forms of life nature is engaged in combining, breaking down, and recombining her store of energy and matter into new forms. The thing we call "life" is nothing other than a state of equilibrium which endures for a short span of years between the two opposing tendencies of nature—the one that builds up, and the one that tears down. In old age, the tearing-down process has already gained the ascendency, and when death intervenes, the equilibrium is finally upset by the complete stoppage of the building-up process, so that nothing remains but complete disintegration. The energy thus released may be converted into grass or trees or animal life; or it may lie dormant until caught up again in the crucible of nature's laboratory. But whatever happens, the man—the *You* and the *I*—like the lump of coal that has been burned, is gone—irrevocably dispersed. All the King's horses and all the King's men cannot restore it to its former unity.

The idea that man is a being set apart, distinct from all the rest of nature, is born of man's emotions, of his loves and hates, of his hopes and fears, and of the primitive conceptions of undeveloped minds. The *You* and the *I* which is known to our friends does not consist of an immaterial something called a "soul" which cannot be conceived. We know perfectly well what we mean when we talk about this *You* and this *Me*: and it is equally plain that the whole fabric that makes up our separate personalities is destroyed, dispersed, disintegrated beyond repair by what we call "death."

As a matter of fact, does *anyone* really believe in a future life? The faith does not simply involve the persistence of activity, but it has been stretched and magnified to mean a future world infinitely better than the earth. In this far-off land no troubles will harass the body or the soul. Eternity will be an eternity of bliss. Heaven, a land made much more delightful because of the union with those who have gone before. This doctrine has been taught so persistently through the years that men and women of strong faith in their dying moments have seen relatives and friends, long since dead, who have come to lead them to their heavenly home.

Does this conduct of the intense disciple show that he really believes that death is a glad deliverance? Why do men and women who are suffering torture on earth seek to prolong their days of agony? Why do victims of cancer being slowly eaten alive for months and years prefer enduring such pain rather than going to a land of bliss? Why will the afflicted travel all over the world and be cut to pieces by inches that they may stay a few weeks longer, in agony and torture? The one answer that is made to this query is that the afflicted struggle to live because it is their duty to hang fast to mortal life, no matter what the pain or the expected joy in heaven. The answer is not true. The afflicted cling to life because they doubt their faith, and do not wish to let go of what they have, terrible as it is.

Those who refuse to give up the idea of immortality declare that their nature never creates a desire without providing the means for its satisfaction. They likewise insist that all people, from the rudest to the most civilized, yearn for another life. As a matter of fact, nature creates many desires which she does not satisfy; most of the wishes of men meet no fruition. But nature does not create any emotion demanding a future life. The only yearning that the individual has is to keep on living—which is a very different thing. This urge is found in every animal, in every plant. It is simply the momentum of a living structure: or, as Schopenhauer put it, "the will to live." What we long for is a continuation of our present state of existence, not an uncertain reincarnation in a mysterious world of which we know nothing. The idea of another life is created after men are convinced that this life ends.

I am not unmindful of those who base their hope of a future life on what they claim are the evidences furnished by the investigation of spiritualism. So far as having any prejudice against this doctrine, I have no more desire to disbelieve than I have as to any other theories of a future life. In fact, for many years, I have searched here for evidence that man still lives after all our senses show that he is dead. For more than fifty years until almost ten years past, I have given some attention to spiritualism. I have read most of the important books of scientists: Alfred Russel Wallace, Crooks, Oliver Lodge, and the books of many other men of ability and integrity who believed that they had found their dead friends who had come back to them. Likewise, I have for years investigated what are called spiritual phenomena. I am satisfied that if any intelligent man, in possession of his senses, thoroughly investigates spiritualism, he will find that there no evidence to support his faith. At least nine-tenths of the phenomena can be set down as pure fraud and imposition. The evidence comes in the main from mediums who are ignorant, and whose tricks are clumsy in the extreme. Perhaps one-tenth of the manifestations are not the result of fraud but the evidence is entirely inadequate to prove the cause of the phenomena. It is possible that there are phenomena which no one can explain. I have many times seen what are called manifestations of spirit-return that I could not explain, but all of these failed utterly to convince me of the communication of disembodies spirits. It does not follow that because the manifestations are strange and weird, and for the present unexplainable, that those phenomena show that life persists after death. In the realm of these manifestations, the evidence of scientists is worth no more than the evidence of other men. Most likely it is worth much less. The truth is that real scientists, outside of their special field, are more helpless than other men in detecting frauds and tricks. It is likewise true that most of the men of science, like Sir Oliver Lodge, have come to their conviction late in life, and under some great stress, which is calculated to unsettle the mind, in the particular field to which they appeal.

Sir Oliver Lodge lost his son in the Great War. This was a sore bereavement to this eminent scientist. When one considers the greatness of Lodge, the clearness with which he discusses every scientific theory with which he deals, and then reads his book called *Raymond*, in which he tells of his meetings with his beloved son, it is not difficult to see that as to this bereavement his mind was unsettled and he is reaching out in the darkness to find what he so strongly wants.

Is it possible that any sort of proof could prove the existence of an individual after his decay? Suppose that some good fairy, distressed at my unbelief, should come to me with the offer to produce any evidence that I desired to satisfy me that I would see my loved ones after death; suppose I should tell this fairy that my father had been dead for twenty years; that I followed his lifeless body to the crematory where he was converted into ashes; that I desired to have him brought back to me as a living entity, and to stay in my house for a year, that I might not be deceived. Assume that when the year had passed I should go out and tell my neighbors and friends that my father had been living in my house, although he died two score years ago; suppose that they believed implicitly in my integrity and my judgment; even then, could I convince one person that my statement was true? Would they be right in doubting my word? After all, which is the more reasonable, that the dead have come back to life, or that I have become insane? All of my friends would say: "Poor fellow, I am sorry he has lost his mind." Against the universal experience of mankind and nature, the dementia or the insanity of one man, or a thousand men, could count as nothing. The insane asylums of the world are filled with men who have these dreams and visions which are realities to them, but which no one else believes, because they are entirely at variance with well-known facts.

All men recognize the hopelessness of finding any evidence that the individual will persist beyond the grave. As a last resort, we are told that it is better that the doctrine be believed even if it is not true. We are assured that without this faith, life is only desolation and despair. However that may be, it remains that many of the conclusions of logic are not pleasant to contemplate; still, so long as men think and feel, at least some of them will use their faculties as best they can. For if we are to believe things that are not true, who is to write our creed? Is it safe to leave it to any man or organization to pick out the errors that we must accept? The whole history of the world has answered this question in a way that cannot be mistaken.

And after all, is the belief in immortality necessary or even desirable for man? Millions of men and women have no such faith; they go on with their daily tasks and feel joy and sorrow without the lure of immortal life. The things that really affect the happiness of the individual are the matters of daily living. They are the companionship of friends, the games and contemplations. They are misunderstandings and cruel judgments, false friends and debts, poverty and disease. They are our joys in our living companions and our sorrows over those who die. Whatever our faith, we mainly live in the present—in the here and now. Those who hold the view that man is mortal are never troubled by metaphysical problems. At the end of the day's labor we are glad to lose our consciousness in sleep; and intellectually, at least, we look forward to the long rest from the stresses and storms that are always incidental to existence.

When we fully understand the brevity of life, its fleeting joys and unavoidable pains; when we accept the facts that all men and women are approaching an inevitable doom: the consciousness of it should make us more kindly and considerate of each other. This feeling should make men and women use their best efforts to help their fellow travelers on the road, to make the path brighter and easier as we journey on. It should bring a closer kinship, a better understanding, and a deeper sympathy for the wayfarers who must live a common life and die a common death.

5

Death, Nothingness, and Subjectivity

Thomas W. Clark

In the first section of our next reading, Thomas W. Clark corrects what he calls "the error of anticipating nothingness." This error, he says, is a result of the "subliminal logic that persuades us that dying leads us into 'the void'." He then observes that, "from our point of view as subjects of experience, there are no gaps during the course of our conscious lives": for subjects of experience, awareness is constant throughout life. He calls this circumstance *personal subjective continuity*, and he takes it as evidence that "consciousness, as a strictly physical phenomenon instantiated by the brain, creates a world subjectively immune to its own disappearance."

This sounds like Epicurus: for the dead, there is nothing that it is like to be dead, and since there is no first-person experience of death, it is neither good nor bad for the dead. It also sounds like the words of the author of the biblical book of Ecclesiastes: "For the living know that they shall die; but the dead know not anything ... neither have they any more a portion for ever in any thing that is done under the sun."[1]

---

[1]*Ecclesiastes* 9:5–6 (King James Translation). But the error that Clark describes—the error of anticipating an experience of no experience at all—is not easy to shake. As we will see, even Titus Lucretius Carus, a devoted follower of Epicurus, fell into the error of describing death as "sleep and quiet" (refer to our Part III reading, line 907).

This is the upshot of the first part of Clark's paper. But of course it is more difficult to accustom ourselves to this view than to state it.

Clark then points out that, although your death is the end of a particular *experiencer*, it is not the end of *experience* per se. From the perspective of scientific naturalism at least, it is "a mundane, although contingent fact of life" that other subjects of experience continue to exist after you die, and new ones come into existence.

In addition to individual subjective continuity, Clark writes, there is also a "shared sense of always having been present." He calls this *generic subjective continuity*. Clark produces a thought experiment intended to show that awareness is subjectively continuous in this shared or generic sense, too. Just as in the case of personal subjective continuity, so also for generic subjective continuity, "awareness—for itself, in its generic aspect of 'always having been present'—is immune to interruption," even across objective discontinuities in the existence of particular conscious beings. The point seems to be that the very act of imagining anything at all, even imagining something that existed before the beginning of your conscious life or something that will exist after you die, requires a perspective broader than your particular context of awareness. And this broader perspective, too, is subjectively immune to its own disappearance. Thus, he writes, "generic subjective continuity holds across any objective discontinuities in the existence of conscious beings."

Toward the end of the paper Clark suggests that, from a naturalistic perspective, generic subjective continuity is the closest one can come to belief in immortality. Even if we dispense with the idea of an immaterial soul and an indivisible self, the consolation of generic subjective continuity may be within our grasp, provided we "wear our personalities more lightly."

Thomas W. Clark is a former Research Associate at the Institute for Behavioral Health at Brandeis University and Director for the Center for Naturalism, Naturalism.org. "Death, Nothingness, and Subjectivity" first appeared in *The Humanist: A Magazine of Critical Inquiry and Social Concern* in 2006. Available online: http://www.naturalism. org/philosophy/death/death-nothingness-and-subjectivity (accessed January 6, 2018). The article is reprinted with kind permission of the author.

Introduction

"For only death annihilates all sense, all becoming, to replace them with nonsense and absolute cessation."

—F. Gonzalez-Cruzzi, "Days of the Dead," in *The New Yorker*, November 1993.

"Personally, I should not care for immortality in the least. Nothing better than oblivion exists, since in oblivion there is no wish unfulfilled. We had it before we were born, yet did not complain. Shall we then whine because we know it will return? It is Elysium enough for me."

—H.P. Lovecraft

The words quoted above distill a common secular conception of death. If we decline the traditional religious reassurances of an afterlife, or their fuzzy new age equivalents, and instead take the hard-boiled and thoroughly modern materialist view of death, then we likely end up with Gonzalez-Cruzzi, and perhaps with Lovecraft. Rejecting visions of reunions with loved ones or of crossing over into the light, we anticipate the opposite: darkness, silence, an engulfing emptiness, a peaceful oblivion. But we would be wrong.

The topic of our fate after death is a touchy subject, but nevertheless the error of anticipating nothingness needs rectifying. This misconception is so widespread and so psychologically debilitating for those facing death (all of us, sooner or later) it is worth a careful look at the faulty, rather subliminal logic which persuades us that dying leads us into "the void."

Here, again, is the view at issue: When we die, what's next is *nothing*; death is an abyss, a black hole, the end of experience; it is eternal nothingness, the permanent extinction of being. And here, in a nutshell, is the error contained in the view: It is to *reify* nothingness—make it a positive condition or quality (e.g., of "blackness")—and then to place the individual in it after death, so that we somehow fall *into* nothingness, to remain there eternally. It is to illicitly project the subject that died into a situation following death, a situation of no experiences, of what might be called "positive nothingness." Epicurus deftly refuted this mistake millennia ago, saying "When I am, death is not, and when death is, I am not," but regrettably his pearl of wisdom has been largely overlooked or forgotten. In what follows I will try to refine this insight and, using a thought experiment, make its implications vivid.

Not that there haven't been more recent attempts to counter the myth of nothingness, notably by the philosopher Paul Edwards in his classic 1969 paper "Existentialism and Death: A Survey of Some Confusions and Absurdities." Below I will produce my own examples of those bewitched by the vision of the void, but before continuing I must bow to Edwards' "who's who" of thinkers that have fallen into this particular conceptual trap. He quotes Shakespeare, Heine, Seneca, Swinburne, Houseman, Mencken, Bertrand Russell, Clarence Darrow, James Baldwin, and others, all to the effect that, as Swinburne put it, death is "eternal night." Those who anticipate nothingness at death are at least in some pretty exalted company.

If, as I will argue, nothingness cannot be anything positively existent, that is, if it truly (as the term would indicate) doesn't exist, then the situation at death cannot involve falling into it. Those skeptical of the soul and an afterlife need not fear (or cannot look forward to, if such is their preference) blackness and emptiness. There is no eternal absence of experience, no black hole which swallows up the unfortunate victim of death. If we conscientiously eliminate the tendency to project ourselves into a situation following death, and if we drop the notion of positive nothingness, then this picture loses plausibility and a rather different one emerges.

Do people still really believe, as I claim they do, in a kind of positive nothingness? I will present enough examples to show that, beyond Edwards' celebrities, many do harbor such a misconception. In developing a plausible alternative, my operating assumptions and guiding philosophy will be resolutely naturalistic, materialist, and non-dualist. I assume only a single universe of interconnected phenomena, a universe devoid of souls, spirits, mental essences, and the like. In particular, persons, on this account, are not possessed of any essential core identity (an indivisible self or soul), but consist only of relatively stable constellations of dispositions and traits, both physical and psychological. Although some conclusions I reach may end up sounding counterintuitive to those inclined to naturalism, it won't be because the argument departs from naturalistic assumptions. And for readers who are skeptical about naturalism, these conclusions may not be so unpalatable as my starting point might lead them to suppose.

Anticipating nothingness

The late Isaac Asimov, interviewed in Bill Moyers' series "A World of Ideas," questioned the traditional religious picture of our fate after death: "When I die I won't go to heaven or hell, there will just be nothingness." Asimov's naturalistically based skepticism about heaven or hell is common among secularists (there is no evidence for such realms) but he commits an equally common fallacy in his blithe assumption about nothingness, namely that it could "be." By substituting nothingness for heaven and hell, Asimov implies that it awaits us after death. Indeed the word itself, with the suffix "ness," conjures up the strange notion of "that stuff which does not exist." In using it we may start to think, in a rather casual, unreflective way, that there exists something that doesn't exist, but of course this is not a little contradictory. We must simply see that nothingness doesn't exist, period.

Harvard philosopher Robert Nozick, in his book *The Examined Life*, expresses much the same view as Asimov, and in much the same context. He debunks, in a very respectful tone, the wishful thinking that supposes there will be an afterlife involving the memories and personality of a currently existing person. "It might be nice to believe such a theory, but isn't the truth starker? This life is the only existence there is; afterward there is nothing." Although he probably doesn't mean to, with these words Nozick may suggest to the unwary that "nothing" is something like a state into which we go and never return. But, as Paul Edwards explained in "Existentialism and Death," death is *not* a state, it is not a condition in which we end up after dying. Of course I'm not denying that we die and disappear, only that we go *into* something called non-existence, nothing, or nothingness.

My richest example is offered by the late novelist Anthony Burgess in his memoirs, *You've Had Your Time: The Second Part of the Confessions*. The following paragraph from his meditations about death contains several nice variations on the "nothingness" theme.

> Am I happy? Probably not. Having passed the prescribed biblical age limit, I have to think of death and I do not like the thought. There is a vestigial fear of hell, and even of purgatory, and no amount of rereading rationalist authors can expunge it. If there is only darkness after death, then that darkness is the ultimate reality and that love of life that I intermittently possess is no preparation for it. In face of the approaching blackness, which Winston Churchill facetiously termed black velvet, concerning oneself with a world that is soon to fade out like a television image in a power cut seems mere frivolity. But rage against the dying of the light is only human, especially when there are still things to be done, and my rage sometimes sounds to myself like madness. It is not only a question of works never to be written, it is a matter of things unlearned. I have started to learn Japanese, but it is too late; I have started to read Hebrew, but my eyes will not take in the jots and tittles. How can one fade out in peace, carrying vast ignorance into a state of total ignorance?

Listing the thematic variations, we have: "darkness after death," "approaching blackness," "black velvet," "a world that is soon to fade out," "the dying of the light," "a state of total ignorance." All these express Burgess' expectation that death will mean entering a realm devoid of experience and qualities, a state something like losing all sensation (Gonzalez-Cruzzi's "non-sense"), all perception, all thought. He is raging against the imminent arrival of Nothingness, the eternal experience of no experience in which the subject somehow witnesses, permanently, its own extinction. But death rules out any such experience or witnessing, unless of course we covertly believe, as Burgess seems to, that in death we persist as some sort of pseudo-subject, to whom eternity presents itself as "black velvet." Burgess, as well as Nozick and Asimov, all deny that they continue on in any form, so their picture of the subject trapped in nothingness after death is rather contradictory. Since death really is the end of the individual, it cannot mean the arrival of darkness as witnessed by some personal remnant.

Two more brief examples, which I believe are typical of those who face death without the traditional reassurances of an afterlife. Arthur W. Frank, author of *At The Will Of The Body: Reflections on Illness*, wrote about his heart attack that "Afterward I felt always at risk of one false step, or heartbeat, plunging me over the side again. I will never lose that immanence of nothingness, the certainty of mortality." And Larry Josephs, an AIDS patient, wrote in the *Times* that "…I hope that when the time comes to face death, I will feel stronger, and less afraid of falling into an empty black abyss."

Although the fear of death is undoubtedly biological and hence unavoidable to some extent, the fear of nothingness, of the black abyss, can be dealt with successfully. This involves seeing, and then actually feeling, if possible, that your death is not the end of experience. It is the end of *this experiencer* most definitely, but that end is not followed by the dying of the light. Experience, I will argue, is quite impervious to the hooded figure who leads his unwilling charges into the night.

Continuity and being present

In order to make this clear it will be helpful to consider some facts about ordinary experience. First is the initially somewhat surprising fact that, from our point of view as subjects of experience, there are no gaps during the course of our conscious lives. Despite the fact that we are frequently and regularly unconscious (asleep, perhaps drugged, knocked out, etc.) these unconscious periods do not represent subjective pauses between periods of consciousness. That is, for the subject there is an instantaneous transition from the experience preceding the unconscious interval to the experience immediately following it. On the operating table we hear ourselves mumble our last admonition to the anesthesiologist not to overdo the pentathol and the next instant we are aware of the fluorescent lights in the recovery room. Or we experience a last vague thought before falling asleep and the next experience (barring a dream, another sort of experience) is hearing the neighbor's dog at 6 a.m. As much as we know that time has passed, nevertheless for us there has been no gap or interval between the two experiences which bracket a period of unconsciousness. I will call this fact about experience "personal subjective continuity".

Next, note that this continuity proceeds from our first experience as a child until the instant of death. For the subject, life is a single block of experience, marked by the rhythm of days, weeks, months, and years, and highlighted by personal and social watersheds. Although it may seem obvious and even tautological, for the purposes of what follows I want to emphasize that during our lives we never find ourselves absent from the scene. We may occasionally have the *impression* of having experienced or "undergone" a period of unconsciousness, but of course this is impossible. For the subject, awareness is constant throughout life; the "nothingness" of unconsciousness cannot be an experienced actuality.

But what about the time periods before and after this subjectively continuous block of experience, that is, before birth and after death? Don't these represent some sort of emptiness or "blank" for the subject, since, after all, it doesn't exist in either? To think that they might, as I've pointed out, is to confuse non-existence with a state that we somehow primitively subsist in, as an impotent ego confronted with blackness. Certainly we don't ordinarily think of the time *before* we come into existence as an abyss from which we manage to escape; we simply find ourselves present in the world. We cannot contrast the fact of being conscious with some prior state of non-experience.

The same is true of the time after death. There will be no future personal state of non-experience to which we can compare our present state of being conscious. All we have, as subjects, is this block of experience. We know, of course, that it is a finite block, but *since that's all we have, we cannot experience its finitude.* As much as we can know with certainty that this particular collection of memories, desires, intentions, and habits will cease, this cessation will not be a concrete fact for us, but can only be hearsay, so to speak. Hence (and this may start to sound a little fishy) as far as we're concerned as subjects, we're always situated here in the midst of experience.

Even given all this, when we imagine our death being imminent (a minute or two away, let us suppose) it is still difficult not to ask the questions "What will happen to me?" or "What's next?" and then anticipate the onset of nothingness. It is extraordinarily tempting to project ourselves—*this* locus of awareness—into the future, entering the blackness or emptiness of non-experience. But since we've ruled out nothingness or non-experience as the fate of subjectivity what, then, are plausible answers to such questions? The first one we can dispense with fairly readily. The "me" characterized by personality and memory simply ends. No longer will experience occur in the context of such personality and memory. The second question ("What's next?") is a little trickier, because, unless we suppose that my death is coincident with the end of the entire universe, we can't responsibly answer "nothing." Nothing is precisely what can't happen next. What happens next must be *something*, and part of that something consists in various sorts of consciousness. In the very ordinary sense that other centers of awareness exist and come into being, *experience* continues after my death. This is the something (along with many other things) which follows the end of my particular set of experiences.

Burgess suggests, when facing death, that "concerning oneself with a world that is soon to fade out like a television image in a power cut seems mere frivolity." But we know, as persons who have survived and witnessed, perhaps, the death of others, that the world does not fade out. It continues on in all sorts of ways, including the persistence of our particular subjective worlds. Death ends individual subjectivities while at the same time others are continuing or being created.

As I tried to make clear above, subjectivities—centers of awareness—don't have beginnings and endings for themselves, rather they simply find themselves in the world. From their perspective, it's as if they have always been present, always here; as if the various worlds evoked by consciousness were always "in place." Of course we know that they are not always in place from an objective standpoint, but their own non-being is never an experienced actuality for them. This fact, along with the fact that other subjectivities succeed us after we die, suggests an alternative to the intuition of impending nothingness in the face of death. (Be warned that this suggestion will likely seem obscure until it gets fleshed out using the thought experiment below.) Instead of anticipating nothingness at death, I propose that we should anticipate the *subjective sense of always having been present*, experienced within a different context, the context provided by those subjectivities which exist or come into being.

In proposing this I don't mean to suggest that there exist some supernatural, death-defying connections between consciousnesses which could somehow preserve elements of memory or personality. This is not at all what I have in mind, since material evidence suggests that everything a person consists of—a living body, awareness, personality, memories, preferences, expectations, etc.—is erased at death. Personal subjective continuity as I defined it above requires that experiences be those of a *particular* person; hence, this sort of continuity is bounded by death. So when I say that *you* should look forward, at death, to the "subjective sense of always having been present," I am speaking rather loosely, for it is not you—not *this* set of personal characteristics—that will experience "being present." Rather, it will be another set of characteristics (in fact, countless sets) with the capacity, perhaps, for completely different sorts of experience. But, despite these (perhaps radical) differences, it will share the qualitatively *very same sense* of always having been here, and, like you, will never experience its cessation.

Transformation and generic subjectivity

To help make this shared, continuing sense of "always having been present" more concrete, I want to embark on a thought experiment of the Rip Van Winkle variety. So imagine, in the perhaps not so distant future, that we develop the technology to reliably stop and then restart biological processes. One could, if one wished, be put "on hold" for an indefinite period, and then be "started up" again. (Some trusting and perhaps naive souls have already had their brains or entire bodies frozen in the expectation of just such technology.) In essence, one is put to sleep and then awakened after however many years, memories and personality intact.

From the point of view of the subject, such a suspension of consciousness would seem no different from a normal night's sleep, or, for that matter, an afternoon nap. The length of the unconscious interval—minutes, years, or centuries—makes no difference. There is simply the last experience before being suspended, and then the first experience upon reactivation, with no experienced gap or interval of nothingness in between. In principle a subject could lie dormant for millions of years, to awaken with no sense of time having passed, except, of course, the clues given by the changed circumstances experienced upon regaining consciousness. Personal subjective continuity would have been preserved across the eons.

Next, suppose that during the unconscious period (the length of which is unimportant for the point I'm about to make) changes in memories or personality, or both, take place, either deliberately or through some inadvertent process of degradation. I go to sleep as TC and wake up as TC/mod. (Readers are encouraged to substitute their own initials in what follows.) If the changes aren't too radical, then I (and others) will be able to re-identify myself as TC, albeit a modified version, whose differences from the original I might or might not be able to pinpoint myself. ("Funny, I don't remember ever having liked calf's liver before. Was I always this grumpy? I wonder if this suspension technique really worked as well as they claimed. Maybe some unscrupulous technician fiddled with my hypothalamus while I was under. Still, all in all, I seem relatively intact.") Assuming this sort of re-identification is possible, personal subjective continuity is still preserved across the unconscious interval. There would be no subjective gap or pause between the last experience of TC and the first experience of TC/mod. For TC/mod, TC was never not here. There is simply one block of experience, the context of which suffered an abrupt but manageable alteration when TC woke up as TC/mod.

An interesting series of question now arises, questions which may generate some visceral understanding of what I mean by expecting the sense of always having been present. First, how much of a change between TC and TC/mod is necessary to destroy personal subjective continuity? At what point, that is, would we start to say "Well, TC 'died' and a stranger now inhabits his body; experience ended for TC and now occurs for someone else"? It is not at all obvious where to draw the line. But let's assume we did draw it somewhere, for instance at the failure to recognize family and friends, or perhaps a vastly changed personality and the claim to be not TC but someone else altogether. Imagine changes so radical that everyone agrees it is not TC that confronts us upon awakening; he no longer exists. Given this rather unorthodox way of dying, *what happens to the intuition that now, for TC there is "nothing"?*

We have seen that, given small or moderate changes in memory and personality, there is no subjective gap or "positive nothingness" between successive experiences on either side of the unconscious period. Instead, there is an instantaneous transition from one to another. (TC/mod says "I'm still here, more or less like before. Seems like I went to sleep just a second ago.") Given this, it seems wrong to suppose that, at some point further along on the continuum of change (the point at which we decide someone else exists), TC's last experience before unconsciousness is not still *instantly followed* by more experiences. These occur within a substantially or perhaps radically altered context, that of the consciousness of the new person who awakens. These experiences may not be TC's experiences, but there has been no subjective cessation of experience, no black abyss of nothingness for TC. Destroying personal subjective continuity (i.e. ending a particular subject by means of the transformation envisioned here) doesn't result in the creation of some positive absence of experience "between" subjects into which the unfortunate TC falls or out of which the new person emerges. Rather, it just changes the context of experience radically enough so that we, and the person who wakes up, decide TC no longer exists. Death in this case is a matter of convention, not biology, and it hasn't interrupted awareness, only changed its context.

Although this transformation has disrupted the personal subjective continuity imparted by a stable context of memory and personality, there is another sort of continuity or sameness, that created by the shared sense of always having been present. Such *generic subjective continuity* is independent of the context of memory and personality (that is, of being a particular person), and it amounts simply to the fact that, whoever wakes up feels as if they've always been here, that there has been no subjective blank or emptiness "in front" of their current experience. We can, I think, imagine going to sleep, being radically transformed, and having someone else wake up, with no worry about falling into nothingness, even though we no longer exist. The first experience of TC/rad (a radically changed TC, no longer identifiable as the same person) would follow directly on the heels of the last experience of TC. If there are no subjective gaps of positive nothingness between successive experiences of a single individual, then there won't be such a gap between a person's last experience and the first experience of his or her radically transformed successor. That first experience occurs within a context of memory and personality which establishes the same sense of always having been present generated by the original person's consciousness.

But of course the difficulty here is that it seems arbitrary, or simply false, to say that TC/rad's experience *instantly follows* TC's last experience if there is no connection of memory or personality, but only some bodily continuity.

(And if we wish, we can imagine that drastic changes in body as well are engineered during the unconscious period, so that TC/rad looks nothing like his predecessor.) The objective facts are that TC has a last experience, then sometime later TC/rad has a first experience. But despite the lack of personal subjective continuity, despite the fact that we may decide at some point on the continuum of change (in memory, personality, and body) that TC no longer exists to have experiences, experience doesn't end *for* him, that is, there is no onset of nothingness. What we have instead is a transformation of the *subject itself*, a transformation of the context of awareness, while experience chugs along, oblivious of the unconscious interval during which the transformation took place. It's not that TC/rad's experience follows TC's in the sense of being connected to it by virtue of memory or personality, but that there is no *subjective* interval or gap between them experienced by either person. This is expressed in the fact that TC/rad, like TC, feels like he's always been present. However radical the change in context, and however long the unconscious interval, it seems that awareness—for itself, in its generic aspect of "always having been present"—is immune to interruption.

Death and birth

Let us call TC's fate in becoming TC/rad "death by transformation." My claim is that awareness is subjectively continuous, in this generic sense, across such a transformation. Considered from "its" point of view, experience never stops even though objectively speaking (from the "outside") one context for it ends and later on, as much later as you care to imagine, another context picks up. The next step in my argument is to apply this conclusion to ordinary death and birth. Instead of being transformed into some sort of successor, imagine that TC is allowed by a careless technician to lapse from unconsciousness into irreversible brain death. Somewhere, sometime later, a fresh consciousness comes into being, either naturally or by artifice. Except that the physical incarnations of TC and this other consciousness have no causal connection, this situation is the same as death by transformation. That is, one context of awareness has lapsed and another very different one begins. During the objective interval there has been no subjective hiatus in awareness; only the context of experience has changed.

   This thesis implies that even if all centers of awareness were extinguished and the next conscious creature appeared millions of years hence (perhaps in a galaxy far, far away) there would still be no subjective interregnum.

Subjectivity would jump that (objective) gap just as easily as it jumps the gap from our last experience before sleep to the first upon awakening. All the boring eons that pass without the existence of a subject will be irrelevant for the subject that comes into being. Nor will they count as "nothingness" for all the conscious entities which ceased to exist. Subjectivity, awareness, consciousness, experience—whatever we call it—never stops arising as far as *it* is concerned.

At this point it is likely that our intuitions about experience "jumping the gap" have been stretched beyond the breaking point. We have moved from the fairly uncontroversial fact of the continuity of one person's experience (no subjective gaps in consciousness during a lifetime) to this seemingly outlandish notion that consciousness, for itself, is impervious to death or indeed to any sort of objective interruption. But let me quickly reiterate my main points in order to reinstate some plausibility. (1) It is a mundane, although contingent, fact of life that when I die other subjects exist, hence subjectivity certainly is immune to *my* death in *these* circumstances. (2) If I am unconscious for any length of time I don't experience that interval; I am always "present"; this is personal subjective continuity. (3) If, after a period of unconsciousness, the transformed person who wakes up is not me there still won't be any perceived gap in awareness. The person who wakes up feels, as I did (hence "still" feels), that they've always been present. There has been no prior experience of not being present for them, nor when I stop existing do I have such an experience; this is generic subjective continuity. (4) Death and birth are "functionally equivalent" to the sort of transformation in (3), so again there will be no perceived gap, no nothingness of non-experience into which the subject might fall. Generic subjective continuity holds across any objective discontinuities in the existence of conscious beings.

Points (3) and (4) are certainly the most difficult to accept, and accepting them really depends on whether we are willing to slide down the slippery slope of the transformation thought experiment. If you don't buy the idea of a soul or indivisible self it's an easy trip. From a naturalistic perspective the self is nothing more than a contingent collection of fairly stable personality traits, memories, and physical characteristics. Thus the difference between my transformation into someone still recognizably me and someone barely not me is not a difference which would prevent awareness from jumping the gap. If there is no nothingness between experiences in the first case, then there is no nothingness in the second.

The reason (3) may have some intuitive plausibility is that we can generalize from our own ordinary experience of subjective continuity to cases in which we may not be quite sure who it is that wakes up. We can then see that even significant changes in the context of experience won't create subjective gaps. It is the absence of such gaps, resulting in the continuing shared sense of always having been present, that constitutes generic continuity.

Point (4) seems plausible only if we accept what I call generic continuity in the *extreme* case of (3) (a completely different person wakes up) and then buy the notion that there is no real difference between death by transformation and ordinary death. This equivalence is difficult to accept since in ordinary death there is no causal "successor" person which "takes over" the consciousness relinquished by the person who dies. But keep in mind that in our thought experiment the successor consciousness might be activated long after the original person was put to sleep, have very different physical and personal traits, and be somewhere else altogether. The only connecting link is presumably some bodily "shell," any of the parts of which (including the brain) might be changed or replaced. The most extreme case of (3) looks a lot, then, like ordinary death, except that there is a very attenuated successor that comes into existence by virtue of a radical transformation. Ordinary death and birth amount, I think, to such radical transformations of subjectivity, except that there is no obvious candidate for a successor. My point is, however, that we don't need such a candidate to insure the generic continuity of experience. We need only see that the continuity is that of subjectivity itself, abstracted from any particular context, and it finds concrete expression in the fact that none of us has ever experienced (or will ever experience) not being here.

Despite my naturalistic and materialist caveats at the beginning of this essay, such a conclusion may still seem to have a mystical ring. It may seem as though I give too much weight to the subjective sense of always having been present, and, in claiming that subjectivity, for itself, always "is," I ignore the vast times and spaces in which no consciousness exists at all. Nevertheless, I believe a materialist can see that consciousness, as a strictly physical phenomenon instantiated by the brain, creates a world subjectively immune to its own disappearance. It is the very finitude of a self-reflective cognitive system that bars it from witnessing its own beginning or ending, and hence prevents there being, *for it*, any condition other than existing. Its ending is only an event, and its non-existence a current fact, for other perspectives. After death we won't experience non-being, we won't "fade to black." We continue as the generic subjectivity that always finds itself here, in the various contexts of awareness that the physical universe manages to create. So when I recommend that you look forward to the (continuing) sense of always having been here, construe that "you" not as a particular person, but as that condition of awareness, which although manifesting itself in finite subjectivities, nevertheless always finds itself present.

To identify ourselves with generic subjectivity is perhaps as far as the naturalistic materialist can go towards accepting some sort of immortality. It isn't conventional immortality (not even as good as living in others' memory, some might think), since there is no "one" who survives, just the persistence of subjectivity for itself. It might be objected that in countering the myth of positive nothingness I go too far in claiming some sort of positive *connection* between subjectivities, albeit a connection that doesn't preserve the individual. I might be construed as saying, to borrow the language of a different tradition, that an eternal Subject exists, ever-present in all contexts of experience. I wouldn't endorse such a construal since it posits an entity above and beyond specific consciousnesses for which there is no evidence; nevertheless such language captures something of the feel for subjectivity and death I want to convey.

It is possible that this view may make it easier to cope with the prospect of personal extinction, since, if we accept it, we can no longer anticipate being hurled into oblivion, to face the eternal blackness that so unsettled Burgess (and, I suspect, secretly bedevils many atheists and agnostics). We may wear our personalities more lightly, seeing ourselves as simply variations on a theme of subjectivity which is in no danger of being extinguished by our passing. Of course we cannot completely put aside our biologically given aversion to the prospect of death, but we can ask, at its approach, why we are so attached to *this* context of consciousness. Why, if experience continues anyway, is it so terribly important that it continue within this set of personal characteristics, memories, and body? If we are no longer haunted by nothingness, then dying may seem more like the radical refreshment of subjectivity than its extinction.

For Discussion or Essays

- In the *Phaedo*, Simmias was surprised when Socrates stated that no philosopher worthy of the name fears death. Why, according to Socrates, was this the case? Are you convinced by Socrates' argument? Why or why not?
- Epicurus wrote that "a right understanding that death is nothing to us makes the mortality of life enjoyable, not by adding to life an unlimited time, but by taking away the yearning after immortality." Do you agree with this statement? Explain.
- Both the author of the *Phaedo* and the author of the Letter to Menoeceus, each in his own way, emphasize the importance of studying philosophy, "the love of wisdom," in order to accept the prospect of dying. Compare and contrast the two views.
- Compare and evaluate Holmes and Darrow when it comes to their respective views about the immortality of the soul. Which of their presentations is more convincing overall? Explain.
- What does Thomas W. Clark mean by "context of awareness"?
- Clark wrote that "subjectivities—centers of awareness—don't have beginnings or endings for themselves, rather they simply find themselves in the world." Why doesn't your earliest memory count, for you yourself, as a beginning of you as a subject?
- A student once remarked that Clark's advice to identify ourselves with generic subjectivity amounts to little more than the recommendation to remind ourselves that *Life goes on*. But this platitude, the student said, offers cold comfort. Do you agree? Why or why not?

Further Readings on Personal Survival and Immortality

Augustine, Keith. "The Case against Immortality." *Skeptic Magazine* 5, no. 2 (1997): 81–87. Augustine surveys many of the objections to notions of personal survival, including problems with bodily continuity, astral bodies, and age regression. He also turns a critical eye to alleged evidence of survival from paranormal research, including alleged past-life memories, out-of-body experiences, and near-death experiences.

Edwards, Paul. "Existentialism and Death: A Survey of Some Confusions and Absurdities." In *Philosophy, Science, and Method*, edited by S. Morgenbesser, P. Suppes, and M. White, 473–505. New York: St. Martin's Press, 1969. Thomas W. Clark, in the reading included above, describes Edwards' controversial paper as an attempt to "counter the myth of nothingness."

Flew, Antony. "Immortality." In *The Encyclopedia of Philosophy*, edited by Paul Edwards, Vol. 3, 139–50. New York: Macmillan, 1967. Interestingly, Flew, who over the course of most of his career promoted atheism, came to reconsider his view in the last years of his life, conceding that there might well be a deity, a designer, and creator of the world order. Even so, he does not appear to have reversed his opposition to any notion of life after death.

Hume, David. "The Immortality of the Soul." In *The Writings of David Hume*, edited by James Fieser. Internet Release, 1995. The original text was completed around 1755. Of special interest is Hume's discussion of what he calls "the physical arguments from the analogy of nature," which he describes as "really the only philosophical arguments which ought to be admitted with regard to this question [of the immortality of the soul]."

Lamont, Corliss. *The Illusion of Immortality*, 5th ed. New York: Unger/Continuum, 1990. First published in 1934, the fifth edition (1935) includes an introduction by the influential American philosopher John Dewey. In this landmark book, Lamont (1902–95) examines the many conceptual problems with notions of personal survival, including problems of describing what exactly it is that is said to survive, and where exactly it is supposed to abide. Toward the end of the book he concludes that "It is best not only to disbelieve in immortality, but to *believe in mortality*."

In a 1988 interview, he stated that "The idea of immorality is really something that encourages war," because "young men going into battle think that if they're killed they're going straight to heaven."

Paul-Henri Thiry, d'Holbach. *Le Bon Sens*. First published in 1772, the book has appeared in various English translations and editions, and is available online. See especially §100–103 and 107–108, wherein the author attacks the dogmas of the immortality of the soul and another life.

Russell, Bertrand. "Death as the Final Event of the Self." In *Why I Am Not a Christian*, 88–93. London: George Allen & Unwin Ltd., 1957. First published in 1927.

Part II

Rebirth

Introduction to Part II:
Survival in a Different Body

As a person puts on new garments, giving up old ones, similarly, the soul accepts new material bodies, giving up the old and useless ones.

—*Bhagavad-Gita*, Chapter 2, Verse 22

When he dies and is turned to ashes,
Whence is he to appear again?

—Jayanta Bhatta (ca. ninth century AD)[1]

The cultural anthropologist Paul Radin (1883–1959) wrote that "the belief in some form of reincarnation [is] universally present in all simple food-gathering and fishing-hunting civilizations."[2] Others have claimed that the belief in reincarnation (or *rebirth*) is universal, or nearly so, not only among "primitive man," but across a much broader range of cultures. A professor of anthropology at Princeton University, for example, has claimed that "an overwhelming number of societies the world over have rebirth eschatologies."[3] This sort of sweeping claim about rebirth as a "cultural universal" is not unusual. Whether or not the claim is true, it might be a safer bet to say that the belief in rebirth is universally present among undergraduates at American universities.

The doctrine of rebirth has its appeals, but it is also beset with daunting conceptual and ethical problems. Both of these points will become clear in the following readings, as we examine the doctrine at closer quarters.

---

[1]Quoted by Theodor Stcherbatsky, "History of Materialism in India," in *Studies in the History of Indian Philosophy*, ed. Debiprasad Chattopadhyaya (Atlantic Highlands, NJ: Humanities Press, 1980), vol. 2, 32–41. The citation is from p. 38. (MM has slightly revised the English translation.)
[2]Paul Radin, *Primitive Religion: Its Nature and Origin* (New York: Viking Press, 1937), 270.
[3]Gananath Obeyesekere, *Imagining Karma* (Berkeley and Los Angeles: University of California Press, 2002), 17. An eschatology is a doctrine that is concerned with the ultimate fate of the soul or of humankind.

Candidate survivors

When it comes to the possibility of personal survival, one of the first questions that arises is: *What exactly is it that is supposed to survive the death of the body?* What is it that is supposed to continue to be conscious or to have experiences after a human dies? Connected to this question are a number of other questions, including the question *where* does whatever survives survive? Let us recall that Plato's answer to these questions is that, when death overtakes a burdensome body, an immaterial and immortal soul continues to exist on a different plane, in the non-material realm of ideas or pure forms.

Plato's answer has been enormously influential over the centuries, and its influence continues to this day. In the readings that follow, it will become clear that other answers, too, continue to exert their power on the popular imagination. In the remainder of this Introduction we will consider how the doctrine of rebirth answers the question of what sort of thing is supposed to survive death. In the final section, we will say a few words about the doctrine of rebirth and the problem of justice.

In his *Meditations on First Philosophy* (1641), the French philosopher René Descartes presented an ingenious argument to support the claim that we can know for certain that our souls are immaterial and immortal. According to Descartes, I can be sure of nothing so much as that *I am a thing that thinks.* As a thing that thinks, I have no length, width, height, or mass; I am as simple as a geometric point. But if this is the case, then I have no parts to fall apart! And since (as Descartes assumed) things come to an end only by falling apart, then as a thing that thinks, I never come to an end.

Like Plato, Descartes exemplifies a view of the mind as a fundamentally different sort of thing, a distinct substance, from the body. This view is called *mind-body dualism.* Descartes' detractors have described his view of the relationship of an immaterial mind with a material body as a picture of "a ghost in a machine," and they are quick to point out that it comes with its own tricky problems. It is not at all clear, for example, how an immaterial mind could ever interact with the material furniture that we seem always to be bumping into. If the mind and the body are essentially distinct substances, then how could making one's mind up to raise your left hand result in raising that hand? And how could the physical act of sitting on a tack result in the feeling of pain? Thus, mind-body dualism is plagued by, among other things, the problem of how the mind could ever interact with the body or with any other material objects.

According to an even older view, what survives is *something physical about you as a person*, and this physical something is your spirit or soul. Ancient Hebrews, and Greeks, too, thought of the soul as "breath"—*ruach* in Hebrew and *pneuma* in Greek. They thought of the soul as a fine, hot, mist-like substance, or something finer still, which leaves the body after you die but continues to exist as a ghostly, somewhat-physical soul or spirit with a shape but no solidity. As we will see in Part Four, Titus Lucretius Carus believed this, too. Clearly this is a very different view from Plato's.

According to a more modern version of this story, what survives is your "energy." This sort of New Age talk trades on the scientific cachet of the word *energy*, while stripping the word of its scientifically useful meaning and giving it a suitably blurry "spiritual" spin. Physicists think of energy as the ability of a physical system to do work on other physical systems; accordingly, energy is an observable, measurable physical phenomenon. This clearly has nothing to do with the New Age view of mind or soul as a mysterious "energy."[4]

A third possibility for personal survival—assuming this formulation is intelligible enough to count as a possibility at all—holds that what survives is a somewhat disembodied soul or spirit, with a shape and location, but otherwise no physicality. On the one hand, such spooky entities are subtle enough to walk through walls; on the other hand, they are stout enough to slam doors, lift candelabras, and make bumps in the night—to the great consternation of overnight guests in haunted mansions. In view of these puzzling abilities and limitations, hardheaded thinkers since at least as early as the English philosopher Thomas Hobbes (1588–1679) have dismissed the very notion of *incorporeal spirits* as a contradiction in terms.[5]

In response, perhaps, to some of these objections, other writers have claimed that before we die we have not one but two bodies: the physical body, as well as a ghostly "astral body," which in this life is usually

---

[4]Moreover, Einstein famously described the convertibility of mass to energy, and vice versa. It is not clear, then, why it would be any more "spiritual" (let alone true) to say that your soul or spirit is energy than it is to say that it is matter.

[5]In a chapter entitled "Of Religion" from his great book *Leviathan* (1651), Hobbes wrote that, "though men may put together words of contradictory signification, as *Spirit*, and *Incorporeall*; yet they can never have the imagination of any thing answering to them" (Thomas Hobbes, *Leviathan*, ed. C.B. Macpherson (London and New York: Penguin Books, 1968), 171).

conterminous with our familiar physical bodies, though it occasionally strays. The astral body, which is not composed of any sort of matter that physics could ever get to the bottom of, is what is supposed to survive after biological death.

To say that such bodies exist is either to make an empirical claim or no claim at all. If it is an empirical claim, then the physical sciences should, at least in principle, be able to provide evidence of astral bodies. Although such bodies are alleged to surround us, it is not clear that anyone has presented good evidence that these entities have ever spontaneously interfered with radiographic equipment, magnetometers, high-speed photography, microscopes, or any other instruments of physics research. This observation should count as strong disconfirmation of the claim that subtle bodies or astral bodies are real, since proponents of that positive claim bear the burden of proof. As the British philosopher Peter Geach has observed, if "subtle bodies" produce no physical effects, they are not bodies at all.[6] If on the other hand it is claimed that astral bodies are composed of a spiritual substance that even an "ideally completed physics" of the future could not get to the bottom of, then most of the alleged evidence from psychical research counts for nothing, and it is unclear how we could ever have any reliable evidence for their existence.

In view of these conceptual and scientific problems, the doctrine of rebirth might appear to be more plausible than the astral body, "breath," or "energy" doctrines of survival. Whether or not this turns out to be the case, the doctrine of rebirth brings its own set of problems. Reading the claims of recent Western proponents of rebirth, one sometimes hears the claim that the doctrine is more *scientific*, in some sense of the word, than other posthumous scenarios, too. Perhaps this impression is due to the association of rebirth with the doctrine of *karma*, with its alleged emphasis on cause and effect, exemplified in the commonsensical adage, *What goes around comes around*.[7] In any case, after the dramatic expansion of our knowledge of the brain in recent years (a trend noted in the General Introduction), rebirth as an empirical claim sounds less plausible today than in the past.[8]

---

[6]Peter Geach, *God and the Soul* (New York: Schocken Books, 1969), 18.

[7]*Karma* is the doctrine that a person's actions in this and previous states of existence decide their fate in future lives. Notice that it is a doctrine distinct from rebirth. We will encounter the term in our readings below.

[8]The American essayist Adam Gopnick recently described how influential proponents of an updated American Buddhism recommend stripping it of the "unsustainable belief" in reincarnation and

The most commonly accepted interpretations of rebirth, two of which we will encounter in our Part II readings, require that something important about a person must *transfer* from one body to another one. That "something" must be the bearer of something essential to the person: her consciousness, her karma, or whatever. Thus, the doctrine of rebirth depicts human beings (and perhaps other living things as well) as a loose combination of two elements: a material body, on the one hand, and something immaterial, on the other. As such, the strengths and weaknesses of mind-body dualism are the strengths and weaknesses of reincarnation.

Where do survivors survive?

We will take up these conceptual problems in our readings below, but let us set them aside for the moment. For now, let us raise an obvious question: if a soul, disembodied or not, survives the death of the body, then *where* does it abide?

As we have seen, Plato's answer is that the native habitat of our immaterial souls is an unchanging realm of eternal forms. By contrast, some popular religions present us with pictures of teeming netherworlds, heavens, hells, purgatories, and paradises. When we try to imagine any of these, though, we seem always to fall back to a *place* somewhere. Questions of posthumous survival seem always to be linked in our imaginations to pictures of where that survival takes place, whether on Earth or elsewhere. Moreover, these questions raise further "logistical" questions,[9] including the "transportation problem" of how the soul, or whatever it is that survives, makes its way from the deceased animal to the soul's posthumous abode, and the related "destination problem" of the location of that abode. Aeronautics, satellite imagery, and meteorology rule out the possibility that the soul rises like smoke or water vapor to a realm above Earth. We are, therefore, in the market for alternative suggestions.

In any case, when it comes to the destination problem there are at least two proposed solutions: (i) rebirth or resurrection on Earth, or above it or

---

karma, just as some Christian thinkers these days "try to tiptoe past the doctrines of Heaven and Hell" as actual places where people go (Adam Gopnick, "American Nirvana: Is There a Science of Buddhism?" in *The New Yorker* (August 2017): 69–74).

[9]Logistics: the careful organization of a complicated activity so that it happens in a successful way.

below it, or elsewhere in more-or-less familiar space, and (ii) afterlife in an immaterial, non-spatial, or even non-temporal realm. In scenario (ii), the Next World is sometimes described as a dimension that is somehow undetectable to us, or as a "state" without spatial dimension. It is, to put it mildly, difficult to figure out what to do with such formulations.[10]

To complicate matters, one could imagine scenarios involving combinations of these two sorts of posthumous domains. Plato, for example, seems to have entertained the possibility of both, in the career of a single soul: after the death of the body, the soul makes its way to another realm before returning to terrestrial life in another body. Or to take the example of our first reading below, the *Katha Upanishad* appears to depict cycles of individual death-and-rebirth in and around Earth, leading to the ultimate goal of impersonal survival of the True Self "everywhere at once." Some Christians and Muslims, by contrast, combine a belief in physical resurrection on Judgment Day, with eternal life—that is to say, life "outside of time"—in God's presence.[11] Others contrast life everlasting for God's elect in heaven or on earth, on the one hand, to a "death" that appears to be something like extinction of personhood, on the other. Still others hold that death is non-survival, but that on the Day of Judgment the dead are bodily raised from the grave to be judged, after which the elect will dwell as psychophysical persons in an Earthly paradise. (We will return to the topics of resurrection and life everlasting in Part III.) To take yet another example, the Buddhist doctrine of nirvana is often conceived as impersonal survival somewhere or nowhere

---

[10]And even if we could somehow set this objection aside, we appear to face further difficulties when it comes to the continuity of personal identity: how could any person in such a dimension or state have enough in common with a human person to establish that the former is the same person as the latter? We will encounter the problem of continuity of personal identity in several readings to come.

[11]Often, as in some of the readings in this book, the word *eternity* is taken to mean something like "forever and ever." This is what American poet Emily Dickinson described when she wrote that Forever is composed of nows. (*The Complete Poems of Emily Dickinson*, ed. Thomas H. Johnson (New York and London: Little, Brown and Company, 1960), 307.) In philosophical theology, by contrast, "eternity" is often used to mean "existence outside of time." The latter meaning raises an obvious problem for talk about "eternal life": as philosopher of religion Charles Seymour notes, "it does not make much sense to say that we, who now exist in time, will after death come to be timeless. What is timelessly true is, of course, unchanging. If our existence in heaven and hell is timeless, then it is an unchanging truth that we exist in heaven or hell. But this cannot be an unchanging truth, since we have not yet arrived at our afterlife destination. [...] Clearly, then, our life after death will be, strictly speaking, everlasting rather than eternal" (Charles Seymour, "Hell, Justice, and Freedom," *International Journal for Philosophy of Religion* 43 (1998): 69–86. (See the entry in the Further Readings section at the end of Part Three below.) The citation appears on p. 84, fn 9. Seymour cites (Peter Geach, *Providence and Evil* (Cambridge: Cambridge University Press, 1977), 130–32).

in particular; however, others have described it as something close to non-survival.[12] We will pick up this discussion in the Walpola Rahula reading below.

Rebirth and the problem of justice

The conceptual problems with the doctrine of rebirth may be daunting, but it has its advantages, too. One of the most notable advantages of the doctrine, and one reason why some people cling to pictures of personal survival in other forms, too, has little to do with an alleged fear of "the void." Rather, it has to do with what we will call the *problem of justice*.[13]

According to Clarence Darrow and many others, including the psychoanalyst Sigmund Freud,[14] wish fulfillment accounts for the pervasiveness and perseverance of belief in life after death. Darrow's fellow nonbeliever and younger contemporary, Corliss Lamont, described the belief in survival as not merely an error, but as a *delusion*—an error motivated by wishful thinking. Wishful thinking with reference to the survival hypothesis can take at least three forms: the supposed fear of first-person non-existence; the fear of losing loved ones or the yearning to be reunited with them, and the yearning for divine retribution and reward, in view of the all-too-obvious injustices here on Earth.

Seen in this light, "moral arguments" for personal survival, including arguments for rebirth, resemble *argumenta ad misericordiam*—arguments that fallaciously appeal to pity. Plato appears to have committed this fallacy when (in a passage from *Phaedo* not included in our reading in Part I), he has his character Socrates say, "I have good hope that some future awaits men after death, as we have been told for years, a much better future for the good than for the wicked."[15] Arguments based on such hopes may be

---

[12]Antony Flew, *Merely Mortal? Can You Survive Your Own Death?* (Amherst, NY: Prometheus Books, 2000), 2–4.

[13]I have no research conclusions at hand to support this conjecture, but it seems likely, in view of anecdotal evidence, including discussions with students. In an essay entitled "The Immortality of the Soul" (1755), David Hume discusses the closely related issue of moral arguments for the survival hypothesis, with reference to God's justice. Also refer to the discussion of the problem of justice in Paul Edwards, *Reincarnation: A Critical Examination* (Amherst, NY: Prometheus Books, 1996), 29–34.

[14]Most famously in Freud's work *The Future of an Illusion* (1927).

[15]Plato, *Phaedo*, 63c.

emotionally satisfying, but their conclusions do not follow reliably from their premises.[16]

According to the doctrine of rebirth-plus-karma, after a thing dies it is reborn—either immediately or eventually, on earth or elsewhere—to a station appropriate to its actions in previous lives. More virtuous deeds get you a higher perch on the tree of life the next time around, and perhaps better circumstances in this or another life, too. Thus, we are presented with a cosmic mechanism that somehow registers the morally relevant actions and inactions of every human or every sentient being, and ascribes to each of these karmically significant actions an automatic compensatory response, a reward or punishment.

Notable among the things that are thereby explained away is a fact of life that is more-than-obvious to the poor and powerless majority of adult humans, namely, that *life is not fair*. Most of us have observed that bad things happen to good people, and—just as outrageously—that good things come to evil people. It is deeply repugnant to many people, at least outside of the United States, to believe that, for example, schoolchildren who have been immolated in a drone strike will share the same posthumous fate as the sublimely unaffected drone operator in an air-conditioned cubicle seven thousand miles away. The doctrine of rebirth-plus-karma proposes that we are, each in his or her turn, alternately victims and victimizers, reaping what we sew: the schoolchild was once the moral equivalent of a drone operator, and the drone operator is a beneficiary of a previous life of virtue. Thus, "everything balances out" morally in a morally structured cosmos.

Like the familiar doctrine of divine judgment that we will examine in Part III, rebirth-plus-karma helps us to convince ourselves that, appearances notwithstanding, things are as they should be. Like divine judgment and pictures of heaven and hell, rebirth-plus-karma depicts a *moralized cosmic order*, one that "makes things right" in the face of what would otherwise appear to be morally senseless suffering on Earth. Like the doctrine of divine judgment, karma provides a measure of relief from reflections on the wicked ways of the world; but unlike divine judgment, rebirth-plus-karma avoids the old, unanswerable question: How could an infinitely good and powerful

---

[16]Just because the belief may be buoyed by pity, however, this does not mean that it is false. The fact that you fervently wish to be united with loved ones "who have gone before us," does not by itself foreclose the possibility that you may get your wish. To claim otherwise is to commit another error of reasoning, in this case the *genetic fallacy*, which is the sort of faulty reasoning that holds that a belief is unacceptable just because of its origin (in this case, a wish).

God countenance the world as it is? Rebirth-plus-karma reassures us of the justice—indeed the *moral perfection at every moment!*[17]—of the passing scene: whoever we are, and whether we languish in pain or bask in comfort, we get what we deserve. The infant who will die of a parasitic disease is bearing her just karmic burden, and similarly in the case of the rapacious executive officer of the pharmaceutical company, a man who lives a long life of comfort, privilege, and public adulation. In view of these considerations, perhaps the doctrine of rebirth-plus-karma provides an especially elegant, socially conservative solution to the problem of justice.[18]

---

[17]"No matter what happens, whether we help the underdog or not, whether our efforts at making lives less full of suffering and sorrow succeed or not, the ultimate outcome will be just, in the sense that every human being will be getting exactly—no more and no less—what he deserves" (Edwards, *Reincarnation*, 43). It should be added, however, that, knowing the operation of the law of karma, a person will strive to enhance her karmic stature by performing acts of kindness and charity. Edwards does not mention this salutary effect of belief in karma.

[18]Notice that the doctrine of rebirth alone does not solve the problem of justice, because one could imagine rebirth taking place in a morally arbitrary manner, without any connection to the deeds of previous lives. The doctrine of rebirth is distinct from the doctrine of *karma*, and it is the latter that purports to express a built-in cosmic law of moral consequences for actions.

6

The Katha Upanishad: Death as a Teacher

Anonymous

Translated by Eknath Easwaran

Katha is a Sanskrit word that means "distress." The Katha Upanishad is an important text within the ancient body of literature called Vedanta. It tells the story of a meeting between a young boy, Nachiketa, and Yama, the Lord of Death himself. Yama informs his young student that "*Ātman* (Soul, Self) exists," and recommends the precept "seek Self-knowledge which is Highest Bliss." As we will see, these teachings differ greatly from the assertions of Buddhists, for whom "Soul, Self does not exist," and from the Buddhist precept that one should seek "Emptiness (*Śūnyatā*), which is Highest Bliss."

A few words by way of background and explanation: As the story opens, Nachiketa's father, Vajasravasa, is performing a sacrifice called *Sarvadakshina*, which is supposed to be a preparation for the last stage of spiritual life. In the ritual, the performer is supposed to offer up his wealth. In those days, cows were among the most precious of possessions, and so Vajasrava felt obliged to give away his cows. Observing the sacrificial ritual, Nachiketa notices that his father is giving away only exhausted old cows that give no milk and are not capable of bearing calves. He is performing the purely outward form of the offering, and he is doing it out of a desire to gain heavenly enjoyment. But he is violating the ritual's inner spirit, and in the course of doing this, he is offering that which is unworthy. Vajasrava's self-interested cleverness distresses Nachiketa. Even worse, as Nachiketa notices, his father is supposed to offer up his son, Nachiketa himself, but he has failed to do so. This is why Nachiketa asks, "Oh father, to whom are you going to offer me up?"

At first his father ignores Nachiketa's question, but the boy insists, repeating the question three times. Finally, the exasperated father says, "Nachiketa, I give you to the God of Death." Vajasrava utters these words in anger, but Nachiketa decides to obey his father's words by going to the House of the God of Death, Yama. The repentant father begs his son not to go, but Nachiketa reminds his father that their ancestors never went back on their word, and so it is unseemly that his father should do so.

Upon reaching the House of Death, the boy finds that Yama is not at home. For three days and nights the young boy waits at the doorstep without food, water, or sleep. When Yama returns, he is grieved to see that Nachiketa had not been welcomed properly. To redress this breech of hospitality, the gracious God of Death grants his guest three wishes.

The boy's first wish is to be discharged from the abode of death, to be allowed to return to his father, and for his father to be favorably disposed toward him. The second wish is to know how one could reach heaven, "where there is no sorrow, old age or death." In response to the second wish, Yama provides all the details of the heavenly fire ritual, performance of which would take one to heaven. For the third wish, Nachiketa asks to learn the mystery of what comes after dying.

Yama is reluctant to grant this wish. Not even the gods know what comes after dying. Yama tries to convince Nachiketa to make a different wish, suggesting many sons, riches, and sources of pleasure instead. But Nachiketa insists: though he is young, he knows that all earthly treasures and heavenly pleasures come to an end sooner or later, and he will settle for nothing less than knowledge of the proper path to be taken.

Yama is pleased with the boy's refusal to pursue the path of enjoyment and his choice to take the path of truth and goodness. So ends the first section of the six sections that make up this work. What follows, beginning with the second section, is Yama's teaching about knowledge of the all-knowing self, and the attainment of immortality. One must discriminate the Soul from the body, which is the seat of desire. After the body dies, it is the all-knowing Soul that remains: it is beyond cause and effect; it was never born and will never die.

Thus having learned this wisdom from Yama, Nachiketa is freed from the cycle of birth, death, and rebirth.

———————

First section

1   Once, long ago, Vajasravasa gave away his possessions to gain religious merit.

2   He had a son named Nachiketa who, though only a boy, was full of faith in the scriptures. Nachiketa thought when the offerings were made:

3   "What merit can one obtain by giving away cows that are too old to give milk?"

4   To help his father understand this, Nachiketa said: "To whom will you offer me?" He asked this again and again. "To death I give you!" said his father in anger.

5   The son thought: "I will go, the first of many who will die, in the midst of many who are dying, on a mission to Yama, king of death.

6   See how it was with those who came before, and how it will be with those who are living. Like corn, mortals ripen and fall; like corn they come up again."
Nachiketa went to Yama's abode, but the king of death was not there. He waited three days. When Yama returned, he heard a voice say:

7   "When a spiritual guest enters the house,
Like a bright flame, he must be received well,

8   With water to wash his feet. Far from wise
Are those who are not hospitable
To such a guest. They will lose all their hopes,
The religious merit they have acquired,
Their sons and their cattle."

Yama

9   O spiritual guest, I grant you three boons
To atone for the three inhospitable nights
You have spent in my abode.
Ask for three boons, one for each night.

Nachiketa

10   O king of death, as the first of these boons
Grant that my father's anger be appeased,

So he may recognize me when I return
And receive me with love.

Yama

11   I grant that your father, the son of Uddalaka and Aruna,
Will love you as in the past. When he sees you
Released from the jaws of death, he will sleep
Again with a mind at peace.

Nachiketa

12   There is no fear at all in heaven; for you
Are not there, neither old age nor death.
Passing beyond hunger and thirst and pain,
All rejoice in the kingdom of heaven.

13   You know the fire sacrifice that leads to heaven,
king of death. I have full faith
In you and ask for instruction. Let this
Be your second boon to me.

Yama

14   Yes, I do know, Nachiketa, and shall
Teach you the fire sacrifice that leads
To heaven and sustains the world, that knowledge
Concealed in the heart. Now listen.

The Narrator

15   Then the king of death taught Nachiketa how to perform the fire
sacrifice, how to erect the altar for worshipping the fire from which
the universe evolves. When the boy repeated his instruction, the dread
king of death was well pleased and said:

Yama

16   Let me give you a special boon: this sacrifice
Shall be called by your name, Nachiketa.
Accept from me this many-colored chain too.

17 Those who have thrice performed this sacrifice,
And who have realized their unity with father, mother,
And teacher, and discharged the three duties
Of studying the scriptures, ritual worship
And giving alms to those in need—they rise above
Birth and death. Knowing the god of fire
Born of Brahman, they attain perfect peace.

18 Those who carry out this triple duty
Conscious of its full meaning will shake off
The dread noose of death and transcend sorrow
To enjoy the world of heaven.

19 Thus have I granted you the second boon,
Nachiketa, the secret of the fire
That leads to heaven. It will have your name.
Ask now, Nachiketa, for the third boon.

Nachiketa

20 When a person dies, there arises this doubt:
"He still exists," say some; "he does not,"
Say others. I want you to teach me the truth.
This is my third boon.

Yama

21 This doubt haunted even the gods of old;
For the secret of death is hard to know.
Nachiketa, ask for some other boon
And release me from my promise.

Nachiketa

22 This doubt haunted even the gods of old;
For it is hard to know, O Death, as you say.
I can have no greater teacher than you,
And there is no boon equal to this.

Yama

23 Ask for sons and grandsons who will live
A hundred years. Ask for herds of cattle,
Elephants and horses, gold and vast land,
And ask to live as long as you desire.

24 Or, if you can think of anything more
Desirable, ask for that, with wealth and
Long life as well. Nachiketa, be the ruler
Of a great kingdom, and I will give you
The utmost capacity to enjoy

25 The pleasures of life. Ask for beautiful
Women of loveliness rarely seen on earth,
Riding in chariots, skilled in music,
To attend on you. But Nachiketa,
Don't ask me about the secret of death.

Nachiketa

26 These pleasures last but until tomorrow,
And they wear out the vital powers of life.
How fleeting is all life on earth! Therefore
Keep your horses and chariots, dancing

27 And music, for yourself. Never can mortals
Be made happy by wealth. How can we be
Desirous of wealth when we see your face
And know we cannot live while you are here?
This is the boon I choose and ask you for.

28 Having approached an immortal like you,
How can I, subject to old age and death,
Ever try to rejoice in a long life
For the sake of the senses' fleeting pleasures?

29 Dispel this doubt of mine, O king of death:
Does a person live after death or does he not?
Nachiketa asks for no other boon
Than the secret of this great mystery.

Second section

Having tested young Nachiketa and found him fit to receive spiritual instruction, Yama, king of death, said:

Yama

1   The joy of the *Ātman* ever abides,
    But not what seems pleasant to the senses.
    Both these, differing in their purpose, prompt
    Man to action. All is well for those who choose
    The joy of the *Ātman*, but they miss
    The goal of life who prefer the pleasant.

2   Perennial joy or passing pleasure?
    This is the choice one is to make always.
    The wise recognize these two, but not
    The ignorant. The first welcome what leads
    To abiding joy, though painful at the time.
    The latter run, goaded by their senses,
    After what seems immediate pleasure.

3   Well have you renounced these passing pleasures
    So dear to the senses, Nachiketa,
    And turned your back on the way of the world
    Which makes mankind forget the goal of life.

4   Far apart are wisdom and ignorance.
    The first leads one to Self-realization;
    The second makes one more and more
    Estranged from his real Self. I regard you,
    Nachiketa, worthy of instruction,
    For passing pleasures tempt you not at all.

5   Ignorant of their ignorance, yet wise
    In their own esteem, these deluded men
    Proud of their vain learning go round and round

6   Like the blind led by the blind. Far beyond
    Their eyes, hypnotized by the world of sense,
    Opens the way to immortality.
    "I am my body; when my body dies,

I die." Living in this superstition
They fall life after life under my sway.

7 It is but few who hear about the Self.
Fewer still dedicate their lives to its
Realization. Wonderful is the one
Who speaks about the Self; rare are they
Who make it the supreme goal of their lives.
Blessed are they who, through an illumined
Teacher, attain to Self-realization.

8 The truth of the Self cannot come through one
Who has not realized that he is the Self.
The intellect cannot reveal the Self
Beyond its duality of subject
And object. They who see themselves in all
And all in them help others through spiritual
Osmosis to realize the Self themselves.

9 This awakening you have known comes not
Through logic and scholarship, but from
Close association with a realized teacher.
Wise are you, Nachiketa, because you seek
The Self eternal. May we have more
Seekers like you!

Nachiketa

10 I know that earthly treasures are transient
And never can I reach the eternal through them.
Hence have I renounced all my desires for earthly treasures
To win the eternal through your instruction.

Yama

11 I spread before your eyes, Nachiketa,
The fulfillment of all worldly desires:
Power to dominate the earth, delights
Celestial gained through religious rites,
Miraculous powers beyond time and space.
These with will and wisdom have you renounced.

12 The wise, realizing through meditation
    The timeless Self, beyond all perception,
    Hidden in the cave of the heart,
    Leave pain and pleasure far behind.

13 Those who know they are neither body nor mind
    But the immemorial Self, the divine
    Principle of existence, find the source
    Of all joy and live in joy abiding.
    I see the gates of joy are opening
    For you, Nachiketa.

Nachiketa

14 Teach me of That you see as beyond right
    And wrong, cause and effect, past and future.

Yama

15 I will give you the Word; all the scriptures
    I will glorify, all spiritual disciplines
    I will express—disciplines that aspirants practice,
    Leading lives of sense-restraint and self-denial.

16 It is OM.[1] This symbol of the Godhead
    Is the highest. Realizing it one finds
    Complete fulfillment of all one's longings.

17 It is of the greatest support to all seekers.
    Those in whose hearts OM reverberates
    Unceasingly are indeed blessed
    And deeply loved as one who is the Self.

18 The all-knowing Self was never born,
    Nor will it die. Beyond cause and effect,
    This Self is eternal and immutable.
    When the body dies, the Self does not die.

19 If the slayer believes that he can slay
    Or the slain believes that he can be slain,

---

[1]Or *Aum* (ॐ), a sacred sound in the Hindu religion. —MM

Neither knows the truth. The eternal Self
Slays not, nor is ever slain.

20 Hidden in the heart of every creature
Exists the Self, subtler than the subtlest,
Greater than the greatest. They go beyond
Sorrow who extinguish their self-will
And behold the glory of the Self
Through the grace of the Lord of Love.

21 Though one sits in meditation in a
Particular place, the Self within
Can exercise his influence far away.
Though still, he moves everything everywhere.

22 When the wise realize the Self
Formless in the midst of forms, changeless
In the midst of change, omnipresent
And supreme, they go beyond sorrow.

23 The Self cannot be known through study
Of the scriptures, nor through the intellect,
Nor through hearing learned discourses.
The Self can be attained only by those
Whom the Self chooses. Verily unto them
Does the Self reveal himself.

24 The Self cannot be known by anyone
Who desists not from unrighteous ways,
Controls not his senses, stills not his mind,
And practices not meditation.

25 None else can know the omnipresent Self,
Whose glory sweeps away the rituals
Of the priest and the prowess of the warrior
And puts death itself to death.

Third section

1 In the secret cave of the heart, two are seated
By life's fountain. The separate ego
Drinks of the sweet and bitter stuff,

Liking the sweet, disliking the bitter,
While the supreme Self drinks sweet and bitter
Neither liking this nor disliking that.
The ego gropes in darkness, while the Self
Lives in light. So declare the illumined sages
And the householders who worship
The sacred fire in the name of the Lord.

2 May we light the fire of Nachiketa
That burns out the ego and enables us
To pass from fearful fragmentation
To fearless fullness in the changeless whole.

3 Know the Self as lord of the chariot,
The body as the chariot itself,
The discriminating intellect as charioteer,
And the mind as reins.

4 The senses, say the wise, are the horses;
Selfish desires are the roads they travel.
When the Self is confused with the body,
Mind, and senses, they point out, he[2] seems
To enjoy pleasure and suffer sorrow.

5 When one lacks discrimination
And his mind is undisciplined, the senses
Run hither and thither like wild horses.

6 But they obey the rein like trained horses,
When one has discrimination and has made
The mind one-pointed.

7 Those who lack discrimination,
With little control over their thoughts
and far from pure,
Reach not the pure state of immortality

8 But wander from death to death (saṁsāra);
But those who have discrimination,
with a still mind and a pure heart,
reach journey's end,
Never again to fall into the jaws of death.

---

[2]Presumably, the lord of the chariot. —MM

9   With a discriminating intellect
    As charioteer and a trained mind as reins,
    They attain the supreme goal of life
    To be united with the Lord of Love.

10 The senses derive from objects of sense perception,
    Sense objects from mind, mind from intellect.
    And intellect from ego;

11 Ego from undifferentiated consciousness,
    And consciousness from Brahman.
    Brahman is the first cause and last refuge.

12 Brahman, the hidden Self in everyone
    Does not shine forth. He is revealed only
    To those who keep their mind one-pointed
    On the Lord of Love and thus develop
    A superconscious manner of knowing.

13 Meditation enables them to go
    Deeper and deeper into consciousness,
    From the world of words to the world of thoughts,
    Then beyond thoughts to wisdom in the Self.

14 Get up! Wake up! Seek the guidance of an
    Illumined teacher and realize the Self.
    Sharp like a razor's edge, the sages say,
    Is the path, difficult to traverse.

15 The supreme Self is beyond name and form,
    Beyond the senses, inexhaustible,
    Without beginning, without end, beyond
    Time, space, and causality, eternal,
    Immutable. Those who realize the Self
    Are forever free from the jaws of death.

16 The wise, who gain experiential knowledge
    Of this timeless tale of Nachiketa,
    Narrated by Death, attain the glory
    Of living in spiritual awareness.

17 Those who, full of devotion, recite this
    Supreme mystery at a spiritual
    Gathering, are fit for eternal life.
    They are indeed fit for eternal life.

Fourth section

1 The self-existent Lord (*svayambhū*) pierced the senses
   To turn outward. Thus we look to the world
   Outside and see not the Self within us.
   A sage withdrew his senses from the world
   Of change and, seeking immortality,
   Looked within and beheld the deathless Self.

2 The immature run after sense pleasures
   And fall into the widespread net of death.
   But the wise, knowing the Self as deathless,
   Seek not the changeless in the world of change.

3 That through which one enjoys form, taste, smell, sound,
   Touch, and sexual union is the Self.
   Can there be anything not known to That
   Who is the One in all? Know One, know all.

4 That through which one enjoys the waking
   And sleeping states is the Self. To know That
   As consciousness is to go beyond sorrow.

5 Those who know the Self as enjoyer
   Of the honey from the flowers of the senses,
   Ever present within, ruler of time,
   Go beyond fear. For this Self is supreme!

6 The god of creation, Brahma,
   Born of the Godhead through meditation
   Before the waters of life were created,
   Who stands in the heart of every creature,
   Is the Self indeed. For this Self is supreme!

7 The goddess of energy, Aditi,
   Born of the Godhead through vitality,
   Mother of all the cosmic forces
   Who stands in the heart of every creature,
   Is the Self indeed. For this Self is supreme!

8 The god of fire, Agni, hidden between
   Two firesticks like a child well protected
   In the mother's womb, whom we adore
   Every day in meditation,
   Is the Self indeed. For this Self is supreme!

9   That which is the source of the sun
     And of every power in the cosmos, beyond which
     There is neither going nor coming,
     Is the Self indeed. For this Self is supreme!

10   What is here is also there; what is there,
     Also here. Who sees multiplicity
     But not the one indivisible Self
     Must wander on and on from death to death.

11   Only the one-pointed mind attains
     This state of unity. There is no one
     But the Self. Who sees multiplicity
     But not the one indivisible Self
     Must wander on and on from death to death.

12   That thumb-sized being enshrined in the heart,
     Ruler of time, past and future,
     To see whom is to go beyond all fear,
     Is the Self indeed. For this Self is supreme!

13   That thumb-sized being, a flame without smoke,
     Ruler of time, past and future,
     The same on this day as on tomorrow,
     Is the Self indeed. For this Self is supreme!

14   As the rain on a mountain peak runs off
     The slopes on all sides, so those who see
     Only the seeming multiplicity of life
     Run after things on every side.

15   As pure water poured into pure water
     Becomes the very same, so does the Self
     Of the illumined man or woman, Nachiketa,
     Verily become one with the Godhead.

Fifth section

1   There is a city with eleven gates
     Of which the ruler is the unborn Self,
     Whose light forever shines. They go beyond
     Sorrow who meditate on the Self
     And are freed from the cycle of birth and death.
     For this Self is supreme!

2 The Self is the sun shining in the sky,
The wind blowing in space; he is the fire
At the altar and in the home the guest;
He dwells in human beings, in gods, in truth,
And in the vast firmament; he is the fish
Born in water, the plant growing in the earth,
The river flowing down from the mountain.
For this Self is supreme!

3 The adorable one who is seated
In the heart rules the breath of life.
Unto him all the senses pay their homage.

4 When the dweller in the body breaks out
In freedom from the bonds of flesh, what remains?
For this Self is supreme!

5 We live not by the breath that flows in
And flows out, but by him who causes the breath
To flow in and flow out.

6 Now, O Nachiketa, I will tell you
Of this unseen, eternal Brahman, and
What befalls the Self after death.

7 Of those unaware of the Self, some are born as
Embodied creatures while others remain
In a lower stage of evolution,
As determined by their own need for growth (*karma*).

8 That which is awake even in our sleep,
Giving form in dreams to the objects of
Sense craving, that indeed is pure light,
Brahman the immortal, who contains all
The cosmos, and beyond whom none can go.
For this Self is supreme!

9 As the same fire assumes different shapes
When it consumes objects differing in shape,
So does the one Self take the shape
Of every creature in whom he is present.

10 As the same air assumes different shapes
When it enters objects differing in shape,
So does the one Self take the shape
Of every creature in whom he is present.

11 As the sun, who is the eye of the world,
    Cannot be tainted by the defects in our eyes
    Or by the objects it looks on,
    So the one Self, dwelling in all, cannot
    Be tainted by the evils of the world.
    For this Self transcends all!

12 The ruler supreme, inner Self (*antarātman*) of all,
    Multiplies his oneness into many.
    Eternal joy is theirs who see the Self
    In their own hearts. To none else does it come!

13 Changeless amidst the things that pass away,
    Pure consciousness in all who are conscious,
    The One answers the prayers of many.
    Eternal peace is theirs who see the Self
    In their own hearts. To none else does it come!

Nachiketa

14 How can I know that blissful Self, supreme,
    Inexpressible, realized by the wise?
    Is he the light, or does he reflect light?

Yama

15 There shines not the sun, neither moon nor star
    Nor flash of lightning, nor fire lit on earth.
    The Self is the light reflected by all.
    He shining, everything shines after him.

Sixth section

1 The Tree of Eternity has its roots above
   And its branches on earth below.
   Its pure root is Brahman the immortal
   From whom all the worlds draw their life, and whom
   None can transcend. For this Self is supreme!

2 The cosmos comes forth from Brahman and moves
   In him. With his power it reverberates

Like thunder crashing in the sky. Those who realize him
Pass beyond the sway of death.

3 In fear of him fire burns, in fear of him
The sun shines, the clouds rain, and the winds blow.
In fear of him death stalks about to kill.

4 If one fails to realize Brahman in this life
Before the physical sheath is shed,
He must again put on a body
In the world of embodied creatures.

5 Brahman can be seen, as in a mirror
In a pure heart; in the world of the ancestors
As in a dream; in the gandharva world[3]
As the reflections in trembling waters;
And clear as light in the realm of Brahma.

6 Knowing the senses to be separate
From the Self, and the sense experience
To be fleeting, the wise grieve no more.

7 Above the senses is the mind,
Above the mind is the intellect,
Above that is the ego, and above the ego
Is the unmanifested Cause.

8 And beyond is Brahman, omnipresent,
Attributeless. Realizing him one is released
From the cycle of birth and death.

9 He is formless, and can never be seen
With these two eyes. But he reveals himself
In the heart made pure through meditation
And sense-restraint. Realizing him one is released
From the cycle of birth and death.

10 When the five senses are stilled, when the mind
Is stilled, when the intellect is stilled,
That is called the highest state by the wise.

---

[3]A heavenly domain inhabited by male demigods who are represented as skilled singers and dancers and as messengers between the human and divine worlds. —MM

11 They say yoga is this complete stillness
In which one enters the state of unity,
Never to become separate again.
If one is not established in this state,
The sense of unity will come and go.

12 The state of oneness cannot be attained
Through words or thoughts or through the eye.
How can it be attained except through one
Who is established in this state himself?

13 There are two selves, the separate ego
And the indivisible *Ātman*. When
One rises above *I* and *me* and *mine*,
The *Ātman* is revealed as one's real Self.

14 When all desires that surge in the heart
Are renounced, the mortal becomes immortal.

15 When all the knots that strangle the heart
Are loosened, the mortal becomes immortal.
This sums up the teaching of the scriptures.

16 From the heart there radiate a hundred
And one vital tracks. One of them rises
To the crown of the head. This way leads
To immortality, the others to death.

17 The Lord of Love, not larger than the thumb,
Is ever enshrined in the hearts of all.
Draw him clear out of the physical sheath
As one draws the stalk from the munja grass.
Know thyself to be pure and immortal!
Know thyself to be pure and immortal!

The Narrator

18 Nachiketa learned from the king of death
The whole discipline of meditation.
Freeing himself from all separateness,
He won immortality in Brahman,
So blessed is everyone who knows the Self!
OM shanti shanti shanti.

7

The Questions of King Milinda

Anonymous

Translated by T.W. Rhys Davids

What follows is a dialogue that is said to have taken place in the first or second century BC, between the Buddhist sage Nagasena and King Milinda (Menander I or possibly II), the Greco-Indian ruler of Bactria, an area centered in the northern part of present-day Afghanistan. The dialogue takes place in the king's palace, in the presence of 500 Yonakas, or Bactrian Greek soldiers. The Buddhist sage presents a picture of the human self or soul as a heap of mental and physical events, "name" and "form," respectively. The events in this heap form the illusion of a discrete and unitary self or soul. We erroneously identify this fictitious entity as our selves, which we believe will continue to exist after this life.

But if the self is a fiction as Nagasena says, then how are we to account for the Buddhist belief in rebirth? What is it that is reborn? Nagasena explains that name and form continue to exist, as long as the heap of events includes desires and aversions: these attachments give rise to subsequent name-and-form heaps. Liberation from the cycle of death and rebirth does not consist of extinction of the self— let alone the realization of a true self, as described in the Katha Upanishad. Rather, liberation consists of extinction of attachments and of the illusion of the enduring and unitary self.

After the dialogue, according to Buddhist tradition, Milinda handed his kingdom over to his son and devoted himself to Buddhist practice.

Now Milinda the king went up to where the venerable Nâgasena was, and addressed him with the greetings and compliments of friendship and courtesy, and took his seat respectfully apart. And Nâgasena reciprocated his courtesy, so that the heart of the king was propitiated.

And Milinda began by asking, "How is your Reverence known, and what, Sir, is your name?"

"I am known as Nâgasena, O king, and it is by that name that my brethren in the faith address me. But although parents, O king, give such a name as Nâgasena, or Sûrasena, or Vîrasena, or Sîhasena, yet this, Sire—Nâgasena and so on—is only a generally understood term, a designation in common use. For there is no permanent individuality (no soul) involved in the matter."

Then Milinda called upon the *Yonakas* and the brethren to witness: "This Nâgasena says there is no permanent individuality (no soul) implied in his name. Is it now even possible to approve him in that?" And turning to Nâgasena, he said: "If, most reverend Nâgasena, there be no permanent individuality (no soul) involved in the matter, who is it, pray, who gives to you members of the Order your robes and food and lodging and necessaries for the sick? Who is it who enjoys such things when given? Who is it who lives a life of righteousness? Who is it who devotes himself to meditation? Who is it who attains to the goal of the Excellent Way, to the Nirvâna of Arahatship?[1] And who is it who destroys living creatures? Who is it who takes what is not his own? Who is it who lives an evil life of worldly lusts, who speaks lies, who drinks strong drink, who (in a word) commits any one of the five sins which work out their bitter fruit even in this life? If that be so there is neither merit nor demerit; there is neither doer nor causer of good or evil deeds; there is neither fruit nor result of good or evil Karma. If, most reverend Nâgasena, we are to think that were a man to kill you there would be no murder, then it follows that there are no real masters or teachers in your Order, and that your ordinations are void. You tell me that your brethren in the Order are in the habit of addressing you as Nâgasena. Now what is that Nâgasena? Do you mean to say that the hair is Nâgasena?"

"I don't say that, great king."

"Or the hairs on the body, perhaps?"

"Certainly not."

---

[1]In Theravada Buddhism, *Arahatship* is the state of an *Arahat*, a "perfected person" who has achieved Nirvāṇa. —MM

"Or is it the nails, the teeth, the skin, the flesh, the nerves, the bones, the marrow, the kidneys, the heart, the liver, the abdomen, the spleen, the lungs, the larger intestines, the lower intestines, the stomach, the fæces, the bile, the phlegm, the pus, the blood, the sweat, the fat, the tears, the serum, the saliva, the mucus, the oil that lubricates the joints, the urine, or the brain, or any or all of these, that is Nâgasena?"

And to each of these he answered no.

"Is it the outward form then (Rûpa) that is Nâgasena, or the sensations (Vedanâ), or the ideas (Saññâ), or the confections (the constituent elements of character, Samkhârâ), or the consciousness (Vigññâna), that is Nâgasena?"

And to each of these also he answered no.

"Then is it all these *skandhas*[2] combined that are Nâgasena?"

"No, great king."

"But is there anything outside the Five *skandhas* that is Nâgasena?"

And still he answered no.

"Then thus, ask as I may, I can discover no Nâgasena. Nâgasena is a mere empty sound. Who then is the Nâgasena that we see before us? It is a falsehood that your reverence has spoken, an untruth!"

And the venerable Nâgasena said to Milinda the king: "You, Sire, have been brought up in great luxury, as beseems your noble birth. If you were to walk this dry weather on the hot and sandy ground, trampling under foot the gritty, gravelly grains of the hard sand, your feet would hurt you. And as your body would be in pain, your mind would be disturbed, and you would experience a sense of bodily suffering. How then did you come, on foot, or in a chariot?"

"I did not come, Sir, on foot. I came in a carriage."

"Then if you came in a carriage, Sir, explain to me what that is. Is it the pole that is the chariot?"

"I did not say that."

"Is it the axle that is the chariot?"

"Certainly not."

"Is it the wheels, or the framework, or the ropes, or the yoke, or the spokes of the wheels, or the goad, that are the chariot?"

And to all these he still answered no.

"Then is it all these parts of it that are the chariot?"

---

[2]Types of elements of the heap, that is, forms, feelings, perceptions, impulses, and consciousness. —MM

"No, Sir."

"But is there anything outside them that is the chariot?"

And still he answered no.

"Then thus, ask as I may, I can discover no chariot. *Chariot* is a mere empty sound. What then is the chariot you say you came in? It is a falsehood that your Majesty has spoken, an untruth! There is no such thing as a chariot! You are king over all India, a mighty monarch. Of whom then are you afraid that you speak untruth?" And he called upon the Yonakas and the brethren to witness, saying: "Milinda the king here has said that he came by carriage. But when asked in that case to explain what the carriage was, he is unable to establish what he averred. Is it, forsooth, possible to approve him in that?"

When he had thus spoken the five hundred Yonakas shouted their applause, and said to the king: "Now let your Majesty get out of that if you can!"

And Milinda the king replied to Nâgasena, and said: "I have spoken no untruth, reverend Sir. It is on account of its having all these things—the pole, and the axle, the wheels, and the framework, the ropes, the yoke, the spokes, and the goad—that it comes under the generally understood term, the designation in common use, of 'chariot.'"

"Very good! Your Majesty has rightly grasped the meaning of 'chariot.' And even so it is on account of all those things you questioned me about— the thirty-two kinds of organic matter in a human body, and the five constituent elements of being—that I come under the generally understood term, the designation in common use, of 'Nâgasena.' For it was said, Sire, by our Sister Vagirâ in the presence of the Blessed One:

> Just as it is by the condition precedent of the co-existence of its various parts that the word 'chariot' is used, just so is it that when the *skandhas* are there we talk of a 'being.'"

"Most wonderful, Nâgasena, and most strange. Well has the puzzle put to you, most difficult though it was, been solved. Were the Buddha himself here he would approve your answer. Well done, well done, Nâgasena!"

8

The World Outlook of the People

Madhava Acharya

Translated by E.B. Cowell

Charvaka (Çārvāka) was one of several skeptical and materialist schools of thought in ancient India. The Charvakan doctrine can be summarized negatively as follows: "no God, no rebirth (*samsara*), no karma, no duty, no fruits of merit, no sin." In another Charvakan text, we read that

> There is no world but this;
> There is no heaven and no hell;
> The realm of Shiva and like regions,
> are invented by stupid imposters.

— *Sarvasiddhanta Samgraha*, Verse 8

Our reading dates to the fourteenth century AD, but the views described are much older than that. Traces of materialism, in opposition to supernaturalism and the Vedas, appear in the earliest recordings of Indian thought. Early references in the Vedas suggest that a figure named Bṛhaspati set about refuting the claims of other schools of thought, without attempting to construct a positive system of philosophy. By the seventh century AD, materialism and skepticism were evolving into a formal school of thought that remained intact in the following centuries.

It should not come as a surprise that rulers suppressed materialist thought throughout the centuries, and this may account in part for the scarcity of original texts of materialist philosophy. What we know of Charvakan teachings has been compiled from secondary literature, notably commentaries and summaries by Vedantic and Buddhist opponents of Charvaka.[1]

The Hindu statesman and philosopher Madhava Acharya (fl. c. 1380) produced one of these commentaries. Acharya is best known as the author of the *Sarvadarsana Samgraha, The Compendium of Speculations*, of which our reading forms the first part. In the *Compendium*, Acharya reviewed sixteen of the most prominent philosophical systems in the South of India in his day, and he did so with extraordinary intellectual detachment. Assuming that Acharya's presentation is accurate, it is one of the most complete descriptions of Charvaka thought that has come down to us. The reader should keep in mind, though, that Acharya was not himself a follower of the Charvakan philosophy. In the Prologue to the *Compendium*, he invokes the god Shiva:

> I worship Shiva, the abode of eternal knowledge, the storehouse of supreme felicity; by whom the earth and the rest were produced, in him only has this all a maker.

Thus, Acharya assumes a position that is inimical to Charvaka. This point will help us to understand the first line of the text below: Acharya is saying, perhaps with tongue in cheek, that, although he has just dedicated his study to Shiva, "the storehouse of supreme felicity," Charvaka has "utterly abolished" the very notion of this or any other Divine Being.

[H]ow can we attribute to the Divine Being the giving of supreme felicity, when such a notion has been utterly abolished by Charvaka, the crest-gem of the atheistical school, the follower of the doctrine of Bṛhaspati?[2] The efforts

---

[1]Debiprasad Chattopadhyaya, *Lokāyata: A Study in Ancient Indian Materialism*, eighth ed. (New Delhi: People's Publishing House, 2006), 7. Still, the economist Amartya Sen has claimed that there is a larger volume of atheistic and skeptical writings in Pali and Sanskrit than in any other classical language, including Greek, Latin, Hebrew, and Arabic. Among these writings Sen includes the texts of Buddhism, which he described as the only agnostic world religion ever to have emerged.
[2]Some scholars believe that Bṛhaspati expounded Charvakan philosophy around 600 BC, in a work known as the *Bṛhaspati Sūtra*. Neither this work nor any other original works of Charvaka have come down to us.—MM

of Charvaka are indeed hard to be eradicated, for most living beings hold by the current refrain:

> While life is yours, live joyously.
> None can escape Death's searching eye.
> When once this frame of ours they burn,
> How shall it e'er again return?

The mass of men, in accordance with the Śāstras [works of literature] of policy and enjoyment—considering wealth and desire the only ends of man, and denying the existence of any object belonging to a future world—are found to follow only the doctrine of Charvaka. Hence another name for that school is *Locāyata*, a name well accordant with the thing signified.[3]

In this school the four elements, earth, etc., are the original principles; from these alone, when transformed into the body, intelligence is produced, just as the inebriating power is developed from the mixing of certain ingredients; and when these are destroyed, intelligence at once perishes also. They quote the Śruti for this: "Springing forth from these elements, itself solid knowledge, it is destroyed when they are destroyed: after death no intelligence remains." Therefore the soul is only the body distinguished by the attribute of intelligence, since there is no evidence for any soul distinct from the body, as such cannot be proved, since this school holds that perception is the only source of knowledge and does not allow inference, etc.

The only end of man is enjoyment produced by sensual pleasures. Nor may you say that such cannot be called the end of man as they are always mixed with some kind of pain, because it is our wisdom to enjoy the pure pleasure as far as we can, and to avoid the pain which inevitably accompanies it; just as the man who desires fish takes the fish with their scales and bones, and having taken as many as he wants, desists; or just as the man who desires rice, takes the rice, straw and all, and having taken as much as he wants, desists. It is not therefore for us, through a fear of pain, to reject the pleasure which our nature instinctively recognizes as congenial. Men do not refrain from sowing rice, because forsooth there are wild animals to devour it; nor do they refuse to set the cooking-pots on the fire, because forsooth there are beggars to pester us for a share of the contents. If any one were so timid as to

---

[3]*Locāyata* translates as "the world-outlook of the people."—MM

forsake a visible pleasure, he would indeed be foolish like a beast, as has been said by the poet:

> The pleasure which arises to men from contact with sensible objects is to be relinquished as accompanied by pain—such is the reasoning of fools. The berries of paddy, rich with the finest white grains: What man, seeking his true interest, would fling this away because it is covered with husk and dust?

You might object that, if there be no such thing as happiness in a future world, then why should men of wisdom engage in the *agnihotra* and other sacrifices, which can only be performed with great expenditure of money and bodily fatigue? Your objection cannot be accepted as any proof to the contrary, since the *agnihotra*, etc., are only useful as means of livelihood, for the Veda is tainted by the three faults of untruth, self-contradiction, and tautology; then again the impostors who call themselves Vaidic pundits are mutually destructive, as the authority of the jñána-kánda is overthrown by those who maintain that of the karma-kánda, while those who maintain the authority of the jñána-kánda reject that of the karma-kánda; and lastly, the three Vedas themselves are only the incoherent rhapsodies of knaves, and to this effect runs the popular saying:

> The Agnihotra, the three Vedas, the ascetic's three staves, and smearing oneself with ashes—
>
> Bṛhaspati says these are but means of livelihood for those who have no manliness nor sense.

Hence it follows that there is no other hell than mundane pain produced by purely mundane causes, as thorns, etc.; the only Supreme is the earthly monarch whose existence is proved by all the world's eyesight; and the only Liberation is the dissolution of the body. By holding the doctrine that the soul is identical with the body, such phrases as "I am thin," "I am black," etc., are at once intelligible, as the attributes of thinness, etc., and self-consciousness will reside in the same subject [that is, the body…]

All this has been thus summed up:

> In this school there are four elements, earth, water, fire, and air. And from these four elements alone is intelligence produced, just like the intoxicating power from kiṇwa, etc., mixed together. Since in "I am fat," "I am lean," these attributes abide in the same subject, and since fatness, etc., reside only in the body, it alone is the soul and no other. And such phrases as "my body" are only significant metaphorically.

"Be it so," says the opponent; "your wish would be gained if inference, etc., had no force of proof; but then they have this force; else, if they had not, then how, on perceiving smoke, should the thoughts of the intelligent immediately proceed to fire; or why, on hearing another say, 'There are fruits on the bank of the river,' do those who desire fruit proceed at once to the shore?"

All this, however, is only the inflation of the world of fancy.

Those who maintain the authority of inference accept the *sign* or middle term as the causer of knowledge, which middle term must be found in the minor and be itself invariably connected with the major.[4] Now this invariable connection must be a relation destitute of any condition accepted or disputed; and this connection does not possess its power of causing inference by virtue of its *existence*, as the eye, etc., are the cause of perception, but by virtue of its being *known*. What then is the means of this connection's being known?

We will first show that it is not *perception*. Now perception is held to be of two kinds, external and internal [*i.e.*, as produced by the external senses, or by the inner sense, mind]. The former is not the required means; for although it is possible that the actual contact of the senses and the object will produce the knowledge of the particular object thus brought in contact, yet as there can never be such contact in the case of the past or the future, the universal proposition [literally, the knowledge of the invariable concomitance (as of smoke by fire)] which was to embrace the invariable connection of the middle and major terms in every case becomes impossible to be known. Nor may you maintain that this knowledge of the universal proposition has the general class as its object, because if so, there might arise a doubt as to the existence of the invariable connection in this particular case [as, for instance, in this particular smoke as implying fire].

Nor is internal perception the means, since you cannot establish that the mind has any power to act independently towards an external object, since all allow that it is dependent on the external senses, as has been said by one of the logicians, "The eye, etc., have their objects as described; but mind externally is dependent on the others."

Nor can *inference* be the means of the knowledge of the universal proposition, since in the case of this inference we should also require another

---

[4]As in the case of some Buddhist texts, and as in the case of David Hume much later, Charvakan skepticism extended to the process of *inference*, the attempt to establish a universal proposition from the relation of cause and effect or genus and species. The rest of our excerpt, until the final two or three paragraphs, is a skeptical attack on the reliability of inference.—MM

inference to establish it, and so on, and hence would arise the fallacy of an *ad infinitum* retrogression.

Nor can *testimony* be the means thereof, since we may either allege in reply, in accordance with the Vaiśeshika doctrine of Kaṇáda, that this is included in the topic of inference; or else we may hold that this fresh proof of testimony is unable to leap over the old barrier that stopped the progress of inference, since it depends itself on the recognition of a *sign* [...] and, moreover, there is no more reason for our believing on another's word that smoke and fire are invariably connected, than for our receiving the *ipse dixit* ("he himself said it"; a dogmatic and unproven statement) of Manu, etc. [which, of course, we Charvakans reject].

And again, if testimony were to be accepted as the only means of the knowledge of the universal proposition, then in the case of a man to whom the fact of the invariable connection between the middle and major terms had not been pointed out by another person, there could be no inference of one thing [as fire] on seeing another thing [as smoke]; hence, on your own showing, the whole topic of inference for oneself [the properly logical, as distinguished from the rhetorical argument] would have to end in mere idle words.

Then again *comparisons*, etc., must be utterly rejected as the means of the knowledge of the universal proposition, since it is impossible that they can produce the knowledge of the unconditioned connection [*i.e.*, the universal proposition], because their end is to produce the knowledge of quite another connection, viz., the relation of a name to something so named.

Again, this same absence of a condition, which has been given as the definition of an invariable connection [*i.e.*, a universal proposition], can itself never be known; since it is impossible to establish that all conditions must be objects of perception; and therefore, although the absence of perceptible things may be itself perceptible, the absence of non-perceptible things must be itself non-perceptible; and thus, since we must here too have recourse to inference, etc., we cannot leap over the obstacle which has already been planted to bar them. Again, we must accept as the definition of the condition, "it is that which is reciprocal or equipollent in extension with the major term though not constantly accompanying the middle." These three distinguishing clauses, "not constantly accompanying the middle term," "constantly accompanying the major term," and "being constantly accompanied by it" [*i.e.*, reciprocal], are needed in the full definition to stop respectively three such fallacious conditions, in the argument to prove the non-eternity of sound, as "being produced," "the nature of a jar," and "the not causing audition;" wherefore the definition holds [...]

But since the knowledge of the condition must here precede the knowledge of the condition's absence, it is only when there is the knowledge of the condition, that the knowledge of the universality of the proposition is possible, *i.e.*, a knowledge in the form of such a connection between the middle term and major term as is distinguished by the absence of any such condition; and on the other hand, the knowledge of the condition depends upon the knowledge of the invariable connection. Thus we fasten on our opponents as with adamantine glue the thunderbolt-like fallacy of reasoning in a circle. Hence by the impossibility of knowing the universality of a proposition it becomes impossible to establish inference, etc.

The step which the mind takes from the knowledge of smoke, etc., to the knowledge of fire, etc., can be accounted for by its being based on a former perception or by its being an error; and that in some cases this step is justified by the result, is accidental just like the coincidence of effects observed in the employment of gems, charms, drugs, etc.

From this it follows that fate, etc., do not exist, since these can only be proved by inference. But an opponent will say, if you thus do not allow *adrishṭa*,[5] the various phenomena of the world become destitute of any cause.

But we cannot accept this objection as valid, since these phenomena can all be produced spontaneously from the inherent nature of things. Thus it has been said:

The fire is hot, the water cold, refreshing cool the breeze of morn.
By whom came this variety? From their own nature was it born.

And all this has also been said by Bṛhaspati:

There is no heaven, no final liberation, nor any soul in another world. Nor do the actions of the four castes, orders, etc., produce any real effect. The *Agnihotra*, the three Vedas, the ascetic's three staves, and smearing one's self with ashes—these were made by Nature as the livelihood of those destitute of knowledge and manliness. If a beast slain in the *Jyotishṭoma* rite will itself go to heaven, why then does not the sacrificer forthwith offer his own father? If the Śrāddha produces gratification to beings who are dead, then here, too, in the case of travellers when they start, it is needless to give provisions for the journey. If beings in heaven are gratified by our offering the Śrāddha here,

---

[5]Fate, or the unseen power of one's past karma in one's present life.—MM

then why not give the food down below to those who are standing on the housetop? While life remains let a man live happily, let him feed on ghee even though he runs in debt. When once the body becomes ashes, how can it ever return again? If he who departs from the body goes to another world, how is it that he comes not back again, restless for love of his kindred? Hence it is only as a means of livelihood that Brahmans have established here all these ceremonies for the dead; there is no other fruit anywhere. The three authors of the Vedas were buffoons, knaves, and demons. All the well-known formulæ of the pandits, jarpharí, turpharí, etc.,[6] and all the obscene rites for the queen commanded in the Aśwamedha—these were invented by buffoons, and so too with all the various kinds of presents to the priests, while the eating of flesh was similarly commanded by night-prowling demons.

Hence, in kindness to the mass of living beings, we must fly for refuge to the doctrine of Charvaka. Such is the pleasant consummation.

---

[6]Apparently, the reference is to an elaborate horse sacrifice, performed by a victorious king. The sacrifice takes place over the course of a year and one-half, and involves the consumption of its flesh.—MM

9

Nirodha, the Cessation of *Dukkha*

Walpola Rahula

The Sanskrit word *dukkha* means "bone out of joint," or "unsatisfactoriness," but it is often translated as "suffering." Dukkha can be everything from sharp physical pain to anxiety, disappointment, or just boredom. Even our moments of greatest happiness are diminished by the anticipation that they will come to an end—and that, too, is dukkha. The contention that life is dukkha is the first of the Four Noble Truths of Buddhism.

The second Noble Truth is *Samudaya*, the source of dukkha. This is, in a word, thirst, or attachment. According to Rahula, desire and the will-to-continue-existing are "a tremendous force" that does not end with death; rather, they take on other forms and produce rebirth. But as we recall from *The Questions of King Milinda*, a central tenet of Buddhism is the doctrine that in reality there is no permanent, unchanging self or the soul.[1]

If there is no continuing self that is reborn, then of what does rebirth consist? This was the question that King Milinda posed to the Venerable Nagasena. The answer is that rebirth is merely the continuation of desire without a subject; nothing substantive passes from one moment to the next and from one life to the next; nevertheless, the series of lives and moments continues. The series

---

[1]David Hume came to the same conclusion in his argument for what has come to be called "the bundle theory of the self" (*A Treatise on Human Nature* [1739], Book I, Part IV: "Of Personal Identity").

is nothing but movement, but movement itself is a kind of continuity. Accordingly, as Rahula says, the extinction of rebirth is "the cessation of continuity." In our reading, the author describes how it is that this movement may be brought to an end. This is the Third Noble Truth of Buddhism, *Nirodha*, the cessation of dukkha.

Notice that for orthodox Buddhists, as for the doctrine presented in the Katha Upanishad, rebirth is not something to be desired. On the contrary, these doctrines, and their various contemplative, meditational, and devotional practices, aim at the cessation or extinction of rebirth.

The Fourth Noble Truth, *Magga*, is the path to extinction of dukkha, which is the path to the extinction of the illusion of self. Rahula writes that "Nirvāṇa is definitely not annihilation of self, because there is no self to annihilate." "If at all," he continues, "It is the annihilation of the illusion, of the false idea of self."

Walpola Rahula (1907–1978) was a Buddhist monk, a scholar of Theravada Buddhism at Northwestern University, and an outspoken socialist. Our reading is from his influential book, *What the Buddha Taught* (1959).

The third Noble Truth is that there is emancipation, liberation, freedom from suffering, from the continuity of *dukkha*. This is called the Noble Truth of the Cessation of *dukkha*, which is *Nibbāna*, more popularly known in its Sanskrit form of *Nirvāṇa*.

To eliminate *dukkha* completely one has to eliminate the main root of *dukkha*, which is "thirst" (*taṇhā*), as we saw earlier. Therefore Nirvāṇa is known also by the term *Taṇhakkhaya* "Extinction of Thirst."

Now you will ask: But what is Nirvāṇa? Volumes have been written in reply to this quite natural and simple question; they have, more and more, only confused the issue rather than clarified it. The only reasonable reply to give to the question is that it can never be answered completely and satisfactorily in words, because human language is too poor to express the real nature of the Absolute Truth or Ultimate Reality, which is Nirvāṇa. Language is created and used by masses of human beings to express things and ideas experienced by their sense organs and their mind. A supramundane experience like that of the Absolute Truth is not of such a category. Therefore there cannot be words to express that experience, just as the fish had no words in his vocabulary to express the nature of the solid land. The tortoise told his friend the fish that he (the tortoise) just returned to the lake after a walk on the land. "Of course" the fish said, "You mean swimming." The tortoise tried to explain that one couldn't swim on the land, that it was solid, and that one walked on it. But the fish insisted that there could be nothing like it, that it must be liquid like his lake, with waves, and that one must be able to dive and swim there.

Words are symbols representing things and ideas known to us; and these symbols do not and cannot convey the true nature of even ordinary things. Language is considered deceptive and misleading in the matter of understanding of the Truth. So the *Lankāvatāra-sūtra* says that ignorant people get stuck in words like an elephant in the mud.

Nevertheless we cannot do without language. But if Nirvāṇa is to be expressed and explained in positive terms, we are likely immediately to grasp an idea associated with those terms, which may be quite the contrary. Therefore it is generally expressed in negative terms—a less dangerous mode perhaps.[2] So it is often referred to by such negative terms as "Extinction of Thirst" (*Taṇhakkhaya*), "Uncompound" (*Asaṃkhata*), "Unconditioned," "Absence of Desire," "Cessation" (*Nirodha*), and "Blowing Out" or "Extinction" (*Nirvāṇa*).

Let us consider a few definitions and descriptions of Nirvāṇa as found in the original Pali[3] texts:

"It is the complete cessation of that very "thirst" (*taṇhā*), giving it up, renouncing it, emancipation from it, detachment from it."

"Calming of all conditioned things, giving up of all defilements, extinction of "thirst," detachment, cessation, Nirvāṇa."

"O bhikkhus,[4] what is the Absolute (*Asaṃkhata*, Unconditioned)? It is, O bhikkhus, the extinction of desire (*rāgakkhayo*), the extinction of hatred (*dosakkhayo*), the extinction of illusion (*mohakkhayo*). This O bhikkhus, is called the Absolute."

"O Rādha, the extinction of "thirst" is Nirvāṇa."

"O bhikkhus, whatever there may be things conditioned or unconditioned, among them detachment (*virāga*) is the highest. That is to say, freedom

---

[2]Sometimes positive terms are used to denote Nirvāṇa, words like "auspicious" (*Siva*), "Good" (*Khema*), "Safety (*Suddhi*), "Purity" (*Dīpa*), "Island" (*Sarana*), "Refuge" (*Tāṇa*), "Protection" (*Pāra*), "Opposite Shore," "Other Side," "Peace" (*Santi*), and "Tranquility." There are thirty-two synonyms for Nirvāṇa in the *Asaṃkhata-saṃyutta* of the *Saṃyutta-nikāya*. They are mostly metaphorical.
[3]One of the ancient languages of the Buddhist scriptures. —MM
[4]A bhikkhu is a Buddhist monk. —MM

from conceit, destruction of thirst, the uprooting of attachment, the cutting off of continuity, the extinction of "thirst" (*taṇhā*), detachment, cessation, Nirvāṇa."

The reply of Sāriputta, the chief disciple of the Buddha, to a direct question "What is Nirvāṇa?" posed by a Parivrājaka, is identical with the definition of *Asaṃkhata* given by the Buddha (above): "The extinction of desire, the extinction of hatred, the extinction of illusion."

"The abandoning and destruction of desire and craving for these Five Aggregates of Attachment:[5] that is the cessation of *dukkha*."

"The cessation of Continuity and becoming (*Bhavanirodha*) is Nirvāṇa."

And further, referring to Nirvāṇa the Buddha says:

"O bhikkhus, there is the unborn, ungrown, and unconditioned. Were there not the unborn, ungrown, and unconditioned, there would be no escape for the born, grown, and conditioned. Since there is the unborn, ungrown, and unconditioned, so there is escape for the born, grown, and conditioned."

"Here the four elements of solidity, fluidity, heat and motion have no place; the notions of length and breadth, the subtle and the gross, good and evil, name and form are altogether destroyed; neither this world nor the other, nor coming, going or standing, neither death nor birth, nor sense-objects are to be found."

Because Nirvāṇa is thus expressed in negative terms, there are many who have got a wrong notion that it is negative, and expresses self-annihilation.[6] Nirvāṇa is definitely no annihilation of self, because there is no self no annihilate. If at all, it is the annihilation of the illusion, of the false idea of self.

It is incorrect to say that Nirvāṇa is negative or positive. The ideas of "negative" and "positive" are relative, and are within the realm of duality. These terms cannot be applied to Nirvāṇa, Absolute Truth, which is beyond duality and relativity.

A negative word need not necessarily indicate a negative state. The Pali of Sanskrit word for health is *ārogya*, a negative term, which literally means "absence of illness." But *ārogya* (health) does not represent a negative state. The word "Immortal" (or its Sanskrit equivalent *Amṛta* or Pali *Amata*), which also is a synonym for Nirvāṇa, is negative, but it does not denote a

---

[5]Refer to the discussion of the Five *Skandhas*, in *The Questions of King Milinda*, above. —MM

[6]Readers will have noticed that Rahula uses the word *negative* in two distinct meanings: sometimes he uses the word to mean "privation" or "absence," and at other times (but sometimes in the same sentence) the word is a synonym for "bad" or "undesirable." —MM

negative state. The negation of negative values is not negative. One of the well-known synonyms for Nirvāṇa is "Freedom" (Pali *Mutti*, Sanskrit *Mukti*). Nobody would say that freedom is negative. But even freedom has a negative side: freedom is always a liberation from something which is obstructive, which is evil, which is negative. But freedom is not negative. So Nirvāṇa, *Mutti* or *Vimutti*, the Absolute Freedom, is freedom from all evil, freedom from craving, hatred and ignorance, freedom from all terms of duality, relativity, time and space.

We may get some idea of Nirvāṇa as Absolute Truth from the *Dhātuvibhaṅga-sutta* (No. 140) of the *Majjhima-nikāya*. This extremely important discourse was delivered by the Buddha to Pukkusāti, whom the Master found to be intelligent and earnest, in the quiet of the night in a potter's shed. The essence of the relevant portions of the sutta (or sutra) is as follows:

A man is composed of six elements: solidity, fluidity, heat, motion, space and consciousness. He analyses them and finds that none of them is "mine," or me, or "my self." He understands how consciousness appears and disappears, how pleasant, unpleasant, and neutral sensations appear and disappear. Through this knowledge his mind becomes detached. Then he finds within him a pure equanimity (*upekhā*), which he can direct towards the attainment of any high spiritual state, and he knows that thus this pure equanimity will last for a long period. But then he thinks:

"If I focus this purified and cleansed equanimity on the Sphere of Infinite Space and develop a mind conforming thereto, that is a mental creation (*saṃkhataṃ*). If I focus this purified and cleansed equanimity on the Sphere of Infinite Consciousness … on the Sphere of Nothingness … or on the Sphere of Neither-perception nor Non-perception and develop a mind conforming thereto, that is a mental creation." Then he neither mentally creates nor wills continuity and becoming (*bhava*) or annihilation (*vibhava*). As he does not construct or does not will continuity and becoming or annihilation, he does not cling to anything in the world; as he does not cling, he is not anxious; as he is not anxious, he is completely calmed within (fully blown out within *paccattaṃ yeva parinibbāyati*). And he knows: "Finished is birth, lived is pure life, what should be done is done, nothing more is left to be done."

Now, when he experiences a pleasant, unpleasant, or neutral sensation, he knows that it is impermanent, that it does not bind him, that it is not experienced with passion. Whatever may be the sensation, he experiences it without being bound to it (*visaṃyutto*). He knows that all those sensations will be pacified with the dissolution of the body, just as the flame of a lamp goes out when oil and wick give out.

"Therefore, O bhikkhu, a person so endowed is endowed with the absolute wisdom, for the knowledge of the extinction of all *dukkha* is the absolute noble wisdom."

"This his deliverance, founded on Truth, is unshakable. O bhikkhu, that which is unreality (*mosadhamma*) is false; that which is reality (*amosadhamma*), Nirvāṇa, is Truth (*Sacca*). Therefore, O bhikkhu, a person so endowed is endowed with this Absolute Truth. For the Absolute Noble Truth (*paramaṃ ariyasaccaṃ*) is Nirvāṇa, which is Reality."

Elsewhere the Buddha unequivocally uses the word Truth in place of Nirvāṇa: "I will teach you the Truth and the Path leading to the Truth."[7] Here Truth definitely means Nirvāṇa.

Now, what is Absolute Truth? According to Buddhism, the Absolute Truth is that there is nothing absolute in the world, that everything is relative, conditioned and impermanent, and that there is no unchanging, everlasting, absolute substance like Self, Soul, or *Ātman* within or without. This is the Absolute Truth. Truth is never negative, though there is a popular expression as negative truth. The realization of this Truth, i.e., to see things as they are (*yathābhūtaṃ*) without illusion or ignorance (*avijjā*), is the extinction of craving "thirst" (*Taṇhakkhaya*), and the cessation (*Nirodha*) of *dukkha*, which is Nirvāṇa. It is interesting and useful to remember here the Mahāyāna view[8] of Nirvāṇa as not being different from *Saṃsāra*.[9] The same thing is Saṃsāra or Nirvāṇa according to the way you look at it—subjectively or objectively. This Mahāyāna view was probably developed out of the ideas found in the original Theravāda Pali texts, to which we have just referred in our brief discussion.

It is incorrect to think that Nirvāṇa is the natural result of the extinction of craving. Nirvāṇa is not the result of anything. If it would be a result, then it would be an effect produced by a cause. It would be *saṃkhata* "produced" and "conditioned." Nirvāṇa is neither cause nor effect. It is beyond cause and effect. Truth is not a result nor an effect. It is not produced like a mystic, spiritual, mental state, such as *dhyāna* or *samādhi*. TRUTH IS. NIRVĀṆA IS. The only thing you can do is to see it, to realize it. There is a path leading to

---

[7] *Saṃyutta-nikāya* V, Pali Text Society of London edition, 369.

[8] The view of the "Great Vehicle" tradition of Buddhism, which differs somewhat from Rahula's own Theravada tradition. —MM

[9] The cycle of death and rebirth, to which life in the material realm is bound. —MM

the realization of Nirvāṇa. But Nirvāṇa is not the result of this path. You may get to the mountain along a path, but the mountain is not the result, not an effect of the path. You may see a light, but the light is not the result of your eyesight.

People often ask: What is there after Nirvāṇa? This question cannot arise, because Nirvāṇa is the Ultimate Truth. If it is Ultimate, there can be nothing after it. If there is anything after Nirvāṇa, then that will be the Ultimate Truth and not Nirvāṇa. A monk named Rādha put this question to the Buddha in a different form: "For what purpose (or end) is Nirvāṇa?" This question presupposes something after Nirvāṇa, when it postulates some purpose or end for it. So the Buddha answered: "O Rādha, this question could not catch its limit (i.e., it is beside the point). One lives the holy life with Nirvāṇa as its final plunge (into the Absolute Truth), as its goal, as its ultimate end."[10]

Some popular inaccurately phrased expressions like "The Buddha entered into Nirvāṇa or Parinirvāṇa after his death" have given rise to many imaginary speculations about Nirvāṇa. The moment you hear the phrase that "the Buddha entered into Nirvāṇa or Parinirvāṇa," you take Nirvāṇa to be a state, or a realm, or a position in which there is some sort of existence, and try to imagine it in terms of the senses of the word "existence" as it is known to you. This popular expression "entered into Nirvāṇa" has no equivalent in the original texts. There is no such thing as "entering into Nirvāṇa after death." There is a word *parinibbuto* used to denote the death of the Buddha or an Arahant[11] who has realized Nirvāṇa, but it does not mean "entering into Nirvāṇa." *Parinibbuto* simply means "fully passed away," "fully blown out" or "fully extinct," because the Buddha or an Arahant has no re-existence after his death.

Now another question arises: What happens to the Buddha or an Arahant after his death, *parinirvāṇa*? This comes under the category of unanswered questions (*avyākata*). Even when the Buddha spoke about this, he indicated that no words in our vocabulary could express what happens to an Arahant after his death. In reply to a Parivrājaka named Vaccha, the Buddha said that terms like "born" or "not born" do not apply in the case of an Arahant, because those things—matter, sensation, perception, mental activities,

---

[10]*Saṃyutta-nikāya* III, Pali Text Society of London edition, 189.
[11]Refer to the note on the term *Arahat* (the Sanskrit form of the Pali word *Arahant*), in *The Questions of King Milinda*, above. In Rahula's Theravada tradition of Buddhism, an Arahant is a "perfected one" who has realized Nirvāṇa. —MM

consciousness—with which the terms like "born" and "not born" are associated, are completely destroyed and uprooted, never to rise again after his death.

An Arahant after his death is often compared to a fire gone out when the supply of wood is over, or to the flame of a lamp gone out when the wick and oil are finished. Here it should be clearly and distinctly understood, without any confusion, that what is compared to a flame or a fire gone out is *not* Nirvāṇa, but the "being" composed of the Five Aggregates who realized Nirvāṇa. This point has to be emphasized because many people, even some great scholars, have misunderstood and misinterpreted this simile as referring to Nirvāṇa. Nirvāṇa is never compared to a fire or a lamp gone out.

There is another popular question: If there is no Self, no *Ātman,* who realizes Nirvāṇa? Before we go on to Nirvāṇa, let us ask the question: Who thinks now, if there is no Self? We have seen earlier that it is the thought that thinks, that there is no thinker behind the thought. In the same way, it is wisdom (*paññā*), realization, that realizes. There is no other self behind the realization. In the discussion of the origin of *dukkha* we saw that whatever it may be—whether being, or thing, or system—if it is of the nature of arising, it has within itself the nature, the germ, of its cessation, its destruction. Now *dukkha, Saṃsāra,* the cycle of continuity, is of the nature of arising; it must also be of the nature of cessation. Dukkha arises because of "thirst" (*taṇhā*), and it ceases because of wisdom (*paññā*). "Thirst" and wisdom are both within the Five Aggregates, as we saw earlier.

Thus, the germ of their arising as well as that of their cessation are both within the Five Aggregates. This is the real meaning of the Buddha's well-known statement: "Within this fathom-long sentient body itself, I postulate the world, the arising of the world, the cessation of the world, and the path leading to the cessation of the world." This means that all the Four Noble Truths are found within the Five Aggregates, i.e., within ourselves. (Here the word "world" (*loka*) is used in place of *dukkha*). This also means that there is no external power that produces the arising and the cessation of *dukkha*.

When wisdom is developed and cultivated according to the Fourth Noble Truth (the next to be taken up), it sees the secret of life, the reality of things as they are. When the secret is discovered, when the Truth is seen, all the forces which feverishly produce the continuity of *Saṃsāra* in illusion become calm and incapable of producing any more karma-formations, because there is no more illusion, no more "thirst" for continuity. It is like a mental disease which is cured when the cause or the secret of the malady is discovered and seen by the patient.

In almost all religions the *summum bonum*[12] can be attained only after death. But Nirvāṇa can be realized in this very life; it is not necessary to wait till you die to "attain" it.

He who has realized the Truth, Nirvāṇa, is the happiest being in the world. He is free from all "complexes" and obsessions, the worries and troubles that torment others. His mental health is perfect. He does not repent the past, nor does he brood over the future. He lives fully in the present. Therefore he appreciates and enjoys things in the purest sense without self-projections. He is joyful, exultant, enjoying the pure life, his faculties pleased, free from anxiety, serene and peaceful. As he is free from selfish desire, hatred, ignorance, conceit, pride, and all such "defilements," he is pure and gentle, full of universal love, compassion, kindness, sympathy, understanding and tolerance. His service to others is of the purest, for he has no thought of self. He gains nothing, accumulates nothing, not even anything spiritual, because he is free from the illusion of Self, and the "thirst" for becoming.

Nirvāṇa is beyond all terms of duality and relativity. It is therefore beyond our conceptions of good and evil, right and wrong, existence and non-existence. Even the word "happiness" (*sukha*) which is used to describe Nirvāṇa has an entirely different sense here. Sāriputta once said: "O friend, Nirvāṇa is happiness! Nirvāṇa is happiness!" Then Udāyi asked: "But, friend Sāriputta, what happiness can it be if there is no sensation?" Sāriputta's reply was highly philosophical and beyond ordinary comprehension: "That there is no sensation itself is happiness."

Nirvāṇa is beyond logic and reasoning (*atakkāvacara*). However much we may engage, often as a vain intellectual pastime, in highly speculative discussions regarding Nirvāṇa or Ultimate Truth or Reality, we shall never understand it that way. A child in the kindergarten should not quarrel about the theory of relativity. Instead, if he follows his studies patiently and diligently, one day he may understand it. Nirvāṇa is "to be realized by the wise within themselves" (*paccattaṃ veditabbo viññūhi*). If we follow the Path patiently and with diligence, train and purify ourselves earnestly, and attain the necessary spiritual development, we may one day realize it within ourselves–without taxing ourselves with puzzling and high-sounding words.

Let us therefore now turn to the Path which leads to the realization of Nirvāṇa.

---

[12]The highest good. —MM

For Discussion or Essays

- Compare and contrast the *Katha Upanishad* to the *Milinda Pañha*, focusing on the role of karma in their respective accounts of liberation from the cycle of death and rebirth.
- Compare and contrast the *parable of the chariot* in the Third Section of the *Katha Upanishad* (verses 3-9) to the famous passage about the chariot in *The Questions of King Milinda*. According to Yama, what is it that attains liberation (*moksha*)? According to Nagasena, what is it that attains the goal of Nirvāṇa? How, then, do these two goals, *moksha* and Nirvāṇa, differ?
- In his book *Reincarnation: A Critical Examination*, the American philosopher Paul Edwards claimed that, unlike physical laws, the doctrine of karma is empirically unverifiable and explains nothing. Is this true? Can you describe a way to confirm or refute the hypothesis of rebirth and karma?
- Starting in the middle of our selection from "The World Outlook of the People," Madhava Acharya presents the Charvakans' skeptical attack against "the authority of inference." How does this attack against inference bolster the Charvakan claims that there is no life but this life and that the doctrine of karma is not worth believing?
- "While life is yours, live joyously," the Charvakans advise: "The only end of man is enjoyment produced by sensual pleasures … it is our wisdom to enjoy the pure pleasure as far as we can, and to avoid the pain which inevitably accompanies it." Compare and contrast the Charvakan view to our reading from Walpola Rahula. Is Charvaka compatible with the First Noble Truth of Buddhism, which says that life is *dukkha*? Explain.
- Walpola Rahula writes that, because Nirvāṇa is the Ultimate Truth, there can be nothing after it. He also warns against viewing Nirvāṇa as "a state, or a realm, or a position in which there is some sort of existence." Moreover, in Nirvāṇa there is no sensation, and it is "beyond our conceptions" of existence and nonexistence. Judging from Rahula's presentation, how are we to distinguish between Nirvāṇa and non-survival? (Keep in mind Rahula's view that there is no self to be annihilated.)
- We seem to understand perfectly well what "I walk" and "I talk" mean. Does this observation cast doubt on the Buddhist claim that we have no selves? Explain.
- How do you know that your best friend has a self? Do you likewise know that your best friend's dog has a self?

Further Readings on Rebirth

Blackmore, Susan. "Out-of-the-Body Experience." In *The Oxford Companion to the Mind*, edited by Richard L. Gregory, 571–73. New York: Oxford University Press, 1987. Blackmore is a formidable opponent of the claim that empirical evidence confirms rebirth.

Edwards, Paul. *Reincarnation: A Critical Examination*. Amherst, NY: Prometheus Books, 2002. Edwards, too, is a forceful skeptic when it comes to doctrines of rebirth.

Obayashi, Hiroshi, ed. *Death and Afterlife: Perspectives of World Religion*. Westport, CT: Praeger Press, 1992. This is a work of comparative religious studies, not philosophy. Religious traditions surveyed include "nonliterate and ancient religions" from Africa, Mesopotamia, Egypt, and Greece; the Hebrew Scriptures and Jewish traditions; the New Testament and Christian traditions; Islam; Hinduism; Theravada Buddhism; Tantric Buddhism, and Chinese religions.

Stevenson, Ian. *Where Reincarnation and Biology Intersect*. Westport, CT: Praeger Publishers, 1997. Paul Edwards describes Stevenson, a practicing physician, as one of the ablest recent defenders of the doctrine of reincarnation.

Tertullian. "The Refutation of the Pythagorean Doctrine of Transmigration." In *Immortality*, edited by Paul Edwards, 88–90. Amherst, NY: Prometheus Books, 1997. Tertullian (c. 160–AD 220) argued against rebirth, as the doctrine appeared in the thought of the Greek philosopher Pythagoras, and also in the writings of some Christians, including perhaps Tertullian's fellow Church Father, Origen of Alexandria.

The Tibetan Book of the Dead: First Complete Translation. Translated by Gyurme Dorje. Edited by Graham Coleman with Thupten Jinpa. New York: Viking, 2005. The title of this work translated from Tibetan is *The Great Liberation by Hearing in the Intermediate States*, or the shortened transliteration *Bardo Thodol*. According to tradition, the Tantric master Padmasambhava composed it in the eighth century AD. The book is a detailed guide to the intermediate state of consciousness (the *bardo* in Tibetan) between dying and the next birth cycle.

Part III

Resurrection and the Afterlife

Introduction to Part III:
Resurrection and the Afterlife

The last enemy that shall be destroyed is death.

I Corinthians, 15:26 (KJV)

And the Trumpet will be blown and behold! From the graves they will come out quickly to their Lord.

The Qur'an, 36:51

One reason why many educated people in the West find the doctrine of rebirth and karma attractive might be that it purports to describe a sort of automatic moral compensatory mechanism at work naturally, without divine intervention. As we noted in the Introduction to Part II, people find comfort in the belief that the cosmos has a built-in moral structure, one that rewards virtuous actions and punishes the vicious. As we have also seen, though, the doctrine of rebirth is beset with many conceptual difficulties, including the "logistical" problems mentioned in Part II, as well as the general problems that all versions of mind-body dualism face, including how to account for the interaction of mind and body. These problems might or might not be surmountable. But even if they are not surmountable—even if a human soul does not fully constitute a person, and even if fully constituted persons turn out to be inseparable from their bodies—we are not done with the possibility of posthumous survival. Hundreds of millions of Christians and Muslims profess to believe that life everlasting is within reach, thanks to God's grace and mercy.

The doctrine of Resurrection at Judgment Day, known by Christians who subscribe to the Nicene Creed[1] as General Resurrection of the Dead, provides a picture of the afterlife and of the human soul that is very different

---

[1]The profession of faith originally adopted by a council of Christian bishops who convened at the city of Nicaea (in present-day Turkey) in 325. The Creed states that Christ "will come again with glory to judge the living and the dead," and that believers "look forward to the resurrection of the dead, and to life in the world to come." Although most Christian denominations accept the Creed, we should bear in mind that some Christians accept other accounts of the afterlife.

from the views we encountered in Part II. In its broadest outlines, this doctrine holds that a Day of Judgment will come, on Earth or somewhere else, when God will raise the dead from the grave, to face punishment or reward in the afterlife. Those to be judged will include the living, too, as well as those whom God has brought back to life, or souls that have existed in one or another intermediate state between bodily death and resurrection.[2] Details differ from one denomination and sect to another, and they lie quite outside our philosophical concerns at present. What the various interpretations share in common is the belief that, thanks to God's grace, we may attain life everlasting even if our souls, like our bodies, are not immortal by nature.

Historically, various doctrines of resurrection, like doctrines of rebirth, have been connected to particular conceptions of the human person. According to a common Christian view, a person, in the fullest sense of the word, is a soul inextricably united with a body. This is the view that we will encounter below, in our reading from Thomas Aquinas. A person, then, is a *psychophysical unity*, and the death of the body puts an end to this unity, and thus an end to the person. The soul might or might not continue to exist and to be a center of experience after bodily death, but death does away with personhood, or at least diminishes it. Full personhood will be restored with the resurrection of the body and the reunion of body and soul on the Day of Judgment. On that day, God will raise the dead from the grave, to judge both the quick and the erstwhile dead, and to reward the righteous and punish the wicked.[3]

The main authority for the doctrine of resurrection is revealed Scripture, whether it be the Hebrew Scriptures, the New Testament, or the Qur'an. Moreover, resurrection is a miracle—a supernatural occurrence for which science can provide little insight. Thus, believers are not obliged to yield to

---

[2]Christian thinkers have posited three main scenarios when it comes to the intermediate state: *mortalism* holds that the entire human being is nonexistent until the general resurrection; *soul sleep* holds that the soul continues to exist but is unconscious; and *soul rest* holds that, at least for the just, the soul, in heaven perhaps, retains its awareness. Islamic scriptures describe a realm of incorporeal beings, the *Barzakh*, which separates bodily death from the Day of Judgment. Doctrines of rebirth, too, may require an intermediate state between death and rebirth, as Plato hinted in the *Phaedo*. The *Tibetan Book of the Dead*, for example, describes an intermediate "Bardo World" between death and rebirth, and offers advice about how to comport oneself there (refer to the Further Readings item at the end of Part II). For an insightful discussion of intermediate states and the philosophical problems that come with them, see Edwards, *Reincarnation*, 238–52.

[3]With reference to divine retribution in the afterlife, consider, for example, the New Testament book of *Matthew* 25:46: "And these will go away into eternal punishment, but the righteous into eternal life."

the authority of contemporary biology, astronomy, and physics when they conflict with the doctrine of resurrection.

Of course, this is not to say that the belief in resurrection is home free. Indeed, as we will see, philosophers who defend resurrection have a big job just trying to square the doctrine with God-given reason. The readings in Part III explore the doctrine of resurrection and related beliefs about the afterlife, in their most general outlines.

Before we proceed, though, one may well ask whether the doctrine of bodily resurrection is a topic for philosophical examination at all. There is, obviously, the question *why* a philosopher should believe in this or any other miraculous occurrence. But even more fundamentally, there is the question *whether we can even make sense of the claims that comprise the doctrine*, notably the question: if what is resurrected is a psychophysical unity, then how are we to imagine the "physical" part of this unity? At the time of resurrection, "my" body, this body, will have ceased its vital functions, and it will be in some state of dissolution—a corpse perhaps, or ashes, or perhaps widely scattered atoms. So what are we to make of this new physical embodiment, the resurrection body?

At this point, further questions arise (though nonphilosophers rarely pose them)—hard questions about the continuity of personal identity. In what sense could *you* be reconstituted as a psychophysical unity with a resurrection body? Will this physical body somehow be constituted of the very atoms of your body at the time of death? But *which* of these atoms? Surely not the atoms that constitute a person's body just before death: if that were the case, then the first job at hand for a resurrected cancer victim would be to die again of cancer.[4] But if not this, then which atoms, at which stage of your life, are you to be resurrected with? The atoms that constituted a previous state of your body on, say, your 33rd birthday? But why at this age rather than another? And what if you never reach your 33rd birthday? Once again the problem of personal continuity reasserts itself: if the "pscyho-" aspect of you at the age of your death were united with a "physical" recreation at age 33, then how could the result count as *you*? Recall Thomas W. Clark's thought experiment: wouldn't any person so radically modified thereby cease to exist as the same person?

One response to these questions might be to remind ourselves that resurrection is an act of divine intervention, dependent upon God's unfathomable will, and God will somehow sort things out fairly. Deferring

---

[4]Similarly, is a person who dies with dementia to be resurrected as a dotard?

to divine will might sound like an intellectual evasion, but in at least one respect proponents of this doctrine enjoy an advantage over proponents of rebirth: claims of psychical researchers notwithstanding, contemporary physics and neuroscience preclude the sort of radical dualism that rebirth demands. The miracle of bodily resurrection does an end-run around this problem. (Admittedly, though, the maneuver is not likely to satisfy scientific naturalists.)

But how do persons, as psychophysical unities, continue to exist after resurrection? And where? Here, once again, we encounter the "destination problem": some believers hold that, for most of us at least, life everlasting will take place on a renewed Earth some time after the Day of Judgment; others say that it will take place in heaven or hell somewhere, perhaps in the blue firmament, or in an underworld somewhere beneath the surface of Earth, or on another planet, or in another dimension of one sort or another, somewhere beyond our mundane experience.

As soon as we settle on a location for the Hereafter, we face the now-familiar "transportation problem": how does the person (or the soul, self, or what have you) get from the place where the death has occurred to the Hereafter? Remarkably little has been written about the destination problem and the closely related transportation problem that it poses.[5]

More than one of our authors in Part III attempt to tackle these problems, starting with Thomas Aquinas. The great thirteenth-century priest and scholar produced arguments that depict men and women as naturally embodied "incorruptible" souls. As such, men and women are qualified for bodily resurrection.

In the next reading, "Of a Particular Providence and of a Future State," David Hume deploys his imperturbable skepticism against the claims that the gods are architects, authors, and supreme governors of the world who punish the vicious and reward the virtuous. Moreover, Hume argues, it is doubtful that this life is but "a porch, which leads to a greater and vastly different building."

Even for some recent philosophers of religion who are believers, the traditional view of bodily resurrection is too problematic to sustain. In the third reading, the late Welsh philosopher H.H. Price produces a highly speculative account of survival of "discarnate minds" in a dreamlike "image world." His version of the Afterlife is far removed from the traditional

---

[5]The Further Readings section for Part III includes several sources that discuss this problem.

doctrine of bodily resurrection, but it retains several key features of the traditional doctrine, notably communication and interaction among persons in the Next World, and even provisions for a sort of posthumous reward and punishment. Price claims that his account of personal survival is at least intelligible, and that it solves or skirts the destination and transportation problems.

In our last reading in Part III, the late American philosopher Lynne Rudder Baker defends a version of resurrection that is closer to the traditional Christian account. On the day of the Resurrection, she suggests, God will create a body for every deceased person, and each of these bodies will *constitute* its respective person (in a sense that she will explain), but will not be *identical* to the corrupted earthly body. Each of these resurrection bodies will have the complexity to "subserve" the deceased person's states, and will be related to her or his biological body in a way that will constitute the resurrected person. In this way, Baker suggests, personal identity will be preserved in the afterlife. Like Price, Baker makes no claim, at least in the reading included here, that her version of bodily resurrection is true; rather, she claims, she has shown that at least one version of bodily resurrection is at least intelligible.

10

Resurrection of the Same Body

Thomas Aquinas

Translated by Fathers of the English Dominican Province

The author of our next reading is Thomas Aquinas (c. 1224–1274), one of the most prolific and influential thinkers of Europe. Aquinas produced a vast body of writing on a wide range of philosophical fields, including scriptural commentary, theology, logic, metaphysics, philosophical anthropology, ethics, and philosophy of law, but his best-known work is the *Summa Theologiae*, written between 1265 and 1274. The reading below consists of passages from Question 75 of the First Part of the *Summa*, Articles 1, 4, 5, and 6.

Aquinas wrote the *Summa Theologiae* for the instruction of students and nonspecialists; nevertheless, he addresses difficult metaphysical problems and he uses a technical vocabulary that (despite your editor's best efforts) readers will find daunting. Still, our brief selection from Aquinas is well worth the effort of reading. Aquinas makes his case, systematically and in a tightly argued manner, for a harmony of faith and reason on questions of the nature and fate of human beings. In each of the four sections or Articles of our reading, he first poses a question, then he presents objections and arguments, usually against the view he will defend, and toward the end of each article he replies to these objections, providing his own argument in response to the question. Aquinas considers four questions here: *Is the human soul a material body or not? Does the human soul constitute the "inward man"? Is the human soul composed of both matter and form? And Is the human soul corruptible?*

Aquinas was greatly influenced by Plato in many ways; however, his view of a human being is much closer to the views of Plato's brilliant student, Aristotle (384–322 BC): According to Aristotle, a human being is not identical to her or his soul; rather, each man or woman has a "bodily substance," in addition to an incorruptible (which is to say, *immortal*) soul. Developing this idea, Aquinas believed that, although the human soul continues to "subsist" after bodily death, it is not "complete in nature"; to be complete, it must be "the form of the body." Immortality, for a human being, ultimately depends on the soul being joined with a body in the afterlife. And this, says Aquinas, can only happen as a result of a Divine action, namely resurrection.

Question 75. Man who is composed of a spiritual and a corporeal substance: and in the first place, concerning what belongs to the essence of the soul.

Article 1. Whether the soul is a body?

Objection 1. It would seem that the soul is a body. For the soul is the moving principle of the body. Nor does it move unless moved.

First, because seemingly nothing can move unless it is itself moved, since nothing gives what it has not; for instance, what is not hot does not give heat. Secondly, because if there be anything that moves and is not moved, it must be the cause of eternal, unchanging movement, as we find proved (in Aristotle's *Physics* viii, 6); and this does not appear to be the case in the movement of an animal, which is caused by the soul. Therefore the soul is a mover moved. But every mover moved is a body. Therefore the soul is a body.

Objection 2. Further, all knowledge is caused by means of a likeness. But there can be no likeness of a body to an incorporeal thing. If, therefore, the soul were not a body, it could not have knowledge of corporeal things.

Objection 3. Further, between the mover and the moved there must be contact. But contact is only between bodies. Since, therefore, the soul moves the body, it seems that the soul must be a body.

On the contrary, Saint Augustine says (in *De Trinitate* vi, 6) that the soul "is simple in comparison with the body, inasmuch as it does not occupy space by its bulk." I answer that, to seek the nature of the soul, we must premise that the soul is defined as the first principle of life of those things which live: for we call living things "animate," [i.e. having a soul], and those things which have no life, "inanimate." Now life is shown principally by two actions, knowledge and movement. The philosophers of old,[1] not being able to rise above their imagination, supposed that the principle of these actions was something corporeal: for they asserted that only bodies were real things; and that what is not corporeal is nothing: hence they maintained that the soul is something corporeal. This opinion can be proved to be false in many ways; but we shall make use of only one proof, based on universal and certain principles, which shows clearly that the soul is not a body.

It is manifest that not every principle of vital action is a soul, for then the eye would be a soul, as it is a principle of vision; and the same might be applied to the other instruments of the soul: but it is the "first" principle of life, which we call the soul. Now, though a body may be considered to be a principle of life, or to be a living thing, as the heart is a principle of life in an animal, yet nothing corporeal can be the *first* principle of life. For it is clear that to be a principle of life, or to be a living thing, does not belong to a body as such; since, if that were the case, every body[2] would be a living thing, or a principle of life. Therefore a body is competent to be a living thing or even a principle of life, as "such" a body. Now [the fact] that it is actually such a body, it owes to some principle which is called its *act*. Therefore the soul, which is the first principle of life, is not a body, but the act of a body; thus heat, which is the principle of calefaction, is not a body, but an act of a body.

Reply to Objection 1. As everything which is in motion must be moved by something else, a process which cannot be prolonged indefinitely, we must allow that not every mover is moved. For, since to be moved is to pass from potentiality to actuality, the mover gives what it has to the thing moved, inasmuch as it causes it to be in act. But, as is shown in *Physics* viii, 6, there is a mover which is altogether immovable, and not moved either essentially, or accidentally; and such a mover can cause an invariable

---

[1]A reference to the earliest Greek philosophers, the *physikoi*. —MM
[2]That is to say, every physical object. —MM

movement.[3] There is, however, another kind of mover, which, though not moved essentially, is moved accidentally; and for this reason it does not cause an invariable movement; such a mover, is the soul. There is, again, another mover, which is moved essentially—namely, the body. And because the philosophers of old believed that nothing existed but bodies, they maintained that every mover is moved; and that the soul is moved directly, and is a body.

Reply to Objection 2. The likeness of a thing known is not of necessity actually in the nature of the knower; but given a thing which knows potentially, and afterwards knows actually, the likeness of the thing known must be in the nature of the knower, not actually, but only potentially; thus color is not actually in the pupil of the eye, but only potentially. Hence it is necessary, not that the likeness of corporeal things should be actually in the nature of the soul, but that there be a potentiality in the soul for such a likeness. But the ancient philosophers omitted to distinguish between actuality and potentiality; and so they held that the soul must be a body in order to have knowledge of a body; and that it must be composed of the principles of which all bodies are formed in order to know all bodies.

Reply to Objection 3. There are two kinds of contact; of "quantity," and of "power." By the former a body can be touched only by a body; by the latter a body can be touched by an incorporeal thing, which moves that body.

[…]

Article 4. Whether the soul is man?

Objection 1. It would seem that the soul is man. For it is written (*II Corinthians* 4:16): "Though our outward man is corrupted, yet the inward man is renewed day by day." But that which is within man is the soul. Therefore the soul is the inward man.

Objection 2. Further, the human soul is a substance. But it is not a universal substance. Therefore it is a particular substance. Therefore it is a "hypostasis" or a person; and it can only be a human person. Therefore the soul is man; for a human person is a man.

On the contrary, Saint Augustine (De Civ. Dei xix, 3) commends Varro as holding "that man is not a mere soul, nor a mere body; but both soul and body."

---

[3]Aquinas, of course, identifies this first unmoved mover as God. —MM

I answer that, the assertion "the soul is man," can be taken in two senses. First, that man is a soul; though this particular man, Socrates, for instance, is not a soul, but composed of soul and body. I say this, forasmuch as some held that the form alone belongs to the species; while matter is part of the individual, and not the species. This cannot be true; for to the nature of the species belongs what the definition signifies; and in natural things the definition does not signify the form only, but the form and the matter. Hence in natural things the matter is part of the species [...] For as it belongs to the notion of this particular man to be composed of this soul, of this flesh, and of these bones; so it belongs to the notion of man to be composed of soul, flesh, and bones; for whatever belongs in common to the substance of all the individuals contained under a given species, must belong to the substance of the species.

It may also be understood in this sense, that this soul is this man; and this could be held if it were supposed that the operation of the sensitive soul were proper to it, apart from the body; because in that case all the operations which are attributed to man would belong to the soul only; and whatever performs the operations proper to a thing, is that thing; wherefore that which performs the operations of a man is man. But it has been shown above (Article 3) that sensation is not the operation of the soul only. Since, then, sensation is an operation of man, but not proper [or unique] to him, it is clear that man is not a soul only, but something composed of soul and body. Plato, by supposing that sensation was proper to the soul, could maintain man to be a soul making use of the body.

Reply to Objection 1. According to the Philosopher (Aristotle, *Ethics* ix, 8), a thing seems to be chiefly what is principle in it; thus what the governor of a state does, the state is said to do. In this way sometimes what is principle in man is said to be man; sometimes, indeed, the intellectual part which, in accordance with truth, is called the "inward" man; and sometimes the sensitive part with the body is called man in the opinion of those whose observation does not go beyond the senses. And this is called the "outward" man.

Reply to Objection 2. Not every particular substance is a hypostasis or a person, but that which has the complete nature of its species. Hence a hand, or a foot, is not called a hypostasis, or a person; nor, likewise, is the soul alone so called, since it is a part of the human species.[4]

---

[4] The term *human species* does not refer to an animal species, as we commonly use the term today. For Aquinas, the term means something like "a human type," or "the idea of what a human is." —MM

Article 5. Whether the soul is composed of matter and form?

[…][5]

I answer that, the soul has no matter. We may consider this question in two ways.

First, from the notion of a soul in general; for it belongs to the notion of a soul to be the form of a body. Now, either it is a form by virtue of itself, in its entirety, or by virtue of some part of itself. If by virtue of itself in its entirety, then it is impossible that any part of it should be matter, if by matter we understand something purely potential: for a form, as such, is an act; and that which is purely potentiality cannot be part of an act, since potentiality is repugnant to actuality as being opposite thereto. If, however, it be a form by virtue of a part of itself, then we call that part the soul: and that matter, which it actualizes first, we call the "primary animate."

Secondly, we may proceed from the specific notion of the human soul inasmuch as it is intellectual. For it is clear that whatever is received into something is received according to the condition of the recipient. Now a thing is known in as far as its form is in the knower. But the intellectual soul knows a thing in its nature absolutely: for instance, it knows a stone absolutely as a stone; and therefore the form of a stone absolutely, as to its proper formal idea, is in the intellectual soul. Therefore the intellectual soul itself is an absolute form, and not something composed of matter and form. For if the intellectual soul were composed of matter and form, the forms of things would be received into it as individuals, and so it would only know the individual: just as it happens with the sensitive powers which receive forms in a corporeal organ; since matter is the principle by which forms are individualized. It follows, therefore, that the intellectual soul, and every intellectual substance which has knowledge of forms absolutely, is exempt from composition of matter and form.

[…]

Article 6. Whether the human soul is incorruptible?

Objection 1. It would seem that the human soul is corruptible. For those things that have a like beginning and process seemingly have a like end.

---

[5]The objections have been omitted. —MM

But the beginning, by generation, of men is like that of animals, for they are made from the earth. And the process of life is alike in both; because "all things breathe alike, and man hath nothing more than the beast," as it is written (Ecclesiastes 3:19). Therefore, as the same text concludes, "the death of man and beast is one, and the condition of both is equal." But the souls of brute animals are corruptible. Therefore, also, the human soul is corruptible.

Objection 2. Further, whatever is out of nothing can return to nothingness; because the end should correspond to the beginning. But as it is written (Wisdom 2:2), "We are born of nothing"; which is true, not only of the body, but also of the soul. Therefore, as is concluded in the same passage, "After this we shall be as if we had not been," even as to our soul.

Objection 3. Further, nothing is without its own proper operation. But the operation proper to the soul, which is to understand through a phantasm,[6] cannot be without the body. For the soul understands nothing without a phantasm; and there is no phantasm without the body as the Philosopher says (Aristotle, *De Anima* i, 1). Therefore the soul cannot survive the dissolution of the body.

On the contrary, Dionysius says (*The Divine Names* iv) that human souls owe to Divine goodness that they are "intellectual," and that they have "an incorruptible substantial life."

I answer that, we must assert that the intellectual principle which we call the human soul is incorruptible. For a thing may be corrupted in two ways— *per se*, and accidentally. Now it is impossible for any substance to be generated or corrupted accidentally, that is, by the generation or corruption of something else. For generation and corruption belong to a thing, just as existence belongs to it, which is acquired by generation and lost by corruption. Therefore, whatever has existence *per se* cannot be generated or corrupted except *per se*; while things which do not subsist, such as accidents and material forms, acquire existence or lose it through the generation or corruption of composite things. Now it was shown above (Articles 2 and 3) that the souls of brutes are not self-subsistent, whereas the human soul is; so that the souls of brutes are corrupted, when their bodies are corrupted; while the human soul could not be corrupted unless it were corrupted *per se*. This, indeed, is impossible, not only as regards the human soul, but also as regards

---

[6] According to Aquinas, whenever we are conscious of the idea of a corporeal thing (whether imaginary or not), a "phantasm" or "likeness of a particular thing" must also be present in consciousness. This is true whether the idea is of a unicorn or of "something real" like a horse. —MM

anything subsistent that is a form alone. For it is clear that what belongs to a thing by virtue of itself is inseparable from it; but existence belongs to a form, which is an act, by virtue of itself. Wherefore matter acquires actual existence as it acquires the form; while it is corrupted so far as the form is separated from it. But it is impossible for a form to be separated from itself; and therefore it is impossible for a subsistent form to cease to exist.

Granted even that the soul is composed of matter and form, as some pretend, we should nevertheless have to maintain that it is incorruptible. For corruption is found only where there is contrariety; since generation and corruption are from contraries and into contraries. Wherefore the heavenly bodies, since they have no matter subject to contrariety, are incorruptible. Now there can be no contrariety in the intellectual soul; for it receives according to the manner of its existence, and those things which it receives are without contrariety; for the notions even of contraries are not themselves contrary, since contraries belong to the same knowledge. Therefore it is impossible for the intellectual soul to be corruptible. Moreover we may take a sign of this from the fact that everything naturally aspires to existence after its own manner. Now, in things that have knowledge, desire ensues upon knowledge. The senses indeed do not know existence, except under the conditions of "here" and "now," whereas the intellect apprehends existence absolutely, and for all time; so that everything that has an intellect naturally desires always to exist. But a natural desire cannot be in vain. Therefore every intellectual substance is incorruptible.

Reply to Objection 1. Solomon reasons thus in the person of the foolish, as expressed in the words of Wisdom 2. Therefore the saying that man and animals have a like beginning in generation is true of the body; for all animals alike are made of earth. But it is not true of the soul. For the souls of brutes are produced by some power of the body; whereas the human soul is produced by God. To signify this it is written as to other animals: "Let the earth bring forth the living soul" (Genesis 1:24): while of man it is written (Genesis 2:7) that "He breathed into his face the breath of life." And so in Ecclesiastes 12:7 it is concluded: "(Before) the dust return into its earth from whence it was; and the spirit return to God Who gave it." Again the process of life is alike as to the body, concerning which it is written (Ecclesiastes 3:19): "All things breathe alike," and (Wisdom 2:2), "The breath in our nostrils is smoke." But the process is not alike of the soul; for man is intelligent, whereas animals are not. Hence it is false to say: "Man has nothing more than beasts." Thus death comes to both alike as to the body, by not as to the soul.

Reply to Objection 2. As a thing can be created by reason, not of a passive potentiality, but only of the active potentiality of the Creator, Who can produce something out of nothing, so when we say that a thing can be reduced to nothing, we do not imply in the creature a potentiality to non-existence, but in the Creator the power of ceasing to sustain existence. But a thing is said to be corruptible because there is in it a potentiality to non-existence.

Reply to Objection 3. To understand through a phantasm is the proper operation of the soul by virtue of its union with the body. After separation from the body it will have another mode of understanding, similar to other substances separated from bodies, as will appear later on (in Question 89).

11

Of a Particular Providence and of a Future State

David Hume

In the following reading, the Scottish Enlightenment thinker David Hume (1711–1776) examines the question whether we can ever be justified in positing the existence of a "superlative intelligence and benevolence," a "supreme governor of the world, who guides the course of events, and punishes the vicious with infamy and disappointment, and rewards the virtuous," whether in this life or in "a future state." With a wink and a nod to the reader, Hume claims to be reporting on a conversation with "a friend who loves skeptical paradoxes." His friend, he writes, has agreed to take on the character of Epicurus addressing the ancient Athenians, to argue that experience and reason provide no support for supreme providence and a future state.

Hume takes pains to assure us that Epicurus' skepticism does not "loosen ... the ties of morality," and poses no danger to the social order. With reference to posthumous survival, as with other matters unseen, we must give up on reason, and satisfy ourselves with the authority of divinely revealed scripture. (Hume, of course, could not himself take the advice that he puts into the mouth of his "friend.")

Hume died peacefully on April 18, 1776. A few weeks before his death, he told his friend James Boswell that he believed that the hope for life after death is a "most unreasonable fancy." We read in eulogies and letters that Hume was cheerful right to the end of his life—fully lucid and unflinching in his disbelief in an afterlife. This disturbed some of his religious acquaintances, but it impressed several friends who visited him in his last days. "Upon the whole," his friend the economist Adam Smith wrote, "I have always considered him, both in his lifetime and since his death, as approaching as nearly to the idea of a perfectly wise and virtuous man, as perhaps the nature of human frailty will permit."[1]

I was lately engaged in conversation with a friend who loves skeptical paradoxes; where, though he advanced many principles, of which I can by no means approve, yet as they seem to be curious, and to bear some relation to the chain of reasoning carried on throughout this enquiry, I shall here copy them from my memory as accurately as I can, in order to submit them to the judgment of the reader.

Our conversation began with my admiring the singular good fortune of philosophy, which, as it requires entire liberty above all other privileges, and chiefly flourishes from the free opposition of sentiments and argumentation, received its first birth in an age and country of freedom and toleration, and was never cramped, even in its most extravagant principles, by any creeds, concessions, or penal statutes. For, except the banishment of Protagoras and the death of Socrates, which last event proceeded partly from other motives, there are scarcely any instances to be met with, in ancient history, of this bigoted jealousy, with which the present age is so much infested. Epicurus lived at Athens to an advanced age, in peace and tranquility: Epicureans were even admitted to receive the sacerdotal character, and to officiate at the altar, in the most sacred rites of the established religion: and the public encouragement of pensions and salaries was afforded equally, by the wisest of all the Roman emperors,[2] to the professors of every sect of philosophy. How requisite such kind of treatment was to philosophy, in her early youth, will easily be conceived, if we reflect that, even at present, when she may be supposed more hardy and robust, she bears with much difficulty the

---

[1] In the days just before he died, Hume wrote a brief memoir entitled "My Own Life. " Less than ten typeset pages in length, it is the nearest thing to an autobiography that he ever produced. The memoir is included in *An Inquiry concerning Human Understanding*, ed. Charles W. Hendel (Indianapolis: The Bobbs-Merrill Company, Inc., 1955), 3–11.

[2] Hume is referring to Marcus Aurelius (121–AD 180), an emperor with a reputation for wise leadership and toleration. Aurelius was a student of Stoic philosophy, but he encouraged toleration of many schools of thought, including Epicureanism. —MM

inclemency of the seasons, and those harsh winds of calumny and persecution, which blow upon her.

You admire, says my friend, as the singular good fortune of philosophy, what seems to result from the natural course of things, and to be unavoidable in every age and nation. This pertinacious bigotry, of which you complain, as so fatal to philosophy, is really her offspring, who, after allying with superstition, separates himself entirely from the interest of his parent, and becomes her most inveterate enemy and persecutor. Speculative dogmas of religion, the present occasions of such furious dispute, could not possibly be conceived or admitted in the early ages of the world; when mankind, being wholly illiterate, formed an idea of religion more suitable to their weak apprehension, and composed their sacred tenets of such tales chiefly as were the objects of traditional belief, more than of argument or disputation. After the first alarm, therefore, was over, which arose from the new paradoxes and principles of the philosophers; these teachers seem ever after, during the ages of antiquity, to have lived in great harmony with the established superstition, and to have made a fair partition of mankind between them; the former claiming all the learned and wise, the latter possessing all the vulgar and illiterate.

It seems then, say I, that you leave politics entirely out of the question, and never suppose, that a wise magistrate can justly be jealous of certain tenets of philosophy, such as those of Epicurus, which, denying a divine existence, and consequently a providence and a future state, seem to loosen in a great measure the ties of morality, and may be supposed, for that reason, pernicious to the peace of civil society.

I know, replied he, that in fact these persecutions never in any age proceeded from calm reason or from experience of the pernicious consequences of philosophy; but arose entirely from passion and prejudice. But what if I should advance farther, and assert that if Epicurus had been accused before the people by any of the sycophants or informers of those days, he could easily have defended his cause and proved his principles of philosophy to be as salutary as those of his adversaries, who endeavored with such zeal to expose him to the public hatred and jealousy?

I wish, said I, you would try your eloquence upon so extraordinary a topic, and make a speech for Epicurus, which might satisfy, not the mob of Athens, if you will allow that ancient and polite city to have contained any mob, but the more philosophical part of his audience, such as might be supposed capable of comprehending his arguments.

The matter would not be difficult upon such conditions, replied he: and if you please, I shall suppose myself Epicurus for a moment, and make you stand for the Athenian people, and shall deliver you such an harangue as will fill all the urn with white beans, and leave not a black one to gratify the malice of my adversaries.

Very well: pray proceed upon these suppositions.

I come hither, O ye Athenians, to justify in your assembly what I maintain in my school, and I find myself impeached by furious antagonists, instead of reasoning with calm and dispassionate enquirers. Your deliberations, which of right should be directed to questions of public good, and the interest of the commonwealth, are diverted to the disquisitions of speculative philosophy; and these magnificent, but perhaps fruitless enquiries, take place of your more familiar but more useful occupations. But so far as in me lies, I will prevent this abuse. We shall not here dispute concerning the origin and government of worlds. We shall only enquire how far such questions concern the public interest. And if I can persuade you that they are entirely indifferent to the peace of society and security of government, I hope that you will presently send us back to our schools, there to examine, at leisure, the question the most sublime, but at the same time the most speculative of all philosophy.

The religious philosophers, not satisfied with the tradition of your forefathers, and doctrine of your priests (in which I willingly acquiesce), indulge a rash curiosity, in trying how far they can establish religion upon the principles of reason; and they thereby excite, instead of satisfying, the doubts, which naturally arise from a diligent and scrutinous enquiry. They paint, in the most magnificent colors, the order, beauty, and wise arrangement of the universe; and then ask, if such a glorious display of intelligence could proceed from the fortuitous concourse of atoms, or if chance could produce what the greatest genius can never sufficiently admire. I shall not examine the justness of this argument. I shall allow it to be as solid as my antagonists and accusers can desire. It is sufficient, if I can prove, from this very reasoning, that the question is entirely speculative, and that when, in my philosophical disquisitions, I deny a providence and a future state, I undermine not the foundations of society, but advance principles, which they themselves, upon their own topics, if they argue consistently, must allow to be solid and satisfactory.

You then, who are my accusers, have acknowledged that the chief or sole argument for a divine existence (which I never questioned) is derived from the order of nature; where there appear such marks of intelligence and design, that you think it extravagant to assign for its cause, either chance, or the blind and unguided force of matter. You allow that this is an argument drawn from effects to causes. From the order of the work, you infer that there must have been project and forethought in the workman. If you cannot make out this point, you allow that your conclusion fails; and you pretend not to establish the conclusion in a greater latitude than the phenomena of nature will justify. These are your concessions. I desire you to mark the consequences.

When we infer any particular cause from an effect, we must proportion the one to the other, and can never be allowed to ascribe to the cause any qualities but what are exactly sufficient to produce the effect. A body of ten ounces raised in any scale may serve as a proof, that the counterbalancing weight exceeds ten ounces; but can never afford a reason that it exceeds a hundred. If the cause, assigned for any effect, be not sufficient to produce it, we must either reject that cause or add to it such qualities as will give it a just proportion to the effect. But if we ascribe to it farther qualities, or affirm it capable of producing other effects, we can only indulge the license of conjecture, and arbitrarily suppose the existence of qualities and energies, without reason or authority.

The same rule holds, whether the cause assigned be brute unconscious matter, or a rational intelligent being. If the cause be known only by the effect, we never ought to ascribe to it any qualities beyond what are precisely requisite to produce the effect: nor can we, by any rules of just reasoning, return back from the cause, and infer other effects from it, beyond those by which alone it is known to us. No one, merely from the sight of one of Zeuxis's pictures, could know that he was also a statuary or architect, and was an artist no less skillful in stone and marble than in colors. The talents and taste displayed in the particular work before us; these we may safely conclude the workman to be possessed of. The cause must be proportioned to the effect, and if we exactly and precisely proportion it, we shall never find in it any qualities, that point farther, or afford an inference concerning any other design or performance. Such qualities must be somewhat beyond what is merely requisite for producing the effect, which we examine.

Allowing, therefore, the gods to be the authors of the existence or order of the universe, it follows, that they possess that precise degree of power, intelligence, and benevolence, which appears in their workmanship; but nothing farther can ever be proved, except we call in the assistance of exaggeration and flattery to supply the defects of argument and reasoning. So far as the traces of any attributes, at present, appear, so far may we conclude these attributes to exist. The supposition of farther attributes is mere hypothesis; much more the supposition that, in distant regions of space or periods of time, there has been, or will be, a more magnificent display of these attributes, and a scheme of administration more suitable to such imaginary virtues. We can never be allowed to mount up from the universe, the effect, to Jupiter, the cause, and then descend downwards, to infer any new effect from that cause, as if the present effects alone were not entirely worthy of the glorious attributes, which we ascribe to that deity. The knowledge of the cause being derived solely from the effect, they must be exactly adjusted to each other, and the one can never refer to anything farther, or be the foundation of any new inference and conclusion.

You find certain phenomena in nature. You seek a cause or author. You imagine that you have found him. You afterwards become so enamored of this offspring of your brain that you imagine it impossible, but he must produce something greater and more perfect than the present scene of things, which is so full of ill and disorder. You forget that this superlative intelligence and benevolence are entirely imaginary, or, at least, without any foundation in reason, and that you have no ground to ascribe to him any qualities but what you see he has actually exerted and displayed in his productions. Let your gods, therefore, O philosophers, be suited to the present appearances of nature: and presume not to alter these appearances by arbitrary suppositions, in order to suit them to the attributes, which you so fondly ascribe to your deities.

When priests and poets, supported by your authority, O Athenians, talk of a golden or silver age, which preceded the present state of vice and misery, I hear them with attention and with reverence. But when philosophers, who pretend to neglect authority and to cultivate reason, hold the same discourse, I pay them not, I own, the same obsequious submission and pious deference. I ask who carried them into the celestial regions, who admitted them into the councils of the gods, who opened to them the book of fate that they thus rashly affirm, that their deities have executed, or will execute, any purpose beyond what has actually appeared? If they tell me that they have mounted on the steps or by the gradual ascent of reason, and by drawing inferences from effects to causes, I still insist that they have aided the ascent of reason by the wings of imagination; otherwise, they could not thus change their manner of inference and argue from causes to effects, presuming that a more perfect production than the present world would be more suitable to such perfect beings as the gods, and forgetting that they have no reason to ascribe to these celestial beings any perfection or any attribute, but what can be found in the present world.

Hence all the fruitless industry to account for the ill appearances of nature, and save the honor of the gods, while we must acknowledge the reality of that evil and disorder with which the world so much abounds. The obstinate and intractable qualities of matter, we are told, or the observance of general laws, or some such reason, is the sole cause, which controlled the power and benevolence of Jupiter, and obliged him to create mankind and every sensible creature so imperfect and so unhappy. These attributes then, are, it seems, beforehand, taken for granted, in their greatest latitude. And upon that supposition, I own that such conjectures may, perhaps, be admitted as plausible solutions of the ill phenomena. But still I ask: Why take these attributes for granted, or why ascribe to the cause any qualities but what actually appear in the effect? Why torture your brain to justify the course of nature upon suppositions, which, for aught you know, may be entirely imaginary, and of which there are to be found no traces in the course of nature?

The religious hypothesis, therefore, must be considered only as a particular method of accounting for the visible phenomena of the universe: but no just reasoner will ever presume to infer from it any single fact, and alter or add to the phenomena, in any single particular. If you think that the appearances of things prove such causes, it is allowable for you to draw an inference concerning the existence of these causes. In such complicated and sublime subjects, every one should be indulged in the liberty of conjecture and argument. But here you ought to rest. If you come backward, and arguing from your inferred causes, conclude, that any other fact has existed, or will exist, in the course of nature, which may serve as a fuller display of particular attributes; I must admonish you, that you have departed from the method of reasoning, attached to the present subject, and have certainly added something to the attributes of the cause, beyond what appears in the effect; otherwise you could never, with tolerable sense or propriety, add anything to the effect, in order to render it more worthy of the cause.

Where, then, is the odiousness of that doctrine, which I teach in my school, or rather, which I examine in my gardens? Or what do you find in this whole question, wherein the security of good morals, or the peace and order of society, is in the least concerned?

I deny a providence, you say, and supreme governor of the world, who guides the course of events, and punishes the vicious with infamy and disappointment, and rewards the virtuous with honor and success in all their undertakings. But surely, I deny not the course itself of events, which lies open to every one's inquiry and examination. I acknowledge that, in the present order of things, virtue is attended with more peace of mind than vice, and meets with a more favorable reception from the world. I am sensible that, according to the past experience of mankind, friendship is the chief joy of human life, and moderation the only source of tranquility and happiness. I never balance between the virtuous and the vicious course of life, but am sensible that, to a well-disposed mind, every advantage is on the side of the former. And what can you say more, allowing all your suppositions and reasonings? You tell me, indeed, that this disposition of things proceeds from intelligence and design. But whatever it proceeds from, the disposition itself, on which depends our happiness or misery, and consequently our conduct and deportment in life is still the same. It is still open for me, as well as you, to regulate my behavior, by my experience of past events. And if you affirm that, while a divine providence is allowed and a supreme distributive justice in the universe, I ought to expect some more particular reward of the good, and punishment of the bad beyond the ordinary course of events; I here find the same fallacy, which I have before endeavored to detect. You persist in imagining that, if we grant that divine existence for which you so earnestly contend, you may safely infer consequences from it, and add something to the experienced order of nature, by arguing from the attributes, which you ascribe to your gods. You seem not to remember that all your reasonings on this subject can only be drawn from effects to causes, and that every argument deducted from causes to effects must of necessity be a gross sophism, since it is impossible for you to know anything of the cause but what you have antecedently, not inferred, but discovered to the full, in the effect.

But what must a philosopher think of those vain reasoners who instead of regarding the present scene of things as the sole object of their contemplation, so far reverse the whole course of nature, as to render this life merely a passage to something farther: a porch, which leads to a greater and vastly different building; a prologue, which serves only to introduce the piece and give it more grace and propriety? Whence, do you think, can such philosophers derive their idea of the gods? From their own conceit and imagination surely. For if they derived it from the present phenomena, it would never point to anything farther, but must be exactly adjusted to them. That the divinity may possibly be endowed with attributes, which we have never seen exerted; may be governed by principles of action, which we cannot discover to be satisfied: all this will freely be allowed. But still this is mere possibility and hypothesis. We never can have reason to infer any attributes or any principles of action in him, but so far as we know them to have been exerted and satisfied.

Are there any marks of a distributive justice in the world? If you answer in the affirmative, I conclude that, since justice here exerts itself, it is satisfied. If you reply in the negative, I conclude that you have then no reason to ascribe justice, in our sense of it, to the gods. If you hold a medium between affirmation and negation, by saying that the justice of the gods, at present, exerts itself in part, but not in its full extent; I answer that you have no reason to give it any particular extent, but only so far as you see it, at present, exert itself.

Thus I bring the dispute, O Athenians, to a short issue with my antagonists. The course of nature lies open to my contemplation as well as to theirs. The experienced train of events is the great standard by which we all regulate our conduct. Nothing else can be appealed to in the field or in the senate. Nothing else ought ever to be heard of in the school or in the closet. In vain would our limited understanding break through those boundaries, which are too narrow for our fond imagination. While we argue from the course of nature, and infer a particular intelligent cause, which first bestowed and still preserves order in the universe, we embrace a principle, which is both uncertain and useless. It is uncertain, because the subject lies entirely beyond the reach of human experience. It is useless, because our knowledge of this cause being derived entirely from the course of nature, we can never, according to the rules of just reasoning, return back from the cause with any new inference, or making additions to the common and experienced course of nature, establish any new principles of conduct and behavior.

I observe (said I, finding he had finished his harangue) that you neglect not the artifice of the demagogues of old, and as you were pleased to make me stand for the people, you insinuate yourself into my favor by embracing those principles to which you know I have always expressed a particular attachment. But allowing you to make experience (as indeed I think you ought) the only standard of our judgment concerning this, and all other questions of fact, I doubt not but, from the very same experience to which you appeal, it may be possible to refute this reasoning, which you have put into the mouth of Epicurus. If you saw, for instance, a half-finished building surrounded with heaps of brick and stone and mortar, and all the instruments of masonry, could you not infer from the effect, that it was a work of design and contrivance? And could you not return again, from this inferred cause, to infer new additions to the effect, and conclude that the building would soon be finished, and receive all the further improvements, which art could bestow upon it? If you saw upon the seashore the print of one human foot, you would conclude that a man had passed that way, and that he had also left the traces of the other foot, though effaced by the rolling of the sands or inundation of the waters. Why then do you refuse to admit the same method of reasoning with regard to the order of nature? Consider the world and the present life only as an imperfect building, from which you can infer a superior intelligence, and arguing from that superior intelligence, which can leave nothing imperfect, why may you not infer a more finished scheme or plan, which will receive its completion in some distant point of space or time? Are not these methods of reasoning exactly similar? And under what pretense can you embrace the one, while you reject the other?

The infinite difference of the subjects, replied he, is a sufficient foundation for this difference in my conclusions. In works of human art and contrivance, it is allowable to advance from the effect to the cause, and returning back from the cause, to form new inferences concerning the effect, and examine the alterations, which it has probably undergone, or may still undergo. But what is the foundation of this method of reasoning? Plainly this, that man is a being whom we know by experience, whose motives and designs we are acquainted with, and whose projects and inclinations have a certain connection and coherence, according to the laws which nature has established for the government of such a creature. When, therefore, we find that any work has proceeded from the skill and industry of man, as we are otherwise acquainted with the nature of the animal, we can draw a hundred inferences concerning what may be expected from him, and these inferences will all be founded in experience and observation. But did we know man only from the single work or production which we examine, it were impossible for us to argue in this manner, because our knowledge of all the qualities, which we ascribe to him, being in that case derived from the production, it is impossible they could point to anything farther or be the foundation of any new inference. The print of a foot in the sand can only prove, when considered alone, that there was some figure adapted to it, by which it was produced: but the print of a human foot proves likewise, from our other experience, that there was probably another foot, which also left its impression, though effaced by time or other accidents. Here we mount from the effect to the cause, and descending again from the cause, infer alterations in the effect; but this is not a continuation of the same simple chain of reasoning. We comprehend in this case a hundred other experiences and observations, concerning the usual figure and members of that species of animal, without which this method of argument must be considered as fallacious and sophistical.

The case is not the same with our reasonings from the works of nature. The Deity is known to us only by his productions, and is a single being in the universe, not comprehended under any species or genus, from whose experienced attributes or qualities we can, by analogy, infer any attribute or quality in him. As the universe shews wisdom and goodness, we infer wisdom and goodness. As it shews a particular degree of these perfections, we infer a particular degree of them, precisely adapted to the effect which we examine. But farther attributes or farther degrees of the same attributes, we can never be authorized to infer or suppose, by any rules of just reasoning. Now, without some such license of supposition, it is impossible for us to argue from the cause, or infer any alteration in the effect, beyond what has immediately fallen under our observation. Greater good produced by this Being must still prove a greater degree of goodness: a more impartial distribution of rewards and punishments must proceed from a greater regard to justice and equity. Every supposed addition to the works of nature makes an addition to the attributes of the Author of nature; and consequently, being entirely unsupported by any reason or argument, can never be admitted but as mere conjecture and hypothesis.[3]

The great source of our mistake in this subject, and of the unbounded license of conjecture, which we indulge, is that we tacitly consider ourselves as in the place of the Supreme Being, and conclude that he will, on every occasion, observe the same conduct, which we ourselves, in his situation, would have embraced as reasonable and eligible. But, besides that the

---

[3]In general, it may, I think, be established as a maxim, that where any cause is known only by its particular effects, it must be impossible to infer any new effects from that cause; since the qualities, which are requisite to produce these new effects along with the former, must either be different, or superior, or of more extensive operation, than those which simply produced the effect, whence alone the cause is supposed to be known to us. We can never, therefore, have any reason to suppose the existence of these qualities. To say that the new effects proceed only from a continuation of the same energy, which is already known from the first effects, will not remove the difficulty. For even granting this to be the case (which can seldom be supposed), the very continuation and exertion of a like energy (for it is impossible it can be absolutely the same), I say, this exertion of a like energy, in a different period of space and time, is a very arbitrary supposition, and what there cannot possibly be any traces of it in the effects, from which all our knowledge of the cause is originally derived. Let the inferred cause be exactly proportioned (as it should be) to the known effect; and it is impossible that it can possess any qualities, from which new or different effects can be inferred. (Hume's note)

ordinary course of nature may convince us that almost everything is regulated by principles and maxims very different from ours; besides this, I say, it must evidently appear contrary to all rules of analogy to reason from the intentions and projects of men to those of a Being so different, and so much superior. In human nature, there is a certain experienced coherence of designs and inclinations, so that when, from any fact, we have discovered one intention of any man, it may often be reasonable, from experience, to infer another, and draw a long chain of conclusions concerning his past or future conduct. But this method of reasoning can never have place with regard to a Being so remote and incomprehensible, who bears much less analogy to any other being in the universe than the sun to a waxen taper, and who discovers himself only by some faint traces or outlines, beyond which we have no authority to ascribe to him any attribute or perfection. What we imagine to be a superior perfection may really be a defect. Or were it ever so much a perfection, the ascribing of it to the Supreme Being, where it appears not to have been really exerted, to the full, in his works, savors more of flattery and panegyric than of just reasoning and sound philosophy. All the philosophy, therefore, in the world, and all the religion, which is nothing but a species of philosophy, will never be able to carry us beyond the usual course of experience, or give us measures of conduct and behavior different from those which are furnished by reflections on common life. No new fact can ever be inferred from the religious hypothesis; no event foreseen or foretold; no reward or punishment expected or dreaded, beyond what is already known by practice and observation. So that my apology for Epicurus will still appear solid and satisfactory; nor have the political interests of society any connection with the philosophical disputes concerning metaphysics and religion.

There is still one circumstance, replied I, which you seem to have overlooked. Though I should allow your premises, I must deny your conclusion. You conclude that religious doctrines and reasonings can have no influence on life, because they ought to have no influence, never considering, that men reason not in the same manner you do, but draw many consequences from the belief of a divine Existence, and suppose that the Deity will inflict punishments on vice and bestow rewards on virtue, beyond what appear in the ordinary course of nature. Whether this reasoning of theirs be just or not, is no matter. Its influence on their life and conduct must still be the same. And those who attempt to disabuse them of such prejudices may, for aught I know, be good reasoners, but I cannot allow them to be good citizens and politicians, since they free men from one restraint upon their passions and make the infringement of the laws of society, in one respect, more easy and secure.

After all, I may perhaps agree to your general conclusion in favor of liberty, though upon different premises from those on which you endeavor to found it. I think that the state ought to tolerate every principle of philosophy, nor is there an instance that any government has suffered in its political interests by such indulgence. There is no enthusiasm among philosophers; their doctrines are not very alluring to the people, and no restraint can be put upon their reasonings but what must be of dangerous consequence to the sciences, and even to the state, by paving the way for persecution and oppression in points where the generality of mankind are more deeply interested and concerned.

But there occurs to me (continued I) with regard to your main topic, a difficulty, which I shall just propose to you without insisting on it, lest it lead into reasonings of too nice and delicate a nature. In a word, I much doubt whether it be possible for a cause to be known only by its effect (as you have all along supposed) or to be of so singular and particular a nature as to have no parallel and no similarity with any other cause or object, that has ever fallen under our observation. It is only when two species of objects are found to be constantly conjoined that we can infer the one from the other; and were an effect presented, which was entirely singular and could not be comprehended under any known species, I do not see that we could form any conjecture or inference at all concerning its cause. If experience and observation and analogy be, indeed, the only guides which we can reasonably follow in inferences of this nature; both the effect and cause must bear a similarity and resemblance to other effects and causes, which we know, and which we have found, in many instances, to be conjoined with each other. I leave it to your own reflection to pursue the consequences of this principle. I shall just observe that, as the antagonists of Epicurus always suppose the universe, an effect quite singular and unparalleled, to be the proof of a Deity, a cause no less singular and unparalleled; your reasonings, upon that supposition, seem, at least, to merit our attention. There is, I own, some difficulty how we can ever return from the cause to the effect, and, reasoning from our ideas of the former, infer any alteration on the latter, or any addition to it.

12

The Soul Survives and Functions after Death

H.H. Price

Some opponents of the survival hypothesis have claimed that it is not really a hypothesis at all, because it is unintelligible: the very suggestion that a person could continue to exist after bodily death, the opponents say, is like claiming that a road could continue after it ends.[1] Since there cannot be evidence for something that is unintelligible to us, there could be no more evidence for survival than there could be for a married bachelor.

Toward the beginning of our next reading, the late Welsh philosopher Henry Habberley Price (1899–1984) rejects the claim that there is anything "self-contradictory or logically absurd in the hypothesis that memories, desires, and images can exist in the absence of a physical brain." He then sets out to describe a version of disembodied survival that meets a necessary precondition for being true, namely that it be conceivable, internally coherent. He does not propose to prove that the survival hypothesis is true; rather, he presents a version of an afterlife that he believes meets today's standards of rationality. This may sound like a modest goal, but as we will see, it is a tall order to fill.

Price imagines a "Next World" inhabited by "discarnate human personalities" that create "an after-death world of mental images," including memories and desires. Mental images take the place of sensory input, creating a more or less coherent "after-death world of

---

[1]Rosenberg, *Thinking Clearly about Death*, 33.

mental images." This version of survival would permit the existence of more than one after-death world; indeed, it might permit the existence of many such image-worlds. Numerous discarnate minds, moreover, might communicate telepathically, within a shared image-world; thus, each image-world need not necessarily be wholly private, one for each discarnate mind.

The "next world," he writes, is "a kind of dream-world," a world in which disembodied human minds have experiences consisting of memory-generated mental images. The mental images that make up the Next World have no spatial relation to objects in the physical world: they are, he says, "in a space of their own." Nevertheless, they are as real as any objects in this world. Disembodied or discarnate beings—beings lacking bodies—would entertain mental images (visual, auditory, olfactory, and tactile) that would be real to those who have them and give the impression of perceiving physical objects. The matter of what is real and unreal is contextual, not a matter of physicality. Thus, he explains, "imaging" does the same work in the next world as perceiving does in this world. (One might compare this next world to the realm of Forms described in the *Phaedo*.)

Price suggests that the location of this world has nothing to do with a change of place but with a change of consciousness. He describes some general features of this image world, and also the disembodied human minds that inhabit it. "In" the Next World, a person's memories and at least some aspects of her or his personality will persist, and imaging, centered on a fundamental body image, would replace sense-perception.

Finally, Price's world of mental images need not be entirely "private," the product of one mind alone. It might be the joint product of many telepathically interacting minds, expressing desires and entertaining memories. Like-minded persons might be brought together by their memories and personalities, to constitute several such worlds, or perhaps even many of them. Thus, there might be many "semi-public" worlds, each of which is a world of intersubjective interactions and communication, just like the physical world.

Image-worlds are dependent on the memories and desires of the discarnate minds that inhabit those worlds, and these memories and desires, or at least many of them, will have arisen in this physical world. Thus, memories and desires from life in this physical world will, to a large extent, determine what sort of image-world the corresponding discarnate minds will experience. Many telepathically interacting minds, each expressing his or her own desires and memories, might in some cases give rise to affirmation and harmony. In other cases, though—cases involving perhaps desires and memories that have arisen for people in this life—they might give rise to recrimination and acute conflict among discarnate personalities. Thus, the Next World that Price imagines might provide some sort of reward or punishment for the moral choices we make in this world.

To describe this scenario as highly speculative would be an understatement. But Price believes that it is at least intelligible. If he has successfully described a version of discarnate survival, then, he argues, "supernormal" evidence for the survival hypothesis might be forthcoming.

I am here only concerned with the conception of Survival; with the *meaning* of the Survival Hypothesis, and not with its truth or falsity. When we consider the Survival Hypothesis, whether we believe it or disbelieve it, what is it that we have in mind? Can we form any idea, even a rough and provisional one, of what a disembodied human life might be like? Supposing we cannot, it will follow that what is called the Survival Hypothesis is a mere set of words and not a hypothesis at all. The evidence adduced in favor of it might still be evidence for something, and perhaps for something important, but we should no longer have the right to claim that it is evidence for Survival. There cannot be evidence for something which is completely unintelligible to us.

Now let us consider the situation in which we find ourselves after seventy years of psychical research. A very great deal of work has been done on the problem of Survival … Yet there are the widest differences of opinion about the result. A number of intelligent persons would maintain that we now have a very large mass of evidence in favor of Survival; that some of it is of very good quality indeed, and cannot be explained away unless we suppose that the supernormal cognitive powers of some embodied human minds are vastly more extensive and more accurate than we can easily believe them to be; in short, that on the evidence available the Survival Hypothesis is more probable than not. Some people—and not all of them are silly or credulous— would even maintain that the Survival Hypothesis is proved, or as near to being so as any empirical hypothesis can be. On the other hand, there are also many intelligent persons who entirely reject these conclusions. Some of them, no doubt, have not taken the trouble to examine the evidence.

But others of them have; they may even have given years of study to it. They would agree that the evidence is evidence of *something*, and very likely of something important. But, they would say, it cannot be evidence of Survival; there *must* be some alternative explanation of it, however difficult it may be to find out. Why do they take this line? I think it is because they find the very conception of Survival unintelligible. The very idea of a "discarnate human personality" seems to them a muddled or absurd one; indeed not an idea at all, but just a phrase—an emotionally exciting one, no doubt—to which no clear meaning can be given . . .

Now why should it be thought that the very idea of life after death is unintelligible? Surely it is easy enough to conceive (whether or not it is true) that experiences might occur after Jones's death which are linked with experiences which he had before his death, in such a way that his personal identity is preserved. But, it will be said, the idea of after-death *experiences* is just the difficulty. What kind of experiences could they conceivably be? In a disembodied state, the supply of sensory stimuli is perforce cut off, because the supposed experiment has no sense organs and no nervous system. There can therefore be no sense-perception. One has no means of being aware of material objects any longer; and if one has not, it is hard to see how one could have any emotions or wishes either. For all the emotions and wishes we have in this present life are concerned directly or indirectly with material objects, including of course our own organisms and other organisms, especially other human ones. In short, one could only be said to have experiences at all, if one is aware of some sort of a *world*. In this way, the idea of Survival is bound up with the idea of "another world" or a "next world." Anyone who maintains that the idea of Survival is after all intelligible must also be claiming that we can form some conception, however rough and provisional, of what "the next world" or "the other world" might be like . . .

The Next World, I think, might be conceived as a kind of dream-world. When we are asleep, sensory stimuli are cut off, or at any rate are prevented from having their normal effects upon our brain-centers. But we still manage to have experiences. It is true that sense-perception no longer occurs, but something sufficiently like it does. In sleep, our image-producing powers, which are more or less inhibited in waking life by a continuous bombardment of sensory stimuli, are released from this inhibition. And then we are provided with a multitude of objects of awareness, about which we employ our thoughts and towards which we have desires and emotions. Those objects which we are aware of behave in a way which seems very queer to us when we wake up. The laws of their behavior are not the laws of physics.

But however queer their behavior is, it does not at all disconcert us at the time, and our personal identity is not broken.

In other words, my suggestion is that the Next World, if there is one, might be a world of mental images. Nor need such a world be so "thin and unsubstantial" as you might think. Paradoxical as it may sound, there is nothing imaginary about a mental image. It is an actual entity, as real as anything can be. The seeming paradox arises from the ambiguity of the verb "to imagine." It does sometimes mean "to have mental images." But more usually it means "to entertain propositions without believing them," and very often they are false propositions, and moreover we disbelieve them in the act of entertaining them. This is what happens, for example, when we read Shakespeare's play *The Tempest,* and that is why we say that Prospero and Ariel are "imaginary characters." Mental images are not in this sense imaginary at all. We do actually experience them, and they are no more imaginary than sensations. To avoid the paradox, though at the cost of some pedantry, it would be well to distinguish between *imagining* and *imaging,* and to have two different adjectives "imaginary" and "imagy." In this terminology, it is imaging, and not imagining, that I wish to talk about; and the Next World, as I am trying to conceive of it, is an *imagy* world, but not on that account an imaginary one.

Indeed, to those who experience it an image-world would be just as "real" as this present world is; and perhaps so like it, that they would have considerable difficulty in realizing that they were dead. We are, of course, sometimes told in mediumistic communications that quite a lot of people do find it difficult to realize that they are dead; and this is just what we should expect if the Next World is an image-world . . . So far as I can see, there might be a set of visual images related to each other perspectively, with front views and side views and back views all fitting neatly together in the way that ordinary visual appearances do now. Such a group of images might contain tactual images too. Similarly it might contain auditory images and smell images. Such a family of inter-related images would make a pretty good object. It would be quite a satisfactory substitute for the material objects which we perceive in this present life. And a whole world composed of such families of mental images would make a perfectly good world.

It is possible, however, and indeed likely, that some of those images would be what Francis Galton called *generic* images. An image representing a dog or a tree need not necessarily be an exact replica of some individual dog or tree one has perceived. It might rather be a representation of a *typical* dog or tree. Our memories are more specific on some subjects than on others. How specific they are, depends probably on the degree of interest we had in the individual objects or events at the time when we perceived them … Left to our own resources, as we should be in the Other World, with nothing but our memories to depend on, we should probably be able to form only generic images of such objects. In this respect, an image-world would not be an exact replica of this one, not even of those parts of this one which we have actually perceived. To some extent it would be, so to speak, a generalized picture, rather than a detailed reproduction.

Let us now put our question in another way, and ask what kind of experience a disembodied human mind might be supposed to have. We can then answer that it might be an experience in which *imaging* replaces sense perception; "replaces" it, in the sense that imaging would perform much the same function as sense-perception performs now, by providing us with objects about which we could have thoughts, emotions, and wishes. There is no reason why we should not be "as much alive," or at any rate *feel* as much alive, in an image-world as we do now in this present material world, which we perceive by means of our sense organs and nervous systems. And so the use of the word "survival" ("life after death"") would be perfectly justifiable.

It will be objected, perhaps, that one cannot be said to be alive unless one has a body. But what is meant here by "alive"? It is surely conceivable (whether or not it is true) that *experiences* should occur which are not causally connected with a physical organism. If they did, should we or should we not say that "life" was occurring? I do not think it matters much whether we answer Yes or No. It is purely a question of definition. If you define "life" in terms of certain very complicated physico-chemical processes, as some people would, then of course life after death is by definition impossible, because there is no longer anything to be alive. In that case, the problem of survival (*life* after bodily death) is misnamed. Instead, it ought to be called the problem of after-death *experiences*. And this is in fact the problem with which all investigators of the subject have been concerned. After all, what people want to know, when they ask whether we survive death, is simply whether experiences occur after death, or what likelihood, if any, there is that they do; and whether such experiences, if they do occur, are linked with each other and with *ante mortem* ones in such a way that personal identity is preserved. It is not physico-chemical processes which interest us, when we ask such questions. But there is another sense of the words "life" and "alive" which may be called the psychological sense; and in this sense "being alive" just *means* "having experiences of certain sorts." In this psychological sense of the word "life" it is perfectly intelligible to ask whether there is life after death, even though life in the physiological sense does *ex hypothesi* come to an end when someone dies. Or, if you like, the question is whether one could *feel* alive after bodily death, even though (by hypothesis) one would not *be* alive at that time. It will be just enough to satisfy most of us if the *feeling* of being alive continues after death. It will not make a halfpennyworth of difference that one will not then *be* alive in the physiological or biochemical sense of the word.

It may be said, however, that "feeling alive" (life in the psychological sense) cannot just be equated with having experiences in general. Feeling alive, surely, consists in having experiences of a special sort, namely *organic sensations*— bodily feelings of various sorts. In our present experience, these bodily feelings are not as a rule separately attended to unless they are unusually intense or unusually painful. They are a kind of undifferentiated mass in the background of consciousness. All the same, it would be said, they constitute our feeling of being alive; and if they were absent (as surely they must be when the body is dead) the feeling of being alive could not be there.

I am not at all sure that this argument is as strong as it looks. I think we should still feel alive—or alive enough—provided we experienced emotions and wishes, even if no organic sensations accompanied these experiences, as they do now. But in case I am wrong here, I would suggest that *images* of organic sensations could perfectly well provide what is needed. We can quite well image to ourselves what it feels like to be in a warm bath, even when we are not actually in one; and a person who has been crippled can image what it felt like to climb a mountain. Moreover, I would ask whether we do not feel alive when we are dreaming. It seems to me that we obviously do—or at any rate we feel quite alive enough to go on.

This is not all. In an image-world, a dream-like world such as I am trying to describe, there is no reason at all why there should not be *visual* images resembling the body which one had in this present world. In this present life (for all who are not blind) visual percepts of one's own body form as it were the constant center of one's perceptual world. It is perfectly possible that visual images of one's own body might perform the same function in the next. They might form the continuing center or nucleus of one's image world, remaining more or less constant while other images altered. If this were so, we should have an additional reason for expecting that recently dead people would find it difficult to realize that they were dead, that is, disembodied. To all appearances they *would* have bodies just as they had before, and pretty much the same ones. But, of course, they might discover in time that these image-bodies were subject to rather peculiar causal laws. For example, it might be found that in an image world our wishes tend ipso facto to fulfill themselves in a way they do not now. A wish to go to Oxford might be immediately followed by the occurrence of a vivid and detailed set of Oxford-like images; even though, at the moment before, one's images had resembled Piccadilly Circus or the palace of the Dalai Lama in Tibet. In that case, one would realize that "going somewhere"—transferring one's body from one place to another—was a rather different process from what it had been in the physical world. Reflecting on such experiences, one might come to the conclusion that one's body was not after all the same as the physical body one had before death. One might conclude perhaps that it must be a "spiritual" or "psychical" body, closely resembling the old body in appearance, but possessed of rather different causal properties. It has been said, of course, that phrases like "spiritual body" or "psychical body" are utterly unintelligible, and that no conceivable empirical meaning could be given to such expressions. But I would suggest that they might be a way (rather a misleading way perhaps) of referring to a set of body-like images.

I think, then, that there is no difficulty in conceiving that the experience of feeling alive could occur in the absence of a physical organism; or, if you prefer to put it so, a disembodied personality could *be* alive in the psychological sense, even though by definition it would not be alive in the physiological or biochemical sense.

Moreover, I do not see why disembodiment need involve the destruction of personal identity. It is, of course, sometimes supposed that personal identity depends on the continuance of a background of organic sensation—the "mass of bodily feeling" mentioned before. (This may be called the Somato-centric Analysis of personal identity.) We must notice, however, that this background of organic sensation is not literally the same from one period of time to another. The very most that can happen is that the organic sensations which form the background of my experience now should be *exactly similar* to those which were the background of my experience a minute ago. And as a matter of fact the present ones need not *all* be exactly similar to the previous ones. I might have a twinge of toothache now which I did not have then. I may even have an overall feeling of lassitude now which I did not have a minute ago, so that the whole mass of bodily feeling, and not merely one part of it, is rather different; and this would not interrupt my personal identity at all. The most that is required is only that the majority (not all) of my organic sensations should be closely (not exactly) similar to those I previously had. And even this is only needed if the two occasions are close together in my private time series; the organic sensations I have now might well be very unlike those I used to have when I was one year old: I say "in my private time series." For when I wake up after eight hours of dreamless sleep my personal identity is not broken, though in the physical or public time series there has been a long interval between the last organic sensations I experienced before falling asleep, and the first ones I experience when I wake up. But if similarity, and not literal sameness, is all that is required of this "continuing organic background," it seems to me that the continuity of it could be perfectly well preserved if there were organic *images* after death very like the organic *sensations* which occurred before death.

As a matter of fact, this whole "somato-centric" analysis of personal identity appears to me highly disputable. I should have thought that Locke was much nearer the truth when he said that personal identity depends on memory. But I have tried to show that even if the "somato-centric" theory of personal identity is right, there is no reason why personal identity need be broken by bodily death, provided there are images after death which sufficiently resemble the organic sensations one had before; and this is very like what happens when one falls asleep and begins dreaming.

There is, however, another argument against the conceivability of a disembodied person, to which some present-day Linguistic Philosophers would attach great weight. It is neatly expressed by Mr. A.G.N. Flew when he says, "People are what you meet" . . .

As a matter of fact, however, we can quite easily conceive that "meeting" of a kind might still be possible between discarnate experiencers. And therefore, even if we do make it part of the definition of "a person," that he is capable of being met by others, it will still make sense to speak of "discarnate persons," provided we allow that telepathy is possible between them. It is true that a special sort of telepathy would be needed; the sort which in this life produces *telepathic apparitions*. It would not be sufficient that A's thoughts or emotions should be telepathically affected by B's. If such telepathy were sufficiently prolonged and continuous, and especially if it were reciprocal, it would indeed have some of the characteristics of social intercourse; but I do not think we should call it "meeting," at any rate in Mr. Flew's sense of the word. It would be necessary, in addition, that A should be aware of something which could be called "B's body," or should have an experience not too unlike the experience of *seeing* another person in this life. This additional condition would be satisfied if A experienced a telepathic apparition of B. It would be necessary, further, that the telepathic apparition by means of which B "announces himself" (if one may put it so) should be recognizably similar on different occasions. And if it were a case of meeting some person *again* whom one had previously known in this world, the telepathic apparition would have to be recognizably similar to the physical body which that person had when he was still alive.

There is no reason why an image-world should not contain a number of images which are telepathic apparitions; and if it did, one could quite intelligently speak of "meeting other persons" in such a world. All the experiences I have when I meet another person in this present life could still occur, with only this difference, that percepts would be replaced by images. It would also be possible for another person to "meet" me in the same manner, if I, as telepathic agent, could cause him to experience a suitable telepathic apparition, sufficiently resembling the body I used to have when he formerly "met" me in this life.

I now turn to another problem which may have troubled some of you. If there be a next world, *where* is it? . . . Surely the next world, if it exists, must be somewhere; and, yet, it seems, there is nowhere for it to be.

The answer to this difficulty is easy if we conceive of the Next World in the way I have suggested, as a dream-like world of mental images. Mental images, including dream images, are in a space of their own. They do have spatial properties. Visual images, for instance, have extension and shape, and they have spatial relations to one another. But they have no spatial relation to objects in the physical world. If I dream of a tiger, my tiger-image has extension and shape. The dark stripes have spatial relations to the yellow parts, and to each other; the nose has a spatial relation to the tail. Again, the tiger image as a whole may have spatial relations to another image in my dream, for example to an image resembling a palm tree. But suppose we have to ask how far it is from the foot of my bed, whether it is three inches long, or longer, or shorter; is it not obvious that these questions are absurd ones? We cannot answer them, not because we lack the necessary information or find it impracticable to make the necessary measurements, but because the questions themselves have no meaning. In the space of the physical world these images are nowhere at all. But in relation to other images of mine, each of them is somewhere. Each of them is extended, and its parts are in spatial relations to one another. There is no a priori reason why all extended entities must be in physical space.

If we now apply these considerations to the Next World, as I am conceiving of it, we see that the question "where is it?" simply does not arise. An image-world would have a space of its own. We could not find it anywhere in the space of the physical world, but this would not in the least prevent it from being a spatial world all the same. If you like, it would be its own "where" . . .

It follows that when we speak of "passing" from this world to the next, this passage is not to be thought of as any sort of movement in space. It should rather be thought of as a change of consciousness, analogous to the change which occurs when we "pass" from waking experience to dreaming. It would be a change from the perceptual type of consciousness to another type of consciousness in which perception ceases and imaging replaces it, but unlike the change from waking consciousness to dreaming in being irreversible . . .

I now turn to another difficulty. It may be felt that an image-world is somehow a deception and a sham, not a *real* world at all. I have said that it would be a kind of dream-world. Now when one has a dream in this life, surely the things one is aware of in the dream are not *real* things. No doubt the dreamer really does have various mental images. These images do actually occur. But this is not all that happens. As a result of having these images, the dreamer believes, or takes for granted, that various material objects exist and various physical events occur; and these beliefs are mistaken. For example, he believes that there is a wall in front of him and that by a mere effort of will he succeeds in flying over the top of it. But the wall did not really exist, and he did not really fly over the top of it. He was in a state of delusion. Because of the images which he did really have, there *seemed* to him to be various objects and events which did not really exist at all. Similarly, you may argue, it may *seem* to discarnate minds (if indeed there are such) that there is a world in which they live, and a world not unlike this one. If they have mental images of the appropriate sort, it may even *seem* to them that they have bodies not unlike the ones they had in this life. But surely they will be mistaken . . .

I would suggest, however, that this argument about the "delusiveness" or "unreality" of an image-world is based on a confusion.

One may doubt whether there is any clear meaning in using the words "real" and "unreal" *tout court*, in this perfectly general and unspecified way. One may properly say, "this is real silver, and that is not," "this is a real pearl and that is not;" or again "this is a real pool of water, and that is only a mirage." The point here is that something X is mistakenly believed to be something else Y, because it does resemble Y in some respects. It makes perfectly good sense, then, to say that X is not really Y. This piece of plated brass is not real silver, true enough. It only looks like silver. But for all that, it cannot be called "unreal" in the unqualified sense, in the sense of not existing at all. Even the mirage is something, though it is not the pool of water you took it to be. It is a perfectly good set of visual appearances, though it is not related to other appearances in the way you thought it was; for example, it does not have the relations to tactual appearances, or to visual appearances from other places, which you expected it to have. You may properly say that the mirage is not a real pool of water, or even that it is not a real physical object, and that anyone who thinks it is must be in a state of delusion. But there is no clear meaning in saying that it is just "unreal" *tout court,* without any further specification or explanation. In short, when the word "unreal" is applied to something, one means that it is different from something else, with which it might be mistakenly identified; what that something else is may not be explicitly stated, but it can be gathered from the context.

What, then, could people mean by saying that a next world such as I have described would be "unreal"? If they are saying anything intelligible, they must mean that it is different from something else, something else which it does resemble in some respects, and might therefore be confused with. And what is that something else? It is this present physical world in which we now live. An image-world, then, is only "unreal" in the sense that it is not really physical, though it might be mistakenly thought to be physical by some of those who experience it. But this only amounts to saying that the world I am describing would be an *other* world, other than this present physical world, which is just what it ought to be; other than this present physical world, and yet sufficiently like it to be possibly confused with it, because images do resemble percepts. And what would this otherness consist in? First, in the fact that it is in a *space* which is other than physical space; secondly, and still more important, in the fact that the *causal laws* of an image-world would be different from the laws of physics. And this is also our ground for saying that the events we experience in dreams are "unreal," that is, not really physical, though mistakenly believed by the dreamer to be so. They do in some ways closely resemble physical events, and that is why the mistake is possible. But the causal laws of their occurrence are quite different, as we recognize when we wake up; and just occasionally we recognize it even while we are still asleep . . .

Let us now try to explore the conception of a world of mental images a little more fully. Would it not be a *"subjective"* world? And surely there would be many *different* next worlds, not just one; and each of them would be private. Indeed, would there not be as many next worlds as there are discarnate minds, and each of them wholly private to the mind which experiences it? In short, it may seem that each of us, when dead, would have his own dream world, and there would be no common or public Next World at all.

"Subjective," perhaps, is rather a slippery word. Certainly, an image world would have to be subjective in the sense of being mind-dependent, dependent for its existence upon mental processes of one sort or another; images, after all, are mental entities. But I do not think that such a world need be completely private, if telepathy occurs in the next life … It is reasonable to suppose that in a disembodied state telepathy would occur more frequently than it does now. It seems likely that in this present life our telepathic powers are constantly being inhibited by our need to adjust ourselves to our physical environment. It even seems likely that many telepathic "impressions" which we receive at the unconscious level are shut out from consciousness by a kind of biologically-motivated censorship. Once the pressure of biological needs is removed, we might expect that telepathy would occur continually, and manifest itself in consciousness by modifying and adding to the images which one experiences. (Even in this life, after all, some dreams are telepathic.)

If this is right, an image-world such as I am describing would not be the product of one single mind only, nor would it be purely private. It would be the joint-product of a group of telepathically-interacting minds and public to all of them. Nevertheless, one would not expect it to have unrestricted publicity. It is likely that there would still be *many* next worlds, a different one for each group of like-minded personalities. I admit I am not quite sure what might be meant by "like-minded" and "unlike-minded" in this connection. Perhaps we could say that two personalities are like-minded if their memories or their characters are sufficiently similar. It might be that Nero and Marcus Aurelius do not have a world in common, but Socrates and Marcus Aurelius do.

So far, we have a picture of many "semi-public" next worlds, if one may put it so; each of them composed of mental images, and yet not wholly private for all that, but public to a limited group of telepathically-interacting minds. Or, if you like, after death everyone does have his own dream, but there is still some overlap between one person's dream and another's, because of telepathy.

I have said that such a world would be mind-dependent, even though dependent on a group of minds rather than a single mind. In what way would it be mind-dependent? Presumably in the same way as dreams are now. It would be dependent on the *memories* and the *desires* of the persons who experienced it. Their memories and their desires would determine what sort of images they had. If I may put it so, the "stuff" or "material" of such a world would come in the end from one's memories, and the "form" of it from one's desires. To use another analogy, memory would provide the pigments, and desire would paint the picture. One might expect, I think, that desires which had been unsatisfied in one's earthly life would play an especially important part in the process. That may seem an agreeable prospect. But there is another which is less agreeable. Desires which had been *repressed* in one's earthly life, because it was too painful or too disgraceful to admit that one had them, might also play a part, and perhaps an important part, in determining what images one would have in the next. And the same might be true of repressed memories. It may be suggested that what Freud (in one stage of his thought) called "the censor"—the force or barrier or mechanism which keeps some of our desires and memories out of consciousness, or only lets them in when they disguise themselves in symbolic and distorted forms—operates only in this present life and not in the next. However we conceive of "the censor," it does seem to be a device for enabling us to adapt ourselves to our environment. And when we no longer have an environment, one would expect that the barrier would come down.

We can now see that an after-death world of mental images can also be quite reasonably described in the terminology of the Hindu thinkers as "a world of desire" (*Kama Loka*). Indeed, this is just what we should expect if we assume that dreams, in this present life, are the best available clue to what the next life might be like. Such a world could also be described as "a world of memories"; because imaging, in the end, is a function of memory, one of the ways in which our memory-dispositions manifest themselves. But this description would be less apt, even though correct as far as it goes. To use the same rather inadequate language as before, the "materials" out of which an image-world is composed would have to come from the memories of the mind or group of minds whose world it is. But it would be their desires (including those repressed in earthly life) which determined the ways in which these memories were used, the precise kind of dream which was built up out of them or on the basis of them.

It will, of course, be objected that memories cannot exist in the absence of a physical brain, nor yet desires, nor images either. But this proposition, however plausible, is after all just an empirical hypothesis, not a necessary truth. Certainly there is empirical evidence in favor of it. But there is also empirical evidence against it. Broadly speaking one might say, perhaps, that the "normal" evidence tends to support this Materialistic or Epiphenomenalist[2] theory of memories, images, and desires, whereas the "supernormal" evidence on the whole tends to weaken the Materialist or Epiphenomenalist theory of human personality (of which this hypothesis about the brain-dependent character of memories, images and desires is a part). Moreover, any evidence which directly supports the Survival Hypothesis (and there is quite a lot of evidence which does, provided we are prepared to admit that the Survival Hypothesis is intelligible at all) is to that extent evidence against the Materialistic conception of human personality.

In this lecture, I am not of course trying to argue in favor of the Survival Hypothesis. I am only concerned with the more modest task of trying to make it intelligible. All I want to maintain, then, is that there is nothing self-contradictory or logically absurd in the hypothesis that memories, desires, and images can exist in the absence of a physical brain. The hypothesis may, of course, be false. My point is only that it is not absurd; or, if you like, that it is at any rate intelligible, whether true or not.

---

[2]In the philosophy of mind, *epiphenomenalism* is the view that physical events cause all mental events, but that mental events can cause neither physical events nor other mental events. Thus, according to this view, memories cannot cause other mental events. Epiphenomenalism, then, conflicts with Price's account of an image-world of telepathically communicating discarnate personalities. —MM

13

Persons and the Metaphysics of Resurrection

Lynne Rudder Baker

The late Lynne Rudder Baker (1944–2017), a distinguished professor of philosophy at the University of Massachusetts Amherst, made important contributions to metaphysics, philosophy of mind, and philosophy of religion. In our next reading, she writes that she wants to "focus on the Christian doctrine of resurrection, and to find the best metaphysics to support it." For Christians and others, resurrection is a miracle. If this is the case, as Scripture indicates, then we cannot expect a full philosophical or scientific explanation of resurrection; rather, "the best we can hope for is a metaphysics consistent with and congenial to the doctrine [of resurrection]." Like H.H. Price and other recent philosophers of religion, then, Baker agrees that "the best that metaphysics can do is to show how resurrection is metaphysically possible," even if, as a supernatural phenomenon (Price) or a miracle (Baker), it defies physics.

   As we have seen, when it comes to the doctrine of resurrection and to accounts of afterlife more broadly, much depends on how one conceives of whatever it is that is supposed to survive death. Baker writes that where dualists see a relation between minds and bodies, she sees a relation between persons and bodies.

   The defining characteristic of a person, she writes, is not just being conscious but having what she calls *a first-person perspective*: if "one can think about oneself as oneself and think about one's thoughts as one's own," she writes, then one is a person. Baker agrees with dualists like Plato and Descartes that persons are not identical to their bodies—they could have bodies different from the ones they happen to have. As she puts it, a person is not a biological "genus" (or category). Nevertheless, she agrees with the materialists that persons necessarily "come with" bodies: they are necessarily embodied. In her view, then, a person is not identical to a body; nevertheless, a body constitutes a person, in a way that she explains. This is her "constitution view" of persons.

In the second half of the paper, Baker argues the merits of the constitution view when it comes to Christian resurrection. The Christian doctrine, she says, requires that three conditions be met: (i) the very same person who exists on earth is to exist in an afterlife; (ii) the person must, at least ultimately, have some kind of bodily life after death; and (iii) the soul is not naturally immortal (and so, as mentioned above, resurrection is a miracle). Baker lists seven candidates for a metaphysics of resurrection, and then examines them at closer quarters, one-by-one, arguing that the constitution view is the only candidate that meets her three requirements for Christian resurrection.

Human persons are not just pure subjects, as Descartes viewed them, or as the Katha Upanishad describes the all-knowing self. Rather, human persons are distinguished from other kinds of persons because they are "constituted by" human bodies. Thus, for Baker, a person has two essential properties: *embodiment* and *a first-person perspective*. Embodiment, however, does not imply that a person must always be constituted by the same body that she was born with.

Let us note that the view of resurrection that Baker defends is compatible with bodily resurrection on Earth. Thus, her view has the advantage that it could answer the *Where?* question that the survival hypothesis raises regarding the whereabouts of the afterlife.

"But what, then, am I?" Descartes famously asked. Although many of us today reject Descartes' equally famous answer –"I am an immaterial mind"— Descartes was right, I believe, to identify himself with a thinking thing, a thing who "doubts, understands, affirms, denies, wills, refuses, and which also imagines and senses."[1] But neither an immaterial mind nor a material

---

[1]Rene Descartes, *Meditations on First Philosophy*, trans. Donald A. Cress (Indianapolis: Hackett Publishing Co., 1979), 19.

brain is the thing that thinks. The thing that thinks is the person. Just as your legs and feet are the limbs by means of which you walk, you the person—not your legs and feet—are the walker; so too the brain is the organ by means of which you think, but you the person—not your brain—are the thinker.

Where Cartesians see a relation between minds and bodies, I see a relation between persons and bodies. Understanding "person" to refer to entities like you and me, it is obvious that persons exist. And just as clearly there are bodies. So, the important philosophical question—whose answer cannot be read off neuro- physiology or scientific psychology—is this: What is a person? What is the relation between a person and her body?[2]

On the answer that I shall propose—I call it "the constitution view"—persons are not identical to their bodies, nor to parts of their bodies (e.g. brains), nor to their bodies plus something else (e.g. immaterial souls). In "logical space" there is room for another possibility, which I shall develop and defend. I shall explore the idea that a person is constituted by a body, where constitution is not identity. On such a constitutional account of persons and bodies, it is necessary that human persons are embodied; but it is not necessary that they have the bodies that they in fact have. Thus, the view that I shall develop shares with the Cartesian dualist the claim that persons are not identical to their bodies (I could have a different body from the one that I do have), and it shares with the classical materialist the claim that, necessarily, human persons are embodied. After setting out this constitution view, I shall turn to the metaphysics of resurrection.

First, let me comment on the term "human being." Some philosophers use "'human being" to denote a biological kind.[3] Others use it to denote a partly psychological kind.[4] I use "human being" in the latter way, to name a partly psychological kind, a human person. All human persons are human beings, and vice versa.

---

[2]Peter van Inwagen has argued that many philosophical uses of "her body" are nonsensical. "Philosophers and the Words 'Human Body'," in Peter van Inwagen (ed.), *Time and Cause* (Dordrecht: Reidel, 1980), 283–99. Michael Tye offers a rebuttal in "In Defense of the Words 'Human Body'," in *Philosophical Studies* 38 (1980): 177–82. I take a human organism to be a kind of body. Wherever I use the term "human body," the reader may substitute the term "human organism." My concern is with the relation between human persons and human organisms (i.e., human bodies).

[3]For example, John Perry says that "'human being" is a purely biological notion. John Perry, "The Importance of Being Identical," in Amelie Oksenberg Rorty (ed.), *The Identities of Persons* (Berkeley: University of California Press, 1976), 70.

[4]For example, Mark Johnston says: "'Human being' names a partly psychological kind, whereas 'human organism' … names a purely biological kind." Mark Johnston, "Human Beings," *Journal of Philosophy* 84 (1987): 64.

The constitution view of human persons

What makes a human person a *person* is having what I'll call a "first-person perspective." What makes a human person *human* is being constituted by a human body.

A first-person perspective is the defining characteristic of all persons, human or not.[5] From a (robust) first-person point of view, one can think about oneself as oneself and think about one's thoughts as one's own. In English, we not only use first-person pronouns to refer to ourselves "from the inside" so to speak (e.g. "I'm happy") but also to attribute to ourselves first-person reference (e.g. "I wonder whether I'll be happy in ten years"). The second occurrence of "I" in "I wonder whether I'll be happy in ten years" directs attention to the person *per se,* without recourse to any name, description, or other third-person referential device to identify who is being thought about. The first-person perspective opens up a distinction between thinking of oneself in the first person and thinking of oneself in the third person. Once someone can make this distinction, she can think of herself as a subject in a world of things different from herself. And since human persons are necessarily embodied, a person can think of her body, as well as her thoughts, from her first-person perspective.

A being may be conscious without having a first-person perspective. Non-human primates and other higher animals are conscious, and they have psychological states like believing, fearing, and desiring. They have points of view (e.g. "'danger in that direction"), but they cannot conceive of themselves as the subjects of such thoughts. They cannot *conceive of* themselves in the first person. (We have every reason to think that they do not wonder how they will die.) So, being conscious, having psychological states like beliefs and desires, and having a point of view are not sufficient conditions for being a person.

To be a person—whether God, an angel, a human person, or a Martian person—one must have a first-person perspective. *Person* is a non-biological genus, of which there may be several species: human, divine,

---

[5]I give an account of the conditions under which something has a first-person perspective in Lynne Rudder Baker, *Persons and Bodies: A Constitution View* (Cambridge: Cambridge University Press, 2000).

bionic, Martian, etc. It is in virtue of having a first-person perspective that an entity is a person. So, what makes something a person is not the "stuff" it is made of. It does not matter whether something is made of organic material or silicon or, in the case of God, no material "stuff" at all. In short, *person* is an ontological kind whose defining characteristic is a first-person perspective.

Babies are not born with the kind of *robust* first-person perspective that I have been describing, but they are born with what I call "rudimentary first-person perspectives": they are sentient; they imitate; they behave in ways which require attribution of beliefs and desires to explain. An organism comes to constitute a person when it develops a *rudimentary* first-person perspective, provided that the organism is of a kind that normally develops a robust first-person perspective. Human babies are persons in virtue of having rudimentary first-person perspectives and of being members of the human species. Members of the human species—unlike non-human animals who may also have rudimentary first-person perspectives—normally develop robust first-person perspectives as they mature and learn a language. A human organism that has a rudimentary or a robust first-person perspective at time *t* constitutes a person at time *t*.[6]

At the other end of human life, a person who becomes demented still has a first-person perspective. Patients who are severely mentally handicapped (e.g. with late Alzheimer's disease) still can conceive of themselves as "I." If you think that you don't exist (Cotard's syndrome), you have a first-person perspective. Your existence on earth comes to an end with the *permanent and irretrievable* loss of the ability to think of yourself from the first person. As long as it is physically possible for a patient (even in a coma) to regain the ability to think of herself in the first-person way, there is a person. When the physical possibility of that ability is forever lost (as in the case of Terry Schiavo), but the brain stem is still functioning, then there is no person there, but only an organism.

A first-person perspective is the basis of all self-consciousness. It makes possible an inner life, a life of thoughts that one realizes are one's own. The appearance of first-person perspectives in a world makes an ontological difference in that world: a world populated with beings with inner lives is

---

[6]For details on the idea of a rudimentary first-person perspective, as well as a defense of the idea based on evidence from developmental psychology, see Lynne Rudder Baker, "When Does a Person Begin?" *Social Philosophy and Policy* 22 (2005): 25–48.

ontologically richer than a world populated with no beings with inner lives. But what is ontologically distinctive about being a person—namely, a first-person perspective—does not have to be secured by an immaterial substance like a soul.

Human persons differ from non-bodily or immaterial persons (if there are any) in that human persons are not just pure subjects; they do not exist unembodied. So, myself includes my body. And persons' bodies are the objects of first-person reference. If Smith wonders whether she has cancer, she is wondering about her body from a first-person perspective. She is not wondering whether there is a malignant tumor in some particular body identified by a third-person demonstrative pronoun or description; she is wondering whether there is a malignant tumor in her own body, considered as herself. This is different from wondering about a material possession, say. If Smith wonders whether her car will run, she wonders about a particular car, which she identifies by a description or a third-person demonstrative reference. Without a third-person way to think about the car, she could not wonder about its battery. But if Smith *is* wondering how she will die, she can think of her body as her own without recourse to any name or description or second- or third-person demonstrative pronoun. And reference without recourse to the familiar third-person devices is the mark of first-person reference.

Human persons—who, like all persons, have first-person perspectives— are distinguished from other kinds of persons in that human persons are constituted by human bodies that are the objects of their first-person thoughts. A human person is a person who is constituted by a human body during some part of her existence. (I say "is constituted by a human body during some part of her existence" to avoid issues raised by the Incarnation. The orthodox Christian view is that the eternal second person of the Trinity is identical with Jesus Christ, who is both fully human and fully divine. How this could be so is ultimately a mystery that requires special treatment far beyond the scope of this paper.)

Putting that issue aside, a human person is constituted by a biological entity—an organism, a member of the species *homo sapiens*—that is physically able to support first-person intentional states.[7] (It is up to

---

[7] Unlike David Wiggins, I do not distinguish between an animal and an animal body. In David Wiggins *Sameness and Substance* (Oxford: Basil Blackwell, 1980), 167, he says, "My claim is that by *person* we mean *a certain sort of animal.*" Then, he distinguishes the animal (that I supposedly am) from the body (that supposedly constitutes it). On the other hand, I think that an animal *is* (identical

neuro-scientists, not philosophers, to determine the biological conditions under which a human being is able to support first-person intentional states.)

A human person—Smith, say—must have a biological body that she can think about in a first-person way. Smith can think of a biological body in the first-person way if she can entertain thoughts about that body without aid of a name, or description, or third-person pronoun. Even if she is totally paralyzed, Smith has a first-person relation to her body if she can entertain the thought, "I wonder if I'll ever be able to move my legs again." To put it differently, Smith can think of a biological body in the first-person way if she can conceive of its properties as her own. For example, Smith's thoughts about how photogenic she (herself) is, or her worries about her (own) state of health—thoughts that she would express with first-person pronouns—make first-person reference to her body as her own. Since a body constitutes a person, a first-person reference to one's body is *ipso* facto a first-person reference to oneself.

So, what makes a particular body Smith's, rather than someone else's, is that it is the body that Smith can think of and refer to in a first-person way, "from the inside." The body to which Smith has a first-person relation is the body some of whose parts she (normally) can move without moving anything else, the body that she tends when she is in pain, and the body that expresses her intentional states. States like pain, longing, sadness, hope, fear, frustration, worry, effort, and joy as well as states like believing, desiring, and intending are expressed through posture, facial expression, sounds, and other bodily motions.

The body that expresses Smith's intentional states is the body to which Smith has a first-person relation. Smith's first-person relation to her body at t does not imply that Smith is actually thinking of her body at t; indeed, Smith may believe at t that she is disembodied. The body to which Smith has a first-person relation is the body whose sweaty hands manifest the fact that Smith is nervous, and the body whose stomach's being tied in knots expresses the fact that Smith is frightened, or the body that would move if Smith carried out her decision to leave the room. Smith's body at time t distinguishes Smith from all other persons at t. What distinguishes me now from all other

---

to) a body of a special self-sustaining and self-organizing sort, and I distinguish the animal/body from the person. Also, I take an animal to be a member of its species whether it is alive or dead. How could an animal lose species-membership on dying? It simply becomes a dead member of its species. See Fred Feldman, *Confrontations with the Reaper* (New York: Oxford University Press, 1992).

coexisting persons—even physical and psychological replicas of me, if there are any—is that at this time, I have a first-person relation to this body and to no other; and any replica of me at this time has a first-person relation to some other body, but not to this one.

The body to which I have a first-person relation constitutes me. But what is constitution? Elsewhere,[8] I have a more rigorous account of the relation of constitution, but the general idea of constitution is this: when various things are in various circumstances, new things—new kinds of things, with new causal powers—come into existence. Every concrete object is of (what I call) a primary kind. A thing has its primary-kind property essentially. So, kind membership (or species membership) is not contingent. The relation of constitution unites things of different primary kinds, and hence things with different essential properties. For example, a human organism is essentially a member of the human species; a person essentially has a first-person perspective.[9] A human person is a person constituted by a human organism.

Constitution is everywhere: pieces of paper constitute dollar bills; strands of DNA constitute genes; pieces of cloth constitute flags; pieces of bronze constitute statues. Constitution is never identity: the piece of cloth that constituted the first Union Flag could exist in a world without nations; hence that piece of cloth could exist without constituting a flag, and the first Union Flag is not identical to the piece of cloth that constituted it. Similarly, the piece of bronze that constituted Myron's statue Discobolus could have existed in a world without art; hence that piece of bronze could have existed without constituting a statue.[10]

The non-identity of persons and their bodies may be seen in another way—in a way that has no parallel for statues. Despite the similarities between persons and statues, there is a major difference between them: Persons have bodies that change drastically over the course of a person's life,

---

[8]"Unity without Identity: A New Look at Material Constitution," in Peter A. French and Howard K. Wettstein (eds), *New Directions in Philosophy*, Midwest Studies in Philosophy 23 (Malden, MA: Blackwell Publishers, Inc., 1999), 144–65. For a related view, see Wiggins, *Sameness and Substance*.
[9]Here I am not talking about entities that are human organisms or persons derivatively. An entity *x* has F derivatively only if *x* has F in virtue of its constitution-relations. See Baker, *Persons and Bodies*, chapter 2.
[10]For detailed arguments against the view that Discobolus and that piece of bronze that constituted it are identical (contingently or necessarily), see Lynne Rudder Baker, "Why Constitution Is Not Identity," *The Journal of Philosophy* 94 (1997): 599–622.

but pieces of marble that constitute statues change very little. To put it the other way around: if the piece of marble that constitutes Michelangelo's David were to change significantly, the statue David would no longer exist; but Smith's body alters radically while Smith endures.

Leaving aside the analogy between persons and statues, consider another argument against the person/ body identity theory, based on criteria for individuating bodies and persons. Criteria of individuation may be vague, but they are not totally elastic. Smith's body is a human body in virtue of being a member of the species *homo sapiens*. What makes something a human body are its biological properties; its career may be followed from beginning to end without respect to whether or not it is any person's body. Similarly, its persistence conditions are independent of whether or not it is any person's body. The identity of a human body is independent of whether it is Smith's or any other person's body.[11]

In the natural course of things, our organic bodies undergo full atomic replacement over some years, and we persons survive this total replacement without interruption in mental functioning. It seems possible that we could equally survive gradual replacement of organic cells by bionic cells—until finally the body that sustains us is no longer an organic body. Exactly how much replacement of parts a human body may undergo and still remain a *human* body is somewhat vague, but if a body is mostly made up of inorganic material and is not sustained by organic processes, it is not a member of the species *homo sapiens*. The non-organic body that ends up constituting Smith now is a different body from the organic body that was a member of the species *homo sapiens*.

Consider the organic body that Smith was born with. Call it "OB." Suppose that the organs of OB were totally replaced over a period of time by bionic parts, until what remained was a fully bionic, non-biological body that resembled OB in appearance, that moved in ways indistinguishable from OB, that emitted sounds that we took to be English sentences that reported memories of things that had happened to Smith, and indeed that we took to be professions that this person was Smith. Is the bionic body the same body as Smith's biological body OB? No. OB was a carbon-based body

---

[11]Moreover, since organisms do not lose their membership in their species at death, a human body remains a human body whether alive or dead. In an ordinary, nonviolent death, one and the same human body persists through the change: it is first alive, and then it is dead.

that was a member of the species *homo sapiens*. The bionic body is not a member of any biological species. Would Smith still exist? Of course. Otherwise Smith's possessions and property should be taken from the bionic-body-Smith and distributed to Smith's heirs. After the organ replacement, Smith would still exist but would no longer be constituted by OB; rather, Smith would be constituted by a bionic body. (I really do not like bizarre thought-experiments, but I think that we are actually close to bringing this thought experiment to fruition. There are now devices implanted in brains that allow paralyzed people to operate computers by their thoughts, cochlear implants allow deaf people to "'hear," and so on. Moreover, it's easy to imagine billionaires seeking "whole-body" replacements to prevent ageing.)

The point is that this is a realistic example that shows that a single person may be constituted by different bodies at different times: Smith had a first-person relation to a biological body at one time, and to a bionic body at a later time, and a biological body is essentially organic, and is not numerically identical to any bionic body. Note that spatio-temporal continuity in general does not signal sameness of entity: Very slowly, atoms could be added or taken away from Smith's biological body until it was indistinguishable from a turnip or a bookcase. In that case, it would no longer be the same body, and presumably Smith would no longer be with us. Indeed, there may be a period of time during which it is indeterminate whether there is a human body or not. I have argued elsewhere that everything that we encounter in the natural world comes into existence gradually; hence, everything that we interact with has vague temporal boundaries.

To sum up: on the constitution view, a human person is constituted by a particular biological body, but the person is not identical to the body. What distinguishes persons from all other beings is that they have first-person perspectives essentially. The persistence conditions of a human person are determined by the property in virtue of which she is a person—viz. the property of having a first-person perspective: a human person could cease to have an organic body without ceasing to exist. But she could not cease to be a person without ceasing to exist.

On the constitution view, then, a human person and the organic body that constitutes her differ in persistence conditions without there being any actual physical intrinsic difference between them. The persistence conditions of animals—all animals, human or not—are biological; and the persistence conditions of persons—all persons, human or not—are not biological.

On the metaphysics of resurrection

All the great monotheistic religions—Judaism, Christianity, and Islam—have doctrines of an afterlife. These are religious doctrines, whose grounding in scripture and tradition leaves open how they should be understood metaphysically. I want to focus on the Christian doctrine of resurrection, and to find the best metaphysics to support it.

To begin, consider three features that characterize the Christian view of resurrection.

First, identity: the very same person who exists on earth is to exist in an afterlife. Individuals exist after death, not in some undifferentiated state merged with the universe, or with an eternal mind, or anything else. Not only is there to be individual existence in the resurrection, but *the very same individuals* are to exist both now and after death. "Survival" in some weaker sense of, say, psychological similarity is not enough. The relation between a person here and now and a person in an afterlife must be identity.

Second, embodiment: resurrection requires some kind of bodily life after death. Post-mortem bodies are different from pre-mortem bodies in that they are said to be "spiritual," "incorruptible," or "glorified." Even if there is an "intermediate state" between death and a general resurrection, in which the soul exists disembodied, those who live after death will ultimately be embodied, according to Christian doctrine.

Third, miracle: life after death, according to Christian doctrine, is a gift from God. Christian doctrine thus contrasts with the Greek idea of immortality as a natural property of the soul. The idea of miracle is built into the Christian doctrine of life after death from the beginning. Since resurrection, if it occurs, is miraculous, we cannot expect a full philosophical account or explanation of it. There will always be some mystery left. The best that we can hope for is a metaphysics consistent with and congenial to the doctrine.

The task for a metaphysics of resurrection is to present a view of human persons whose persistence conditions allow, by means of a miracle, for post-mortem as well as pre-mortem life. The best that metaphysics can do is to show how resurrection is metaphysically possible. That is, any candidate for a metaphysics of resurrection must conceive of human persons in such a way that it is metaphysically possible (even if physically impossible) that one and the same person whose earthly body is corruptible may also exist with a post-mortem body that is incorruptible. That is the task. I shall argue that the constitution view fares better than its competitors in fulfilling that task.

There are a number of candidates for a metaphysics of resurrection:

1 Immaterialism: sameness of person is sameness of soul both before and after death.
2 Animalism: sameness of person is sameness of living organism before and after death.
3 Thomism:[12] sameness of person is sameness of body/soul composite before and after death.
4 The memory criterion, according to which pre- and post-mortem persons are the same person if and only if they are psychologically continuous.
5 The soul-as-software view, according to which sameness of person is analogous to sameness of software.
6 The soul-as-information-bearing-pattern view, according to which sameness of person is sameness of pattern of information.
7 The constitution view, which I explained earlier.

Let's consider each of these.

Immaterialism

Although souls in this world are linked to brains, there is no contradiction, according to Richard Swinburne, in the soul's continuing to exist without a body. Indeed, the soul is the necessary core of a person which must continue if a person is to continue.[13] Since, on Swinburne's view, no natural laws govern what happens to souls after death, there would be no violation of natural law if God were to give to souls life after death, with or without a new body. Swinburne solves the problem of personal identity for this world and the next by appeal to immaterial souls.

There is a metaphysical problem with immaterialism: in virtue of what is a soul the same soul both before and after death? Perhaps the best answer is that souls are individuated by having a "thisness" or haecceity.[14] This is an

---

[12]The relevant view of Thomas Aquinas, discussed in the reading above. —MM
[13]Richard Swinburne, *The Evolution of the Soul* (Oxford: Oxford University Press, 1997), 146.
[14]*Haecceity*, a term from medieval scholastic philosophy, names the alleged property by virtue of which something is a unique or individual thing. —MM

intriguing suggestion that I cannot pursue here. An haecceity view, if otherwise satisfactory, may well be suitable as a metaphysics of resurrection—if it did not leave dangling the question of why resurrection should be bodily.

However, I believe that immaterialism should be rejected. My reason for rejecting immaterialism has less to do with resurrection than with the natural world. Immaterial souls just do not fit with what we know about the natural world. We human persons evolved by natural selection (even if God actualized this world on the basis of His foreknowledge of the outcome). Immaterial souls would simply stand out as surds[15] in the natural world.

Someone may object: "If you dismiss immaterial *souls* on the grounds that they would be surds, then you should dismiss resurrection too. Resurrected persons *would* surely be surds if immaterial souls are." This objection can be met: My opposition to souls concerns their putative existence in the natural world. Resurrected persons, by contrast to immaterial souls, would not be surds in the natural world, because resurrection is not part of the natural order in the first place. Resurrection involves miracles, and miracles require God's specific intervention. We human persons—who, as I mentioned, evolved by natural selection—are part of the natural order, but immaterial souls are not. At least, I do not see how immaterial entities (unlike first-person perspectives, whose evolutionary roots can be seen in chimpanzees) could have evolved by natural selection.

Animalism

According to animalism, a human person is identical to a human animal. Therefore, animalists hold, a human person has the same persistence conditions as a human animal. If animalism is correct, then the story about Smith's having a biological body at one time and a distinct bionic body at another time is incoherent: on the animalist conception, no human person can have numerically distinct bodies at different times. I believe that this disqualifies animalism as part of a metaphysics of resurrection. Here's why.

If any sort of animalism is true, then a human person has her human body essentially. Her body changes cells, size, and shape, but the human person is nothing but that (changing) body. If her body went permanently out of existence, then that person would go permanently out of existence.

---

[15]Irrational things, or things lacking sense. —MM

Here is a simple argument to show that a biological body is not identical to a resurrection body.

Let h be your human biological body, the one that you have now. Let b be your spiritual body, the one that you have in the resurrection. Then:

(1) h is corruptible.
(2) b is incorruptible.
(3) Whatever is corruptible is essentially corruptible.
So, (4) $h \neq b$.

Both the second and third premises may seem open to challenge. Consider the second premise. Someone may hold that resurrection bodies are not really in- corruptible; they remain corruptible, but God just prevents them from actual decay.[16] I have a couple of responses.

First, the suggestion that your resurrection body is the same body as your corruptible earthly body raises the well-known problems of reassembly of earthly bodies that, prior to resurrection, have burned to ashes or decayed or been eaten by animals.[17] I have been convinced by Peter van Inwagen that God could not restore a particular body by reassembling the particles formerly in the body.[18] And the other suggestions about how an earthly body could survive to be a resurrection body without reassembly (Dean Zimmerman's and Van Inwagen's)[19] seem to me much less plausible than the constitution view.

The next response to the claim that resurrection bodies are not incorruptible comes from Paul, who in *I Corinthians* 15, calls resurrection bodies "incorruptible" or "imperishable" or "spiritual," depending on the translation. In *The New English Bible*, Paul says: "What I mean, my brothers, is this: flesh and blood can never possess the kingdom of God, and the perishable cannot possess immortality" (*I Corinthians* 15.50). Although I am leery of proof-texts, Paul's words clearly suggest that resurrection bodies

---

[16]This is a suggestion of David Hershenov's. Hershenov defends a reassembly conception of resurrection.
[17]But see David B. Hershenov, "The Metaphysical Problem of Intermittent Existence and the Possibility of Resurrection," *Faith and Philosophy* 20 (2003): 89–100, and his "Van Inwagen, Zimmerman, and the Materialist Conception of Resurrection," *Religious Studies* 38 (2002): 11–19.
[18]Peter van Inwagen, "The Possibility of Resurrection," in *International Journal for Philosophy of Religion* 9 (1978). Reprinted in Paul Edwards (ed.) *Immortality* (New York: Macmillan, 1992), 242–46.
[19]Dean Zimmerman, "The Compatibility of Materialism and Survival: The 'Falling Elevator' Model," *Faith and Philosophy* 16 (1999): 194–212, and Van Inwagen, "The Possibility of Resurrection."

are not identical to earthly bodies—despite the tradition to the contrary. So, I stand by the second premise: resurrection bodies are incorruptible.

Now consider the third premise. You may think that God, in His omnipotence, could transform a corruptible body into an incorruptible body. I agree. But the transformation would be what Aristotle and Aquinas call a substantial change. The incorruptible body would not be identical to the corruptible body from whence it came. Why not? A corruptible body has different persistence conditions from an incorruptible body. A corruptible body would go completely out of existence under different circumstances from an incorruptible body. Since things have their persistence conditions essentially, a single body cannot change its persistence conditions; so, a single body cannot be corruptible at one time and incorruptible at another time.[20]

To put it another way: earthly bodies are organisms, and organisms are essentially carbon-based. Anything that is carbon-based is corruptible. So, anything that is incorruptible is not carbon-based, and is not an organism, not a human biological body. Since resurrection bodies are incorruptible, they are not carbon- based and hence not identical to organisms, human biological bodies.

God could transform your human body into a resurrection body in the same way that He transformed Lot's wife into a pillar of salt. The pillar of salt, which is not organic, is not identical to Lot's wife's body, which is essentially organic. (Nor, of course, is the pillar of salt identical to Lot's wife.) Nothing that is a pillar of salt is identical to Lot's wife's body. Similarly, if God changed your human biological body into a resurrection body, the resurrection body would not be identical to your human biological body. So, if animalism (or Thomism, for that matter) is true, you would not exist in the resurrection.

If my argument here is correct, then no view of human persons (Like animalism or Thomism) that construes a person's corruptible body to be essential to her is consistent with the doctrine of bodily resurrection.

---

[20]Although I am not considering four-dimensionalism [the philosophical position that an object's persistence through time is importantly like its extension through space —MM] here, a four-dimensionalist may hold that a single person could have corruptible temporal parts during part of her existence and incorruptible temporal parts during another part of her existence. Although so far, your temporal parts are all corruptible, after your death, God could make an incorruptible body and freely decree it to be a temporal pan of your body. Then, in the sense that a four-dimensionalist construes "same body"—that is, as being a sequence of temporal parts—you would have (or rather, be) the same body in the resurrection that you have now. Perhaps so, but there are other reasons beyond the scope of this paper for Christians to reject four-dimensionalism.

Thomism

Thomism takes over Aristotle's notion of a human being as a substance for which the body supplies the matter and the soul supplies the form. According to Thomas [Aquinas], then, a human being is a composite of a rational soul (form) and a body (matter). The human being is a substance; the rational soul is not—it is a substantial form that nonetheless can "subsist" on its own. Before the general resurrection, people who have died are in an "intermediate state," during which the human being (the substance) does not exist. What continues through the intermediate state is the rational soul that subsists (disembodied) until reunited with the body, at which time the human being is recovered.

I think that there are two difficulties with Thomism, considered as a metaphysics of resurrection. The first is the same as with animalism: Thomas requires that a person's resurrection body be numerically identical to his or her earthly body. But (as we just reflected) resurrection bodies and earthly biological bodies have different persistence conditions, and are thus not numerically identical.

The second difficulty is how to individuate disembodied souls. In the case of immaterialism, we could appeal to haecceities, because according to immaterialism, the soul itself is a substance. But according to Thomas, the soul is not a substance. Disembodied souls are individuated by the bodies that they long for and desire to be reunited with. Smith's soul is the one that longs for and desires reunion with a certain body. But what makes a body (mere potency, the *matter* of which the soul is the *form*) the body that Smith's soul longs for? It can only be that Smith's soul longs for "it." But since the body is mere potency, there is no "it " for Smith's soul to long for. Hence, what makes a soul Smith's soul cannot be the body that it longs for. As Caroline Bynum says, "God can make the body of Peter out of the dust that was once the body of Paul."[21] If this is the case, then disembodied souls cannot be individuated at a time by their yearning for certain bodies— because the identity of the body (Smith's, say) will depend upon the identity of the soul. It is difficult to see how Aquinas can combine the Aristotelian view that matter individuates with his view that the soul is a substantial form that can "subsist"—and experience God—apart from a body.

---

[21]Caroline Walker Bynum, *The Resurrection of the Body in Western Christianity* (New York: Columbia University Press, 1995), 260.

Let me pause here and say that I realize that there is scriptural basis for the view that resurrection bodies will be identical to human biological bodies. There are puzzling metaphors in *I Corinthians* 15 and in *II Corinthians* 5, as well as the post-resurrection appearances of Jesus, in which he still seems to have his wounds. On the other hand, the fact that he can walk through locked doors and disappear into thin air may lead us to suppose that resurrection bodies are not identical to human biological bodies. But I don't think that such passages wear their meanings on the sleeve.

The memory criterion, the soul-as-software view, and the soul-as-information-bearing-pattern view

These may be considered together. The memory criterion is familiar from Locke (and his Scottish opponents). What I am calling the soul-as-software view takes seriously a computer metaphor: the soul is software to the hardware of the brain; if persons are identified with souls (software), they can be "'re-embodied, perhaps in a quite different medium," as D.M. Mackay put it.[22] Another materialistic view of the soul (this one from Polkinghorne) conceives of the soul as an "information-bearing pattern, carried at any instant by the matter of my animated body."[23] At death, God will remember the patterns and "its instantiation will be recreated by him" when at the resurrection.[24]

These views share a widely recognized defect: the duplication problem. The problem is that two people (B and C, say) may both be psychologically continuous with (or run the same software, or exhibit the same information-bearing pattern as) a single earlier person, A. If B and C bear exactly the same relationship to A, and if B and C are distinct, then the relation that they both bear to A cannot be identity. A cannot be identical with two distinct objects, and it would be arbitrary to suppose that A is identical to one but

---

[22]D. M. MacKay, "Brain Science and the Soul," in Richard L. Gregory (ed.), *The Oxford Companion to the Mind* (Oxford: Oxford University Press, 1987), 724–25.
[23]John Polkinghorne, *The Faith of a Physicist: Reflections of a Bottom-Up Thinker* (Minneapolis: Fortress Press, 1996), 163.
[24]Ibid., 163.

not the other. Identity is a one-one relation, but person A's (quasi-) memories, software, information-bearing pattern, etc., could be transferred to more than one person. So, sameness of (quasi-) memories, software, or information-bearing pattern cannot suffice for sameness of person. To avoid this problem, defenders of the memory criterion and the like usually add the (ad hoc) requirement that there be no duplication.

However, there is a theological argument, suggested in conversation by my colleague Gareth B. Matthews, that supporters of the memory criterion etc. need not worry about duplication and need not appeal to ad hoc stipulations. I'll call the argument "the Matthews argument." The premises of this argument are explicitly religious. They appeal to God's necessary attributes—viz. that God is essentially just—and to the notion of a judgment after death. If God is essentially just and God judges everyone, then it is metaphysically impossible for God to let a person A branch into persons B and C.

The reason that it would be metaphysically impossible for A to branch into B and C is this. Assume that everyone except Christ deserves punishment. God is essentially just and judges everyone. Suppose that person A branched into persons B and C: both B and C had A's (quasi-) memories (caused in the right way, etc.). Whom does God punish? If God punished B but not C, or C but not B, then God would not be essentially just: B and C are related to A in exactly the same way; it is impossible to be just and to judge B and C differently. On the other hand, if God punished both B and C, then there would be twice the punishment that A deserved, and again God would not be essentially just. Either way, supposing that B and C both had A's (quasi-) memories (caused in the right way), violates God's essential justice in judgment. Since God is essentially just, if A deserves punishment, it is metaphysically impossible for B and C both to have A's (quasi-) memories. So, God's essential justice rules out the metaphysical possibility that A could have a duplicate in the afterlife.

The Matthews argument relies on weighty theological assumptions; but it does rescue the memory criterion from the duplication problem. And it works equally well to save the soul-as-software view and the soul-as-information-bearing-pattern view. So, if the memory criterion (or the soul-as-software view, or the soul-as-information-bearing-pattern view) could be developed in ways that avoid other problems (besides the duplication problem), any of them would be suitable candidates for a metaphysics of resurrection.

The constitution view

Now let me turn to the constitution view, according to which sameness of pre- and post-mortem person is sameness of first-person perspective. In the first place, the constitution view avoids some of the pitfalls of the other candidates for a metaphysics of resurrection. Since human persons are essentially embodied, the constitution view avoids the problem of individuating disembodied souls—a problem that afflicts Thomism. Since a person's identity depends on her first-person perspective, the constitution view avoids the problem of the numerical identity of corruptible and incorruptible bodies—a problem that afflicts both animalism and Thomism.

Still, the constitution view is not home free. What is needed is a criterion for sameness of first-person perspective over time. In virtue of what does a resurrected person have the same first-person perspective as a certain earthly person who was born in, say, 1800? In my opinion, there is no informative non-circular answer to the question: "In virtue of what do person P1at t_1 and person P2 at t_2 have the same first-person perspective over time?" It is just a primitive, unanalyzable fact that some future person is I; but there is a fact of the matter nonetheless.

We can see this by means of an argument from providence. Now, according to the traditional doctrine of providence, God has two kinds of knowledge—free knowledge and natural knowledge. God's free knowledge is knowledge of contingent truths, and His natural knowledge is knowledge of logical and metaphysical necessities. (I'm disregarding the possibility of middle knowledge here.) Again, according to the traditional doctrine of providence, the obtaining of any contingent state of affairs depends on God's free decree. Whether the person with resurrected body 1, or body 2, or some other body, is Smith is a contingent state of affairs. Therefore, which if any of these states of affairs obtains depends on God's free decree. No immaterial soul is needed for there to be a fact of the matter as to whether Smith is the person with resurrected body 1. All that is needed is God's free decree that brings about one contingent state of affairs rather than another. If God decrees that the person with body 1 have Smith's first-person perspective, then Smith is the person with body 1.[25] So, there is a fact of the matter as to which, if any, of

---

[25]Stephen T. Davis, *Risen Indeed: Making Sense of the Resurrection* (Grand Rapids: Eerdmans Publishing Co., 1993), 119–21.

the persons in the resurrection is Smith, even if we creatures cannot know it. On the Christian idea of providence, it is well within God's power to bring it about that a certain resurrected person is identical to Smith.[26]

Notice that the argument from providence provides for the metaphysical impossibility of Smith's being identical to both the person with body 1 and the person with body 2 in the resurrection. For it is part of God's natural knowledge that it is metaphysically impossible for one person to be identical to two persons. And according to the notion of God's natural knowledge, what is metaphysically impossible is not within God's power to bring about. Hence, there is no threat from the duplication problem. Indeed, this argument from providence may be used to support, not only the constitution view, but also immaterialism, the soul-as-software view, the soul-as-information-bearing-pattern view, and the memory criterion, to guarantee a fact of the matter about which person is you in the resurrection. The only views of persons that receive no aid from the argument from providence are those (like animalism and Thomism) that require that incorruptible resurrection bodies be identical to corruptible biological bodies.

The relative merits of the constitution view

The constitution view can deliver the benefits of immaterialism and Thomism without having to postulate immaterial souls, which would be surds in the natural world. In light of the Matthews argument, the memory criterion, the soul-as-software view, and the soul-as-information-bearing-pattern view may be saved from the duplication problem, but none of these is really a fully developed metaphysical theory. The constitution view of persons is superior in that it is integrated into a comprehensive unified view of the natural world.

But the real advantage of the constitution view, at least for Christians, is over animalism. In contrast to animalism, the constitution view does not take being a person to be just a contingent and temporary property of beings

---

[26]The idea of haecceity we find in Duns Scotus seems to offer another possibility: God knows our haecceities in this life, but we do not.

that are fundamentally non-personal (organisms). On animalism, being a person has no ontological significance at all.

Indeed, on the animalist view, our having first-person perspectives (or any mental states at all) is irrelevant to the kind of being that we are. But the Christian story cannot get off the ground without presuppositions about first-person perspectives. On the human side, without first-person perspectives, there would be no sinners and no penitents. Since a person's repentance requires that she realize that she herself has offended, nothing lacking a first-person perspective could possibly repent. On the divine side, Christ's atonement required that Christ suffer, and an important aspect of his suffering was his anticipation of his death (e.g. the agony in the Garden of Gethsemane); and his anticipation of his death would have been impossible without a first-person perspective. This part of Christ's mission specifically required a first-person perspective. What is important about us (and Christ) according to the Christian story is that we have first-person perspectives.

Also, of course, there is Genesis 2:26, according to which God said: "Let us make man in our image, after our likeness." A natural reading of this verse is that we were made to be persons, to be capable of reflective thought about ourselves—in short, to have first-person perspectives. On the animalist view, our first-person perspectives are just contingent features of us. On the constitution view, they are essential to us.

Given how important the first-person perspective is to the Christian story, Christians have good reason to take our having first-person perspectives to be central to the kind of being that we are. Hence, Christians have good reason to endorse the constitution view.[27]

---

[27]This paper was presented as a plenary address at the Society of Christian Philosophers meeting at San Diego University in February 2006. I am very grateful to the SCP and to Gareth B. Matthews and David B. Hershenov for reading drafts of this paper and for making helpful comments.

For Discussion or Essays

- Review Thomas Aquinas' view of a human being as a composite of a rational soul and a material body, then discuss this view, in light of what Lynne Rudder Baker has to say about the alleged problems it poses for a metaphysics of resurrection.
- Explain Hume's friend's disanalogy (his failure of comparison or similarity) between the mind of God and the minds of humans. How might an orthodox believer respond to Hume's claim?
- How far do questions concerning "the origin and government of worlds" concern the public interest? Are such questions really entirely indifferent to the peace of society and the security of government, as Hume appears to claim?
- Discuss H.H. Price's claim that "It is surely conceivable (whether or not it is true) that *experiences* should occur which are not causally connected with a physical organism." Do you agree? Explain.
- Writing in the early 1970s, H.H. Price claimed that "a number of intelligent persons would maintain that we now have a very large mass of evidence in favor of survival," and on the basis of this evidence, "the survival hypothesis is more probable than not." Much of that evidence, he says, comes thanks to "seventy years of psychical research." In the decades since then, neuroscience has produced an understanding of the brain which, however rudimentary it may appear to future generations, is nevertheless much greater than it was forty or fifty years ago. What are we to make of Price's picture of "discarnate minds," in view of the state of neuroscience today?
- H.H. Price claims that it is conceivable that "discarnate minds" might create "an after-death world of mental images," including memories and desires. He claims that, "when we no longer have an environment" we are, at least, relieved of the task of finding our location. In our reading, has Price solved the Destination Problem?
- Review Lynne Rudder Baker's *constitution view* of human persons, as she presents it in the first subsection of her paper.

Is her view compatible with a scientific naturalist account of a human person? In what respects is it or is it not?

- In her section on the metaphysics of resurrection, Baker mentions the "duplication problem": "The problem is that two people [...] may both be psychologically continuous with [...] a single earlier person," or they may both run the same software or exhibit the same information-bearing pattern. Does the duplication problem apply to the doctrine of rebirth that Yama presents in the *Katha Upanishad*? Explain. Does the version of rebirth that we encountered in the *Milinda Panha* face this problem?

Further Readings on Resurrection and the Afterlife

There is enough literature on this topic to fill libraries. Here are several sources that students might find especially relevant and helpful:

Aquinas, St. Thomas. *Summa contra gentiles*, Book IV (in various translations and editions), especially Chapter 79, "That through Christ the Resurrection of the Body is to Come." Aquinas, the prolific Christian thinker who "put a halo on Aristotle," defends bodily resurrection as against a "spiritual resurrection," depicted along the lines of Plato as the soul's liberation from the cage of the body. Aquinas argues that, "the immortality of the soul seems to demand a future resurrection of the body" (Book IV, Ch. 79: 10).

Bukkyo Dendo Kyokai. *The Buddha's Land* (1966). Doctrines of a heavenly afterlife are not confined to the Greeks and the Abrahamic religions of Judaism, Christianity, and Islam. Kyokai introduces us to the heaven depicted by a particular school of Buddhism.

Hick, John H. *Death and Eternal Life*. New York: Harper & Row, 1976. Hick, an influential British philosopher of religion, contrasts Plato's notion of the immortality of the soul to a New Testament view of divine recreation of the person, conceived as a psychophysical unity, body and soul in one. He then sets out to establish that this picture of resurrection as the divine recreation of the individual as a psychophysical "replica" in another space is at least conceivable. Like many of his Christian predecessors, he notably rejects the picture of hell as everlasting torment: this picture, he believes, is inconsistent with belief in a loving God. (Compare to the Charles Seymour item below.)

Idelman Smith, Jane, and Yvonne Haddad. *The Islamic Understanding of Death and Resurrection*. Oxford: Oxford University Press, 2002. This is a guide to Sunni Muslim beliefs about the afterlife, divine reward, and punishment.

van Inwagen, Peter. "The Possibility of Resurrection." In *Immortality*, edited by Paul Edwards, 242–46. Amherst, NY: Prometheus Books, 1992. Inwagen is a Christian philosopher who views resurrection from a perspective close to metaphysical materialism.

Seymour, Charles. "Hell, Justice, and Freedom." *International Journal for Philosophy* 43 (1998): 69–86. The author, a professor of philosophy at the University of Notre Dame, defends the doctrine of hell against the "argument from justice," which concludes that a just God would not punish human sin with eternal damnation. Seymour argues that it is conceivable that a person, imbued with free will, may continue to sin even after bodily death, and for any number of reasons, including force of habit, may continue to bring suffering on herself for an indefinitely long period of time.

Swinburne, Richard. "A Theodicy of Heaven and Hell." In *The Existence and Nature of God*, edited by Alfred J. Freddoso, 37–54. Notre Dame: University of Notre Dame Press, 1983. Swinburne, a British philosopher of religion, is one of the most influential contemporary practitioners of Christian apologetics.

A Note on Key Passages from Christian and Muslim Scriptures:

Some of the most-cited *New Testament* passages on the topic of the afterlife are the following: Matthew 10:28; 1 Corinthians 15:14, 19, *and* 35–55 ("Death, where is thy sting?"); 1 Thessalonians 4:13-18; 2 Thessalonians 1:8–9. "everlasting destruction from the presence of the Lord"; Revelation 20:15; 21:1-8; 221:3-4. Other key passages regarding resurrection and posthumous judgment include Isaiah 26:19; Daniel 12:2; Matthew 23:33; John 3:36; Acts 24:15; 1 Corinthians 2:9; and Revelation 20:6, 12-15.

Key passages in the *Qur'an* describing the Day of Judgment[1] and the afterlife include Sura I:5; S. III:185–86; S. VIII:50–51; S. XVI:27–34; S. XXIII:14–16, 100–04; S. LV:46–78, and S. LXXVIII:17–37.

---

[1] *Yaom al-Qiyyamah; Yaom ad-Din.*

Part IV

Problems with Immortality

Introduction to Part IV:
Problems with Immortality

For that which befalleth the sons of men befalleth beasts; even one thing befalleth them: as the one dieth, so dieth the other; yea, they have all one breath; so that a man hath no preeminence above a beast; for all is vanity.

All go unto one place; all are of the dust, and all turn to dust again.

—Ecclesiates 3:19 (King James Version)

Why, you do not even know what will happen tomorrow. What is your life? You are a mist that appears for a little while and then vanishes.

—The General Epistle of James 4:14 (King James Version)

So far, we have considered arguments for and against survival and the immortality of the soul, and the question of what could survive after we die. In Part IV we will shift our focus to the question whether immortality would really be better than non-survival.

We begin with Book III of Titus Lucretius Carus' magnificent book-length poem, *De rerum natura*, or *On the Nature of Things*. We have already mentioned that Lucretius (c. 99–c. 55 BC) was a follower of the Greek philosopher Epicurus. Like Epicurus, Lucretius taught that there is no divine interference in the natural order of things. Rather than seeking solace in childish wishful thinking about immortality and divine judgment, Lucretius prescribed the study of "metaphysics," or perhaps of philosophy and what we today would call natural sciences, to fight our supposed fear of death.[1]

Toward the end of our selection, the poet introduces us to the *symmetry argument*, which draws a parallel between the eons before conception and the eons after dying. If the thought of the former time does not cause us grief, then why should we dread the prospect of the latter time? Lucretius

---

[1]Samuel Scheffler, a philosopher we will encounter in Part Five, examined the limitations of the Epicurus–Lucretius strategy of "using metaphysics to fight fear," in Niko Kolodny (ed.), *Death & the Afterlife* (Oxford: Oxford University Press, 2013), 83–87.

wants to convince us that, in the words of Epicurus, "The wise person does not deprecate life nor does he fear the cessation of life."[2]

For some people, though, mortality seems to be something that is impossible to come to terms with. Our next reading is a riveting article by the Spanish philosopher Miguel de Unamuno. This author could not disagree more strongly with Epicurus' claim that *Death is nothing to us*. Unamuno makes his case for the immortality of the soul, and that "It is better to live in pain than to cease to be in peace."

Then, in a provocative and justly famous paper, the late English philosopher Bernard Williams (1929–2003) explores the question whether immortality, even if it were conceivable, would be desirable at all. The answer to the question might seem obvious at first, but let us recall Walpola Rahula's discussion of the Four Noble Truths of Buddhism, and let us consider what the fourteenth-century Japanese poet Kenko had to say:

> If man were never to fade away like the dews of Adashino, never to vanish like the smoke over Toribeyama, but lingered on forever in the world, how things would lose their power to move us![3]

As his point of departure, Williams draws from "The Makropulos Secret," a play by the Czech writer Karel Čapek (1890–1938),[4] about EM, a woman who, in the course of 300 years of life without aging, has lost the desire to live any longer. To make sense of this, Williams distinguishes between *conditional desires* and *categorical desires*. A "positive" categorical desire is a reason to go on living. Williams claims that an individual with an immortal life would, like EM, eventually lose her positive categorical desires and would find immortality insufferably wearisome.

Next, in "Immortality without Boredom," Lisa Bortolotti and Yujin Nagasawa find reason to doubt Williams' contention that persons with indefinitely extended lives would inevitably lose the desires and goals that provide reasons to live. Distinguishing between *habitual boredom* and *situational boredom*, they conclude that Williams has not made a convincing case for the necessity of boredom in an indefinitely extended life, of the sort that EM led.

---

[2]Refer to the Letter to Menoeceus, in Part I.
[3]From *Essays in Idleness* (*Tsurezuregusa*). Yoshida Kenko (c. 1283–1350) was an author, a functionary in the Japanese imperial court, and a Buddhist monk. The citation, trans. Donald Keene, is from Phillip Lopate, *The Art of the Personal Essay* (New York: Anchor Books, 1995), 31.
[4]Refer to the item in the Further Readings section at the end of Part IV.

In previous readings we have encountered powerful arguments against the survival hypothesis. But even if it turns out that after we die we no longer exist as persons, there remains at least one other possibility—a bizarre one—when it comes to life "after" death. *Eternal return* is the doctrine that the same events occurring in the same sequence have occurred infinitely many times in the past and will occur infinitely many times in the future. The idea of eternal return is perhaps too speculative to be taken seriously as a "scientific hypothesis"; nevertheless, as we will see, some contemporary physicists find it strangely compelling. The German philosopher Friedrich Nietzsche believed that the rare sort of person who could embrace the "thought of eternal return" is the sort of person who could raise himself or herself above the level of those who are "human, all too human," and live life without regret. In our reading, Swedish philosopher Lars Bergström explores some philosophical implications of eternal return, as the doctrine has a bearing on death. In the course of his discussion, Bergström mentions the relevant views of several thinkers we have already encountered, including Unamuno and Bernard Williams.

14

On Mortality and the Soul

Lucretius

Translated by Anthony M. Esolen

In our next reading, we encounter the view that the soul is inseparable from the body, and that when the body dies so does the soul. Our reading is from Book III of the six books that comprise the soaring didactic poem, *On the Nature of Things* (*De rerum natura*). Writing in Latin, the author, Roman poet Titus Lucretius Carus (c. 99–55 BC), presents us with sweeping vistas of life for mortal humans, reconciled to their mortality, living fearlessly in a universe of matter in motion, without beginning or end.

Scholars believe that Lucretius wrote *On the Nature of Things* in the mid-first century BC, a time of civil war, slave rebellions, and vicious reprisals by the wealthy and powerful against the poor. Amid this fire and carnage, many Romans sought solace in the misty realms of religious cults. Lucretius, however, would have none of this. Following his hero Epicurus, he taught that the gods have no influence on the natural order of things. In their ignorance, humans fabricated the gods, only to live in fear of them:

> And just like children, trembling, are afraid
> Of all things in the dark, so sometimes we in broad daylight
> Fear things imaginary as what babes dread in the night.

But we can put "the shadowy terrors of the mind to flight" by "observing Nature's laws and looking on her face." Once we grant that the soul will also die, "Death, then, is nothing to us," Lucretius writes, echoing his precursor Epicurus.

In David Hume's essay from Part III, we read that "The Soul therefore if immortal, existed before our birth; and if the former existence no ways concerned us, neither will the latter." This is a version of the *symmetry argument* that Lucretius presented eighteen centuries earlier. Why, Lucretius asks, should we be any more concerned about nonexistence after we die than we are about the eons that preceded our birth or conception?

Lucretius does not deny that many people live with morbid fear of physical decomposition, whether gradual or abrupt, and that others dread the prospect of pain-wracked or forlorn circumstances in their final days. We dread the abrupt abandonment of unfinished projects, too, and the deprivation of "the good things of life," or the prospect of dying without having left something behind as evidence that we had once existed. Lucretius acknowledges all of this.

Nor does Lucretius claim that *the death of others* is nothing to us. We dread the loss of loved ones, and we worry about the health and happiness of our loved ones and of fellow humans and perhaps other species, too. But this, too, is fear of losing the good things of life, and arguably, you can be deprived of something only if you exist.[1] If Lucretius is right, then our present dread of losing these things cannot qualify as dread of death, properly speaking.

[...]   30

I've taught of the first fabric of all things,
And how of their own the atoms of various shapes
Fly driven along in endless motion, how
All things can be created out of them;
Next, in my verse, it's clear I should shed light
Upon the nature of the mind and soul;
And pitch that fear of the underworld headlong
Which troubles human life from the inmost wells,
Muddying all our affairs with the black of death,
Leaving behind no pleasure pure and clear.   40

----

[1]In a paper included in Part V, Thomas Nagel will dispute this claim.

For though men preach that sickness or a life
Of infamous vice ought sooner to be feared
Than the realm of death, and say they know their souls
Are nothing but blood (or air, if the fancy strikes them),
And don't need our philosophy at all,
Turn your thoughts this way and you'll see it's just
Swagger and bluster and not firm belief:
Men driven out of their country and kept far
From human sight, men tarred by crime and scandal,
Wretched in every way, still hang to life,   50
Pathetic, and invoke ancestral shades,
And slaughter black cattle and send the spirits down
To the gods of the dead. In bitter times
They turn their minds more keenly toward religion.
All the more, in danger and doubt, when things go wrong,
We should keep our eye on the man, see what he is—
For that's the spell that snatches his mask and makes him
Cry out at last from the heart. The truth remains.
And greed and the blind craving for rank, which drive
Pitiful men to overleap the bounds   60
Of law, drive friends-in-evil and their henchmen
To struggle night and day with the utmost strain
To fight to the heights of wealth—these sores of life
Are fed in no small part by fear of death.
To be despised, to feel the pinch for money
Are ills that seem to linger at Death's door,
Far from the sweetness of a steadfast life.
And so, spurred on by groundless fears, men strive
To escape, to hustle themselves far out of their reach,
And from the blood of countrymen they forge   70
Riches, and double them, heaping slaughter on slaughter.
With a bloodthirsty glee they bury their own brothers
And hate and fear to eat at a cousin's table.
In the same way, from the same fear, men often
Grow lean with envy. There he is, that powerbroker,
That rising star attracting every gaze
While *they* 're bogged down in the mud (they whine) and darkness.
Some waste away for statues and a name.
And often from fear of dying, men will be
Seized with disgust for life, will hate the light,   80
So with sorrowing hearts they pass their sentence, death,

Forgetting that all their cares spring from this fear—
This puts their shame to rout, this breaks the bonds
Of friendship and subverts all piety.
And men have sold the land that gave them birth,
Sold their dear parents, to shun the underworld.
For as little boys tremble and fear whatever's lurking
In the blind dark, so we in the light of day
Tremble at what is no more terrible than
What little boys dream in the dark and fear will come.   90
And so this darkness and terror of the mind
Shall not by the sun's rays, by the bright lances of daylight
Be scattered, but by Nature and her law.

First I say that the soul, which we call "mind,"
The site of judgment, governor of life,
Is one more human part no less than hands
And feet and eyes are part of the whole creature . . .
The mind's sense is not situate in one place
But is a certain life-giving state of the body
Called "harmony" by the Greeks, enabling us   100
To live and feel, without a part for "mind,"
As often it's said good health belongs to the body
And yet health's no one part of the healthy man.
So they place the mind's power in no certain part-
But I think they veer far off and stray from truth.
For often the body—and that's in plain sight—suffers
While we feel gladness in some hidden part,
And the reverse in turn is often true,
That a man's soul-sick with a body whole and glad,
Just as when, though the gout should pinch your foot,   110
Your head may meanwhile feel no pain at all.
More: when the limbs are poured out in soft sleep
And the laden body lies insensible,
There still is something else in us which then
Is tumbled this way and that, and takes inside
All the turns of gladness and idle cares of the heart.
Now, to show you that the "anima," the life spirit,
Is a body part, and that bodies do not feel
By virtue of harmony: cut away much of the body
And often life still lingers in our limbs,   120
But that same life, when the tiny atoms of heat
Flee, and the mouth releases its last breath,

Deserts the blood at once and leaves the bones.
This ought to show you that not all atoms play
The same parts, with the same sustaining powers;
Rather the seeds of air and the moist warmth
Take care that life may linger in the limbs.
So there's a vital breath and warmth in the body,
Which, when it leaves us, leaves us full of death.
Therefore, as the mind and soul are found to be   130
A sort of bodily part, let the musicians
Keep that "harmony" name they've filched from Helicon
Or from wherever they've dragged it and applied it
To something which had lacked a proper name.
Let them have it, whatever. You attend the rest.

Now I assert, the spirit and the soul
Are held conjoint and form one common nature,
But the captain, so to speak, and lord of the body
Is the judgment, which we call the soul or mind.
It sits fixed in the center of the breast.   140
Here alarm bucks loose, and dread, and round these regions
Gladness caresses. Here, then, is the mind, the soul.
The other, the spirit, sown broadcast through the body,
Obeys and moves to the mind's sway and will.
The mind thinks by itself, joys in itself,
Even when nothing is stirring the spirit or body.
And as when our head or eye is stricken with
Some trying pain, we're still not torture-crossed
Throughout the body, so the mind itself
Will grieve or flourish in gladness while the spirit,   150
Spread through the frame, is touched by nothing new.
But when the fear that troubles the mind is more
Vehement, we see the spirit in all the members
Agree, and the body blanches and beads of sweat
Break out all over, the tongue-tied voice cracks, falters,
It's dusk with the eyes, ears ring, limbs buckle and give,
And yes, we see men terrified in mind
Crumple—so anyone should easily learn
That the spirit and mind are one, for when spirit is struck
By the force of the mind, it thrusts and hurls the body.   160

This reasoning also shows that mind and spirit
Are corporeal. When they can shove the limbs,

Snatching the sleeping body and discomposing
The features, wheeling and steering the whole person
(None of which, we see, can come to pass without
Touch, and all touch implies a body), must
You not confess, the soul's corporeal?

And more: you'll notice the soul, as one with the body,
Is affected the same and shares the body's feeling.
If your life's not dashed by the force of a quivering lance   170
Thrust home to split the bones and muscles open,
Still languor will follow, and the soothing swoon to the earth,
And as you lie on the ground your mind's a whirl
With willing and not willing to arise.
The soul must therefore be corporeal, since
Corporeal lances jab it and make it stagger.

What sorts of atoms constitute the soul
And where they come from, I'll explain to you.
To start, I say that the soul is super-subtle,
Composed of tiniest particles. Consider,   180
To prove the truth of my hypothesis,
That nothing we see can happen so swiftly as
The mind imagines and initiates.
Quicker therefore the mind will spur itself
Than anything we see before our eyes.
But since it's so quick to move, it must consist
Of the roundest and tiniest seeds, so that a small
Impulse can drive them forward into motion.
For water will ripple under the littlest impulse,
Made up of tiny and turnable tumbling figures.   190
By contrast, honey stands thick, sticks, won't budge,
Its juice more sluggish, motion more reluctant.
For all its wealth of atoms clogs and clings
Together; no surprise, as it's not made
Of atoms so smooth or subtle or round and rolling.
And a puff—half-held and light—can send your mound
Of poppy seed spilling and scattering down from the summit;
By contrast, a rock heap or cornstalk rick
Won't. And so the smaller the bodies and smoother,
The more a thing enjoys mobility.   200
But then whatever you come upon that's heavy,
Rough, sharp—to that extent these things stand stable.

Now, therefore, since we've found the soul to be
Exceedingly mobile, it must then consist
Of atoms awfully tiny and smooth and rolling.
This knowledge, my good reader, you will find
Useful and opportune in many matters.

This too will help establish the soul's nature,
How finely woven it is and what small space
Would hold it, if it could be gathered up: 210
That as soon as the imperturbable peace of Death
Lays hold of a man, and the mind and soul have departed,
You detect nothing dwindling from the body,
Nothing to see or to weigh. Death guarantees
All, save life-giving sense and the moist warm breath.
Thus all the soul must of necessity
Be made of the tiniest seeds, be interwoven
So fully with veins, flesh, muscle that when it leaves
The body deserted, the outer contour is
Preserved intact and not a jot the lighter.   220
It's like bouquets of wine that evanesce,
Or the sweet breath of perfume that floats away,
Or savors that abandon any body.
Still to the eyes these things look none the smaller
And not a grain of weight seems drawn away:
No wonder, for many and tiny seeds create
Aroma and savor, diffuse through the whole body.
So again and again I say the mind and spirit
Are made up of the tiniest, tiniest seeds,
For when they flee they steal no weight away.   230

But don't think that our souls are one and simple.
A sort of light breath leaves us when we die,
Breath mingled with heat, and heat in turn with air;
No warmth at all without a mix of air.
For since warmth's thinly woven, there must be
Many air-atoms moving in and through it.
So then we find three elements in the soul.
Yet, all told, will these three suffice to make
Sensation? The mind grants none of them the power
Of sense-bearing motion—still less the power of thought!   240

Therefore to these we're forced to add a fourth
Element—this one has no name at all,

There's nothing finer or more readily moving,
Nothing made up of smaller or smoother atoms—
And *this* first deals to the limbs the sense-bearing motions.
For its small atoms are the first to stir;
Then warmth and the invisible power of breath
Are moved, then air, then everything falls into motion,
The blood is shaken to life, all the flesh tingles
With every sensation, and last, the bones and marrow   250
Feel joy (if it's joy they feel!) or burning passion.
And it's no harmless matter if sickness seeps
Or pain cuts to the marrow; for such brawls
Will follow, that life will have no room, and the soul
Will fly, torn up through all the pores of the body.
But usually the skin's a sort of shield;
That gives us strength to keep our hold on life.

And now, how these are jumbled, in what manner
They are arranged and thrive, I wish to explain—
Checked though I am by our spare native tongue.   260
What I can briefly touch upon, I will.

The atoms race between and amongst each other,
Each element with its motion, so none can ever
Be sundered and set aside to do its work;
Instead they're like four forces in one body.
As in the flesh of any living creature
There are color and smell and taste, yet all of these
Add up to make the single finished body;
So warmth, air, and the invisible power of breath
Mingle and make one nature, along with that   270
Quickest of elements that moves the others,
Then sense-bearing motions in our flesh arise.
This fourth is subtle, hidden, penetrating;
There's not a thing more subtle in our bodies;
It is itself the soul of all the soul.
As mingled throughout the frame of the whole body
Are the hidden powers of the soul and spirit,
Since they are made of small and scanty atoms,
So too your nameless element, made of the smallest
Atoms, lies hidden and itself is as   280
The soul of the soul, and sweeps like a lord through the body.
In just the same way, breath and air and warmth
Must mingle in the limbs and blend their powers,

One more withdrawn than the next, or thrust to the fore,
So that a uniformity appears;
Lest warmth and breath and the power of air, of their own,
Sunder and separate and destroy sensation.

There's that warmth too in the soul, which it puts to use
When it seethes in rage and the dagger-eyes flash fire.
There's the chill breath, that chattering friend of fear,   290
Which rattles the limbs and sets the bones to shaking.
There's finally that state of the calm air
For the easy heart and countenance at peace.
More heat's in the forging of those whose hearts are keen
For anger, and come to a quick and raging boil;
The prime example is the truculent lion
Who bursts his ribs with the growl, whose big roar often
Can't make the anger of his heart subside.
But the soul of a deer is shaken in the breeze,
Quivers through all his flesh and stirs cold breath   300
To make the members tremble into motion.
While cows, by contrast, live in the calm air;
No smoking firebrand ever sears their hearts
With anger, spewing soot and darkness; they
Are not transfixed or frozen into fear;
Their place, between the deer and the savage lions.
So too with men. Take them and train them alike,
Make them polished and learned; there will still remain
The first and native traces of each soul.
You can't yank up these vices by the roots: 310
This man careens headfirst into fits of rage,
While that man's sooner pinched with a little fear,
And a third takes it all too placidly.
And in many other matters the natures of men—
The various habits that hound them—have to differ.
I cannot now expose the unseen cause,
Or find as many names as there are shapes
Of atoms, whence these differences arise.
But this I can affirm: so picayune
Are the traces of those natural faults which reason   320
Can't clear away, that nothing hinders us
From leading calm lives worthy of the gods.

And so the soul's enclosed by the whole body;
It is the body's guard and cause of health.

They twine together with common roots, nor can
One be plucked loose without destroying both.
As easily could you tear the aroma from
A lump of myrrh, and not destroy its essence,
As you could draw the soul and spirit from
The body, and not have it all dissolve.   330
For from the beginning they share the seat of life,
Their atoms so interwoven; nor, it's clear,
Can the body or the soul, all by itself,
Without the power of the other, feel sensation,
But from those common motions sprung from both,
Sensation is kindled and fanned high in our flesh.
Furthermore, body is never born alone,
Never grows alone or lasts long after death.
It's not like heated water that releases
Its heat as steam, while the water remains intact,   340
Not rent by the release—not so, I tell you,
Can the limbs, abandoned, suffer the soul's separation,
But rent to the core they die and rot away.
From the earliest age the mutual touchings of
The soul and body learn the vital motions,
Even while dwelling deep in the mother's womb,
So that divorce must sicken and kill both;
Then, since their wedlock brings them health, you should
See that their natures also must be wedded.

Next: if someone denies that the body feels,   350
But trusts that the soul diffused through the whole body
Catches that motion we've been calling "sense,"
Well, he just fights the plain facts and the truth.
For how can the body's feeling be explained
Unless the facts of that experience teach us?
"But the body lacks all sense when the soul's departed."
So? It loses what in life was never its own,
And loses much besides, when it's thrust from life.

And worse, to say the eyes can't see a thing,
But the soul peeps through them as through open doors,   360
That's hard to do when vision itself refutes it—
Sense ropes us and hustles us down to the eyes themselves—
When in fact we sometimes can't see dazzling things,
The light of vision fettered by the light.
That can't happen with doorways. If they're open

We can seen through them—and they're not distressed.
Finally, if our eyes are really windows,
The soul's sight should be all the keener when
The eyes- those very windows- are removed!

Don't assume, in these matters, what the holy   370
Words of the great Democritus propose:
That atoms of body and soul, matched one by one,
Alternate thus and link themselves together.
For as the atoms of soul are so much smaller
Than those which constitute our flesh and body,
They yield in number too, so sparsely sown
Throughout our frames that you can vouch for this:
The intervals in the fabric of soul-atoms
Are no smaller than the smallest bodies which
Can stir up sense-bearing motions when they strike us.   380
For we can't always feel the cling of dust
Or of chalk kicked up and settling on our limbs,
Of the night fog or the slender filaments
Of a spider's net that tangle us on our way,
Or an old cobweb settling upon our heads,
Or a bird's feather or floating thistledown,
Which are so light they find it hard to fall,
Nor do we feel at once the passage of
Any and every animal, or each footfall
Upon our skin of midges and such things.   390
Much in us must be stirred up first before
The seeds of the soul, diffuse through all our frame,
Can feel that the body's atoms have been jolted,
And hammering, jarring in those nooks and crannies,
Can dash for each other and ram and ricochet.

And the soul's the haughtier lord of life than the spirit,
Keeping tight-barred the battlements of life.
Not for the fleetest moment can the spirit
Reside in us without the soul; it follows
Like a meek friend, and scatters to the wind,   400
Leaving the cold limbs to the chill of death.
But if the soul remains, then life remains.
Lop off a man's limbs all about and leave him
A mangled trunk, his members spiritless—
Yet he survives, and breathes the breath of life.
So a man cut off from spirit (in large part,

Not wholly) will yet hang on, will cling to life,
As in a torn-up eye if the pupil's still
Intact, the power of sight's alive and well,
So long as you don't rupture the whole eyeball,   410
Or cut the pupil off from the rest of the eye—
That too must bring about the sight's destruction.
But let the pupil, as tiny as it is,
Be eaten away—light falls, the darkness follows,
Though the rest of the ball is whole and full of light.
Such bonds have ever bound the soul and spirit.

Listen: to show you that a living thing's
Soul is as light as air, is born, must die,
I shall lay forth my hard-won labor of love
In verses worthy of your noble life.   420
Make sure you merge these two under one term,
So if I need a word and I teach that "spirit"
Is mortal, trust I've said that "soul" is too,
Since the two are conjoint in unity.

To begin, then. Since I've shown that the soul, so thin,
So light, is made of the tiniest atoms, much
Smaller than those which make up the clear water
Or clouds or smoke (for in mobility
It far excels and moves at the slightest touch,
Why not? When it's moved by the *shadows* of cloud and smoke,   430
The sort we see as we lie asleep and dream
Of the breath high over the altar, the drifting smoke—
Such things, no doubt, bring images to our minds),
And now too since you mark that when ajar
Is smashed the water spills away and scatters,
And since clouds and smoke will scatter to the winds,
Trust that the soul spills too and perishes
The sooner and melts the quicker into its atoms
Once it's been drawn away from the human body.
In fact if the body—the soul's jar—is smashed   440
Or so attenuated by loss of blood
It can no longer hold the soul inside,
What air do you think will hold the soul, when air
Is slighter than the body and less confining?

What's more, we see the body and mind are born
Together, and grow old and weak together.

For as babies toddle about with bodies soft
And tender, so their minds are wobbly too;
But when the trunk grows ripe with the strength of adulthood
The mind is better endowed, the reason stronger;   450
And last, when the might of Age has crushed the body
And the limbs have fallen, strengthless, beaten down,
Then the native talent hobbles, the tongue wanders,
Thoughts lapse—all powers fail at the same time.
It follows then that soul and spirit too
Dissolve like smoke into that sea of air,
For soul is born with the body and grows with it
And, as I've shown, cracks under the weight of age.

Here we should note that as the body itself
Is racked with violent sickness and sharp pain,   460
So the soul's seized with trouble and fear and sorrow.
It follows that the soul will share in Death.
For when the body is ill the soul will often
Wander; he loses his train of thought, he speaks
Astray, while drowsiness sinks him into a deep
And lasting coma—the head nods, the lids fall.
Where he is, he can hear no voices, recognize
No faces of those who surround him and call him back
To life, dewing their cheeks and lips with tears.
Admit, therefore, the soul dissolves—you must,   470
When the touch of sickness penetrates so far.
And pain and disease are both Death's artisans,
As we've learned so well from watching many die.
Yes, why is it then, when wine has stung a man
To the quick, his blood aglow with the heat it lends him,
The limbs, as a consequence, grow heavy; tripped, tangled,
Legs stagger, the thick speech lags, the thoughts are soused,
Eyes swim, and roaring and sobbing and brawls break out?
And all the rest of this sort of thing that follows,
Why is it? If not that the thrust and throttle of wine   480
Makes a habit of whipping the soul—and this, in the body!
But whatever can be throttled or trip-and-tangled,
Shows us that if a little rougher force
Finds a way in, it will die, its future lost.
Why, the sudden power of sickness before our eyes
Will sometimes strike a man like a thunderbolt—
He crumples, froths at the mouth, moans, thrashes, raves,

Stiffens and wrenches his muscles, writhes and gasps
Fitfully, arms and legs flung to exhaustion.
Sure enough: the violent sickness spreads through the body,   490
Disorders it, drives the soul out, frothing—as waves
Of the salt sea seethe and foam in the battering wind.
Groans are wrung out because the limbs are racked
With pain, but chiefly because the vocal-atoms
Are spit up in a mass on the lips outside,
On the road, you might say, where they're used to go.
The raving comes when the powers of soul and spirit
Are jarred and, as I've shown, wrenched one from the other,
Sundered and torn apart by the same poison.
Then, when the illness has broken, and the black bile   500
Returns to its dens in the corrupted body,
He staggers to his feet, a little queasy,
Returns to his senses and takes the soul back in.
So if these are thrown for a fall—while in the body—
And torn and bruised so badly by such diseases,
Why then do you think that in open air, alone,
They can survive the battering of the wind?
And since we see that the mind, like a sick body,
Can be brought round by medicine and made whole,
That's our prognosis: souls live but to die.   510
You've got to add parts or scramble the order around
Or lift a jot directly from the whole
If you would undertake to change the spirit
Or bend the nature of any living thing.
But what's immortal allows no shuffle of parts,
No jot to trickle in or be skimmed away,
For change that leads a thing beyond its limits
Is instant death to the original.
So if the soul falls ill or is brought round
By medicine, those are signs that it must die,   520
As I've taught. The facts charge on to block the path
Of false reasoning and head off its retreat,
Routing it with a double-pronged rebuttal.

Yes, often we watch a man die by degrees,
Member by member losing the sense of life:
The toes and the toenails first turn black; then the feet,
The legs die; then creeping through all the other limbs
The chilling pace of Death will make its way.

Since the soul is sundered here and doesn't come out
Unscathed or in one piece, it must be mortal.   530
What if you think the soul can draw itself
In from the limbs, contracting its parts into
One, and there stow away the members' senses?
And yet that place where so much soul's collected
Should be super-sensitive! That never happens;
Don't wonder if, as I've said, the soul is sliced
To ribbons and scattered away. Conclude: it dies.
Even if we concede what is flat wrong
And grant that the soul can shrink into one lump
As the dying, little by little, lose the light,   540
Still we must then admit the soul shall die;
Let it die scattered to the winds, grow dull, blank,
All its parts clumping up—it doesn't matter,
When the senses fail him everywhere more and more
And less and less of life remains behind.

And since the mind is just one part of a man,
Fixed in its proper place, like eyes and ears
And the other organs of sense that steer our lives,
And just as a hand or an eye or nose if severed
From us, can neither sense nor even be   550
(Rather resolves directly into rot),
So by itself the soul can't live—it needs
The body, the man who is its vessel, or
Whatever image you can find that joins
More intimately, for the body is bound fast.

Indeed, the living powers of body and soul
Join in their strength, delight in life together.
For without the body, alone, the soul cannot
Make motions that bring forth life; if stripped of soul
The body can't last long or use its senses.   560
Know then, as an eye that's plucked out roots and all
Sees nothing, torn away from the rest of the body,
So too, alone, the spirit can do nothing.
Of course—for mingled in the veins and flesh,
In bone and muscle, the atoms of soul are held
By the whole body and can't leap free in flight
Over great intervals; shut in, they stir
The sense-bearing motions, but cast by death from the body

Into the winds they cannot make those motions
Because they're not confined in the same way.   570
A body, a breathing thing— air would be *that*
If it could bind the soul and lock it into
Motions that stirred in the sinews once, in the body.
So again I argue, if the sheltering body
Is undone, and the breath of life is cast away,
The soul and sense—you must admit—dissolve;
Conjunction is the cause of life for both.

Well then, if the body can't outlast the departure
Of soul, but dwindles into the stench of rot,
Why hesitate to say that the soul is gathered   580
And seeps away like so much smoke spilled out,
That the body, now altered, crumbles into ruin
And falls apart, foundations jolted from
Their proper places, letting the soul seep out
Through all the limbs and winding passageways
And chinks in the wall? So many proofs should show you
That when it leaves the limbs the soul's been split,
Torn into pieces first in the very body
Before it slips out, floating in the wind.
Look, when the bonds of life within are shaken,   590
Though the body is whole, still something will stagger the spirit
So that it strains its moorings to the body;
And the face goes blank as at the final moment,
And all the limbs fall limp and drained of blood;
As when they cry, "He's fallen unconscious!" or
"He's fainted dead away!" and in the panic
They clutch at the last cable of his life.
For the faculties of the mind are cracked and crazed
And reel to the earth with the body—if the stroke
Were slightly heavier, they might be destroyed.   600
How, then, can you doubt that the soul, cast out of the body,
A weakling, in the open, its shields removed,
Not only can't outlast the ages, but
Can't for the tiniest moment stand intact?
Nor does a dying man sense that his soul
Takes its leave of the body safe and sound,
Making its way up the gullet into the throat;
Rather he feels it failing where it dwells
As he knows the other senses in their organs

Are slipping away. But if our souls were deathless   610
He wouldn't wail that he was slipping away—
No—going to shuck his old skin, like a snake!

Then, too, why aren't mind and judgment born
In the head alone or the feet or the hands, but cleave
In all of us to one sure dwelling place?
It must be, every human part is given
A certain place to be born and to endure,
Partitioned among all the various parts,
Not wrong-end-up or cart-before-the-horse!
For effect follows cause reliably;   620
We don't get fire from rivers or frost from flame.

Besides, if the soul by nature is immortal,
And can sense although it's severed from our body,
We'd better, I think, equip it with all five senses.
How else can we imagine for ourselves
That the souls stroll about in the underworld?
Painters and poets have for generations
So introduced those souls, complete with senses.
But separate hands for the soul cannot exist,
Or nose and eyes, or separate ears and tongue—   630
Then by themselves these souls can't feel—or be.

And since we feel that the sense of life belongs
To all the body, and all is filled with soul,
If a sudden stroke should chop us clean in two,
Each part divided wholly from the other,
Surely the force of the soul would be divided
And, severed, along with the body be destroyed.
But whatever can be sliced to fall in halves
Surely denies that it can never die.
Men tell of sickle-wheeled chariots that in a flash   640
Lopped members off and gleamed in a welter of slaughter,
And while the lopped-limb lay on the ground and twitched,
The soul of the man himself, alive and strong,
Could feel no pain, so swift was the attack,
His mind so zealously devout to fight;
He seeks with what's left of his body the battle and slaughter,
Nor grasps that his left arm and shield are lost,
Dragged off by the horses and wheels and hungering sickles,
Or his right is fallen, as he mounts to charge.

Another tries to rise on a missing leg   650
As his dying toes lie scrabbling in the dust.
And a head lopped off from a glowing, living trunk
Preserves its face alive, eyes open, till
It renders up the remnants of its soul.
Or take a serpent—the flicking tongue, the tail
That menaces, body arched to strike; if you please,
Chop its trunk with an axe into many parts;
You'll see those separate hacked-off snake parts writhe
From the sudden wound and spatter the earth with gore,
And the head of the snake will twist about and try   660
To strike at the tail, or gnaw the searing wound.
Say all the soul's in each of the little parts?
But from that line of reasoning this would follow:
One living thing possesses many souls.
Therefore what once was single is now divided
Along with the body, and therefore both must die,
For into many parts they're cut alike.

Besides, if the soul by nature stands immortal
And slips into the body right at birth,
Why can't we recall as well the times gone by,   670
Preserving traces of our former lives?
But if the spirit's power is so altered
That all its hold upon past actions fails,
Well, that, I think, strays not too far from Death.
Therefore you must confess: what once existed
Has died; what now exists was just now formed.
Moreover, if the living power of soul
Is first installed when the body is complete
And we are born and come to the shores of life,
It's hardly fitting that it grow together   680
Along with the members, in the very blood;
Instead it ought to live cooped up, alone,
And somehow flood the body with sensation.
So again I say it: never think the soul
Is free from birth, or from the law of death.
For if it were slipped in from without, it couldn't
Fasten itself to us so thoroughly
(The reverse causes that—the facts are plain,
For soul is so enmeshed with veins, flesh, muscle,
And bone, that even the teeth share in sensation,   690

As the toothache shows and the bracing of ice water
And the harsh crunch of a stone in a loaf of bread),
Nor, so sewn up with the body as it is,
Could it depart intact and loose itself
Safely from all the bones and joints and muscles.
But should you think that, slipped in from without,
The soul seeps through our members, all the more—
So blended with the body—shall it perish.

Whatever seeps will dwindle; therefore death.
It would be strained through all the pores of the body.   700
As food when sent to all the limbs and members
Dies, and shores up another from itself,
So the spirit even if it's whole and new
When it enters the body at birth, must still break down
As all its particles are being sifted
Into the limbs, to make up a new spirit,
This one, the lord of our bodies now, born from
That first which died, dealt out to every joint.
Therefore the soul is not without its day
Of birth, nor shall it lack its funeral.   710

And are there or aren't there soul—seeds left behind
In a lifeless body? If some are lodged inside
It's hardly just to think the soul immortal,
For it retreats, diminished of its parts.
But if its limbs are sound when it escapes,
Not one of them remaining in the body,
Out of what atoms do corpses, the guts gone rancid,
Sigh forth their worms? How can such an army of creatures,
Boneless and bloodless, swell like a tide through the members?
Maybe the souls are slipped from without into   720
The maggots, a soul for each maggot body? If
You think so, you haven't reckoned on why so many
Thousands of souls converge where one retreats!
This research problem it would seem to pose:
Whether, see, all the seeds of the maggot souls
Arrive and build themselves their homes-to-be,
Or are slipped into maggot bodies ready-made.
And you can't prop things up by telling why
They'd bother to do such work. They've got no bodies!
They'd flutter free of hunger and cold and illness!   730
These are the plagues that weary the body— and soul,

Its neighbor, catches many of its evils.
Ah, but let's say they make that awfully useful
Body they enter! How? No way appears.
Thus souls do not make bodies for themselves.
And they don't slip into finished bodies either,
For that will not allow the subtlest weave
Of body and soul, the touch that makes sensation.

Yes, why does violence stalk the sullen brood
Of lions? Or fraud, the fox? And the deer's forefathers   740
Bequeath them their flight and their family limbs that tremble,
And so on and so forth? Why are they all born
With traits and talents proper to each kind,
If not that in accordance with the breed
One sort of soul develops with each body?
But if souls never died and could swap bodies,
All creatures would become a welter of cross-traits:
Noble Hyrcanian hounds would scoot away
From the charge of the antlered stag; trembling in flight
The hawk would flee the swooping of the dove;   750
Men would be foolish and fierce creatures wise.
It's all illogic when they say the soul
Is deathless, only changed by the change of body.
What alters must dissolve. Conclude: it dies.
Its parts are shuffled, straying out of order;
Hence in the members it must also dwindle
And at last die together with the body.
Now if they say that human souls will always
Pass into human bodies, let me ask:
Why does that wise soul make a foolish boy?   760
Why isn't the foal as cunning as the stallion?
Sure, they'll wriggle out, "The mind in a weakling body
Becomes a weakling too." Well then, they must
Admit that the soul dies, since it's so changed
It loses all its prior life and sense.
How can the mind along with the body too
Grow firm and attain that longed-for flower, adulthood,
Unless it was its consort from the first?
And why would it want to leave its wasted limbs?
Afraid to be trapped inside a rotting body?   770
Or its house will cave in, heavy with old age?
These pose no danger—to a deathless thing.

And then, what a laugh! to think that souls stand waiting
When beasts are born or during the rites of Venus,
Innumerable immortals taking numbers
For mortal limbs, crowding, elbowing to see
Who'll be the first to slip himself in or the strongest—
Oh, maybe all the souls are bound by contract:
Whoever swoops in first to be installed
Is first; no scuffing, and no arguments!   780

There are no trees in the sky, in the ocean plains
No clouds; no fish can live in the fields, no blood
Can dwell in a wooden stock, no sap in stone.
Each thing has one sure place to grow and dwell.
Soul cannot spring alone without the body,
Nor, far away from flesh and blood, survive.
For if it could, far sooner might that soul
Dwell in the head or the shoulders or the heels
And be born into whatever part you like—
So long as it stays in the same man, the same "jar."   790
But since there's a certain place inside our bodies
For the spirit, set apart, to dwell and grow,
All the more reason why you must deny
That it can be born or endure outside the body.
Admit then, when the body passes, so
The soul must pass, torn up throughout the body.
Really, to yoke what's mortal to the eternal,
Thinking they can agree and work as one,
Is silliness. For what can be reckoned more
Disjoint, discrepant, dissonant, than that   800
What's mortal, bound with the lasting and immortal,
Should bear up under the storm-whipped surge of life?

More proof: whatever's everlasting must
Either (solid of matter) spit back the punches,
Not suffering anything to pierce and split
Its tight-packed parts within (so durable are
Atoms, whose nature I have shown above),
Or persevere through all eternity
Not struck by a single blow (as empty space
Remains unacting and untouchable),   810
Or last because no wealth of space surrounds it
Where its loosening parts might break away and scatter

(As the everlasting All-in-All), for there
Is no Beyond to fly to, or atoms which
Could loosen it and destroy it with their pounding.
Should the soul be thought immortal all the more
In that it's fortified by living things,
Because the foes of health never invade it
Or the invaders for some reason yield,
Repulsed before we can feel what harm they'd do . . .   820

Besides the fact that the soul falls sick with the body,
A thought of things to come will strike the soul
And starve it hollow, harass it with worry and fear,
While the remorse for old sins gnaws away;
Add the mind's own madness and forgetfulness;
Add that it drowns in the black depths of coma.

Death, then, is nothing to us, no concern,
Once we grant that the soul will also die.
Just as we felt no pain in ages past
When the Carthaginians swarmed to the attack   830
And under the sky's high shores the whole world shook,
Struck by the shocks of war and alarm and riot,
All mankind over land and ocean in
The balance, whether to fall to the rule of either—
So too, when we no longer are, when our
Union of body and soul is put asunder,
Hardly shall anything then, when we are not,
Happen to us at all and stir the senses,
Not if the sea embroiled earth, and heaven the sea!

And even if the soul, ripped from the body,   840
Retained the power to feel, that still would be
Nothing to us, whose beings have been fashioned
By one fit marriage of one body and soul.
And if the Ages should collect our matter
After we die and return our present forms,
Lending us once again the light of life,
Even that won't mean anything to us,
Once our continuation has been snapped.
Who we once were can't touch us now at all;
Nor are we gripped with care for who we'll be.   850
When you reflect on the unmeasured span
Of ages past, how many and various were

The motions of matter, you may rest assured
That the seeds at times were placed in the same order
As these seeds which compose us now; a fact
That the mind can't retain in memory.
There's been a halt—hiatus—in our lives,
And all the motions of sense have gone astray.
Thus if your future is misery and sickness
You've got to exist in that same future time   860
For the ill to catch you. But since death clears the deck,
Forbidding that would-be sufferer to exist,
Nothing at all have we to fear from death;
He who cannot exist cannot feel pain,
Or care if he's never born again, once death
That does not die has seized his dying life.

Now if you happen to see someone resent
That after death he'll be put down to stink
Or be picked apart by beasts or burnt on the pyre,
You'll know that he doesn't ring true, that something hidden   870
Rankles his heart—no matter how often he says
He trusts that there's no feeling after death.
He doesn't grant the premise or conclusion,
Can't pluck himself out of life by the roots and chuck it;
He posits, unknowing, a bit of himself left over.
For when anyone living puts it that his body,
Dead, will be laced by the birds and the wild beasts,
It's himself he pities! He can't cut himself free
From the castoff body—no, he dreams it's him,
Stands by, infects it with his own sensation.   880
So he resents that he was formed to die;
Can't see that when he dies there'll be no other
Him living to moan that he's bereft of him,
Weeping because he's lying scorched or mangled.
If in death it's bad to be treated to wild beasts
And the jaws that rip, I don't see why it's not
Bitter to lie there roasting in brilliant flames
Or to smother in balm and honey or grow stiff
With cold as you lie on your ice-hard bed of stone,
Or be squashed flat by the earth's crushing weight.   890

"Now—now—no happy home, no darling wife
Will greet you, no sweet children race to steal

Kisses, and touch your heart with quiet joy.
You'll never rule the roost or watch your business
Flourish. From you, poor boy, poor boy," they say,
"One bad day's stolen all life has to win."
"Not one desire for any of these things,"
They don't add, "will beset you anymore."
If they could see *that,* and speak accordingly,
Their souls would slip the tight strong clench of fear.   900

"Sure, you enjoy the sleep of death—you're free
Of all the bitter pains that were to come.
But we stand shuddering by your pyre of ash,
Insatiably lamenting; nevermore
Shall this great grief be lifted from our hearts."
Better ask this fellow: what's so very bitter
If the whole business comes to sleep and quiet?
Why waste away with his everlasting tears?

When men lie back and shade their eyes with garland
And tip a few too many, they love to utter   910
Such heartfelt stuff, "Ah, we only go round once, boys!
Soon over the hill—and there's no turning back!"
As if the worst of death were really this,
That the poor souls would be so dry they'd parch
With thirst, or that some other want would catch them!
But no one searches for himself or life
When body and mind together rest in sleep.
For all we'd care, that sleep could be eternal;
No longing for our waking selves would move us.
Yet when we sleep our atoms never stray   920
Far from the sense-bearing motions—for a man
Can snatch himself from bed and gather his wits.
Much less, then, should we be concerned *with* death,
Less than the *nothing* that we think of sleep!
For greater is the whirl and scatter of atoms
Which follows death; no one will wake and rise
Once the cold halt in life has caught him up.

Yes, if Nature herself should suddenly raise her voice
Against one of us, and rebuke him in this way,
"What's the matter, mortal, with you, that you coddle yourself   930
With all this sorrow? Why moan and wail at death?
If your life's been happy and blessed, and all those blessings

Haven't been poured into a leaky pot
To spill away, with nothing left to give thanks for,
Why not, as a man who's feasted full of life,
Retire contented—fool!—and rest in peace?
But if all the blessings squandered on you are gone
And life's so hateful, why add still more? What use?
They'll all turn sour again and come to nothing!
Why don't you strive instead to end your life?   940
For what else can I find or make to please you?
There's nothing—all things always stay the same.
If your body's not shriveled with years and your arms and legs
Still don't hang nerveless, well, things stay the same,
The same, should you go and outlast generations,
Just more of the same, if you never happen to die—"
What shall we say in defense, if not that Nature's
Complaint is just and her indictment true?
And if some high and mighty older man
Should whimper, poor fellow, too sadly that he must go,   950
Let her cry the louder and lash out in reproof!
"Get your sobs out of here, scoundrel, and quit your whining!
You mope—though you've rifled all life has to win;
But since you scorn what's here and crave what's not,
Your life—unfinished, thankless—slips away,
And so you're shocked that Death is waiting now
Before you're stuffed and ready to leave the table.
Give it up, old man, it doesn't become your years.
Come, be content! Give way to your heirs! You must."
Just, would her charge be! Just, her rebuke, her outcry!   960
The old, shoved out, must always cede to the new,
One thing restores another; it must be.
And no one's flung to the pit or the pains of Hell.
We need those atoms for our progeny
Who, though they live life full, shall follow us.
Before you came, men died—and they will die.
One thing gives rise to another, incessantly;
Life's given to no one outright; all must borrow.
Reflect how the span of the endless ancient past
Before our births means nothing at all to us.   970
Here Nature has provided us a mirror
Of the time to come when we at last have died.
Is there horror in the prospect? Any sorrow?
Isn't it freer from care than the sweetest sleep?

But the things that are said to exist in the depths of Hell
Are all, to no surprise, part of our lives.
No fairy-tale Tantalus, frozen in empty fear,
Pathetically shudders under a teetering stone;
Rather here, in life, an empty fear of the gods
Looms, and it's chance that brings the fall we dread.   980
No birds delve into a Tityus Bat in Hell
Or prick for a morsel left in that huge liver[2]
Throughout time everlasting—really now!
Let him stretch out, if you like, immense in bulk,
His splayed limbs spanning not nine acres merely
But the whole globe; nevertheless, he'd not
Be able to suffer everlasting pain
Or offer the food of his body forever and ever.
Our Tityus is here—a man laid flat by love,
Whom the birds peck apart—that's gnawing worry   990
Or other cares that tear us with desire.
In life we've Sisyphus too, before our eyes,
Drunk with campaigning for the rods of power,
And always the people send him home to sulk.
To canvass for power—unattainable, useless—
And ever to sweat and suffer hardship for it,
That's to push and push up a mountain a heavily-leaning
Boulder—which tumbles right back down from the summit
Anyhow, bouncing and bounding down to the plain.
Then to feed forever your ingrate heart, to take   1000
Your fill of the good things, stuffed but still not full
(As the returning seasons in their rounds
Bring us fresh life and harvest and delight,
The fruits of life that never seem to fill us)
That's the old tale, I think, of the ripe young virgins
Gathering water in a leaky pot
That couldn't be filled no matter what they did.
And Cerberus and the Furies, see, and the darkness,
Tartarus[3] belching blasts from his horrible maw,

---

[2]The reference here and in the following lines is to the mythological giant Tityus, who assaulted the goddess Leto while she was on her way to a shrine. For punishment, the gods bound Tityus in the underworld, where two vultures feast forever on his ever-regenerating liver. —MM
[3]In Greek mythology, Tartarus is the name of both a primordial god and an abysmal place of punishment for the wicked. —MM

Really, they can't exist and never have!   1010
But in life infamous fear of punishment for
Infamous crimes is how we pay for evil.
Prison, and being flung from the frightful Rock,
Flogging and chopping, racking, tarring, torching,
Take these away—still the man who knows his sin
Anticipates, and whips himself hot with terror,
And never sees where misery can have
Its terminus, and punishments their limit;
He fears they may grow heavier still in death.
This life of fools, then, *this* is the true Hell.   1020

Sometimes you should remind yourself, "For shame!
The good king Ancus[4] lost the light of day
And he was a far better man than you.
And many other kings and potentates
Have fallen, once commanders of great nations.
Even that ruler who over the ocean once
Laid down a road for legions to bridge the deep,
Taught them to go over the salt gulfs on foot,
Who scorned with a trample of hooves the hissing sea,
Robbed of light, from a dying body poured his soul.[5]   1030
And Scipio, the battle-lightning, the terror of Carthage,
Gave his bones to the earth like the meanest slave.
Include discoverers of truth and beauty,
Include the poets—among whom solely-sceptered
Homer sleeps just as soundly as the rest.
And when ripe age had warned Democritus
That the motions of his memory were fading,
He accosted Death and offered his own head.
Even Epicurus died, his light of life
Run to the finish; the mind who bested all,   1040
Who doused their light as the sunrise dims the stars.
Who are *you* to be reluctant about dying?

---

[4]Ancus Marcius, the fourth king of Rome, ruled in the seventh century BC. He won notable victories over the Latin adversaries of Rome and extended Roman territory to the sea. —MM
[5]The reference appears to be to Persian emperor Xerxes (c. 518–465 BC), who invaded Greece in 480 BC. The campaign involved building a bridge across the Hellespont (the Dardanelles), so that his land army could cross out of Asia Minor. After initial victories, the campaign suffered reversals of fortune and failed to achieve its goal. Later, a commander of Xerxes' royal bodyguard assassinated the Great King by stabbing. —MM

You with your half-dead life still kicking about!
You fritter most of your last years asleep,
You snore when you're awake, and you're always dreaming,
Carrying around a mind that's touchy, panicky,
But you can't tell what's the everlasting trouble,
You're so groggy and worried and jostled on all sides,
And you wander and drift along you don't know where."

If, when men sense a weight upon their minds,   1050
A trouble deep within that wearies them,
They could but recognize the source, and know
Why such huge misery masses in the heart,
They'd never lead their lives as we see now—
As men who never know what they want, who move
From place to place to lay their burden down.

Out of his mansion he's got to go, that fool,
Home bores him to death, and yet he turns right back,
Finding that things are just as dull outside.
Swift, to the villa he spurs his galloping ponies,   1060
Bringing relief—you'd think—to a house afire.
But soon as he touches the villa door, he yawns,
Tries to forget, falls heavily asleep,
Or hurries out to see the town again.
We flee ourselves, whom we can never flee.
Against our will the self we hate clings tight
For we are sick and do not grasp the cause.
If he could see it, he might leave his worries
And strive to understand the nature of things,
For not an hour but all eternity   1070
Is here at issue: what the state will be
Of the time left for each man after death.

What vicious yearning for life, then, makes us hurry
In such a panic, attacked by doubts and dangers?
This much is sure: the end of life awaits us,
The summons must be answered; we must die.
As it is, we lurch in the same ruts; no new pleasure
Is forged for us from drawing out our lives.
Whatever we lack, we want, we think it excels
All else, but when we've grabbed it something new   1080
We thirst for, always panting after life.
Yet we don't know what fortune the years will bring,

What luck we'll have, and what our end will be.
And long life won't allow us to pluck out
One moment from our span beyond the grave
That we might spend a shorter time in death.
Survive this generation and the next—
Nevertheless eternal death awaits,
Nor will the man who died with the sun today
Be nonexistent for less time than he   1090
Who fell last month—or centuries ago.

15

The Hunger of Immortality

Miguel de Unamuno

Translated by J.E. Crawford Flitch

This excerpt comprises Chapter III of Miguel de Unamuno's book *The Tragic Sense of Life* (*Del Sentimiento Trágico de la Vida*), first published in 1913. At the beginning of our reading, the author acknowledges that "gnostics or intellectuals" might accuse him of engaging in mere rhetoric, rather than philosophy. He insists, however, that he is here presenting something of an argument for personal immortality. Unamuno was influenced in some respects by Thomas Aquinas, who advanced several arguments for the immortality of the soul, including the argument from desire. This argument states that, because God does not leave our deepest and most fundamental desires unanswered, our desire to live on after death will not be in vain.

In the end, though, reason can never prove that the soul is immortal or, as Unamuno says, "that the human consciousness shall preserve its indestructibility through the tracts of time to come." As we know by now, this too is a part of Christian belief.

Let us pause to consider this immortal yearning for immortality—even though the gnostics or intellectuals may be able to say that what follows is not philosophy but rhetoric. Moreover, the divine Plato, when he discussed the immortality of the soul in his *Phædo*, said that it was proper to clothe it in legend, $\mu\nu\theta o\lambda o\gamma\epsilon\iota\nu$ [mythology —MM].

First of all let us recall once again—and it will not be for the last time—that saying of Spinoza[1] that every being endeavors to persist in itself, and that this endeavour is its actual essence, and implies indefinite time, and that the soul, in fine, sometimes with a clear and distinct idea, sometimes confusedly, tends to persist in its being with indefinite duration, and is aware of its persistency (Spinoza, *Ethics*, Part III, Propositions VI–X).

It is impossible for us, in effect, to conceive of ourselves as not existing, and no effort is capable of enabling consciousness to realize absolute unconsciousness, its own annihilation. Try, reader, to imagine to yourself, when you are wide awake, the condition of your soul when you are in a deep sleep; try to fill your consciousness with the representation of no-consciousness, and you will see the impossibility of it. The effort to comprehend it causes the most tormenting dizziness. We cannot conceive ourselves as not existing.

The visible universe, the universe that is created by the instinct of self-preservation, becomes all too narrow for me. It is like a cramped cell, against the bars of which my soul beats its wings in vain. Its lack of air stifles me. More, more, and always more! I want to be myself, and yet without ceasing to be myself to be others as well, to merge myself into the totality of things visible and invisible, to extend myself into the illimitable of space and to prolong myself into the infinite of time. Not to be all and for ever is as if not to be—at least, let me be my whole self, and be so for ever and ever. And to be the whole of myself is to be everybody else. Either all or nothing!

All or nothing! And what other meaning can the Shakespearean "To be or not to be" have, or that passage in *Coriolanus* where it is said of Marcius "He wants nothing of a god but eternity"? Eternity, eternity!—that is the supreme desire! The thirst of eternity is what is called love among men, and whosoever loves another wishes to eternalize himself in him. Nothing is real that is not eternal.

From the poets of all ages and from the depths of their souls this tremendous vision of the flowing away of life like water has wrung bitter cries—from Pindar's σκιας οναρ ("dream of a shadow") to Calderón's "life is

---

[1]Unamuno agrees with the great Dutch-Sephardic thinker Baruch Spinoza (1632–77) that each individual thing, by virtue of being *this*, and not *that*, "endeavors" to persist indefinitely through time. This endeavor is the actual essence of the thing itself. When it comes to humans, "you, I, and Spinoza wish never to die and [...] this longing of ours never to die is our actual essence." The essence of man, Unamuno (but not Spinoza) concludes, is not to die. —MM

a dream"[2] and Shakespeare's "we are such stuff as dreams are made on," this last a yet more tragic sentence than Calderón's, for whereas the Castilian only declares that our life is a dream, but not that we ourselves are the dreamers of it, the Englishman makes us ourselves a dream, a dream that dreams.

The vanity of the passing world and love are the two fundamental and heart-penetrating notes of true poetry. And they are two notes of which neither can be sounded without causing the other to vibrate. The feeling of the vanity of the passing world kindles love in us, the only thing that triumphs over the vain and transitory, the only thing that fills life again and eternalizes it. In appearance at any rate, for in reality … And love, above all when it struggles against destiny, overwhelms us with the feeling of the vanity of this world of appearances and gives us a glimpse of another world, in which destiny is overcome and liberty is law.

Everything passes! Such is the refrain of those who have drunk, lips to the spring, of the fountain of life, of those who have tasted of the fruit of the tree of the knowledge of good and evil.

To be, to be forever, to be without ending! Thirst of being, thirst of being more! Hunger of God! Thirst of love eternalizing and eternal! To be for ever! To be God!

"Ye shall be as gods!" we are told in *Genesis* that the serpent said to the first pair of lovers (Genesis 3:5). "If in this life only we have hope in Christ, we are of all men most miserable," wrote the Apostle (1 Corinthians 15:19); and all religion has sprung historically from the cult of the dead—that is to say, from the cult of immortality.

The tragic Portuguese Jew of Amsterdam [Spinoza] wrote that the free man thinks of nothing less than of death; but this free man is a dead man, free from the impulse of life, for want of love, the slave of his liberty. This thought that I must die and the enigma of what will come after death is the very palpitation of my consciousness. When I contemplate the green serenity of the fields or look into the depths of clear eyes through which shines a fellow-soul, my consciousness dilates, I feel the diastole[3] of the soul and am bathed in the flood of the life that flows about me, and I believe in my future; but instantly the voice of mystery whispers to me, "Thou shalt cease to be!"

---

[2]Pindar was a Greek lyric poet of the fifth century BC. *La vida es sueño* was perhaps the best-known play by the great Spanish dramatist Pedro Calderón de la Barca (1600–81). —MM
[3]The phase of the cardiac cycle when the heart refills with blood. —MM

the angel of Death touches me with his wing, and the systole[4] of the soul floods the depths of my spirit with the blood of divinity.

Like Pascal,[5] I do not understand those who assert that they care not a farthing for these things, and this indifference "in a matter that touches themselves, their eternity, their all, exasperates me rather than moves me to compassion, astonishes and shocks me," and he who feels thus "is for me," as for Pascal, whose are the words just quoted, "a monster."

It has been said a thousand times and in a thousand books that ancestor-worship is for the most part the source of primitive religions, and it may be strictly said that what most distinguishes man from the other animals is that, in one form or another, he guards his dead and does not give them over to the neglect of teeming mother earth; he is an animal that guards its dead. And from what does he thus guard them? From what does he so futilely protect them? The wretched consciousness shrinks from its own annihilation, and, just as an animal spirit, newly severed from the womb of the world, finds itself confronted with the world and knows itself distinct from it, so consciousness must needs desire to possess another life than that of the world itself. And so the earth would run the risk of becoming a vast cemetery before the dead themselves should die again.

When mud huts or straw shelters, incapable of resisting the inclemency of the weather, sufficed for the living, tumuli were raised for the dead, and stone was used for sepulchers before it was used for houses. It is the strong-built houses of the dead that have withstood the ages, not the houses of the living; not the temporary lodgings but the permanent habitations.

This cult, not of death but of immortality, originates and preserves religions. In the midst of the delirium of destruction, Robespierre induced the Convention to declare the existence of the Supreme Being and "the consolatory principle of the immortality of the soul," the Incorruptible being dismayed at the idea of having himself one day to turn to corruption.

A disease? Perhaps; but he who pays no heed to his disease is heedless of his health, and man is an animal essentially and substantially diseased. A disease? Perhaps it may be, like life itself to which it is thrall, and perhaps the only health possible may be death; but this disease is the fount of all vigorous health. From the depth of this anguish, from the abyss of the feeling

---

[4]The contraction phase of the cardiac cycle. —MM
[5]Blaise Pascal (1623–62) was a French mathematician and philosopher. —MM

of our mortality, we emerge into the light of another heaven, as from the depth of Hell Dante emerged to behold the stars once again—

e quindi uscimmo a riveder le stelle.[6]

Although this meditation upon mortality may soon induce in us a sense of anguish, it fortifies us in the end. Retire, reader, into yourself and imagine a slow dissolution of yourself—the light dimming about you—all things becoming dumb and soundless, enveloping you in silence—the objects that you handle crumbling away between your hands—the ground slipping from under your feet—your very memory vanishing as if in a swoon—everything melting away from you into nothingness and you yourself also melting away—the very consciousness of nothingness, merely as the phantom harborage of a shadow, not even remaining to you.

I have heard it related of a poor harvester who died in a hospital bed, that when the priest went to anoint his hands with the oil of extreme unction, he refused to open his right hand, which clutched a few dirty coins, not considering that very soon neither his hand nor he himself would be his own any more. And so we close and clench, not our hand, but our heart, seeking to clutch the world in it.

A friend confessed to me that, foreseeing while in the full vigor of physical health the near approach of a violent death, he proposed to concentrate his life and spend the few days which he calculated still remained to him in writing a book. Vanity of vanities!

If at the death of the body which sustains me, and which I call mine to distinguish it from the self that is I, my consciousness returns to the absolute unconsciousness from which it sprang, and if a like fate befalls all my brothers in humanity, then is our toil-worn human race nothing but a fatidical procession of phantoms, going from nothingness to nothingness, and humanitarianism the most inhuman thing known.

And the remedy is not that suggested in the quatrain that runs—

Cada vez que considero
que me tengo de morir,
tiendo la capa en el suelo
y no me harto de dormir.[7]

---

[6]"and then we went out to see the stars."
[7]"Every time I consider/that it is my lot to die,/I spread my cloak upon the floor/ and cannot get enough sleep."

No! The remedy is to consider our mortal destiny without flinching, to fasten our gaze upon the gaze of the Sphinx, for it is thus that the malevolence of its spell is discharmed.

If we all die utterly, wherefore[8] does everything exist? Wherefore? It is the Wherefore of the Sphinx; it is the Wherefore that corrodes the marrow of the soul; it is the begetter of that anguish which gives us the love of hope.

Among the poetic laments of the unhappy Cowper[9] there are some lines written under the oppression of delirium, in which, believing himself to be the mark of the Divine vengeance, he exclaims—

Hell might afford my miseries a shelter.

This is the Puritan sentiment, the preoccupation with sin and predestination; but read the much more terrible words of Sénancour, expressive of the Catholic despair, not the Protestant, when he makes his Obermann say, "*L'homme est périssable. Il se peut; mais périssons en résistant, et, si le néant nous est réservé, ne faisons pas que ce soit une justice.*"[10] And I must confess, painful though the confession be, that in the days of the simple faith of my childhood, descriptions of the tortures of hell, however terrible, never made me tremble, for I always felt that nothingness was much more terrifying. He who suffers lives, and he who lives suffering, even though over the portal of his abode is written "Abandon all hope!" loves and hopes. It is better to live in pain than to cease to be in peace. The truth is that I could not believe in this atrocity of Hell, of an eternity of punishment, nor did I see any more real hell than nothingness and the prospect of it. And I continue in the belief that if we all believed in our salvation from nothingness we should all be better.

What is this *joie de vivre* that they talk about nowadays? Our hunger for God, our thirst of immortality, of survival, will always stifle in us this pitiful enjoyment of the life that passes and abides not. It is the frenzied love of life, the love that would have life to be unending, that most often urges us to long for death. "If it is true that I am to die utterly," we say to ourselves, "then once I am annihilated the world has ended so far as I am concerned—it is finished. Why, then, should it not end forthwith, so that no new consciousnesses,

---

[8]"Why?"
[9]The English poet William Cowper (1731–1800) spent much of his life convinced that he was doomed to eternal damnation. —MM
[10]"Man is mortal. That may be; but perish resisting, and if nothingness is our fate, do not pretend it is justice."

doomed to suffer the tormenting illusion of a transient and merely apparent existence, may come into being? If, the illusion of living being shattered, living for the mere sake of living or for the sake of others who are likewise doomed to die, does not satisfy the soul, what is the good of living? Our best remedy is death." And thus it is that we chant the praises of the never-ending rest because of our dread of it, and speak of liberating death.

Leopardi,[11] the poet of sorrow, of annihilation, having lost the ultimate illusion, that of believing in his immortality—

Peri l'inganno estremo
ch'eterno io mi credei,[12]

spoke to his heart of *l'infinita vanitá del tutto,*[13] and perceived how close is the kinship between love and death, and how "when love is born deep down in the heart, simultaneously a languid and weary desire to die is felt in the breast." The greater part of those who seek death at their own hand are moved thereto by love; it is the supreme longing for life, for more life, the longing to prolong and perpetuate life, that urges them to death, once they are persuaded of the vanity of this longing.

The problem is tragic and eternal, and the more we seek to escape from it, the more it thrusts itself upon us. Four-and-twenty centuries ago, in his dialogue on the immortality of the soul, the serene Plato—but was he serene?—spoke of the uncertainty of our dream of being immortal and of the *risk* that the dream might be vain, and from his own soul there escaped this profound cry—Glorious is the risk!—καλος γαρ ο κινδυνος, glorious is the risk that we are able to run of our souls never dying—a sentence that was the germ of Pascal's famous argument of the wager.

Faced with this risk, I am presented with arguments designed to eliminate it, arguments demonstrating the absurdity of the belief in the immortality of the soul; but these arguments fail to make any impression upon me, for they are reasons and nothing more than reasons, and it is not with reasons that the heart is appeased. I do not want to die—no; I neither want to die nor do I want to want to die; I want to live for ever and ever and ever. I want

---

[11]The poet-philosopher Leopardi (and Pliny and many others besides) described the craving for immortality as over-reach (*pleonexia*), the lust for more than our portion. In this case, the lust is for that which rightfully belongs to the gods. —MM

[12]"I used to believe in the extreme deceit that I was eternal." These are lines from Leopardi's poem *A se Stesso*, "To Himself." —MM

[13]"The infinite vanity of everything."

this "I" to live—this poor "I" that I am and that I feel myself to be here and now, and therefore the problem of the duration of my soul, of my own soul, tortures me.

I am the center of my universe, the center of the universe, and in my supreme anguish I cry with Michelet, "*Mon moi, ils m'arrachent mon moi!*"[14] What is a man profited if he shall gain the whole world and lose his own soul? (*Matthew* 16:26). Egoism, you say? There is nothing more universal than the individual, for what is the property of each is the property of all. Each man is worth more than the whole of humanity, nor will it do to sacrifice each to all save in so far as all sacrifice themselves to each. That which we call egoism is the principle of psychic gravity, the necessary postulate. "Love thy neighbour as thyself," we are told, the presupposition being that each man loves himself; and it is not said "Love thyself." And, nevertheless, we do not know how to love ourselves.

Put aside the persistence of your own self and ponder what they tell you. Sacrifice yourself to your children! And sacrifice yourself to them because they are yours, part and prolongation of yourself, and they in their turn will sacrifice themselves to their children, and these children to theirs, and so it will go on without end, a sterile sacrifice by which nobody profits. I came into the world to create my self, and what is to become of all our selves? Live for the True, the Good, the Beautiful! We shall see presently the supreme vanity and the supreme insincerity of this hypocritical attitude.

"That art thou!" they tell me with the Upanishads. And I answer: Yes, I am that, if that is I and all is mine, and mine the totality of things. As mine I love the All, and I love my neighbor because he lives in me and is part of my consciousness, because he is like me, because he is mine.

Oh, to prolong this blissful moment, to sleep, to eternalize oneself in it! Here and now, in this discreet and diffused light, in this lake of quietude, the storm of the heart appeased and stilled the echoes of the world! Insatiable desire now sleeps and does not even dream; use and wont, blessed use and wont, are the rule of my eternity; my disillusions have died with my memories, and with my hopes my fears.

And they come seeking to deceive us with a deceit of deceits, telling us that nothing is lost, that everything is transformed, shifts and changes, that not the least particle of matter is annihilated, not the least impulse of energy is lost, and there are some who pretend to console us with this! Futile

[14]"My me, they tear my me!"

consolation! It is not my matter or my energy that is the cause of my disquiet, for they are not mine if I myself am not mine—that is, if I am not eternal. No, my longing is not to be submerged in the vast All, in an infinite and eternal Matter or Energy, or in God; not to be possessed by God, but to possess Him, to become myself God, yet without ceasing to be I myself, I who am now speaking to you. Tricks of monism avail us nothing; we crave the substance and not the shadow of immortality.

Materialism, you say? Materialism? Without doubt; but either our spirit is likewise some kind of matter or it is nothing. I dread the idea of having to tear myself away from my flesh; I dread still more the idea of having to tear myself away from everything sensible and material, from all substance. Yes, perhaps this merits the name of materialism; and if I grapple myself to God with all my powers and all my senses, it is that He may carry me in His arms beyond death, looking into these eyes of mine with the light of His heaven when the light of earth is dimming in them for ever. Self-illusion? Talk not to me of illusion—let me live!

They also call this pride—"stinking pride" Leopardi called it—and they ask us who are we, vile earthworms, to pretend to immortality; in virtue of what? Wherefore? By what right? "In virtue of what?" you ask; and I reply, In virtue of what do we now live? "Wherefore?"—and wherefore do we now exist? "By what right?"—and by what right are we? To exist is just as gratuitous as to go on existing for ever. Do not let us talk of merit or of right or of the wherefore of our longing, which is an end in itself, or we shall lose our reason in a vortex of absurdities. I do not claim any right or merit; it is only a necessity; I need it in order to live.

And you, who are you? you ask me; and I reply with Obermann, "For the universe, nothing; for myself, everything!" Pride? Is it pride to want to be immortal? Unhappy men that we are! It is a tragic fate, without a doubt, to have to base the affirmation of immortality upon the insecure and slippery foundation of the desire for immortality; but to condemn this desire on the ground that we believe it to have been proved to be unattainable, without undertaking the proof, is merely supine. I am dreaming … ? Let me dream, if this dream is my life. Do not awaken me from it. I believe in the immortal origin of this yearning for immortality, which is the very substance of my soul. But do I really believe in it … ? And wherefore do you want to be immortal? you ask me, wherefore? Frankly, I do not understand the question, for it is to ask the reason of the reason, the end of the end, the principle of the principle.

But these are things which it is impossible to discuss.

It is related in the book of the *Acts of the Apostles* how wherever Paul went the Jews, moved with envy, were stirred up to persecute him. They stoned him in Iconium and Lystra, cities of Lycaonia, in spite of the wonders that he worked therein; they scourged him in Philippi of Macedonia and persecuted his brethren in Thessalonica and Berea. He arrived at Athens, however, the noble city of the intellectuals, over which brooded the sublime spirit of Plato—the Plato of the gloriousness of the risk of immortality; and there Paul disputed with Epicureans and Stoics. And some said of him, "What doth this babbler (σπερμολογος) mean?" and others, "He seemeth to be a setter forth of strange gods" (*Acts* 17:18), "and they took him and brought him unto Areopagus,[15] saying, May we know what this new doctrine, whereof thou speakest, is? For thou bringest certain strange things to our ears; we would know, therefore, what these things mean" (verses 19-20). And then follows that wonderful characterization of those Athenians of the decadence, those dainty connoisseurs of the curious, "for all the Athenians and strangers which were there spent their time in nothing else, but either to tell or to hear some new thing" (verse 21). A wonderful stroke which depicts for us the condition of mind of those who had learned from the *Odyssey* that the gods plot and achieve the destruction of mortals in order that their posterity may have something to narrate!

Here Paul stands, then, before the subtle Athenians, before the *græuli*, men of culture and tolerance, who are ready to welcome and examine every doctrine, who neither stone nor scourge nor imprison any man for professing these or those doctrines—here he stands where liberty of conscience is respected and every opinion is given an attentive hearing. And he raises his voice in the midst of the Areopagus and speaks to them as it was fitting to speak to the cultured citizens of Athens, and all listen to him, agog to hear the latest novelty. But when he begins to speak to them of the resurrection of the dead their stock of patience and tolerance comes to an end, and some mock him, and others say: "We will hear thee again of this matter!" intending not to hear him. And a similar thing happened to him at Cæsarea when he came before the Roman prætor Felix, likewise a broad-minded and cultured man, who mitigated the hardships of his imprisonment, and wished to hear and did hear him discourse of righteousness and of

---

[15] Areopagus, or the Rock of the god Ares, located northwest of the Acropolis in Athens, was the site of the high Court of Appeal for criminal and civil cases. In Roman times, it was the location of the altar to the Unknown God. It was there that the Apostle Paul spoke. —MM

temperance; but when he spoke of the judgment to come, Felix said, terrified (εμφοβος γενομενος): "Go thy way for this time; when I have a convenient season I will call for thee" (*Acts* 24:22-25). And in his audience before King Agrippa, when Festus the governor heard him speak of the resurrection of the dead, he exclaimed: "Thou art mad, Paul; much learning hath made thee mad" (*Acts* 26:24).

Whatever of truth there may have been in Paul's discourse in the Areopagus, and even if there were none, it is certain that this admirable account plainly shows how far Attic tolerance goes and where the patience of the intellectuals ends. They all listen to you, calmly and smilingly, and at times they encourage you, saying: "That's strange!" or, "He has brains!" or "That's suggestive," or "How fine!" or "Pity that a thing so beautiful should not be true!" or "this makes one think!" But as soon as you speak to them of resurrection and life after death, they lose their patience and cut short your remarks and exclaim, "Enough of this! We will talk about this another day!" And it is about this, my poor Athenians, my intolerant intellectuals, it is about this that I am going to talk to you here.

And even if this belief be absurd, why is its exposition less tolerated than that of others much more absurd? Why this manifest hostility to such a belief? Is it fear? Is it, perhaps, spite provoked by inability to share it?

And sensible men, those who do not intend to let themselves be deceived, keep on dinning into our ears the refrain that it is no use giving way to folly and kicking against the pricks, for what cannot be is impossible. The manly attitude, they say, is to resign oneself to fate; since we are not immortal, do not let us want to be so; let us submit ourselves to reason without tormenting ourselves about what is irremediable, and so making life more gloomy and miserable. This obsession, they add, is a disease. Disease, madness, reason … the everlasting refrain! Very well then—No! I do not submit to reason, and I rebel against it, and I persist in creating by the energy of faith my immortalizing God, and in forcing by my will the stars out of their courses, for if we had faith as a grain of mustard seed we should say to that mountain, "Remove hence," and it would remove, and nothing would be impossible to us (*Matthew* 17:20).

There you have that "thief of energies," as he[16] so obtusely called Christ who sought to wed nihilism with the struggle for existence, and he talks to you about courage. His heart craved the eternal all while his head convinced

---

[16]Unamuno is referring to the German philosopher Friedrich Nietzsche. —MM

him of nothingness, and, desperate and mad to defend himself from himself, he cursed that which he most loved. Because he could not be Christ, he blasphemed against Christ. Bursting with his own self, he wished himself unending and dreamed his theory of eternal recurrence, a sorry counterfeit of immortality, and, full of pity for himself, he abominated all pity. And there are some who say that his is the philosophy of strong men! No, it is not. My health and my strength urge me to perpetuate myself. His is the doctrine of weaklings who aspire to be strong, but not of the strong who are strong. Only the feeble resign themselves to final death and substitute some other desire for the longing for personal immortality. In the strong the zeal for perpetuity overrides the doubt of realizing it, and their superabundance of life overflows upon the other side of death.

Before this terrible mystery of mortality, face to face with the Sphinx, man adopts different attitudes and seeks in various ways to console himself for having been born. And now it occurs to him to take it as a diversion, and he says to himself with Renan that this universe is a spectacle that God presents to Himself, and that it behooves us to carry out the intentions of the great Stage-Manager and contribute to make the spectacle the most brilliant and the most varied that may be. And they have made a religion of art, a cure for the metaphysical evil, and invented the meaningless phrase of art for art's sake.

And it does not suffice them. If the man who tells you that he writes, paints, sculptures, or sings for his own amusement, gives his work to the public, he lies; he lies if he puts his name to his writing, painting, statue, or song. He wishes, at the least, to leave behind a shadow of his spirit, something that may survive him. If the *Imitation of Christ* is anonymous, it is because its author sought the eternity of the soul and did not trouble himself about that of the name. The man of letters who shall tell you that he despises fame is a lying rascal. Of Dante, the author of those three-and-thirty vigorous verses (*Purgatorio* xi:85–117) on the vanity of worldly glory, Boccaccio says that he relished honors and pomp more perhaps than suited with his conspicuous virtue. The keenest desire of his condemned souls is that they may be remembered and talked of here on earth, and this is the chief solace that lightens the darkness of his Inferno. And he himself confessed that his aim in expounding the concept of Monarchy was not merely that he might be of service to others, but that he might win for his own glory the palm of so great prize (*De Monarchia*, lib. i, cap. i). What more? Even of that holy man, seemingly the most indifferent to worldly vanity, the Poor Little One of Assisi, it is related in the *Legenda Trium Sociorum* that he said: *Adhuc adorabor per totum mundum!*—You will see how I shall yet be adored by all the world! (II. *Celano*, i:1). And even of God Himself the theologians say that He created the world for the manifestation of His glory.

When doubts invade us and cloud our faith in the immortality of the soul, a vigorous and painful impulse is given to the anxiety to perpetuate our name and fame, to grasp at least a shadow of immortality. And hence this tremendous struggle to singularize ourselves, to survive in some way in the memory of others and of posterity. It is this struggle, a thousand times more terrible than the struggle for life, that gives its tone, color, and character to our society, in which the medieval faith in the immortal soul is passing away. Each one seeks to affirm himself, if only in appearance.

Once the needs of hunger are satisfied—and they are soon satisfied—the vanity, the necessity—for it is a necessity—arises of imposing ourselves upon and surviving in others. Man habitually sacrifices his life to his purse, but he sacrifices his purse to his vanity. He boasts even of his weaknesses and his misfortunes, for want of anything better to boast of, and is like a child who, in order to attract attention, struts about with a bandaged finger. And vanity, what is it but eagerness for survival?

The vain man is in like case with the avaricious—he takes the means for the end; forgetting the end he pursues the means for its own sake and goes no further. The seeming to be something, conducive to being it, ends by forming our objective. We need that others should believe in our superiority to them in order that we may believe in it ourselves, and upon their belief base our faith in our own persistence, or at least in the persistence of our fame. We are more grateful to him who congratulates us on the skill with which we defend a cause than we are to him who recognizes the truth or the goodness of the cause itself. A rabid mania for originality is rife in the modern intellectual world and characterizes all individual effort. We would rather err with genius than hit the mark with the crowd. Rousseau has said in his *Émile* (book iv):

> Even though philosophers should be in a position to discover the truth, which of them would take any interest in it? Each one knows well that his system is not better founded than the others, but he supports it because it is his. There is not a single one of them who, if he came to know the true and the false, would not prefer the falsehood that he had found to the truth discovered by another. Where is the philosopher who would not willingly deceive mankind for his own glory? Where is he who in the secret of his heart does not propose to himself any other object than to distinguish himself? Provided that he lifts himself above the vulgar, provided that he outshines the brilliance

of his competitors, what does he demand more? The essential thing is to think differently from others. With believers he is an atheist; with atheists he would be a believer.

How much substantial truth there is in these gloomy confessions of this man of painful sincerity!

This violent struggle for the perpetuation of our name extends backwards into the past, just as it aspires to conquer the future; we contend with the dead because we, the living, are obscured beneath their shadow. We are jealous of the geniuses of former times, whose names, standing out like the landmarks of history, rescue the ages from oblivion. The heaven of fame is not very large, and the more there are who enter it the less is the share of each. The great names of the past rob us of our place in it; the space which they fill in the popular memory they usurp from us who aspire to occupy it. And so we rise up in revolt against them, and hence the bitterness with which all those who seek after fame in the world of letters judge those who have already attained it and are in enjoyment of it. If additions continue to be made to the wealth of literature, there will come a day of sifting, and each one fears lest he be caught in the meshes of the sieve. In attacking the masters, irreverent youth is only defending itself; the iconoclast or image-breaker is a Stylite who erects himself as an image, an *icon*. "Comparisons are odious," says the familiar adage, and the reason is that we wish to be unique. Do not tell Fernandez that he is one of the most talented Spaniards of the younger generation, for though he will affect to be gratified by the eulogy he is really annoyed by it; if, however, you tell him that he is the most talented man in Spain—well and good! But even that is not sufficient: one of the worldwide reputations would be more to his liking, but he is only fully satisfied with being esteemed the first in all countries and all ages. The more alone, the nearer to that unsubstantial immortality, the immortality of the name, for great names diminish one another.

What is the meaning of that irritation which we feel when we believe that we are robbed of a phrase, or a thought, or an image, which we believed to be our own, when we are plagiarized? Robbed? Can it indeed be ours once we have given it to the public? Only because it is ours we prize it; and we are fonder of the false money that preserves our impress than of the coin of pure gold from which our effigy and our legend has been effaced. It very commonly happens that it is when the name of a writer is no longer in men's mouths that he most influences his public, his mind being then disseminated and infused in the minds of those who have read him, whereas he was quoted chiefly when his thoughts and sayings, clashing with those generally received, needed the guarantee of a name. What was his now belongs to all, and he lives in all. But for him the garlands have faded, and he believes himself to have failed. He hears no more either the applause or the silent tremor of the heart of those who go on reading him. Ask any sincere artist which he would prefer, whether that his work should perish and his memory survive, or that his work should survive and his memory perish, and you will see what he will tell you, if he is really sincere. When a man does not work merely in order to live and carry on, he works in order to survive. To work for the work's sake is not work but play. And play? We will talk about that later on.

A tremendous passion is this longing that our memory may be rescued, if it is possible, from the oblivion which overtakes others. From it springs envy, the cause, according to the biblical narrative, of the crime with which human history opened: the murder of Abel by his brother Cain. It was not a struggle for bread—it was a struggle to survive in God, in the divine memory. Envy is a thousand times more terrible than hunger, for it is spiritual hunger. If what we call the problem of life, the problem of bread, were once solved, the earth would be turned into a hell by the emergence in a more violent form of the struggle for survival.

For the sake of a name man is ready to sacrifice not only life but happiness—life as a matter of course. "Let me die, but let my fame live!" exclaimed Rodrigo Arias in *Las Mocedades del Cid*[17] when he fell mortally wounded by Don Ordóñez de Lara. "Courage, Girolamo, for you will long be remembered; death is bitter, but fame eternal!" cried Girolamo Olgiati, the disciple of Cola Montano and the murderer, together with his fellow-conspirators Lampugnani and Visconti, of Galeazzo Sforza, tyrant of Milan. And there are some who covet even the gallows for the sake of acquiring fame, even though it be an infamous fame: *avidus malæ famæ*,[18] as Tacitus says.

And this erostratism,[19] what is it at bottom but the longing for immortality, if not for substantial and concrete immortality, at any rate for the shadowy immortality of the name?

---

[17] *The Youth of El Cid.*
[18] "Greedy bad reputation."
[19] To immortalize his name, Erostratus set fire to the temple of Diana in the city-state of Ephesus. —MM

And in this there are degrees. If a man despises the applause of the crowd of today, it is because he seeks to survive in renewed minorities for generations. "Posterity is an accumulation of minorities," said Gounod. He wishes to prolong himself in time rather than in space. The crowd soon overthrows its own idols and the statue lies broken at the foot of the pedestal without anyone heeding it; but those who win the hearts of the elect will long be the objects of a fervent worship in some shrine, small and secluded no doubt, but capable of preserving them from the flood of oblivion. The artist sacrifices the extensiveness of his fame to its duration; he is anxious rather to endure for ever in some little corner than to occupy a brilliant second place in the whole universe; he prefers to be an atom, eternal and conscious of himself, rather than to be for a brief moment the consciousness of the whole universe; he sacrifices infinitude to eternity.

And they keep on wearying our ears with this chorus of Pride! Stinking Pride! Pride, to wish to leave an ineffaceable name? Pride? It is like calling the thirst for riches a thirst for pleasure. No, it is not so much the longing for pleasure that drives us poor folk to seek money as the terror of poverty, just as it was not the desire for glory but the terror of hell that drove men in the Middle Ages to the cloister with its *acedia*.[20] Neither is this wish to leave a name pride, but terror of extinction. We aim at being all because in that we see the only means of escaping from being nothing. We wish to save our memory—at any rate, our memory. How long will it last? At most as long as the human race lasts. And what if we shall save our memory in God?

Unhappy, I know well, are these confessions; but from the depth of unhappiness springs new life, and only by draining the lees of spiritual sorrow can we at last taste the honey that lies at the bottom of the cup of life. Anguish leads us to consolation.

This thirst for eternal life is appeased by many, especially by the simple, at the fountain of religious faith; but to drink of this is not given to all. The institution whose primordial end is to protect this faith in the personal immortality of the soul is Catholicism; but Catholicism has sought to rationalize this faith by converting religion into theology, by offering a philosophy, and a philosophy of the thirteenth century, as a basis for vital belief. This and its consequences we will now proceed to examine.

---

[20] *Acedia*: a state of listlessness or torpor; unconcern with one's status or condition. —MM

16

The Makropulos Case: Reflections on the Tedium of Immortality

Bernard Williams

Not long before his death, the philosopher and poet Walter Kaufmann (1921–1980) observed that "Many people have so little imagination and are so unthoughtful that they think they would enjoy living forever."[1] Our next reading is here to dispel that unthoughtfulness. But first, a few words to set the stage.

Recall that Miguel de Unamuno approvingly quoted the French mathematician and philosopher Blaise Pascal, for whom people who do not crave immortality are "monsters." As it turns out, such monsters are not uncommon; indeed, some of them have claimed that, upon closer inspection, everlasting life would be a curse. We have already met Lucretius. To take another example, in Part III of the novel *Gulliver's Travels* (1726), the Anglo-Irish satirist Jonathan Swift introduces us to the Struldbruggs, from the island of Luggnagg. In most respects they resemble ordinary mortal humans, except that, having grown old, they continue to age forever, losing their mental acuity and gaining numerous vices in the process. As their surroundings

[1]Walter Kaufmann, "Death without Dread," in Tamar Szabo Gendler, Susanna Siegel, and Steven M. Cahn (eds.), *The Elements of Philosophy: Readings from Past and Present* (New York and Oxford: Oxford University Press, 2008), 779.

change and the mortals around them pass like seasonal flowers, the Struldbruggs wind up "living like foreigners in their own country." The funerals of their mortal countrymen are occasions of terrible mourning for the Struldbruggs, because funerals remind them that they are doomed to the unmitigated drudgery of endless old age.

Even if an endless life did not involve the infirmities of old age, it might still be a curse. In the next reading we take a steadier look at the undesirability of life everlasting, even without old age. The author, Bernard Williams (1929–2003), was a fighter pilot in the Royal Air Force before he made his name as one of the "most important British moral philosopher of his time," as *The Times of London* described him. The title of his provocative paper refers to a theatre piece by the Czech writer Karel Čapek.[2] The play, *The Makropulos Secret* (1922), is a work of fiction about EM, a woman who imbibed an elixir of life three hundred years ago, and who has been frozen at the "physical" age of forty-two ever since. She has long since achieved her life goals, endured the loss of her loved ones, and come to conclude that, "it can be a good thing not to live too long." After all those years, "everything is joyless" for her, and life will "still be more of the same" (Lucretius, line 948).

To explain why this would be the case, Williams distinguishes between our ordinary preferences, on the one hand, and *positive categorical desires*, on the other. The latter desires are not merely *conditional preferences*, which hold only so long as the question of continued existence is settled; rather, they are reasons to continue living. Williams suggests that in an immortal life, one would exhaust one's positive categorical desires, and this in turn would make endless life unbearable.

Although Williams agrees with Lucretius on this point, he takes his distance from the Epicurean philosopher in other respects, as we shall see.

This essay started life as a lecture in a series "on the immortality of the soul or kindred spiritual subject."[3] My kindred spiritual subject is, one

---

[2] An early science fiction writer, Čapek (1890–1938) introduced the word *robot* (from modern Czech *robota*, "serf labor") to the public in 1920.
[3] At the University of California, Berkeley, under a benefaction in the names of Agnes and Constantine Foerster. I am grateful to the Committee for inviting me to give the 1972 lecture in this series.

might say, the mortality of the soul. Those among previous lecturers who were philosophers tended, I think, to discuss the question whether we are immortal; that is not my subject, but rather what a good thing it is that we are not. Immortality, or a state without death, would be meaningless, I shall suggest; so, in a sense, death gives the meaning to life. That does not mean that we should not fear death (whatever force that injunction might be taken to have, anyway). Indeed, there are several very different ways in which it could be true at once that death gave the meaning to life and that death was, other things being equal, something to be feared. Some existentialists, for instance, seem to have said that death was what gave meaning to life, if anything did, just because it was the fear of death that gave meaning to life; I shall not follow them. I shall rather pursue the idea that from facts about human desire and happiness and what a human life is, it follows both that immortality would be, where conceivable at all, intolerable, and that (other things being equal) death is reasonably regarded as an evil. Considering whether death can reasonably be regarded as an evil is in fact as near as I shall get to considering whether it should be feared: they are not quite the same question.

My title is that, as it is usually translated into English, of a play by Karel Čapek which was made into an opera by Janacek and which tells of a woman called Elina Makropulos, *alias* Emilia Marty, *alias* Ellian Macgregor, alias a number of other things with the initials "EM," on whom her father, the Court physician to a sixteenth-century Emperor, tried out an elixir of life. At the time of the action she is aged 342. Her unending life has come to a state of boredom, indifference and coldness. Everything is joyless: "in the end it is the same," she says, "singing and silence." She refuses to take the elixir again; she dies; and the formula is deliberately destroyed by a young woman among the protests of some older men.

EM's state suggests at least this, that death is not necessarily an evil, and not just in the sense in which almost everybody would agree to that, where death provides an end to great suffering, but in the more intimate sense that it can be a good thing not to live too long. It suggests more than that, for it suggests that it was not a peculiarity of EM's that an endless life was meaningless. That is something I shall follow out later. First, though, we should put together the suggestion of EM's case, that death is not necessarily an evil, with the claim of some philosophies and religions that death is necessarily not an evil. Notoriously, there have been found two contrary bases on which that claim can be mounted: death is said by some not to be an evil because it is not the end, and by others, because it is. There is perhaps some profound temperamental difference between those who find consolation for the fact of death in the hope that it is only the start of another life, and those who equally find comfort in the conviction that it is the end of the only life there is. That both such temperaments exist means that those who find a diagnosis of the belief in immortality, and indeed a reproach to it, in the idea that it constitutes a consolation, have at best only a statistical fact to support them. While that may be just about enough for the diagnosis, it is not enough for the reproach.

Most famous, perhaps, among those who have found comfort in the second option, the prospect of annihilation, was Lucretius, who, in the steps of Epicurus, and probably from a personal fear of death which in some of his pages seems almost tangible, addresses himself to proving that death is never an evil. Lucretius has two basic arguments for this conclusion, and it is an important feature of them both that the conclusion they offer has the very strong consequence—and seems clearly intended to have the consequence— that, for oneself at least, it is all the same whenever one dies, that a long life is no better than a short one. That is to say, death is never an evil in the sense not merely that there is no-one for whom dying is an evil, but that there is no time at which dying is an evil—sooner or later, it is all the same.

The first argument[4] seeks to interpret the fear of death as a confusion, based on the idea that we shall be there after death to repine our loss of the *praemia vitae,* the rewards and delights of life, and to be upset at the spectacle of our bodies burned, and so forth. The fear of death, it is suggested, must necessarily be the fear of some experiences had when one is dead. But if death is annihilation, then there are no such experiences: in the Epicurean phrase, when death is there, we are not, and when we are there, death is not. So, death being annihilation, there is nothing to fear. The second argument[5] addresses itself directly to the question of whether one dies earlier or later, and says that one will be the same time dead however early or late one dies, and therefore one might as well die earlier as later. And from both arguments we can conclude *nil igitur mors est ad nos, neque pertinent hilum*—death is nothing to us, and does not matter at all.[6]

The second of these arguments seems even on the face of things to contradict the first. For it must imply that if there *were* a finite period of

---

[4]*de Rerum Natura* Book III, line 870 *seq* ("and following pages"), line 898 *seq*. (Refer to the Lucretius reading above. —MM)
[5]Ibid., line 1091.
[6]Ibid., line 830.

death, such that if you died later you would be dead for less time, then there *would* be some point in wanting to die later rather than earlier. But that implication makes sense, surely, only on the supposition that what is wrong with dying consists in something undesirable about the condition of being dead. And that is what is denied by the first argument.

More important than this, the oddness of the second argument can help to focus a difficulty already implicit in the first. The first argument, in locating the objection to dying in a confused objection to being dead, and exposing that in terms of a confusion with being alive, takes it as genuinely true of life that the satisfaction of desire, and possession of the *praemia vitae,* are good things. It is not irrational to be upset by the loss of home, children, possessions—what is irrational is to think of death as, in the relevant sense, *losing* anything. But now if we consider two lives, one very short and cut off before the *praemia* have been acquired, the other fully provided with the *praemia* and containing their enjoyment to a ripe age, it is very difficult to see why the second life, by these standards alone, is not to be thought better than the first. But if it is, then there must be something wrong with the argument which tries to show that there is nothing worse about a short life than a long one. The argument locates the mistake about dying in a mistake about consciousness, it being assumed that what commonsense thinks about the worth of the *praemia vitae* and the sadness of their (conscious) loss is sound enough. But if the *praemia vitae* are valuable; even if we include as necessary to that value consciousness that one possesses them; then surely getting to the point of possessing them is better than not getting to that point, longer enjoyment of them is better than shorter, and more of them, other things being equal, is better than less of them. But if so, then it just will not be true that to die earlier is all the same as to die later, nor that death is never an evil—and the thought that to die later is better than to die earlier will not be dependent on some muddle about thinking that the dead person will be alive to lament his loss. It will depend only on the idea, apparently sound, that if the *praemia vitae* and consciousness of them are good things, then longer consciousness of more *praemia* is better than shorter consciousness of fewer *praemia.*

Is the idea sound? A decent argument, surely, can be marshalled to support it. If I desire something, then, other things being equal, I prefer a state of affairs in which I get it from one in which I do not get it, and (again, other things being equal) plan for a future in which I get it rather than not. But one future, for sure, in which I would not get it would be one in which I was dead. To want something, we may also say, is to that extent to have reason for resisting what excludes having that thing: and death certainly does that, for a very large range of things that one wants.[7] If that is right, then for any of those things, wanting something itself gives one a reason for avoiding death. Even though if I do not succeed, I will not know that, nor what I am missing, from the perspective of the wanting agent it is rational to aim for states of affairs in which his want is satisfied, and hence to regard death as something to be avoided; that is, to regard it as an evil.

It is admittedly true that many of the things I want, I want only on the assumption that I am going to be alive; and some people, for instance some of the old, desperately want certain things when nevertheless they would much rather that they and their wants were dead. It might be suggested that not just these special cases, but really all wants, were conditional on being alive; a situation in which one has ceased to exist is not to be compared with others with respect to desire-satisfaction—rather, if one dies, all bets are off. But surely the claim that all desires are in this sense conditional must be wrong. For consider the idea of a rational forward-looking calculation of suicide: there can be such a thing, even if many suicides are not rational, and even though with some that are, it may be unclear to what extent they are forward-looking (the obscurity of this with regard to suicides of honor is an obscurity in the notion of shame). In such a calculation, a man might consider what lay before him, and decide whether he did or did not want to undergo it. If he does decide to undergo it, then some desire propels him on into the future, and *that* desire at least is not one that operates conditionally on his being alive, since it itself resolves the question of whether he is going to be alive. He has an unconditional, or (as I shall say) a *categorical* desire.

The man who seriously calculates about suicide and rejects it, only just has such a desire, perhaps. But if one is in a state in which the question of suicide does not occur, or occurs only as total fantasy—if, to take just one example, one is happy—one has many such desires, which do not hang from the assumption of one's existence. If they did hang from that assumption, then they would be quite powerless to rule out that assumption's being questioned, or to answer the question if it is raised; but clearly they are not powerless in those directions—on the contrary they are some of the few

---

[7]Obviously the principle is not without exception. For one thing, one can want to be dead: the content of that desire may be obscure, but whatever it is, a man presumably cannot be *prevented* from getting it by dying. More generally, the principle does not apply to what I elsewhere call *non-f desire*: for an account of these (see "Egoism and Altruism," 260 *seq*). They do not affect the present discussion, which is within the limits of egoistic rationality.

things, perhaps the only things, that have power in that direction. Some ascetics have supposed that happiness required reducing one's desires to those necessary for one's existence, that is, to those that one has to have granted that one exists at all; rather, it requires that some of one's desires should be fully categorical, and one's existence itself wanted as something necessary to them.

To suppose that one can in this way categorically want things implies a number of things about the nature of desire. It implies, for one thing, that the reason I have for bringing it about that I get what I want is not merely that of avoiding the unpleasantness of not getting what I want. But that must in any case be right—otherwise we should have to represent every desire as the desire to avoid its own frustration, which is absurd.

About what those categorical desires must be, there is not much of great generality to be said, if one is looking at the happy state of things: except, once more against the ascetic, that there should be not just enough, but more than enough. But the question might be raised, at the impoverished end of things, as to what the minimum categorical desire might be. Could it be *just* the desire to remain alive? The answer is perhaps "no." In saying that, I do not want to deny the existence, the value, or the basic necessity of a sheer reactive drive to self-preservation: humanity would certainly wither if the drive to keep alive were not stronger than any perceived reasons for keeping alive. But if the question is asked, and it is going to be answered calculatively, then the bare categorical desire to stay alive will not sustain the calculation— that desire itself, when things have got that far, has to be sustained or filled out by some desire for something else, even if it is only, at the margin, the desire that future desires of mine will be born and satisfied. But the best insight into the effect of categorical desire is not gained at the impoverished end of things, and hence in situations where the question has actually come up. The question of life being desirable is certainly transcendental in the most modest sense, in that it gets by far its best answer in never being asked at all.

None of this–including the thoughts of the calculative suicide–requires my reflection on a world in which I never occur at all. In the terms of "possible worlds" (which can admittedly be misleading), a man could, on the present account, have a reason from his own point of view to prefer a possible world in which he went on longer to one in which he went on for less long, or–like the suicide–the opposite; but he would have no reason of this kind to prefer a world in which he did not occur at all. Thoughts about his total absence from the world would have to be of a different kind, impersonal reflections on the value *for the world* of his presence or absence: of the same kind, essentially, as he could conduct (or, more probably, not manage to conduct) with regard to anyone else. While he can think egoistically of what it would be for him to live longer or less long, he cannot think egoistically of what it would be for him never to have existed at all. Hence the somber words of Sophocles[8] "Never to have been born counts highest of all" are well met by the old Jewish reply– "But how many are so lucky? Not one in ten thousand."

Lucretius' first argument has been interestingly criticized by Thomas Nagel,[9] on lines different from those that I have been following. Nagel claims that what is wrong with Lucretius' argument is that it rests on the assumption that nothing can be a misfortune for a man unless he knows about it, and that misfortunes must consist in something nasty *for* him. Against this assumption, Nagel cites a number of plausible counter-instances, of circumstances which would normally be thought to constitute a misfortune, though those to whom they happen are and remain ignorant of them (as, for instance, certain situations of betrayal). The difference between Nagel's approach and mine does not, of course, lie in the mere point of whether one admits misfortunes which do not consist of or involve nasty experiences: anyone who rejects Lucretius' argument must admit them. The difference is that the reasons which a man would have for avoiding death are, on the present account, grounded in desires— categorical desires—which he has; he, on the basis of these, has reason to regard possible death as a misfortune to be avoided, and we, looking at things from his point of view, would have reason to regard his actual death as his misfortune. Nagel, however, if I understand him, does not see the misfortune that befalls a man who dies as necessarily grounded in the issue of what desires or sorts of desires he had; just as in the betrayal case, it could be a misfortune for a man to be betrayed, even though he did not have any desire not to be betrayed. If this is a correct account, Nagel's reasoning is one step further away from Utilitarianism on this matter than mine,[10] and rests on an independent kind of value which a sufficiently Utilitarian person might just reject; while my argument cannot merely be

---

[8]*Oedipus at Colonus* (a play by the Greek tragedian Sophocles, c. 496–406 BC), line 1224 *seq.*

[9]"Death," *Nous* IV, no. 1 (1970): 73 *seq.* Reprinted with some alterations in James Rachels ed., *Moral Problems* (New York: Harper & Row, 1975). (Refer to the reading in Part V, below. —MM)

[10]Though my argument does not in any sense imply Utilitarianism; for some further considerations on this, see the final paragraphs of this paper.

rejected by a Utilitarian person, it seems to me, since he must if he is to be consistent, and other things being equal, attach disutility to any situation which he has good reason to prevent, and he certainly has good reason to prevent a situation which involves the non-satisfaction of his desires. Thus, granted categorical desires, death has a disutility for an agent, although that disutility does not, of course, consist in unsatisfactory experiences involved in its occurrence.

The question would remain, of course, with regard to any given agent, whether he had categorical desires. For the present argument, it will do to leave it as a contingent fact that most people do: for they will have a reason, and a perfectly coherent reason, to regard death as a misfortune, while it was Lucretius' claim that no-one could have a coherent reason for so regarding it. There may well be other reasons as well; thus Nagel's reasoning, though different from the more Utilitarian type of reason I have used against Lucretius, seems compatible with it and there are strong reasons to adopt his kind of consideration as well. In fact, further and deeper thought about this question seems likely to fill up the apparent gap between the two sorts of argument; it is hard to believe, for one thing, that the supposed contingent fact that people have categorical desires can really be as contingent as all that. One last point about the two arguments is that they coincide in not offering—as I mentioned earlier—any considerations about worlds in which one does not occur at all; but there is perhaps an additional reason why this should be so in the Utilitarian-type argument, over and above the one it shares with Nagel's. The reason it shares with Nagel's is that the type of misfortune we are concerned with in thinking about X's death is X's misfortune (as opposed to the misfortunes of the state or whatever); and whatever sort of misfortune it may be in a given possible world that X does not occur in it, it is not X's misfortune. They share the feature, then, that for anything to be X's misfortune in a given world, then X must occur in that world. But the Utilitarian-type argument further grounds the misfortune, if there is one, in certain features of X, namely his desires; and if there is no X in a given world, then *a fortiori* there are no such grounds.

But now–if death, other things being equal, is a misfortune; and a longer life is better than a shorter life; and we reject the Lucretian argument that it does not matter when one dies; then it looks as though–other things always being equal–death is at any time an evil, and it is always better to live than die. Nagel indeed, from his point of view, does seem to permit that conclusion, even though he admits some remarks about the natural term of life and the greater misfortune of dying in one's prime. But wider consequences follow.

For if all that is true, then it looks as though it would be not only always better to live, but better to live always, that is, never to die. If Lucretius is wrong, we seem committed to wanting to be immortal.

That would be, as has been repeatedly said, with other things equal. No-one need deny that since, for instance, we grow old and our powers decline, much may happen to increase the reasons for thinking death a good thing. But these are contingencies. We might not age; perhaps, one day, it will be possible for some of us not to age. If that were so, would it not follow then that, more life being *per se* better than less life, we should have reason so far as that went (but not necessarily in terms of other inhabitants) to live for ever? EM indeed bears strong, if fictional, witness against the desirability of that; but perhaps she still labored under some contingent limitations, social or psychological, which might once more be eliminated to bring it about that really other things were equal. Against this, I am going to suggest that the supposed contingencies are not really contingencies; that an endless life would be a meaningless one; and that we could have no reason for living eternally a human life. There is no desirable or significant property which life would have more of, or have more unqualifiedly, if we lasted forever. In some part, we can apply to life Aristotle's marvelous remark about Plato's Form of the Good:[11] "nor would it be any the more good for being eternal: that which lasts long is no whiter than that which perishes in a day." But only in part; for, rejecting Lucretius, we have already admitted that more days may give us more than one day can.

If one pictures living for ever as living as an embodied person in the world rather as it is, it will be a question, and not so trivial as may seem, of what age one eternally is. EM was 342 because for 300 years she had been 42. This choice (if it was a choice) I am personally, and at present, well disposed to salute—if one had to spend eternity at any age, that seems an admirable age to spend it at. Nor would it necessarily be a less good age for a woman: that at least was not EM's problem, that she was too old at the age she continued to be at. Her problem lay in having been at it for too long. Her trouble was it seems, boredom: a boredom connected with the fact that everything that could happen and make sense to one particular human being of 42 had already happened to her. Or, rather, all the sorts of things that could make sense to one woman of a certain character; for EM has a certain character, and indeed, except for her accumulating memories of earlier times, and no

---

[11]*Nicomachean Ethics*, 1096b 4.

doubt some changes of style to suit the passing centuries, seems always to have been much the same sort of person.

There are difficult questions, if one presses the issue, about this constancy of character. How is this accumulation of memories related to this character which she eternally has, and to the character of her existence? Are they much the same kind of events repeated? Then it is itself strange that she allows them to be repeated, accepting the same repetitions, the same limitations—indeed, *accepting* is what it later becomes, when earlier it would not, or even could not, have been that. The repeated patterns of personal relations, for instance, must take on a character of being inescapable. Or is the pattern of her experiences not repetitious in this way, but varied? Then the problem shifts, to the relation between these varied experiences, and the fixed character: how can it remain fixed, through an endless series of very various experiences? The experiences must surely happen to her without really affecting her; she must be, as EM is, detached and withdrawn.

EM, of course, is in a world of people who do not share her condition, and that determines certain features of the life she has to lead, as that any personal relationship requires peculiar kinds of concealment. That, at least, is a form of isolation which would disappear if her condition were generalized. But to suppose more generally that boredom and inner death would be eliminated if everyone were similarly becalmed, is an empty hope: it would be a world of Bourbons, learning nothing and forgetting nothing, and it is unclear how much could even happen.

The more one reflects to any realistic degree on the conditions of EM's unending life, the less it seems a mere contingency that it froze up as it did. That it is not a contingency, is suggested also by the fact that the reflections can sustain themselves independently of any question of the particular character that EM had; it is enough, almost, that she has a human character at all. Perhaps not quite. One sort of character for which the difficulties of unending life would have less significance than they proved to have for EM might be one who at the beginning was more like what she is at the end: cold, withdrawn, already frozen. For him, the prospect of unending cold is presumably less bleak in that he is used to it. But with him, the question can shift to a different place, as to why he wants the unending life at all; for, the more he is at the beginning like EM is at the end, the less place there is for categorical desire to keep him going, and to resist the desire for death. In EM's case, her boredom and distance from life both kill desire and consist in the death of it; one who is already enough like that to sustain life in those conditions may well be one who had nothing to make him want to do so. But even if he has, and we conceive of a person who is stonily resolved to sustain for ever an already stony existence, his possibility will be of no comfort to those, one hopes a larger party, who want to live longer because they want to live more.

To meet the basic anti-Lucretian hope for continuing life which is grounded in categorical desire, EM's unending life in this world is inadequate, and necessarily so relative to just those desires and conceptions of character which go into the hope. That is very important, since it is the most direct response, that which should have been adequate if the hope is both coherent and what it initially seemed to be. It also satisfied one of two important conditions which must be satisfied by anything which is to be adequate as a fulfillment of my anti-Lucretian hope, namely that it should clearly be *me* who lives for ever. The second important condition is that the state in which I survive should be one which, to me looking forward, will be adequately related, in the life it presents, to those aims which I now have in wanting to survive at all. That is a vague formula, and necessarily so, for what exactly that relation will be must depend to some extent on what kind of aims and (as one might say) prospects for myself I now have. What we can say is that since I am propelled forward into longer life by categorical desires, what is promised must hold out some hopes for those desires. The limiting case of this might be that the promised life held out some hope just to that desire mentioned before, that future desires of mine will be born and satisfied; but if that were the only categorical desire that carried me forward into it, at least this seems demanded, that any image I have of those future desires should make it comprehensible to me how in terms of my character they could be my desires.

This second condition, the EM kind of survival failed, on reflection, to satisfy; but at least it is clear why, before reflection, it looked as though it might satisfy the condition—it consists, after all, in just going on in ways in which we are quite used to going on. If we turn away now from EM to more remote kinds of survival, the problems of those two conditions press more heavily right from the beginning. Since the major problems of the EM situation lay in the indefinite extension of one life, a tempting alternative is survival by means of an indefinite series of lives. Most, perhaps all, versions of this belief which have actually existed have immediately failed the first condition: they get nowhere near providing any consideration to mark the difference between rebirth and new birth. But let us suppose the problem, in some way or another, removed; some conditions of bodily continuity, minimally sufficient for personal identity, may be supposed satisfied. (Anyone who thinks that no such conditions could be sufficient, and requires, for instance, conditions of memory, may well find it correspondingly difficult to find an alternative for survival in this direction which both satisfies the first requirement, of identity, and also adequately avoids the difficulties of the EM alternative.) The problem remains of whether this series of psychologically disjoint lives could be an object of hope to one who did not want to die. That is, in my view, a different question from the question of whether it will be him—which is why I distinguished originally two different requirements to be satisfied. But it is a question; and even if the first requirement be supposed satisfied, it is exceedingly unclear that the second can be. This will be so, even if one were to accept the idea, itself problematical, that one could have reason to fear the future pain of someone who was merely bodily continuous with one as one now is.[12]

There are in the first place certain difficulties about how much a man could consistently be allowed to know about the series of his lives, if we are to preserve the psychological disjointedness which is the feature of this model. It might be that each would in fact have to seem to him as though it were his only life, and that he could not have grounds for being sure what, or even that, later lives were to come. If so, then no comfort or hope will be forthcoming in this model to those who want to go on living. More interesting questions, however, concern the man's relation to a future life of which he did get some advance idea. If we could allow the idea that he could fear pain which was going to occur in that life, then we have at least provided him with one kind of reason which might move him to opt out of that life, and destroy himself (being recurrent, under conditions of bodily continuity, would not make one indestructible). But physical pain and its nastiness are to the maximum degree independent of what one's desires and character are, and the degree of identification needed with the later life to reject that aspect of it is absolutely minimal. Beyond that point, however, it is unclear how he is to bring this later character and its desires into a relation to his present ones, so as to be satisfied or the reverse with this marginal promise of continued existence. If he can regard this future life as an object of hope, then equally it must be possible for him to regard it with alarm, or depression, and—as in

---

[12]One possible conclusion from the dilemma discussed in "The Self and the Future" (Bernard Williams, *The Philosophical Review* 79, no. 2 (April 1970): 161–80).

the simple pain case—opt out of it. If we cannot make sense of his entertaining that choice, then we have not made sense of this future life being adequately related to his present life, so that it could, alternatively, be something he might want in wanting not to die. But can we clearly make sense of that choice? For if we—or he—merely wipe out his present character and desires, there is nothing left by which he can judge it at all, at least as something for *him;* while if we leave them in, we—and he—apply something irrelevant to that future life, since (to adapt the Epicurean phrase), when they are there, it is not, and when it is there, they are not. We might imagine him considering the future prospects, and agreeing to go on if he found them congenial. But that is a muddled picture. For whether they are congenial to him as he is now must be beside the point, and the idea that it is not beside the point depends on carrying over into the case features that do not belong to it, as (perhaps) that he will remember later what he wanted in the earlier life. And when we admit that it is beside the point whether the prospects are congenial, then the force of the idea that the future life could be something that he *now* wanted to go on to, fades.

There are important and still obscure issues here,[13] but perhaps enough has been said to cast doubt on this option as coherently satisfying the desire to stay alive. While few will be disposed to think that much can be made of it, I must confess that out of the alternatives it is the only one that for me would, if it made sense, have any attraction—no doubt because it is the only one which has the feature that what one is living at any given point is actually *a life*. It is singular that those systems of belief that get closest to actually accepting recurrence of this sort seem, almost without exception, to look forward to the point when one will be released from it. Such systems seem less interested in continuing one's life than in earning one the right to a superior sort of death.

The serial and disjoint lives are at least more attractive than the attempt which some have made, to combine the best of continuous and of serial existence in a fantasy of very varied lives which are nevertheless cumulatively effective in memory. This might be called the *Teiresias*[14] model. As that case

---

[13]For a detailed discussion of closely related questions, though in a different framework, see Derek Parfit, "Personal Identity," *Philosophical Review* LXXX (1971): 3–27.

[14]In Greek mythology, Teiresias was a prophet from the city of Thebes, whom the goddess Hera transformed into a woman. After living seven years as a woman, he was transformed back into a man, after which he was blinded by the goddess Athena (or in another version, by Hera), and then given seven lifetimes by Zeus. —MM

singularly demonstrates, it has the quality of a fantasy, of emotional pressure trying to combine the uncombinable. One thing that the fantasy has to ignore is the connection, both as cause and as consequence, between having one range of experiences rather than another, wishing to engage in one sort of thing rather than another, and having a character. Teiresias cannot have a character, either continuously through these proceedings, or cumulatively at the end (if there were to be an end) of them: he is not, eventually, a person but a phenomenon.

In discussing the last models, we have moved a little away from the very direct response which EM's case seemed to provide to the hope that one would never die. But perhaps we have moved not nearly far enough. Nothing of this, and nothing much like this, was in the minds of many who have hoped for immortality; for it was not in this world that they hoped to live for ever. As one might say, their hope was not so much that they would never die as that they would live after their death, and while that in its turn can be represented as the hope that one would not really die, or, again, that it was not really oneself that would die, the change of formulation could point to an after-life sufficiently unlike this life, perhaps, to [avoid] the current of doubt that flows from EM's frozen boredom.

But in fact this hope has been and could only be modeled on some image of a more familiar untiring or unresting or unflagging activity or satisfaction; and what is essentially EM's problem, one way or another, remains. In general we can ask, what it is about the imaged activities of an eternal life which would stave off the principle hazard to which EM succumbed, boredom. The Don Juan in Hell joke, that heaven's prospects are tedious and the devil has the best tunes, though a tired fancy in itself, at least serves to show up a real and (I suspect) a profound difficulty, of providing any model of an unending, supposedly satisfying, state or activity which would not rightly prove boring to anyone who remained conscious of himself and who had acquired a character, interests, tastes, and impatiences in the course of living, already, a finite life. The point is not that for such a man boredom would be a tiresome consequence of the supposed states or activities, and that they would be objectionable just on the utilitarian or hedonistic ground that they had this disagreeable feature. If that were all there was to it, we could imagine the feature away, along no doubt with other disagreeable features of human life in its present imperfection. The point is rather that boredom, as sometimes in more ordinary circumstances, would be not just a tiresome effect, but a reaction almost perceptual in character to the poverty of one's relation to the environment. Nothing less will do for eternity than something that makes boredom *unthinkable*. What could that be? Something that could be guaranteed to be at every moment utterly absorbing? But if a man has and retains a character, there is no reason to suppose that there is anything that could be that. If, lacking a conception of the guaranteedly absorbing activity, one tries merely to think away the reaction of boredom, one is no longer supposing an improvement in the circumstances, but merely an impoverishment in his consciousness of them. Just as being bored can be a sign of not noticing, understanding, or appreciating enough, so equally not being bored can be a sign of not noticing, or not reflecting, enough. One might make the immortal man content at every moment, by just stripping off from him consciousness which would have brought discontent by reminding him of other times, other interests, other possibilities. Perhaps, indeed, that is what we have already done, in a more tempting way, by picturing him just now as at every moment totally absorbed—but that is something we shall come back to.

Of course there is in actual life such a thing as justified but necessary boredom. Thus—to take a not entirely typical example—someone who was, or who thought himself, devoted to the radical cause might eventually admit to himself that he found a lot of its rhetoric excruciatingly boring. He might think that he ought not to feel that, that the reaction was wrong, and merely represented an unworthiness of his, an unregenerate remnant of intellectual superiority. However, he might rather feel that it would not necessarily be a better world in which no-one was bored by such rhetoric and that boredom was, indeed, a perfectly worthy reaction to this rhetoric after all this time; but for all that, the rhetoric might be necessary. A man at arms can get a cramp from standing too long at his post, but sentry-duty can after all be necessary. But the threat of monotony in eternal activities could not be dealt with in that way, by regarding immortal boredom as an unavoidable ache derived from standing ceaselessly at one's post. (This is one reason why I said that boredom in eternity would have to be *unthinkable*.) For the question would be unavoidable, in what campaign one was supposed to be serving, what one's ceaseless sentry-watch was for.

Some philosophers have pictured an eternal existence as occupied in something like intense intellectual enquiry. Why that might seem to solve the problem, at least for them, is obvious. The activity is engrossing, self-justifying, affords, as it may appear, endless new perspectives, and by being engrossing enables one to lose oneself. It is that last feature that supposedly makes boredom unthinkable, by providing something that is, in that earlier phrase, at every moment totally absorbing. But if one is totally and perpetually absorbed in such an activity, and loses oneself in it, then as those words suggest, we come back to the problem of satisfying the conditions that it should be me who lives for ever, and that the eternal life should be in prospect of some interest. Let us leave aside the question of people whose characteristic and most personal interests are remote from such pursuits, and for whom, correspondingly, an immortality promised in terms of intellectual activity is going to make heavy demands on some theory of a "real self" which will have to emerge at death. More interesting is the content and value of the promise for a person who *is*, in this life, disposed to those activities. For looking at such a person as he now is, it seems quite unreasonable to suppose that those activities would have the fulfilling or liberating character that they do have for him, if they were in fact all he could do or conceive of doing. If they are genuinely fulfilling, and do not operate (as they can) merely as a compulsive diversion, then the ground and shape of the satisfactions that the intellectual enquiry offers him, will relate to *him*, and not just to the enquiry. The *Platonic introjection*, seeing the satisfactions of studying what is timeless and impersonal as being themselves timeless and impersonal, may be a deep illusion, but it is certainly an illusion.

We can see better into that illusion by considering Spinoza's thought, that intellectual activity was the most active and free state that a man could be in, and that a man who had risen to such activity was in some sense most fully individual, most fully himself. This conclusion has been sympathetically expounded by Stuart Hampshire, who finds on this point a similar doctrine in Spinoza and in Freud:[15] in particular, he writes "[one's] only means of achieving this distinctness as an individual, this freedom in relation to the common order of nature, is the power of the mind freely to follow in its thought an intellectual order." The contrast to this free intellectual activity is "the common condition of men that their conduct and their judgments of value, their desires and aversions, are in each individual determined by unconscious memories"—a process which the same writer has elsewhere associated with our having any character at all as individuals.[16]

Hampshire claims that in pure intellectual activity the mind is most free because it is then least determined by causes outside its immediate states.

---

[15]*Spinoza and the Idea of Freedom,* reprinted in Stuart Hampshire, *Freedom of Mind* (Oxford: Clarendon Press, 1972), 183 *seq;* the two quotations are from 206–07.

[16]"Disposition and Memory," in *Freedom of Mind,* 160 *seq;* see especially 176–77.

I take him to mean that rational activity is that in which the occurrence of an earlier thought maximally explains the occurrence of a later thought, because it is the rational relation between their contents which, granted the occurrence of the first, explains the occurrence of the second. But even the maximal explanatory power, in these terms, of the earlier thought does not extend to total explanation: for it will still require explanation why this thinker on this occasion continued on this rational path of thought at all. Thus I am not sure that the Spinozist consideration which Hampshire advances even gives a very satisfactory sense to the *activity* of the mind. It leaves out, as the last point shows, the driving power which is needed to sustain one even in the most narrowly rational thought. It is still further remote from any notion of creativity, since that, even within a theoretical context, and certainly in an artistic one, precisely implies the origination of ideas which are not fully predictable in terms of the content of existing ideas. But even if it could yield one sense for "activity," it would still offer very little, despite Spinoza's heroic defense of the notion, for *freedom*. Or—to put it another way—even if it offered something for freedom of the intellect, it offers nothing for freedom of the individual. For when freedom is initially understood as the absence of "outside" determination, and in particular understood in those terms as an unquestionable *value*, my freedom is reasonably not taken to include freedom from my past, my character and my desires. To suppose that those are, in the relevant sense, "outside" determinations, is merely to beg the vital question about the boundaries of the self, and not to prove from premises acceptable to any clear-headed man who desires freedom that the boundaries of the self should be drawn round the intellect. On the contrary, the desire for freedom can, and should, be seen as the desire to be free in the exercise and development of character, not as the desire to be free of it. And if Hampshire and others are right in claiming that an individual character springs from and gets its energies from unconscious memories and unclear desires, then the individual must see them too as within the boundaries of the self, and themselves involved in the drive to persist in life and activity.

With this loss, under the Spinozist conception, of the individual's character, there is, contrary to Hampshire's claim, a loss of individuality itself, and certainly of anything that could make an eternity of intellectual activity, so construed, a reasonable object of interest to one concerned with individual immortality. As those who totally wish to lose themselves in the movement can consistently only hope that the movement will go on, so the consistent Spinozist—at least on this account of Spinozism—can only hope that the intellectual activity goes on, something which could be as well realized in the existence of Aristotle's prime mover, perhaps, as in anything to do with Spinoza or any other particular man.

Stepping back now from the extremes of Spinozist abstraction, I shall end by returning to a point from which we set out, the sheer desire to go on living, and shall mention a writer on this subject, Unamuno, whose work *The Tragic Sense of Life*[17] gives perhaps more extreme expression than anyone else has done to that most basic form of the desire to be immortal, the desire not to die.

> I do not want to die—no, I neither want to die nor do I want to want to die; I want to live for ever and ever and ever. I want this "I" to live—this poor "I" that I am and that I feel myself to be here and now, and therefore the problem of the duration of my soul, of my own soul, tortures me.[18]

Although Unamuno frequently refers to Spinoza, the spirit of this is certainly far removed from that of the "sorrowful Jew of Amsterdam." Furthermore, in his clear insistence that what he desperately wants is this life, the life of this self, not to end, Unamuno reveals himself at equal removes from Manicheanism and from Utilitarianism; and that is correct, for the one is only the one-legged descendant of the other. That tradition—Manichean, Orphic, Platonic, Augustinian—which contrasts the spirit and the body in such a sense that the spiritual aims at eternity, truth and salvation, while the body is adjusted to pleasure, the temporary, and eventual dissolution, is still represented, as to fifty per cent, by secular Utilitarianism: it is just one of the original pair of boots left by itself and better regarded now that the other has fallen into disrepair. Bodies are all that we have or are: hence for Utilitarianism it *follows* that the only focus of our arrangements can be the efficient organization of happiness. Immortality, certainly, is out, and so life here should last as long as we determine—or eventually, one may suspect, others will determine—that it is pleasant for us to be around.

Unamuno's outlook is at the opposite pole to this and whatever else may be wrong with it, it salutes the true idea that the meaning of life does not consist either in the management of satisfactions in a body or in an abstract immortality without one. On the one hand he had no time for Manicheanism,

---

[17]*Del sentimiento trágico de la vida*, trans. J. E. Crawford Flitch (London, 1921). Page references are to the Fontana Library edition, 1962. (Refer to the previous reading in this volume.) —MM
[18]Ibid., 60.

and admired the rather brutal Catholic faith which could express its hopes for a future life in the words which he knew on a tombstone in Bilbao:

> Though we are transformed to dust,
> In You, Lord, our faithful hope,
> May we return to live clothed
> In the flesh and skin that covered us.[19]

At the same time, his desire to remain alive extends an almost incomprehensible distance beyond any desire to continue agreeable experiences:

> For myself I can say that as a youth and even as a child I remained unmoved when shown the most moving pictures of hell, for even then nothing appeared quite so horrible to me as nothingness itself.[20]

The most that I have claimed earlier against Lucretius is not enough to make that preference intelligible to me. The fear of sheer nothingness is certainly part of what Lucretius rightly, if too lightly, hoped to exorcise; and the *mere* desire to stay alive, which is here stretched to its limit, is not enough (I suggested before) to answer the question, once the question has come up and requires an answer in rational terms. Yet Unamuno's affirmation of existence even through limitless suffering[21] brings out something which is implicit in the claim against Lucretius. It is not necessarily the prospect of pleasant times that create the motive against dying, but the existence of categorical desire, and categorical desire can drive through both the existence and the prospect of unpleasant times.

Suppose, then, that categorical desire does sustain the desire to live. So long as it remains so, I shall want not to die. Yet I also know, if what has gone before is right, that an eternal life would be unlivable. In part, as EM's case originally suggested, that is because categorical desire will go away from it: in those versions, such as hers, in which I am recognizably myself, I would eventually have had altogether too much of myself. There are good reasons, surely, for dying before that happens. But equally, at times earlier than that moment, there is reason for not dying. Necessarily, it tends to be either too early or too late. EM reminds us that it can be too late, and many, as against

---

[19]Ibid., 79. (Translated by MM.)

[20]Ibid., 28.

[21]An affirmation which takes on a special dignity retrospectively in the light of his own death shortly after his courageous speech against [Spanish Nationalist officer] Millán Astray and the obscene slogan "¡*Viva la Muerte!*" ["Long Live Death!"]. See Hugh Thomas, *The Spanish Civil War* (Harmondsworth: Pelican, 1961), 442–44.

Lucretius, need no reminding that it can be too early. If that is any sort of dilemma, it can, as things still are and if one is exceptionally lucky, be resolved, not by doing anything, but just by dying shortly before the horrors of not doing so become evident. Technical progress may, in more than one direction, make that piece of luck rarer. But as things are, it is possible to be, in contrast to EM, *felix opportunitate mortis*—as it can be appropriately mistranslated, lucky in having the chance to die.

17

Immortality without Boredom

Lisa Bortolotti and Yujin Nagasawa

In our next reading, Lisa Bortolotti and Yujin Nagasawa, both professors of philosophy at the University of Birmingham in the United Kingdom, take issue with Bernard Williams' claim that unavoidable and pervasive boredom would characterize the immortal life of an individual with unchanging categorical desires. This assumption, they say, is "implausible on the basis of considerations of psychological realism." (The term *psychological realism*, as Bortolotti and Nagasawa use it here, appears to mean something like "our best-informed description of human motives.") Our authors write that they "want to suggest that the type of boredom which is likely to emerge from the repetition of similar experiences is not the type of boredom that could have pervasive effects on the desirability and meaningfulness on one's existence." This type of boredom, which arises from poor stimulation or repeated experiences, is *situational boredom*, in contrast to *chronic* or *habitual boredom*. The latter sort of boredom, but not the former, is said to arise "from the *loss* or *outright absence* of categorical desires rather than from their *satisfaction*." In the course of her long years, however, EM has exhausted her categorical desires while repeatedly satisfying them. If EM has lost her categorical desires, then, it must have been for some other reason, not because of habitual boredom acquired in the course of a life lived too long. Bortolotti and Nagasawa conclude that Williams has offered no persuasive argument for the necessity of boredom in the immortal life.

Introduction[1]

The attention on scientific research that has the potential to extend our life span has sparked new interest in the long-standing debate on whether prolonging life or obtaining immortality would be desirable. The main argument against the desirability of immortality, developed by Bernard Williams in 1973, presents us with a dilemma between two scenarios.[2] In the former, an individual with unchanging interests and life goals continues to exist indefinitely. There are only a limited number of experiences she can have, and can wish to have, given her interests and life goals. After satisfying her interests and achieving her goals, she is affected by boredom to the point that her life becomes unbearable, and she no longer wishes to live. In the alternative scenario, the immortal life remains exciting and worth living, because there are new interests to satisfy and new life goals to attain. But sameness of interests and life goals is crucial for personal identity. In this scenario we are presented not with the indefinitely long life of *one* individual, but with the conjunction of many shorter lives belonging to different individuals who have different interests and life goals. In this latter case, the question whether immortality is desirable cannot be meaningfully answered, because, if the subjects of the mini-lives are distinct, none of them individually is immortal.

The first scenario is based on the conviction that the range of experiences worth having by one individual with certain interests and life goals would be limited. In an indefinitely long life, the repetition of such experiences would be inevitable and it would ultimately generate boredom. Allowing interests and life goals to change, as in the second scenario, is only an apparent solution, as it is not compatible with Williams' assumption about personal identity, that what defines one as a unique individual is sameness of interests and life goals.

More recent attacks on the desirability of immortality are inspired by this argument and further articulate the thought, already present in the original

---

[1]The first draft of this paper benefited from comments by Francis Longworth, and discussion with Erik Angner and Larry James during the *Happiness and the Meaning of Life* one-day conference which was held in Birmingham on May 19, 2007. We also acknowledge the intellectual support of the "Dying and Death for the 21st Century" research group at the University of Birmingham.
[2]B. Williams, "The Makropulos Case: Reflections on the Tedium of Immortality" in *Problems of the Self* (Cambridge: Cambridge University Press, 1973), 82–100.

1973 paper, that an indefinitely long life would lack *meaning*. This lack of meaning would be due to the detachment and emptiness caused by repetitive experiences in the absence of interests to satisfy and goals to attain. Williams is concerned with the meaning of life, which is a classic philosophical issue, and treats it as a conceptual problem. The cogency of his argument, however, depends crucially on empirical facts about the quality of the immortal life and about the likely causes and consequences of permanent states of boredom. On the basis of a useful distinction between two types of boredom and classical and recent psychological evidence on boredom proneness and the likely causes of boredom, we shall argue that there is no reason to believe that an indefinitely long life would be necessarily boring to the point of becoming undesirable, even when we concede that such a life would be characterized by the repetition of similar experiences.

The Makropulos case

It is likely that when the technology for prolonging life becomes available, many people will welcome the chance of becoming immortal, but will they live to regret their choice? If we were convinced by the argument that the immortal life would be boring to the point of becoming unbearable and meaningless, then debates about the sustainability of a population with increasing life expectancy, which often presuppose that living longer is a desirable goal for the individual, would be reshaped. Moreover, we would value lifestyle choices aimed at the prevention of dying to a lesser extent and we would be less keen to support and invest into those research projects aimed at achieving longer lives.

Williams' starting point is the idea that "a state of boredom, indifference and coldness" where "everything is joyless" ensues after one has lived the same experiences over and over again. Williams describes the case of Elina Makropulos, a woman who was given the elixir of immortal life by her father and went on to live for over 300 years. Elina is a literary character, created by Karel Čapek for the theatre, and then revisited by Leo Janacek in an opera with the same title, *The Makropulos Case*.[3] Williams' description of the case

---

[3]K. Čapek, "The Makropulos Case," in *Four Plays*, ed. and trans. P. Majer and C. Porter (London: Methuen, 1999), 165–260.

is very sketchy, so we will supplement it here with further details found in Čapek and Janacek.

What is special about Elina? It is important to notice that, both in the play and in the opera, Elina is a character with a distinct personality, life goals and interests that have been present in all stages of her long life. Elina has lived for 300 years without any sign of ageing, and has had an intense love life and a very successful career as an opera singer. But to keep the secret of her unusual longevity, she had to change name and country a number of times, leaving those she loved behind or seeing them die. Maybe because she suffered this type of loss too many times, Elina develops some detachment from the people around her. She claims she does not care for the well-being of her children (she cannot even remember how many she had) and she looks indifferent to the many declarations of love that she receives, treating her suitors with contempt. Other characters in the play accuse her of being unable to love and "cold as a corpse." Towards the end of the opera and the play, Elina expresses the thought that life is beautiful when it is short and that it is the fact that it does not last forever that gives it meaning and direction. In the end, Elina decides not to take the elixir that would give her another 300 years of youth and she dies.

Williams describes her situation as follows:

> Everything that could happen and make sense to one particular human being of forty-two had already happened to her. Or rather, all the sorts of things that could make sense to one woman of a certain character.[4]

Notice that the assumption here is that there is only a limited number of experiences that would enrich and give meaning to a certain stage of a woman's life, unless she could change interests and personality every time she was getting to the bottom of all the meaningful and rewarding experiences available to her. Williams believes that the reason why Elina wants to die is that, after 300 years of being the same age and doing the same things, she is tired. She finds the constant repetition of similar experiences unbearable and, as a consequence, she develops detachment from her own life. She wanted to be a proficient singer, and she achieved that goal. She aspired to love as a companion and as a mother, and she did that, many more times than she thought she would. So any experience of that kind that comes her way seems no longer exciting or enriching.

---

[4]Williams, "The Makropulos Case," 90.

As Williams explicitly recognizes in the paper, the Makropulos case is not a good illustration of what would happen in a world of immortals. In the play, Elina is one of two or three people on Earth who drank the elixir and, as a consequence, had a prolonged existence. Her being different from the people around her is probably partly responsible for her solitude and sense of detachment. Because she cannot share her secret, she feels isolated. In a world where immortality was available to many, this sense of not being understood and of not having anybody to share the concerns of one's life with, would not necessarily apply. But it is of course possible that the other aspects of Elina's experience would be shared in the world of immortals that we are imagining, as these immortal beings would also, presumably, according to Williams, exhaust at some stage the list of experiences that could make their lives meaningful and worthwhile given their interests and life goals.[5] A good illustration of this scenario can be found in the short story written by José Luis Borges, "The Immortal", where an entire community of immortal people is affected by a permanent state of apathy.[6]

The sense of detachment Williams describes in Elina is analyzed in terms of her having exhausted all her *categorical* desires. These are desires that are not conditional on one's continued existence but constitute a reason for wanting to go on living. The desire to eat a piece of carrot cake is (usually) not categorical. That desire alone would not "propel one into the future," that is, it would not be sufficient by itself to give one a reason to continue to live.[7] On the other hand, parents often have the desire to take care of their young children and be there to offer them guidance and support. That desire can play the role of a categorical desire by providing a sufficient reason for wanting to continue to live.

The only way, Williams argues, to be immortal and not develop the form of detachment from one's own life that results from the exhaustion of categorical desires is to have an indefinite number of disjoint lives, rather than to extend one's unique life – but this would not count as the genuine survival of the same person. An extreme scenario of this kind is illustrated in Michel Houellebecq's novel, *The Possibility of an Island*, where immortality is achieved via a cloning technique.[8] Between the human ancestor who is the

---

[5]Ibid., 90.

[6]J. L. Borges, "The Immortal," in *Labyrinths* (London: Penguin, 2000).

[7]Williams, "The Makropulos Case," 86.

[8]M. Houellebecq, *The Possibility of an Island*, trans. G. Bowd (London: Weidenfeld & Nicolson, 2005).

protagonist of the story (Daniel) and his subsequent clones (Daniel2, Daniel3, etc.), who are labeled as "neohumans," there is no physical continuity, strictly speaking, as the clones are new individuals. All they share is the genetic code as all the subsequent clones are derived from the human ancestor's DNA. There is no psychological continuity either, as memories are not transferable. But this problem is obviated by requiring that clones read the life story of their human ancestor and the life stories of the clones who existed before them. Although there is a genetic link between the individuals called 'Daniel', it is obvious that they are different individuals with different life stories, feelings, opinions, interests and desires.

The issue that needs addressing in relation to the Makropulos case is whether Williams is right in thinking that the repetition of potentially rewarding experiences can cause the sense of detachment from one's own life that Elina suffers from. Wisnewski rightly observes that Williams' position is convincing only if we intend by boredom a quite radical state of exhaustion of categorical desires, as opposed to the temporary emotional state that can emerge from repetitive experiences or lack of novel stimulation.[9]

We shall develop this objection further. This is our reconstruction of the first horn of the dilemma in Williams' argument:

1 If you are immortal and have unchanging categorical desires, then you will have similar experiences repeatedly.
2 If you have similar experiences repeatedly, then you will at some stage exhaust all your categorical desires.
3 If you exhaust all your categorical desires, then you will be afflicted by pervasive boredom.
4 If you have pervasive boredom, then you will suffer from lack of motivation to act, feelings of detachment and loss of meaning.
5 If your life is affected by lack of motivation to act, feelings of detachment and loss of meaning, then it is not worth living.

Conclusion: If you are immortal and have unchanging categorical desires, then your life is not worth living.

In the rest of this paper we shall challenge the view that the notion of boredom that derives from the repetition of similar experiences is the notion of boredom that is likely to make life meaningless and undesirable.

---

[9] J. Wisnewski, "Is the Immortal Life worth Living?" *International Journal for Philosophy of Religion* 58 (2005): 27–36.

Situational and habitual boredom

Many of the premises of Williams' argument are vulnerable. In particular, they suffer from lack of support and are implausible on the basis of considerations of psychological realism. Let's briefly consider the claim that we derive from premises (1) and (2), that if we are immortal and have unchanging categorical desires, then we will exhaust our categorical desires.

Wisnewski challenges this aspect of Williams' argument by observing that the type of boredom that would truly make life undesirable, if not unbearable, is not a necessary feature of immortality. Even in the immortal life new situations could emerge in which people who seem to have already exhausted all their categorical desires form new ones without changing any essential feature of their personality. Wisneswski's example is that of a man who has the categorical desire to be the best living musician and, in order to satisfy this desire, he learns to play all musical instruments to perfection. It is conceivable that, once he has achieved this aim, the man first feels satisfied with himself but then he is unable to find further reasons to continue to live. As Wisnewski argues, the invention of a new musical instrument could change this man's situation.

Levy suggests that there are categorical desires that might never be properly exhausted, because their satisfaction involves open-ended activities.[10] The example used is that of valuable activities whose aim "cannot be fixed prior to the activity itself" and "is gradually defined in the course of its pursuit," such as the pursuit of truth and justice or the practice of artistic creativity. What people take truth and justice to be is likely to develop in the course of their activity of discovery and need not be predetermined. The aim of this categorical desire could be a moving target. The claim is that interest in these types of projects could keep people engaged for an indefinitely long time.

The repetition of similar experiences might not give rise to the exhaustion of unchanging categorical desires given the nature of some categorical desires (Levy's open-ended activities) and the potential for having experiences that are similar but not identical to previously valued experiences (as in the case of Wisnewski's musician). Moreover, Williams' argument seems to depend for its persuasiveness on the extent to which the exhaustion

---

[10]N. Levy, "Downshifting and Meaning of Life," *Ratio* XVIII (2005); 176–89; citation at 184–85.

of categorical desires affects the meaningfulness and desirability of one's life. Even conceding that all the categorical desires of a unique individual might at some point be fully satisfied, this condition does not seem to necessarily lead to desiring death as opposed to life. Not having an independent reason to continue to live is not the same as having a reason to bring about one's own death, or even to come to believe that one's life is not worth living. Life might lose its interest if there is nothing that one desires independently of one's own continued existence, but death might be judged as a worse option than a life in which some pleasure is obtained from the satisfaction of conditional desires and in which the possibility of new categorical desires emerging cannot be safely ruled out. For the purposes of the present discussion, though, we shall assume that Williams' distinction between categorical and conditional desires is unproblematic and we shall not put any pressure on premises (4) and (5) of his argument.

Rather, we want to suggest that the type of boredom which is likely to emerge from the repetition of similar experiences is not the type of boredom that could have pervasive effects on the desirability and meaningfulness of ones' existence. Some psychologists call *situational* the type of boredom that arises from poor stimulation or repeated experiences.[11] This type of boredom does not usually have long-term consequences and can be characterised as a state of relatively low arousal which is attributed to an inadequately stimulating situation.[12] A common case of situational boredom is when the subject is bored *with something specific*, i.e. an experience or an activity that might also have been regarded by the subject as very pleasant to start with, but is then perceived as boring because it has been repeated too many times. Gabriel defines these episodes of boredom as "expectable products of a monotonous, repetitious, non-stimulating environment."[13]

The boredom that is manifested in personal dissatisfaction and lack of involvement and that signals low interest in one's present and future life has been called *habitual* (Bargdill) or *chronic* boredom (Eastwood et al.).[14] This type of boredom presents very different phenomenology from situational

---

[11]R. Bargdill, "The Study of Life Boredom," *Journal of Phenomenological Psychology* 31 (2000): 188–219.

[12]W. L. Mikulas and S. Vodanovich, "The Essence of Boredom," *Psychological Record* 43 (1993): 3–12.

[13]M. Gabriel, "Boredom: Exploration of a Developmental Perspective," *Clinical Social Work Journal* 16 (1988): 156–64; citation at 156.

[14]Bargdill, "The Study of Life Boredom."; J. Eastwood, C. Cavaliere, S. Fahlman, and A. Eastwood, "A Desire for Desires: Boredom and Its Relation to Alexithymia," *Personality and Individual Differences* 42 (2007): 1035–45.

boredom: the subject is not bored with something specific, but with life in general. Among the phenomena either correlated with habitual boredom or directly stemming from it, we find inactivity, withdrawal, anxiety, alienation, anti-social behavior, alcohol and drug abuse, and even depression and suicide (Vodanovich 2000). Gabriel observes that in cases of habitual boredom, "boredom does not appear responsive to external influences but rather reflective of a recurrent state of inner life."[15]

The condition that psychologists call habitual or chronic boredom has not escaped philosophical attention. Wisnewski (2005, 31) offers a characterization of habitual boredom by using Williams' own terminology: "we no longer have categorical desires propelling us into the future, and by virtue of this fact, we become bored with life." Overall and Walker refer to this phenomenon as "ennui."[16]

What are the consequences of the distinction between situational and habitual boredom for the argument by Williams? He does not explicitly distinguish between types of boredom in the paper and argues that the state of boredom that is sufficient for making one's existence meaningless and undesirable is due to the exhaustion of categorical desires. Our main strategy will be to resist premises (3), that we are going to be affected by pervasive boredom if we exhaust our categorical desires, because it is an empirical claim with no evidence going for it. If we take seriously the distinction between situational and habitual boredom, Williams' pervasive boredom is more plausibly identified with habitual boredom on the basis of the description of Elina's behaviour. And the best available hypothesis about likely causes of habitual boredom is that it arises from the *loss* or *outright absence* of categorical desires rather than from their *satisfaction*.

If Williams is talking about habitual boredom in his paper, then the claim we derive from premises (2) and (3) of his argument, that if we have repeated experiences, then we develop habitual boredom, also turns out to be implausible, or at best unsupported. The repetition of similar experiences seems to be a trigger for boredom, but there is no empirically grounded connection between the repetition of similar experiences and habitual boredom. These two considerations undermine the very motivation for Williams' argument: if the loss or absence of categorical desires is responsible

---

[15]Gabriel, "Boredom."
[16]C. Overall, *Aging, Death, and Human Longevity* (Berkeley: University of California Press, 2003); M. Walker, "Boredom, Experimental Ethics, and Superlongevity," in *Death and Anti-Death*, ed. C. Tandy, vol. 4 (Palo Alto: Ria University Press, 2006).

for the onset of habitual boredom, and not their exhaustion which would come from the repetition of similar experiences, then habitual boredom does not seem to be a special feature of immortality. The loss or absence of categorical desires, as opposed to their exhaustion, is a phenomenon that affects shorter as well as longer lives.

Boredom and goal satisfaction

A common trend in classic and recent psychological studies of boredom is to treat boredom as a trait rather than a state. It emerges from empirical investigations conducted with subjects affected by boredom that their condition is much less dependent on the contextual factors of their experience than we might think, and is instead positively correlated with character traits or other individual constants. This is thought to be the case especially for habitual boredom. Greenson suggests that habitual boredom is due to an "inhibition of fantasy," whereas Bernstein believes that it comes from a lack of emotional awareness.[17] More recently, Eastwood and colleagues have confirmed a positive correlation between research participants' boredom proneness and their lack of emotional awareness.[18] The study finds that it is possible to predict how prone to boredom individuals are and how difficult it is for them to cope with boredom on the basis of the degree of attention they pay to their thoughts and feelings and their capacity for examining and labeling their moods. On the basis of these results, the hypothesis is that boredom is not caused by "an impoverished environment," but it is "the result of an internal psychological process" which affects some individuals more than others.

Even if we concede that the repetition of similar experiences is an unavoidable feature of the immortal life (premise one), there are no reasons to believe that habitual boredom is a necessary consequence of the repetition of similar experiences (from pre- mises 2 and 3). Although the repetition of similar experiences is regarded as a trigger of situational boredom, it does not seem to be correlated with the behaviors manifested by people affected by habitual boredom. We cannot have reliable evidence on the incidence of

---

[17]R. Greenson, "On Boredom," *Journal of the American Psychoanalytic Association* 1 (1953): 7–21; H. Bernstein, 'Boredom and the Ready Made Life', *Sociological Research* 42 (1975): 512–37.
[18]J. Eastwood, et al., "A Desire for Desires," 1037.

boredom in immortal beings for lack of experimental subjects, but we can study the incidence of boredom-related behaviors in subjects who are exposed to more repetitive lifestyles, such as people in prison.[19] Findings suggest that behaviors associated with boredom are more frequently manifested in these populations, but they do not tell us whether boredom is due to those features of a life in prison that are comparable with likely features of an immortal life (such as repeated similar experiences), or to those features that are specific to, say, the prison situation (where experiences are limited in a specific way, e.g. by lack of freedom and isolation).

Prima facie, the finding that boredom proneness in all its forms, and especially proneness to habitual boredom, depends on personality traits or constants of the individuals who are the subject of experience puts additional pressure on the motivation for Williams' argument: why should we regard boredom as a *necessary* feature of the immortal life? But we are happy to concede that environmental triggers might play an important role in how boredom (including habitual boredom) develops, or even that they might be necessary for its onset. These are empirical claims that need further investigation, but the picture of boredom emerging so far is that it is the result of different factors, some related to constant traits of the individual and some related to low stimulation and the repetition of experiences. Even if constant traits were the most reliable predictor of boredom, one could argue that they would not lead to boredom in the absence of appropriate environmental triggers. If the immortal life is richer of repetitive experiences than the mortal life, the argument goes, then these triggers would be much more abundant in the immortal life, increasing the risk of habitual boredom for all those already pre-disposed to it.

In order to properly evaluate this possibility, though, we need to unpack the thought that the repetition of similar experiences is sufficient for habitual boredom, and consider whether we have any reasons to believe that habitual boredom comes from the exhaustion of categorical desires (premise 3).

---

[19]See A. Sieminska, E. Jassem and K. Konopa, "Prisoners' Attitudes towards Cigarette Smoking and Smoking Cessation: A Questionnaire Study in Poland," *BMC Public Health* 6 (2006): 181–90; R. Richmond, T. Butler, J. Belcher, A. Wodak, K. Wilhelm, and E. Baxter, "Promoting Smoking Cessation among Prisoners: Feasibility of a Multi-Component Intervention," *Australian and New Zealand Journal of Public Health* 30 (2006): 474–78; and L. Rhodes, *Total Confinement: Madness and Reason in the Maximum Security Prison* (Berkeley: University of California Press, 2004); C. Haney, "Mental Health Issues in Long-Term Solitary and 'Supermax' Confinement," *Crime and Delinquency* 49 (2003): 124–56.

Serious doubts can be shed on the link between the exhaustion of categorical desires and habitual boredom. Bargdill has concentrated on habitual boredom and attempted to investigate empirically the possible reasons for it.[20] Utilizing the (admittedly controversial) method of *individual situated narrative*, he analyzed some subjects' accounts of their own experience of boredom and found some common aspects. Either they had never had any life goal, or they had them and failed to satisfy them. In this latter case, Bargdill found a fairly common pattern. At first, subjects had goals that made them interested in their lives, but after encountering some obstacles towards the realization of those goals, they gave them up and changed the direction of their lives accordingly. Bargdill calls this phenomenon "compromising life projects." Instead of recognizing their own responsibility in what was perceived as failing to achieve their life goals, subjects often attributed this responsibility to external factors or other people, often developing anger and frustration.

The psychological literature confirms that habitual boredom has very serious consequences for the well being of the individual suffering from it, often leading to self-destructive and anti-social behavior.[21] If immortals were by necessity affected by habitual boredom, this would definitely constitute a good argument against the desirability of immortality. But for the research participants in Bargdill's study the patterns of behavior characterized as manifestations of habitual boredom were caused by never having had any life goal or having stopped pursuing a life goal without attaining it, and therefore perceiving themselves as failures. The research participants in that study had all, one way or the other, failed to give a direction to their lives.

The case of Elina Makropulos is very different. She had no further life goal to aspire to, because she had already pursued and *satisfied* all her existing life goals. Her circumstances would not be a reason for her to believe that she had failed to give a direction to her life. Elina's story is a story of success, not of failure. The evidence gathered by Bargdill does *not* support any correlation of the type that Williams postulates between goal satisfaction and habitual boredom.

Recall the dilemma we started with. Williams argues that either one has a series of disjoint mini-lives, in each of which one has new categorical desires

---

[20]Bargdill, "The Study of Life Boredom."
[21]Ibid.

to satisfy; or one extends one's own life forever. In the former case, all one's lives would be exciting and worth living, but there would be no sense in which the subject of those lives is a unique individual. The very idea of survival is compromised. In the latter case, the personal identity condition is satisfied, but one's life is doomed to boredom. In the Makropulos case, Elina cannot be different from herself and develop new categorical desires to keep her engaged and motivated. Once she has satisfied all her original categorical desires, she finds that she no longer enjoys her life experiences and is ultimately stuck in an existence devoid of meaning. In order to properly understand Elina's decision to stop living and the way in which she described her pervasive lack of motivation and her withdrawal, we need to assume that she has a version of habitual boredom (as opposed to situational boredom). In support of this reading, Williams characterizes Elina's boredom as a feature of all her perception, as if there was really nothing that could surprise or interest her anymore.

But it is implausible to think that this radical state of boredom stems from the repetition of experiences and the exhaustion of categorical desires. As we have attempted to show by reference to the psychological evidence, although boredom can be triggered in part by the limited range and quality of the subject's experience, it seems to depend heavily on the psychological characteristics of the individual and their capacity to acquire or maintain some life-goals. Elina might not find any reasons to live at the end of her first 300 years, but she is in a very different position from the inmates of maximum security prisons. Although she has been separated from those she loved in the past and she has experienced some limitation of freedom by having to disguise her identity, she has given the direction she wanted to her life and achieved what she had set out to achieve. It is the failure in developing, pursuing and ultimately achieving life goals that is most likely to determine habitual boredom. The view that some of the alleged features of the immortal life, i.e. the repetition of similar experiences and goal exhaustion, are significant factors in the occurrence of habitual boredom is unsupported and unmotivated.

The Makropulos case does illustrate something significant, that *for some individuals* the exhaustion of life goals, together with feelings of isolation and failure of integration, would render life unbearable. But we cannot find in Williams' argument any good reason to believe that in general or by necessity an immortal life would be afflicted by habitual boredom.

Objections

In this final section we shall address some objections to the argument we presented. Here is a first attempt to defend Williams' claim that the immortal life would be necessarily boring. We claimed that detachment from one's own life and loss of meaning are effects of habitual boredom and would not be a typical consequence of situational boredom, but the repetition of similar experiences that could characterize the immortal life is likely to generate situational boredom and at best be only a trigger for habitual boredom. We concluded that there is no good reason to believe that the immortal life would necessarily be plagued by habitual boredom.

An obvious reply is to suggest that situational boredom can give rise to habitual boredom, and therefore a more substantial link can be identified after all between the repetition of similar experiences and the detachment from one's life that makes the Makropulos case so tragic. In the interpretation of the psychological data on boredom we found no persuasive argument that situational and habitual boredom are related in this way and the phenomenology of the two experiences of boredom as it is manifested in first-person reports and third-person descriptions seems to be dramatically different. Ultimately this is an empirical question and we do not mean to rule out *a priori* the possibility that a link between situational and habitual boredom could be identified in the future. If such a link were discovered, then it would be reasonable to expect the immortal life to contain more cases, or more dramatic cases, of habitual boredom. However, in his paper Williams has failed to give us any conceptual or empirical argument for this conclusion, and therefore his way of reaching the conclusion would remain unwarranted, even if the conclusion turned out to be true.

Another related worry could be articulated as follows. We assume that what Williams has in mind, when he argues that immortal life is not worth living, is that the immortal life would be plagued by habitual boredom. However, he could be thinking about a really persistent form of situational boredom, which could be equally harmful if experienced for eternity. In our view, the literary evidence in Williams' paper does not support this reading, given that Williams associates the relevant type of boredom with the exhaustion of categorical desires and with a failure of engagement with *all* available experiences, rather than with a sustained but relatively circumscribed lack of interest. But, even if he had in mind just a persistent form of situational boredom, what is missing in his argument is a reason to believe that situational boredom could be so harmful and generate lack of motivation to act, feelings of detachment and loss of meaning (premise 4). If he thought that situational boredom could have serious effects, but not as serious and damaging as those described in premise 4 of his argument, then his conclusion would remain unsupported. The target of Williams' argument is to show that death is preferable to living for an indefinitely long time.

The argument we just considered is an instance of a more general strategy, aimed at showing that immortality is undesirable because it would be "more of a bad thing." This strategy cannot be used to rescue Williams, because it is not in the spirit of Williams' argument. Williams defends the undesirability of immortality but concedes from the start that all things considered death is a bad thing. The question becomes: how can more of a good thing (life) becomes worse than a bad thing (death)? How can the successful talented passionate Elina lose the desire to live? The arguments aimed at showing that, when life is not that good (e.g. it is afflicted by boredom), having more of it would bring even more misery are not addressing the same problem as Williams' argument.

Finally, we would like to consider a set of methodological objections to our argument. Is the psychological evidence sufficiently authoritative in this context? Is it at all relevant? Let's address authority first. For our objection to Williams to go through we don't need to buy into any specific theory about what boredom is, how it manifests itself, or what causes it. There is a lively debate in the psychological literature about each of these three issues and the jury is out. The studies on boredom proneness differ in their interpretation of which specific trait of an individual might be the determining factor in the occurrence of boredom, but they seem to converge on the view that the factor is a constant trait, and not just the combination of external features of an individual's experience. We only need to claim that this hypothesis about the occurrence of states of boredom is plausible in order to put pressure on the premises of Williams' argument. Reference to the existing psychological evidence is methodologically less objectionable than relying on anecdotal evidence, fiction or intuitions, primarily because of the possibility that, as there are significant individual differences in boredom proneness, there can be divergent intuitions about the nature of boredom and the likely causes of its occurrence. What mechanisms cause boredom and what type of behavior is caused by it are empirical questions, and if empirical data about the phenomenon are available, then the appeal to anecdotes, fiction or intuitions cannot be regarded as a better way to answer those questions.

Let's move to the second methodological worry. Why should empirical data about human behavior in the *mortal* life be of any relevance to human behavior in an immortal life? The change of conditions and circumstances could make an important difference to the quality of human experience. This is a good point, and it is an objection that should invite greater caution in any philosophical discussion of immortality. The psychological evidence on boredom is informative about how humans are likely to behave, but because the data concern mortal beings, they can be only a tentative guide to the experience of boredom in the immortal life. The assumption we make throughout the argument is that human nature would not be drastically changed in this respect if life were to be extended. But if you are worried about the legitimacy of this assumption, Williams makes it too. No fictional scenario can be immune from the worry that we are making inferences about what immortality would be like based on our experiences of the mortal life.

The *necessity* of boredom in the immortal life cannot be defended just by reflecting on the concepts involved, as there is nothing in the mere idea of immortality that suggests the necessity of boredom. The claim that the immortal life would be unavoidably or necessarily boring needs to have some other grounds, and it is based on Williams' views about why people get bored in the mortal life. His views might have an intuitive appeal, but are supported neither by argument nor by the available empirical evidence.

Conclusion

In this paper we had no ambition to offer a comprehensive answer to the question whether the immortal life would be desirable. Rather, we aimed at advancing the debate on the desirability of immortality by reconsidering the claim that the immortal life would necessarily be plagued by boredom. We found this claim unjustified on the basis of the best current understanding of the phenomenon of boredom in the psychological literature. The type of boredom that brings about loss of meaning and detachment from one's life ensues in the absence of life goals or as a result of the failure in pursuing the life goals one has, and it correlates with individual traits and constants. Boredom can be triggered by low stimulation and repeated experiences, and although these triggers can be seen as necessary for boredom to develop, they are not sufficient.

It is possible that the reason why we have not found a correlation between the exhaustion of categorical desires and habitual boredom is that in the mortal life the exhaustion of categorical desires is not such a common phenomenon. It could become a more serious problem for immortals, and evidence that it correlates with habitual boredom could become available then. But Williams has no independent argument to endorse this claim. So, as we stand, we should not rule out the possibility of immortality without boredom.

18

Death and Eternal Recurrence

Lars Bergström

In the next reading, we consider the question *What if, instead of having an immortal soul, we are infinitely mortal?* The doctrine of eternal return (or eternal recurrence) holds that exactly the same events in exactly the same sequence have taken place infinitely many times in the past and will take place infinitely many times in the future. Thus, you have read the previous line infinitely many times in the past and you will read it infinitely many times in the future. The reader might recall Lucretius' lines:

> When you reflect on the unmeasured span
> Of ages past, how many and various were
> The motions of matter, you may rest assured
> That the seeds at times were placed in the same order
> As these seeds which compose us now; a fact
> That the mind can't retain in memory.[1]

By "seeds," Lucretius appears to be referring here to atoms. So he, too, invokes the possibility of Eternal Return.

Some authors have marveled at how pervasive the idea of eternal return has been, across the continents and the centuries, but we need not be too surprised by the recurrence of the idea of eternal recurrence: it is a simple analogy, drawn from day-to-day regularities in a wide range of geographies and social settings: high tide and low tide, night and day, rainy season and dry season, birth and death.

The influential German philosopher Friedrich Nietzsche (1844–1900) once wrote that the thought of eternal return must be accepted

---

[1]Refer to our excerpt from Book III of *On the Nature of Things above*, lines 851–56.

as "an ineluctable implication of impartial science,"[2] but he was probably writing in a deliberately provocative tone. The idea, at least in the versions presented so far, is probably too speculative to be taken seriously as a scientific hypothesis (talk about unfalsifiable!); nevertheless, some contemporary physicists find it strangely compelling. In a 2004 article in *Discover* magazine, for example, science writer Michael D. Lemonick discusses the "ekpyrotic hypothesis," a speculative view of cosmologists Paul Steinhardt and Neil Turok:[3]

> They theorize that the cosmos was never compacted into a single point and did not spring forth in a violent instant. Instead, the universe as we know it is a small cross section of a much grander universe whose true magnitude is hidden in a dimension we cannot perceive. What we think of as the Big Bang, they contend, was the result of a collision between our three-dimensional world and another three-dimensional world less than the width of a proton away from ours [...] Moreover, they say the Big Bang is just the latest in a cycle of cosmic collisions stretching infinitely into the past and into the future. Each collision creates the universe anew.

In the following excerpt, Lars Bergström, Emeritus Professor of Practical Philosophy at the University of Stockholm, explores some philosophical implications of eternal return, as the doctrine has a bearing on our conception of death. Bergström distinguishes between linear time and closed time. Linear time may be represented as a straight line, where the points on the line represent moments or instants of time. Eternal return in linear time would mean that time is infinite, but the history of the universe is finite. Thus, each moment or event x occurs infinitely many times. In the case of closed time, by contrast, time may be represented as a closed curve, or a circle. As we move around the circle, or "through time," we eventually arrive at the very same point or moment that we started from. Thus, although one could say that time forever repeats itself, one could also say that each moment or event in closed time occurs only once.

[2]Walter Kaufman, ed., *The Portable Nietzsche* (New York: The Viking Press, 1968), 111.
[3]"Before the Big Bang," *Discover* 25, no. 2 (February 2004), http://www.discover.com/issues/feb-04/cover/|Space; accessed 6 January 2007. Also see Paul J. Steinhardt and Neil Turok, *Endless Universe: Beyond the Big Bang* (New York: Doubleday, 2007).

With the distinction between linear and circular time in hand, Bergström argues that "the *belief* in closed time—or the belief that closed time is at least a realistic possibility—may make a great difference" for one who believes in it. Here he is taking a cue from Nietzsche, who claimed that the kind of person who could embrace the "thought of eternal return" could embrace life without regret and meet the end accordingly. Bergström then considers the thought of eternal recurrence in closed time with reference to problems of personal identity, justice, and whether eternal return would make things worse for those whose lives are full of suffering. "Under normal circumstances," he writes,

> if the future looks bad, we may nevertheless want to live on because we think that a bad life can be preferable to death. But if we come to believe in eternal recurrence, we may see things differently. Death seems less bad if it is followed by life, and we may wish to avoid the repetition of a bad future.

In the course of the discussion Bergström mentions relevant views of several thinkers we have already encountered, including Miguel de Unamuno, Thomas Nagel, and Bernard Williams.

Many people—perhaps the vast majority of mankind—seem to believe that there is some kind of life after death. This is remarkable, if only because corpses appear to be so completely dead. Some people believe that each person has an immaterial soul that somehow lives on when the body is transformed into a corpse, but this is unlikely in view of the fact that a person's mental life appears to be intimately connected with what happens in his or her brain. Even so, there is perhaps some other way in which we might survive death.

The belief in some kind of afterlife may of course be an instance of wishful thinking, but it is unclear to what extent a life after death is something to be wished for. To wish for good things—at least if one believes that they are at all possible—is perhaps not irrational, but it is not so obvious that life after death would be a good thing. It is very unclear what kind of life it could be. In this paper I shall explore the idea that life after death is exactly the same as life before death. This follows from the theory of *eternal recurrence*. Eternal recurrence—or "eternal return," as it is sometimes called—can be described in different ways; roughly, the basic idea is that the whole history of the universe has happened before and will happen again; cosmic history is cyclic, with no beginning and no end. In particular, whenever someone dies, he or she will be born again in the next cycle of cosmic history. So even if all of us die, our death is never definitive. There is always an afterlife, and this afterlife is just like the life we live before death. In one sense, we are certainly mortal—but, in another sense, we are also immortal.

The idea that everything has happened before and will happen again may seem very implausible, but many philosophers have been attracted to it, and it used to be held by many people in earlier times. For traditional man, time was cyclical in the sense that life consisted in the repetition of archetypes; e.g. each year (often in the spring) men abandoned the past and started all over again, thereby achieving purification and recreation.[4] The distinguished historian of religions Mircea Eliade, in his book *The Myth of the Eternal Return,* writes as follows:

> This cyclical conception of the disappearance and reappearance of humanity is also preserved in the historical cultures. In the third century BC, Berossus [a Babylonian priest and astronomer —MM] popularized the Chaldean doctrine of the "Great Year" in a form that spread through the entire Hellenic world (whence it later passed to the Romans and the Byzantines). According to this doctrine, the universe is eternal but it is periodically destroyed and reconstituted every Great Year (the corresponding number of millennia varies from school to school).[5]

Eliade approvingly quotes another author as follows:

> According to the celebrated Platonic definition, time, which determines and measures the revolution of the celestial spheres, is the moving image of unmoving eternity, which it imitates by revolving in a circle. [...] No event is unique, occurs once and for all (for example the condemnation and death of Socrates), but it has occurred, occurs, and will occur, perpetually; the same individuals have appeared, appear, and reappear at every return of the cycle upon itself. Cosmic duration is repetition and *anakuklosis,* eternal return.[6]

Eliade also says that "the eternal return—the periodic resumption, by all beings, of their former lives [...] is one of the few dogmas of which we know

---

[4]See Mircea Eliade, *The Myth of the Eternal Return,* 85. (Refer to the entry in the Further Readings section at the end of Part IV. —MM)

[5]Eliade, *The Myth of the Eternal Return,* 87.

[6]Ibid., 89. The quotation is from Henri-Charles Puech.

with some certainty that they formed a part of primitive Pythagoreanism";[7] and "the Greek theory of eternal return is the final variant undergone by the myth of the repetition of an archetypal gesture, just as the Platonic doctrine of Ideas was the final version of the archetype concept, and the most fully elaborated."[8]

In later years, the belief in eternal recurrence appears to have become much less widespread. This is probably because of the overwhelming influence of Jewish and Christian conceptions of cosmic history as linear and bounded by two unique events: Creation and Last Judgment.[9] But some philosophers, notably Nietzsche,[10] have been attracted to the idea, and it seems to have been accepted by C. S. Peirce.[11] In one place, Nietzsche sketches an argument for eternal recurrence as follows:

> If the world may be thought of as a certain definite quantity of force and as a certain definite number of centers of force—and every other representation remains indefinite and therefore useless—it follows that, in the great dice game of existence, it must pass through a calculable number of combinations. In infinite time, every possible combination would at some time or another be realized; more: it would be realized an infinite number of times. And since between every combination and its next recurrence all other possible combinations would have to take place, and each of these combinations conditions the entire sequence of combinations in the same series, a circular movement of absolutely identical series is thus demonstrated: the world as a circular movement that has already repeated itself infinitely often and plays its game in infinitum.[12]

---

[7]Ibid., 120.
[8]Ibid., 123. See also Richard Sorabji, *Time, Creation, and the Continuum* (London: Duckworth, 1983), 182ff.
[9]See Milic Capek, "Eternal Return," in *The Encyclopedia of Philosophy*, ed. Paul Edwards (New York and London: Macmillan, 1967), vol. 3, 61–62. But also Eliade, *The Myth of the Eternal Return*, 129–30. Eliade also says: "From the seventeenth century on, linearism and the progressivistic conception of history assert themselves more and more" (145).
[10]See, for example, Lawrence Hatab, *Nietzsche's Life Sentence: Coming to Terms with Eternal Recurrence* (New York and London: Routledge, 2005), and Friedrich Nietzsche, *The Will to Power*, trans. W. Kaufman and R.J. Hollingdale (New York: Random House, 1968), 544–50.
[11]See Capek, "Eternal Return." [Charles Sanders Peirce (1839–1914) was an American logician and philosopher who is associated with pragmatism. —MM] For more contemporary proponents or sympathizers of the doctrine, Eliade points out that "the work of two of the most significant writers of our day—T. S. Eliot and James Joyce—is saturated with nostalgia for the myth of eternal repetition and, in the last analysis, for the abolition of time" (Eliade, *The Myth of the Eternal Return*, 153).
[12]Nietzsche, *The Will to Power*, 549.

Peirce seems to have reasoned in a similar way.[13] Anders Wedberg claims that paragraph 1066 of *The Will to Power*—from which the above quotation is taken—can be interpreted to contain five postulates from which the eternal recurrence can be strictly derived. The five postulates are (in my translation):

P1. Time is the infinite and unbounded sequence of discrete moments $T = \ldots, t_{-2}, t_{-1}, t_0, t_1, t_2, \ldots$ (where a "moment" may be a point or a certain short interval of time).

P2. At each moment in T, there occurs exactly one of the states in the set Σ, where Σ is the finite set of all the possible total states of affairs.

P3. Each state in Σ occurs as some moment in T.

P4. Σ is a finite set $\{s_1, s_2, s_3, \ldots, s_p\}$.

P5. If the same state occurs at t_i and t_j, then there is a state in Σ that occurs at both t_{i+1} and t_{j+1}.

Wedberg shows in detail that, if P1, P2, and P3 are satisfied, then the conjunction of P4 and P5 is equivalent to eternal recurrence, i.e. the thesis that there exists a specific sequence S of the states in Σ, such that the history of the world has the form …SSSSSSS…. But Wedberg also notes that, while Nietzsche himself regarded P4 as the most problematic of the postulates, each of P1, P2, P4, and P5 can very well be questioned.[14]

Most people today may be inclined to dismiss the doctrine of eternal recurrence as pure fantasy. However, one may wonder if it can be refuted by rational arguments. To some extent, this depends upon the exact version of the doctrine, and it also depends upon the nature of time and other cosmological facts—and these are matters upon which there appears to be no solid and convincing consensus among the experts.

---

[13]See Capek, "Eternal Return," 291–92. Capek notes that this reasoning is related to a certain theorem proved by Henri Poincaré, but that Nietzsche grasped this intuitively a few years before it was proved by Poincaré (see p. 291). However, Capek claims that eternal recurrence "is incompatible with our present physical knowledge" (1960, p. 294); for example, he cites "the lack of constancy and the lack of persistence through time of the alleged 'particles' of contemporary physics" and the fact that relativity theory forces us "to deny the existence of events simultaneous in an absolute sense" (p. 293). Capek's reasoning is criticized by Bas van Fraassen ("Čapek on Eternal Recurrence," *Journal of Philosophy* 59 (1962): 371–75.

[14]Anders Wedberg, "*Die ewige Wiederkunft: Ett filosofihistoriskt tidsfördriv*," in *Nio filofiska studier*, ed. H. Wennerberg (Uppsala: Filosofiska förentingen), 69–74.

Recurrence in linear time

We ordinarily think of time as *linear*; that is, we believe it can be represented by a line, where the points on the line represent moments or instants of time.[15] The line may or may not be bounded, in one end or in both. Eternal recurrence in linear time would mean that time is infinite, and that the history of the universe is finite, but occurs over and over again, without beginning and/or without end. Each occurrence of cosmic history[16] is qualitatively exactly like every other, the only difference is that they occur at different times.[17]

Given what we currently believe about the universe, it appears that eternal recurrence in linear time is not to be expected. In particular, physicists seem to hold that the world is not completely deterministic. If it is not, it seems very unlikely that the whole cosmic history would be qualitatively the same whenever it occurs. Besides, even if it were true that whenever it comes to an "end" it always "begins" all over again, we have no reason to believe that it will always begin in exactly the same way as before.

This talk of a beginning and an end of cosmic history may be bewildering. In one sense, eternal recurrence means that there is no beginning and no end. Clearly, however, the idea is that there is a *sequence* of cosmic histories, where every element in the sequence has a beginning and an end, but where there is perhaps no beginning and no end to the sequence itself. We might imagine that each instance of cosmic history begins with a Big Bang and ends with a Big Crunch or Heat Death (maximum entropy). But there seems to be no particular reason why one should expect there to be more than one

---

[15]People disagree about whether time is continuous, dense, or discrete, but this seems to be irrelevant for problems concerning eternal recurrence, so it will not be discussed here.

[16]One may wonder if the notion of a cosmic history makes sense at all, if "time is relative" as in relativity theory. Different reference frames split spacetime differently into space and time. But some physicists seem to believe that there is nevertheless a kind of "universal" or "cosmic" time in the universe, namely the time that is relative to a frame of reference from which the background heat radiation that fills space appears exactly uniform in all directions (see Paul Davies, *About Time: Einstein's Unfinished Revolution* (London: Penguin Books, 1995), 127–29). Besides, even if *clocks* are affected by motion and by gravity, as in relativity theory, it may perhaps be doubted that *time* is therefore likewise affected. This seems to *presuppose* that time is not absolute. There is no consensus on this. For example, J.R. Lucas says: "Time is not the same as change or motion, it is not just what the clocks say. For we are aware of the passage of time, even when we are not aware of any changes in the external world" (*A Treatise of Time and Space*, London: Methuen, 1973), 8).

[17]If time is absolute, this is perhaps a qualitative difference. Otherwise, it can be regarded as merely numerical.

instance of cosmic history—unless one finds it hard to believe that there is simply no time, or just empty (but infinite) time, before and after a single (finite) cosmic history.

Closed time

A completely different idea is that time is not linear, but *closed* (or "circular" or "cyclic"). If so, it can be represented by a circle, or some other closed curve, rather than by a straight line.[18] The idea is that if we move from one instant or moment of time to a later moment, and so on, and so on, we will ultimately arrive at the very same moment that we started from. Someone might express this latter thought by saying that time itself recurs or repeats itself.

However, some philosophers say that a time cannot recur or repeat itself, since this would mean that one and the same time occurs at different times— while in fact each time can occur only once.[19] This objection is not very strong. We may be inclined to agree that a time does not occur at different times, but this is perhaps mainly because a time does not "occur" (at some time) at all. Rather, the idea that a time, t, recurs must be taken to mean that there is some sequence of times, $<x_1, x_2, ..., x_n>$, where each x_{i+1} is later than x_i, such that $t = x_1 = x_n$.[20]

---

[18]Some philosophers may even argue that if there is eternal recurrence, then, in virtue of the Principle of the Identity of Indiscernibles, time *must* be closed. For, according to that Principle, there can be no numerical difference where there is no qualitative difference. Susan Weir, for example, argues in this way ("Closed Time and Causal Loops: A Defence against Mellor," *Analysis*, 48 (1988): 203–09; the reference is to 204). But this, again, seems to presuppose that time is not absolute—for if time is absolute and linear, there is a qualitative difference between different cycles of cosmic history, namely that they occur at different times.

[19]See, for example, Lucas, *A Treatise of Time*, 58 and W.H. Newton-Smith, *The Structure of Time* (London: Routledge & Kegan Paul, 1980), 57. I will come back to the problem of repetition below.

[20]Indeed, there is some indication that Peirce might have believed in closed time. Capek quotes what he calls a "peculiar argument" from Peirce (*Collected Works* I, 498–50) as follows: "since every portion of time is bounded by two instants, there must be a connection of time ring-wise. Events may be limited to a portion of this ring, but the time itself must extend round or else there will be a portion of time, say future time and also past time, not bounded by two instants" (Milic Capek, "The Theory of Eternal Recurrence in Modern Philosophy of Science, with Special Reference to C.S. Peirce," *Journal of Philosophy* 57 (1960): 289–96; the reference here is to 295–96). Wedberg points out that there are formulations in Nietzsche's work that suggests that he sometimes thought of time as closed, even though this is incompatible with his assumption that time is infinite and discrete. Wedberg suggests that Nietzsche might have started with this assumption and then, after having

The relation *later than* is usually taken to be irreflexive, asymmetric, and transitive. But if time is closed, these assumptions are problematic. For irreflexivity as well as asymmetry implies that, for every time *t*, *t* is *not* later than *t*, whereas if times "recur" in the sense just indicated, transitivity would imply that *t* *is* later than *t*. We would have a contradiction on our hands. So it might seem that, if time is closed, either irreflexivity and asymmetry or transitivity must be given up.

We can hardly stay away from the relation *later than* altogether, for this relation (or something equivalent) seems to be absolutely essential for our notion of *time*. However, W.H. Newton-Smith claims that "no two-term relation will be adequate for characterizing order in a closed structure."[21] As a matter of fact, he seems to think that if time is closed, it has no direction— since each time is later than every other time, and each time is even later than itself.[22] This is strange in view of the fact that he himself points out that positing closed time would require a distinction between *locally before*, which is an asymmetric but not transitive relation, and *globally before*, which is reflexive, symmetric, and transitive.[23] Surely, this is on the right track, but Newton-Smith seems to forget about this possibility as soon as he has mentioned it.

Let us stick to the relation *later than*, and let us retain the usual characterization of this relation as irreflexive, asymmetric, and transitive. Let us notice, however, that these properties have to be relativized, explicitly or implicitly, to some set in which the relation in question holds; for a relation may be, e.g., transitive in one set but not in another. Now, if time is closed, it is quite reasonable to assume that *later than* is not connected in the set *T* of all times. For, as we have seen, this would lead to contradictions; e.g. a time would be later than itself (because of transitivity) and not later than itself (because of irreflexivity). But in "local" subsets of *T*, i.e. subsets whose elements are comparatively close to one another, we can still uphold the

---

used it to support eternal recurrence, changed his mind about time under the influence of Leibniz's principle of the Identity of Indiscernibles (see Wedberg, "*Die ewige Wiederkunft*, 80–83).

[21]Newton-Smith, *The Structure of Time*, 59.

[22]The same point is evidenced by the fact that, when he illustrates closed time with a circle, he does not indicate direction with an arrow, as he does in the case of open, linear time (see Newton-Smith, *The Structure of Time*, 58). Lucas has a similar view. He says that "there are difficulties about the order of events in cyclic time. If we take 'before' and 'after' in their usual sense, every event will be both before and after every other event; and it will become impossible [...] to identify them by reference to their temporal ordering. [...] Moreover, even if we could introduce an order into cyclic time, we cannot import a direction" (*A Treatise of Time*, 59–60).

[23]Newton-Smith, *The Structure of Time*, 58–59.

connectedness of the relation. In view of common usage, *later than* should always be taken as irreflexive, asymmetric, and transitive—but if time is closed it should only be applied in local subsets of T.[24]

Suppose time is really closed. Suppose, for example, that the history of the universe starts with a Big Bang and ends with a Big Crunch, which immediately (or after a while) takes us back to the time of the Big Bang and then further to the Big Crunch, and so on forever. Of course, we would never notice, since we only exist for a very small interval of time in the cosmic history. So we would naturally, but falsely, believe that *later than* is transitive without any restriction (and that time is linear). For the times at which we exist constitute a very local subset of the set T of all times.

If, for every time t, there is some sequence of times, $<x_1, x_2, ..., x_n>$, such that $t = x_1 = x_n$ and each x_{i+1} is later than x_i, then time certainly has a direction. The direction is determined by the asymmetric relation *later than*. And even if, in this sense, every instant in closed time will "recur," it will not follow that every time is later than itself. Nor will it follow that for every pair of times, each member is later than the other.

But is there any reason to believe that time is closed? Perhaps not. But neither, it seems, is there any reason to believe that time is linear. For all we know, both alternatives seem equally possible.[25] Both are equally compatible with all possible empirical evidence. Furthermore, it seems unlikely that simplicity could break the tie. In some respect, a straight line may be simpler that a circle, but with the straight line there is also the problem of how, and why, it begins and ends—unless it is of infinite length, which is also problematic and not very simple. Linear time may be simpler in the sense that it appears more "natural" to ordinary people—at least in modern times—but, given the manifest "unnaturalness" of modern cosmology, this is surely not a very relevant consideration. Besides, the fact that people *nowadays* tend to think of time as linear may be primarily due to the overwhelming influence over many centuries of Christian dogma.

---

[24]Notice that this is somewhat different from Newton-Smith's suggestion. He recognizes *two* relations, two senses of "before," while I stick to *one* well-known relation—which may however not be connected in the set of all times (depending upon whether time is closed). His suggestion, as well as mine, removes contradictions, but it seems to me that mine is more natural in view of common usage.

[25]According to Lawrence Hatab, Nietzsche did not try to decide between linear and cyclical time for eternal recurrence. This was partly because Nietzsche's immanent naturalism is incompatible with an external, "God's eye" standpoint from which one can survey all of reality and make the relevant decision (see Hatab, *Nietzsche's Life Sentence*, 71–73).

We may conclude, then, that closed time is a realistic possibility, which in turn appears to imply a plausible version of eternal recurrence.

Objective and subjective perspectives

Some philosophers would still insist that eternal recurrence in closed time is incoherent: if time were closed, they would argue, it would *not* be the case that every time will recur. For example, J.R. Lucas says: "If time really were cyclic, there would not be a recurrence of events [...] not the same sort of event all over again, but the very same event just once."[26] Lucas claims that recurrence presupposes precisely that time is *not* cyclic (closed). Adolf Grünbaum seems to have the same view; he says that "cyclic recurrence affirms the openness of time."[27]

It might be replied that this is just a matter of words. Lucas and Grünbaum may be right as long as "recurrence" is taken in its normal sense, but this normal sense probably reflects our normal, unreflecting belief that time is linear. If we believed that time is closed, the normal sense of "recurrence," in contexts like this, would probably be the one indicated above.

However, there may still be some doubt as to whether this reply has any philosophical substance. Is there any real difference between recurrence in closed time—from now on, unless otherwise indicated, "recurrence" will always mean recurrence of this kind—and no recurrence at all? In particular, if there is a difference, is this difference of any interest to those of us who do not want to die (or, for that matter, to those who want to die)?

We need to distinguish here between objective and subjective differences.[28] From an objective point of view, there is a theoretical difference between

---

[26]Lucas, *A Treatise of Time*, 58.

[27]Adolf Grünbaum, *Philosophical Problems of Space and Time*, 2nd ed. (Boston: Reidel, 1973), 198.

[28]Thomas Nagel has made important contributions to our understanding of this distinction; see, for example, *Mortal Questions* (refer to the Further Readings entry, at the end of Part V), in particular, the chapter entitled "Subjective and Objective" (Nagel, *Mortal Questions*, 196–213). Most of us believe that the ambition to achieve objectivity, especially evident in the natural sciences, leads to an increased and more correct understanding of reality, but Nagel forcefully argues that a purely objective conception of the world can never be complete. The objective facts are not all the facts there are. Many truths are only accessible from a subjective perspective. For example, a complete and objective description of every person in the building where I am now writing this paper does

linear and cyclical time, but this difference is never noticed by anyone. It is not noticed from any subjective point of view. Still, the *prospect* of death may appear quite different to those who believe in closed time than to those who do not. In other words, the *belief* in closed time—or the belief that closed time is at least a realistic possibility—may make a great difference from a subjective perspective.

When the prospect of death is terrifying it is, I suggest, the prospect of not having any future, of never again having any experiences. But the very idea of a *future* is only intelligible from within a subjective perspective. From an external perspective, eternal recurrence in closed time may be just the same as no recurrence at all, but from a subjective point of view it might be a great comfort, since it would remove the prospect of never again having a subjective point of view.

According to Thomas Nagel, "if death is an evil, it is the *loss of life*, rather than the state of being dead, or nonexistent, or unconscious, that is objectionable."[29] This seems to me to be only partly correct. I should not really object to the loss of life, if it were not followed by the permanent state of being dead.[30] The loss of life seems quite tolerable if time is closed, for in that case death is followed by life.

But is that really what happens in closed time? Philosophers like Lucas and Grünbaum may insist that death is *not* followed by life in closed time, since in closed time a person's life occurs only once. From a subjective point of view, it may appear that death will be followed by life in closed time—since the subject will never experience the time between death and life—but this, it might be argued, is an illusion. From an objective or external point of view, this illusion is dissolved; objectively, life is not later than death, since *later than* is only applicable in local subsets of the set of all times. However, as Nagel has argued, the subjective perspective is not (always) illusory and it is not inferior to the objective perspective; "our objective understanding of things [...] is in essence only partial," and "objective reality cannot be

---

not include the fact that *I* am one of these persons—even though this is clearly a fact. Similarly, there may be facts about *time* that are only evident from a subjective perspective—for example, the facts that it is now 10 a.m. and that time now moves very slowly.

[29]Thomas Nagel, *Mortal Questions*, 3.

[30]Nagel says in a footnote: "It is sometimes suggested that what we really mind is the process of *dying*. But I should not really object to dying if it were not followed by death" (Nagel, *Mortal Questions*, 3). By contrast, I should not object to death, if it were followed by life, as in closed time. However, in fairness to Nagel, it should be added that in the paper discussed here he uses "death" and its cognates to mean *permanent* death (see *Mortal Questions*, 1).

analyzed or shut out of existence any more than subjective reality can."[31] From a subjective perspective it certainly seems that death *is* followed by life in closed time.

It may be noticed that eternal recurrence in this sense appears to be subjectively equivalent to a kind of time travel between death and birth: from a subjective perspective, they would feel the same, and both prospects would (therefore) be equally desirable. It would not be time travel performed intentionally or even consciously, but it would be time travel in the sense that the person in question moves from one location in time to another.[32] If this were possible in linear time, it is hard to see why it should be impossible in closed time.

It may be objected that we cannot move in time at all. Some philosophers believe that time's passage is a myth, an illusion, and that it is also an illusion—more or less the same illusion—that we advance through time.[33] Nevertheless, we certainly experience a passage of time. We often express this by saying that time moves or flows, but on second thoughts we would probably be more inclined to say that time does not move any more than space does. It is rather *we* who move; more exactly, our subjective points of view move from one position in space and in time to another, and so on. There is a difference, though. In space, we move around in many different ways and we have the impression that most of the time we move voluntarily, but in time we seem to move along automatically in one direction whether we like it or not. There is nothing we can do about it. We cannot control our movement in time (except, perhaps, by committing suicide). Our impression

---

[31]Nagel, *Mortal Questions*, 212.

[32]Notice that this kind of time travel is not like the kind that occurs in science fiction stories. It does not involve the movement of a *body of a certain age* to an earlier time; rather, it is the movement of a *person* from one time, and from a body with a certain age, to another time, and to a rather different and much younger body. The time traveler is transformed into an earlier version of himself (or herself). So there is no room for any of the usual paradoxes here; for example, the time traveler will not be in a position to kill himself or his parents or grandparents, thereby preventing himself from being born or from being in a position to travel backwards in time. Moreover, in time travel of the science fiction kind, there is a problem of how departure and arrival can be separated by two unequal intervals of time, as, for example, when I travel from the year 2009 back to the year 1954 in a couple of hours (see e.g. David Lewis, "The Paradoxes of Time Travel," *American Philosophical Quarterly* 13 (1976): 145–52; the reference here is to 145). This is not a problem for eternal recurrence in closed time, since there is then only one sequence of times, and one direction of movement in time.

[33]See, for example, J.J.C. Smart, "Time," in *The Encyclopedia of Philosophy*, ed. Paul Edwards (New York and London: Macmillan, 1967), vol. 8, 127.

that time moves (while we do not) can perhaps be explained by the fact that we cannot affect our own movement in time.[34]

But *do* we move in time?

Movement in Time

From an objective point of view, it may be quite correct to say that we do not move in time. In particular, if the world is a four-dimensional manifold of events, ordinary objects and human bodies are a kind of perduring solids or "worms" that are composed of temporal parts, or stages, located at various times and places.[35] Neither the worm itself, nor any of its stages, move in time. They just have some location in time. But from a subjective point of view, we certainly advance through time.[36] The subjective perspective, the point of view of a person—the *subject*, for short—moves along from one stage of a human body to the next, and so on.[37] This is the perspective from which the person refers to times and places by words like "now" and "here"; these words have no place in an objective perspective, they can only be used by a subject.

Nevertheless, J.J.C. Smart and others claim that movement in time is just an illusion. They point out that movement is movement with respect to time, and they ask: if motion in space is feet per second, at what speed is motion in time? Seconds per what?[38] That is a good question, but it seems clear that the answer must involve *two* kinds of time, subjective and objective.[39] Objectively, there is no movement in time, but subjectively we certainly

---

[34]Suppose we always moved uniformly in space, without any control at all over the movement, as if we were looking out of the windows of a moving train. If so, we might be inclined to say that space, or "the landscape," moved or passed by outside the window.

[35]Refer to note 17, about four-dimensionalism, in the Lynne Rudder Baker reading in Part III. —MM

[36]Physicists may not care about this. For example, Davies says: "We can envisage the time dimension stretched out as a line of fate, and a particular instant—'now'—being singled out as a little glowing point. As 'time goes on,' so the light moves steadily up the time line towards the future. Needless to say, physicists can find nothing of this in the objective world." (Davies, *About Time*, 258). On the other hand, if human beings are enduring three-dimensional objects it is hard to see how one can deny that they move in time.

[37]Periods of unconsciousness and multiple personalities are disregarded here.

[38]Smart, "Time," 126.

[39]The distinction between objective and subjective time is not the same as the distinction between external and personal time proposed by David Lewis ("The Paradoxes of Time Travel," 146). For Lewis, personal time is primarily tied to bodily processes and the normal order of the stages of a human body; it has no essential connection to a subjective perspective.

move forward in (objective) time. This is nicely expressed by Hermann Weyl as follows:

> The objective world simply *is*, it does not *happen*. Only to the gaze of my consciousness, crawling upward along the lifeline of my body, does a section of this world come to life as a fleeting image in space which continuously changes in time.[40]

Everyone knows that subjectively some days, weeks and years appear much longer or shorter than others. So our answer to Smart's question should be something like this: in many cases our movement in time is just one objective second per subjective second, but sometimes we move at considerably more or less than one objective second per subjective second. We may not currently have access to any good objective instruments to measure subjective time—to construct such instruments, might be a task for psychologists—but it can hardly be doubted that there is such a thing as subjective time.

However, it has been held, more specifically, that passage of time, or "a moving present," is incompatible with closed time. For example, Robin Le Poidevin says that

> once we introduce the idea of a moving present into the picture of cyclic time, we cannot but imagine the present going around the circle repeatedly, and if the circle represents time itself, then we have to say, thus contradicting ourselves, that each event happens both once and an infinite number of times. We are in fact importing *two* representations of time into the picture: the circle itself, and the motion of the present around it. But we cannot, it seems have both. So there appears to be a tension between the idea of cyclic time on the one hand and the passage of time on the other.[41]

Le Poidevin claims that there is a contradiction here and that time is represented in two incompatible ways. By contrast, I suggest that two different systems of time are involved, one objective and the other subjective. As far as I can see, this does not yield any contradiction. The circle represents objective time, but the movement around the circle is movement in subjective time.

---

[40]Hermann Weyl, *Philosophy of Mathematics and Natural Science* (Princeton: Princeton University Press, 1949), 116.

[41]Robin Le Poidevin, *Travels in Four Dimensions: The Enigmas of Space and Time* (Oxford: Oxford University Press, 2003), 86–87. Let us disregard the strange idea that time—or moments of time—can move; this would seem to involve us in the absurdity that one and the same moment of time can be located at different times. Instead, let us ask whether something like Le Poidevin's argument may be applied to the position outlined above, namely that a *subject* (i.e. a person's subjective perspective) advances through time.

It is misleading to say that "the present" moves around the circle, for "the present" must surely be taken to refer to some time, and times do not move. But as I argued above, *we*, or our subjective points of view, move from one position in objective time to the next, and so on. Of course, for most of the (objective) time we are dead (or, not alive), so nothing happens subjectively; given closed time, we may assume that in subjective time we move directly from death to birth—or to some (objective) time after birth where we begin to have a subjective point of view.

Another point in Le Poidevin's argument is that, if there is a moving present in cyclic time, then we would have to say that "each event happens both once and an infinite number of times." This does not follow. Objectively, as we have repeatedly noted, everything happens just once in closed time. But, from a subjective perspective, since we move forward in objective time, the same events can be expected to occur over and over again in subjective time, if objective time is closed. It can also be expected that this repetition will never be experienced or remembered. But since there is also a kind of eternal repetition in subjective time, we should perhaps think of subjective time as linear rather than closed.

It might be asked how a subject can return to a time where it has already been. Is such time travel at all possible? Well, this is just what must be the case if objective time is closed. But, a skeptic may wonder, in the interval between death and birth, the subject does not exist at all, so how does it move over this interval? This question also seems to involve the problem of personal identity. So let us pass on to that.

Personal identity

It is sometimes said that a person who reappears in a different cycle of cosmic history could not be numerically the same as before. Identity is usually taken to presuppose some kind of continuity, physical or psychological. According to Milič Čapek, the Stoics believed, like Aristotle, that even though Socrates could reappear again and again, the Socrateses would be numerically different (since numerical identity presupposes uninterrupted existence). And St. Thomas rejected eternal recurrence on the ground that re-creation of numerically identical individuals would be contradictory.[42]

---

[42]See Capek, "Eternal Return," 62.

Similarly, Lucas says: "Even if in another cycle there was, or will be, some one qualitatively identical with me, he will not be me unless either I can remember being him or he will be able to remember being me."[43] Clearly, this rules out inter-cycle personal identity under eternal recurrence. If a person has memories from one cycle to another, then there is indeed a kind of psychological continuity, but, on the other hand, this requirement can hardly be satisfied if the cycles are qualitatively exactly similar. One cycle cannot be qualitatively identical with another if it contains memories from the other. Besides, there cannot be memories from one cycle to another in closed time, since there is in fact only one cycle. A person has certain memories at any given time; the moving subject does not acquire any memories *in addition* to that.

In any case, it seems that the problems of combining personal identity with eternal recurrence arise only for the linear time case—and we have argued that linear time is in any case not very promising for eternal recurrence.[44] In cyclical time, on the other hand, it seems that a person simply has to be the same in every instance of the person's life, since there is after all only one instance of this life.

Someone might say that in closed time there is presumably a very long period of time from the death of a person until he or she is born, and it may be asked how the person can retain his or her identity during all that time. This could be seen as a problem, even if it is granted that the person will not subjectively notice the long period between death and birth. (From a subjective point of view, it does not matter whether the interval between death and birth is long or short.)

However, it could be argued that in closed time there is in fact both physical and psychological continuity between the person who dies and the (same) person who is born, even though this continuity works backward in time rather than forward. One may of course question the assumption that the dying person has the same subjective point of view as the newborn baby, but we can hardly doubt that the subject, at any given time in his or her life,

---

[43]Lucas, *A Treatise of Time*, 59.

[44]Besides, the problems may not be overwhelming for linear time either. For the mental in general, and the subjective point of view in particular, might be expected to supervene upon physical traits, and these are the same in different cycles even in linear time (given eternal recurrence). But perhaps we cannot dismiss the possibility that the mere numerical difference in linear time entails that subjective points of view must be different.

is the same as the subject at that time. This should be enough for anyone who wants to be born again to the same life as before.

But is it at all reasonable to want such a thing? This may be doubted. So let us now turn to that question.

Different attitudes towards eternal recurrence

It has been said that eternal recurrence is "a sorry counterfeit of immortality," and that "[w]hat we really long for after death is to go on living this life, this same mortal life, but without its evils, without its tedium—and without death."[45] Similarly, Schopenhauer said that "at the end of his life, no man, if he be sincere and at the same time in possession of his faculties, will ever wish to go through it again. Rather than this, he will much prefer to choose complete non-existence."[46] More recently, Paul Davies says that "the literal reappearance of the same people and events in cycle after cycle, [is] an idea that strikes most people today as utterly sterile and repugnant."[47]

It may be true that what many people want is a prolonged and perfectly happy life, or perhaps just an ordinary human life, but without misfortunes and without end. On the other hand, a life without end would not be an ordinary human life, and it would probably be unbearably boring. Bernard Williams cites the case of a woman in a play who takes an elixir of life until, at the age of three hundred and forty-two, she reaches a state of "boredom, indifference and coldness" and refuses to take the elixir, whereupon she dies.[48]

---

[45]Miguel de Unamuno, *The Tragic Sense of Life* (Princeton: Princeton University Press, 1972), 57 and 252. [Refer to the reading in this volume, above. —MM] Unamuno goes on to say: "And what else is the meaning of that comical notion of eternal recurrence which issued from the tragic inner voice of poor Nietzsche, in his hunger for a concrete, temporal immortality?" (Ibid., 252). As far as I can see, however, Unamuno does not tell us *why* eternal recurrence is a "comical notion" and a "sorry counterfeit of immortality."

[46]Arthur Schopenhauer, *The World as Will and Representation* (I, 324), quoted here from Hatab, *Nietzsche's Life Sentence*, 87.

[47]Davies, *About Time*, 29.

[48]See Bernard Williams, "The Makropulos Case," in *Problems of the Self* (Cambridge: Cambridge University Press, 1973), 82–100. [Refer to the reading in this volume, above. —MM] The woman, Elina Makropulos, is forty-two years old for three hundred years. Richard Sorabji has suggested that her life would have been better if she had grown older for ever, or if she had become a Christian mystic with a sense of timelessness (see Sorabji, *Time, Creation*, 181).

Williams argues that "an endless life would be a meaningless one."[49] He does not discuss eternal recurrence as a possible version of "an endless life," but he considers the possibility that death would be followed by an indefinite or infinite series of psychologically disjoint lives, some kind of reincarnation or metempsychosis, where a person may take on very different personality traits and other characteristics in subsequent lives. He says that "out of the alternatives it is the only one that for me would, if it made sense, have any attraction—no doubt because it is the only [way of avoiding permanent death] which has the feature that what one is living at any given point is actually a *life*."[50] But there are still problems with this: is it really *oneself* that survives in all those different lives, and can one really *want* to live lives that are so different from one's own? Williams also notes that those who believe in reincarnation usually see it as something negative, something that one hopes to be released from as soon as possible.

Eternal recurrence avoids the problematic aspects of reincarnation, but it also retains its desirable features. It provides a way to avoid permanent death, without running the risk of eternal boredom. It satisfies the consideration that "death gives the meaning to life," as Williams puts it.[51] So we can have our cake and eat it too.

Or is there perhaps also something frightening or repugnant in the idea of eternal recurrence? As we have just seen, several people seem to take exception to this idea, but as far as I can see, they seldom give any grounds for this—except perhaps the general ground that life is evil, but this does not seem to apply in the case of those who fear the loss of life.

It appears that Nietzsche tended to oscillate between different attitudes towards eternal recurrence. In one well-known passage, he says the following.

> What if some day or night a demon were to sneak after you in your loneliness and say to you: "This life as you now live it and have lived it, you will have to live once more and innumerable times more; and there will be nothing new in it, but every pain and every joy and every thought and sigh and everything immeasurably small or great in your life must return to you, all in the same succession and sequence—even this spider and this moonlight between the trees, and even this moment and I myself. The eternal hourglass of existence is turned over and over, and you with it, a speck of dust!"

---

[49]Williams, "The Makropulos Case," 89.
[50]Ibid., 93–94.
[51]Ibid., 82.

Would you not throw yourself down and gnash your teeth and curse the demon who spoke thus? Or did you once experience a tremendous moment when you would have answered him: "You are a god, and never did I hear anything more godly." If this thought were to gain possession of you, it would change you, as you are, or perhaps crush you. The question in each and every thing, "Do you want this again and innumerable times again?" would weigh upon your actions as the greatest weight. Or how well disposed would you have to become to yourself and to life to desire nothing more than this ultimate eternal confirmation and seal?[52]

Nietzsche seems to have thought of eternal recurrence, partly at least, as a thought experiment or test. Hatab says: "Nietzsche is putting the perennial question of the meaning of life in the most dramatic and acute form imaginable. It poses the meaning question in terms of whether one will say Yes or No to life as actually lived, with no alternative."[53] In one place, Nietzsche states his position as follows: "My teaching says: Live in such a way that you must *desire* to live again; this is the task—you will live again *in any case*."[54]

Consequences

In order to form an opinion of the desirability of eternal recurrence we need to ask what its consequences would be for human life. However, we should distinguish here between consequences of eternal recurrence itself and consequences of the belief in eternal recurrence. It is mainly the latter that are of importance. Let me give some examples.

Belief in eternal recurrence may affect our attitudes to time. It has been noted that most of us have a bias towards the near and towards the future, at least with regard to pleasure and pain.[55] This bias might be greatly diminished if we believed in eternal recurrence, for presumably in that perspective different stages of our lives would tend to become of more equal importance to us. From a subjective point of view, they may all seem to lie in the future. Consequently, we might even acquire an attitude of temporal neutrality and

---

[52] *The Gay Science*, section 341, here quoted from Hatab, *Nietzsche's Life Sentence*, 66.
[53] Hatab, *Nietzsche's Life Sentence*, 2. But Hatab also says that "Nietzsche always regarded eternal recurrence as more than simply a hypothetical thought experiment pertaining only to human psychology; he always took it to express something about life and the world as such" (9).
[54] Quoted from Hatab, *Nietzsche's Life Sentence*, 117.
[55] See, for example, Derek Parfit, *Reasons and Persons* (Oxford: The Clarendon Press, 1984), 158ff.

this, according to Derek Parfit, would be good for us; we would lose in some ways, but we would also gain, and the gains "would outweigh the losses."[56]

Again, our attitudes to death and dying can be expected to change if we came to believe in eternal recurrence. Not only would there be less fear of death; it also seems quite likely that people would become less eager to prolong their lives when the prospects for a good life are bad. And people may be more prepared to commit suicide. Under normal circumstances, if the future looks bad, we may nevertheless want to live on because we think that a bad life can be preferable to death. But if we come to believe in eternal recurrence, we may see things differently. Death seems less bad if it is followed by life, and we may wish to avoid the repetition of a bad future.

Belief in eternal recurrence may also result in a sense of meaningfulness. The way we live will matter more to us, if we believe that our lives will recur. We need no longer have the feeling that our life ends absurdly, that it has no purpose, that it is a preparation for nothing. For example, at the very end of his *Reveries over Childhood and Youth*, W. B. Yeats writes:

> It is not that I have accomplished too few of my plans, for I am not ambitious; but when I think of all the books I have read, and of the wise words I have heard spoken, and of the anxiety I have given to parents and grandparents, and of the hopes that I have had, all life weighed in the scales of my own life seems to me a preparation for something that never happens.[57]

By contrast, with eternal recurrence life is a preparation for something, namely for lives that will happen again and again in the future. Nietzsche seems to have had a similar thought when he claimed that belief in eternal recurrence would counteract "the paralyzing sense of general disintegration and incompleteness."[58]

Just as a single life can appear to be a preparation for nothing, so the whole history of humanity can seem to be futile since it plays such a small role from the point of view of the universe as a whole. In the words of Bertrand Russell,

> Man is the product of causes which had no prevision of the end they were achieving [... and] all the labors of the ages, all the devotion, all the inspiration, all the noonday brightness of human genius, are destined to extinction in the

---

[56]Parfit, *Reasons and Persons*, 174.
[57]W.B. Yeats, *Autobiographies* (London: Macmillan & Co., 1955), 106.
[58]Nietzsche, *The Will to Power*, 224.

vast death of the solar system, and [...] the whole temple of Man's achievement must inevitably be buried beneath the débris of a universe in ruins[59]

This picture of humanity is chilling, but it may seem rather less chilling to people who believe that time is closed. However, such a reaction is perhaps not very rational, for it is still true that the history of humanity happens only once in closed time. Nevertheless, the reaction may occur. From the point of view of humanity, an endless future with "a universe in ruins" is certainly bleak, but if we believe that this future is not endless, but is instead followed by the past history of the universe, many of us may feel less depressed. If someone finds it more rational to focus on the horror of a "universe in ruins," we need not let that affect us.

So far I have only considered consequences of the *belief* in eternal recurrence, and I am not sure that eternal recurrence itself has any consequences for human life that are worth mentioning. However, it might appear to be a consequence of eternal recurrence that we have no free will. For example, Hatab considers the thought that, "the repetition scheme seems to imply a rigid determinism [...]. Whatever I do next has happened an infinite number of times in the same way, and so there is only one possible future."[60] It is true that eternal recurrence in linear time sits best with determinism and, therefore, absence of free will. But in closed time the situation is different. Here, there is no objective repetition, and no determinism has to be assumed.

Justice

Even if eternal recurrence is an attractive notion for privileged people, it might seem unfair to those who are less privileged. This is one important respect in which eternal recurrence is different from various doctrines of reincarnation that are adhered to in certain religious traditions. Reincarnation—where some part of a living being survives death by being reborn in a new body, with a new personality—allows for compensation of the underprivileged in subsequent lives. But in eternal recurrence, the underprivileged are always underprivileged. Can eternal recurrence be desirable if this is so?

---

[59]Bertrand Russell, "A Free Man's Worship," in *Mysticism and Logic and Other Essays* (London: Longmans, Green, and Co., 1919), 47–48.
[60]Hatab, *Nietzsche's Life Sentence*, 127.

It is perhaps *possible* for this kind of injustice to be explained away. For example, just as someone may lead a great many different lives at different times, if reincarnation occurs, so one might lead many different lives at the *same* time—as long as one is completely unaware of this. This could even amount to a kind of solipsism: there is only one subject, but this subject is incarnated in many different bodies, some of which live at the same time while others live at different times. In other words, without knowing it, the subject plays many different roles—in fact, all the roles there are in all of history. If this were the case, there would be no serious form of injustice. The one and only subject would simply be privileged in some of its roles and underprivileged in others. Under such circumstances, eternal recurrence would not be morally repugnant. But, of course, we do not have much ground for assuming that such circumstances actually obtain.[61]

In any case, eternal recurrence does not seem to make injustices any worse if time is closed. But recurrence would indeed be morally repugnant, if it occurs in linear time. For injustice would be worse, if it is repeated endlessly. In closed time, on the other hand, all injustices in cosmic history occur only once.

Lives not worth living

Injustices might be tolerable as long as everyone lives a good life, but in a world, such as ours, that contains an overwhelming amount of suffering, it may seem morally impossible to wish for eternal recurrence. How can one wish for the recurrence of the Holocaust, for example?

In defense of Nietzsche's position, Hatab seems to think that there is a solution to this problem: "The crucial point is that affirmation does not mean *approving* of everything, but rather affirming the necessity of otherness for the emergence of one's values, which means that affirmation retains opposition to countervalues, retains the space of one's Yes and No."[62] There may be some truth in this, but it does not seem to remove the problem.

However, the problem is neither suffering as such nor the total balance of pleasure over pain in the universe. For a life may be worth living—from the

---

[61]Conversely, we may not have much ground for assuming that they do *not* obtain either.
[62]Hatab, *Nietzsche's Life Sentence*, 139.

point of view of the person living it—even if it contains a lot of suffering and even if it contains more pain than pleasure. And, since other things are equal in eternal recurrence, as long as a person's life is worth living it is worth living each time it is lived. So, eternal recurrence would be desirable if everyone's life is worth living.

But is everyone's life worth living? Some people seem to think so. For example, Thomas Nagel says: "All of us, I believe, are fortunate to have been born."[63] Of course, one can be fortunate to have been born even if one's life, at a certain moment in time, is no longer worth living. Again, a person's life may be worth living even if it would have been better, all things considered, if he had never lived. For example, Hitler's life was perhaps worth living even if the world would have been much better without him. But I take it that someone is fortunate to have been born only if his or her life is worth living. Therefore, if Nagel is right, it seems that everyone's life is worth living and that eternal recurrence is desirable from each individual point of view. I myself find it hard to believe that everyone is fortunate to have been born, but I shall make no attempt to settle that question here.

Eternal recurrence may perhaps be objectively desirable even if many lives are not worth living—provided that *most* people are fortunate to have been born.

In any case, the desire for eternal recurrence can hardly be morally repugnant if time is closed, for in that case everything happens just once. Even if some lives are not worth living, eternal recurrence cannot make things objectively worse.

Conclusion

The arguments that have been sketched above are perhaps not conclusive, but I believe they give at least some support to the view that eternal recurrence is both possible and desirable. The acceptance of this view may

---

[63]Nagel, *Mortal Questions*, 7. Nagel adds: "unless good and ill can be assigned to an embryo, or even to an unconnected pair of gametes, it cannot be said that not to be born is a misfortune." According to Nagel, "life is worth living even when the bad elements of experience are plentiful, and the good ones too meager to outweigh the bad ones on their own" (2), but he also says that "a sufficient quantity of more particular evils can *perhaps* outweigh" the goods that life contains (Ibid., 2, italics mine).

in turn reduce or exterminate the fear of death that many of us feel at least some of the time. Eternal recurrence gives a pretty attractive answer to the question of "what dreams may come, when we have shuffled off this mortal coil." It is perhaps the only intelligible and attractive version of eternal life that we can think of, and even if it presupposes a rather non-standard conception of time, it seems to be fairly compatible with what is known about the world we live in.

For Discussion or Essays

- Compare and contrast Lucretius' sweeping view of the passing scene to the Charvaka perspective that Madhava Acharya has described.

- Unamuno wrote that "Our hunger for God, our thirst of immortality, of survival, will always stifle in us this pitiful enjoyment of the life that passes and abides not." Compare this passage to what Walpola Rahula has to say about *dukkha* in our reading from Part II.

- In Christian theology, the *beatific vision* is a perfect communication of an individual but finite soul with an infinitely great and good God. Thomas Aquinas described it as the "final end" of human beings, the satisfaction of all desires, and perfect happiness. What might Williams have to say about the beatific vision, as a possible posthumous state?

- In Williams' interpretation of the Makropulos Case, EM is supposed to have lost her categorical desires as a result of having repeatedly satisfied these desires in the course of her centuries-long life. Bortolotti and Nagasawa claim, however, that empirical evidence from psychology does not support Williams' interpretation: habitual boredom, they claim, "arises from the *loss* or *outright absence* of categorical desires rather than from their *satisfaction*." Thus, they say, "we cannot find in Williams' argument any good reason to believe that in general or by necessity an immortal life would be afflicted by habitual boredom." Is this claim convincing? Why or why not?

- Another critic of Williams, John Martin Fischer, has suggested that an immortal life with a mix of repeatable pleasures need not be unbearably boring. (Refer to the entry in the Further Readings section.) Fischer has also suggested that *forgetting* might conceivably mitigate the tedium of an immortal life: a variety of activities endlessly repeated might continue to be experienced as pleasant, as long as the individual forgets that she has had the experiences before. Compare and contrast Fischer's version of a desirable immortality to the hypothesis of Eternal Return.

- We have noted that Friedrich Nietzsche believed that the eternal return would make a great deal of difference for anyone strong enough to embrace it. In classroom discussions, though, some students have argued that, on the contrary, believing that events are unique and unrepeated puts one in a position to more powerfully appreciate Nietzsche's point about living without regret and embracing one's fate (*amor fati*). Can you construct an argument for this view? Should it make a difference either way? Explain.

- In Part II, we saw that doctrines of rebirth that are familiar to us today are wedded to the doctrine of karma. This combination depicts a morally comprehensible cosmos, one in which the suffering of good people in this life and the apparent prosperity of evildoers are vindicated, and justice is achieved. Compare this to the justice implications of eternal return, as Lars Bergström describes them.

- Toward the end of Bergström's paper, under the subheading "Justice," the author responds to the accusation that eternal return seems to entail that lives of drudgery, toil, powerlessness, fear, and pain will be infinitely repeated, and thus the underprivileged will be endlessly underprivileged. In your own words, describe Bergström's highly conjectural way of "explaining away" this possibility of infinite injustice. Does Bergström's response offer comfort? "In any case," Bergström writes, "eternal recurrence does not seem to make injustices any worse if time is closed." How might this be so? Are you convinced? Explain.

Further Readings on Problems with Immortality and the Eternal Return

De Beauvoir, Simone. *All Men Are Mortal*. New York: W.W. Norton & Co., 1992. First published in 1946, this "metaphysical novel" by the great French writer de Beauvoir (1908–86) tells the story of Regina, an ambitious and self-absorbed actress who stalks and then befriends the mysterious Italian Count Raymond Fosca. As Regina soon discovers, Fosca has lived 700 years and is cursed to live forever. Like EM in The Makropulos Case, Fosca has long since grown weary of both, daily life and great historical deeds alike. Regina's attention revitalizes him; ultimately, though, Fosca admits that "immortality is a terrible curse," and only death gives meaning to life.

Čapek, Milič. "Eternal Return." In *Encyclopedia of Philosophy*, edited by Paul Edwards, Vol. 3, 61–63. New York: Macmillan, 1967.

Čapek, Karel. "The Makropulos Secret," translated by Yveta Synek Graff and Robert T. Jones. In *Toward the Radical Center: A Karel Čapek Reader*, edited by Peter Kussi, 110–77. Highland Park, NJ: Catbird Press, 1990. Originally published in 1922.

Eliade, Mircea. *The Myth of the Eternal Return: Or, Cosmos and History*. Bollingen Series XLVI. Princeton, NJ: Princeton University Press, 1954.

Fischer, John Martin. "Why Immortality Is Not So Bad." *International Journal of Philosophical Studies* 2, no. 2 (1994): 257–70. Fischer examines Bernard Williams' "necessary boredom thesis"—the thesis that no activity or set of activities, pursued for an indefinitely long period of time, will remain attractive to an individual. Toward the end of his paper, he notes that he cannot see why an everlasting life with a mix of repeatable pleasures would necessarily be boring.

Lemonick, Michael D. "Before the Big Bang." *Discover* 25, no. 2 (February 2004). http://www.discover.com/issues/feb-04/cover/ I Space (accessed January 6, 2007). Lemonick, a writer at *Scientific American*, discusses the maverick theory of cosmologists Paul Steinhardt and Neil Turok, which suggests that the Big Bang is just the latest in a cycle of cosmic collisions stretching infinitely into the past and into the future.

Löwith, Karl. *Nietzsche's Philosophy of the Eternal Recurrence of the Same*. Translated by J. Harvey Lomax. Berkeley: University of California Press, 1997. Löwith makes the case that the thought of eternal return and the figure of the superman are keys to understanding Friedrich Nietzsche's highly original thought.

Nietzsche, Friedrich. *The Will to Power*. Edited by Walter Kaufmann. Translated by Walter Kaufmann and Reginald John Hollingdale. New York: Vintage, 1968. Passages on the Eternal Return, "the *hardest* idea" appear in *The Will to Power*, on pp. 35–36, pp. 544ff., including remarks 1059 and 1066. Other passages on eternal return appear in *Thus Spoke Zarathustra*, *The Gay Science*, and elsewhere in Nietzsche's works.

Rosati, Connie S. "The Makropulos Case Revisited: Reflections on Immortality and Agency." In *The Oxford Handbook of Philosophy of Death*, edited by Ben Bradley, Fred Feldman, and Jens Johansson, 355–90. Oxford and New York: Oxford University Press, 2013. Rosati doubts that we can clearly imagine immortal life; thus, the question "Is it a good thing that we are not immortal?" is "too ill-formed to admit of a determinate answer," of the sort that Bernard Williams has offered. She argues, moreover, that longing for extended existence need not be at odds with satisfying the widespread longing for a meaningful existence.

Part V

Living with Mortality

Introduction to Part V:
Living with Mortality

Death is not an evil, because it frees us from all evils, and while it takes away good things, it also takes away the desire for them. Old age is the supreme evil, because it deprives us of all pleasures, leaving us only the appetite for them, and it brings with it all sufferings. Nevertheless, we fear death, and we desire old age.

—Giacomo Leopardi (1798–1837)

Do not go gentle into that good night.
Rage, rage against the dying of the light.

—Dylan Thomas (1914–1953)

We have reviewed posthumous scenarios of survival: rebirth, resurrection, and even eternal return. Each of these scenarios provides a certain view of the soul, *Ātman*, or the person that survives, even if it be a scanty karmic stream, and some of these scenarios describe posthumous survival environments: life on Earth, or in an extraterrestrial afterlife, or in another realm of dimension entirely. And as we have seen, each of these basic scenarios poses serious philosophical problems, including the relationship between the mind and the body, the destination problem, the transportation problem, and the problem of continuity of personal identity. Perhaps none of these problems, individually or taken together, poses a mortal danger to one or more of the survival accounts we have encountered. Perhaps. In any case, it is appropriate now to consider whether or not the non-survival hypothesis is something we can or should live with.

Hospice nurses are interesting to talk to. Late one night not long ago, I found myself in a small room with such a nurse, a pleasant woman named Bernadette. There we were, this stranger and I, on opposite sides of a bed containing a patient softly sleeping. Though Bernadette was only thirty-three, she had been a nurse for years, and in that time she had seen many people die, ranging in age from the very old to an infant of only several weeks. In a low voice she spoke of her experiences, including scenes that had upset her—scenes of people who had lived eighty or ninety years and more, and who had lingered for months at the edge, but who in their final moments had desperately thrashed and grasped, raging against the dying of the light. Surprisingly many of these people, she said, were religious, but she could not explain why this might be. After all, they were supposed to believe in the afterlife. Perhaps in their last moments they were seized by doubts, or perhaps, as Lucretius noted,[1] religion had made them fearful of divine punishment. Or perhaps, as Bernadette suspected, they had sought solace in religion in the first place because they were the fearful type. It turned out that Bernadette was herself battling Hodgkin's lymphoma. She was a woman of faith, but she smiled and said that she was not afraid.

We are told that the realization that we are mortal has transfixed even the greatest figures, including the hero of one of the oldest extant works of literature. In a version of the *Epic of Gilgamesh* dating back to the eighteenth century BC, Prince Gilgamesh mourns the death of his beloved friend, the tamed wild man Enkidu. The once-brash prince clings to his friend's dead body:

> Enkidu, whom I so loved, who went with me through every hardship,
> The fate of mankind has overtaken him.
> I would not give him up for burial,
> Until a worm fell out of his nose.
> I was frightened […]
>
> My friend whom I loved is turned into clay,
> Enkidu, my friend whom I loved, is turned into clay.
> Shall I too not lie down like him,
> And never get up forever and ever?[2]

Thus mortality, in the form of a worm, confronts Prince Gilgamesh. He will undergo much travail before he accepts his own mortality and redirects his attention to the satisfactions and achievements of his life.

The Roman author Seneca (4 BC–AD 65) infamously counseled that in order to avoid the fear of death "one must think of it constantly." By contrast, the great Portuguese-Jewish philosopher Benedict Spinoza,

---

[1] *On the Nature of Things*, line 1014.
[2] *Epic of Gilgamesh*, trans. and ed. Benjamin R. Foster (New York and London: W. W. Norton & Co., 2001), 74.

whom we met in Part IV, wrote that "A free man thinks of nothing less than death, and his wisdom is not a meditation upon death but upon life."[3] Appropriately, Spinoza did not elaborate very much on this statement, except to add that a free man is "a man who lives according to the dictates of reason alone."[4]

Our readings in Part V are not meditations upon death, but rather considerations of our mortality. We begin with three little stories by the Chinese sage Zhuangzi. They are as charming as they are short.

Next, Thomas Nagel will introduce us to the influential view that death is evil because it deprives us of something good or beneficial. Nagel's argument depends on the claim that we can be harmed without being aware of it: a woman who is brain dead as the result of an automobile accident has undergone a misfortune; similarly, one who has died has undergone a misfortune.

The third reading in Part V is based on a ground-breaking lecture in 2012 by American philosopher Samuel Scheffler. In this selection Scheffler argues, provocatively, that the belief in personal survival actually makes less difference to the conduct of our lives and institutions than does the assumption that people—even people we will never know—will continue to exist after each of us ceases to exist. The failure to believe in personal survival, Scheffler claims, is actually much less likely to undermine our confidence in the importance of our pursuits than is a failure to believe in what Scheffler calls "the collective afterlife."

Next, American moral philosopher Susan Wolf presents her take on Scheffler's paper. She agrees with Scheffler that the survival of humans, including strangers who will exist after we have died, is more important to us that our own survival; however, she does not see how the afterlife conjecture provides much support for these claims. In the course of making her case, Wolf advances her own afterlife conjecture, according to which the human capacity to value, to care for, and to make meaning are likely to prove more resilient, even in the face of doomsday, than Scheffler has portrayed it.

Our last reading is Beverley Clack's insightful paper, "Constructing Death as a Form of Failure: Addressing Mortality in a Neoliberal Age."

---

[3]Benedict Spinoza, *Ethics*, Part Four, Proposition 67 (W. H. White translation).
[4]Spinoza, *Ethics*.

Clack observes that prevailing attitudes toward death reflect larger economic, political, and ideological processes at work here on Earth. The dominant neoliberal account of personhood or subjectivity, she claims, offers a model of success for which death is "the ultimate failure." She then proposes an alternative account of subjectivity, one in keeping with a "social principle for understanding humanity" that reconciles vulnerable subjects with the inevitability of death.

19

"Perfect Happiness"

Zhuangzi

Translated by Herbert A. Giles

Zhuangzi (or Chuang Tzŭ) (369–286 BC?) lived during the Warring States Period in China (from around 480 to 221 BC). These were years of intense conflict among seven main feudal states. Zhuangzi was influenced by his predecessor Laozi (Lao Tzŭ), and his work shows a skeptical stance. The following three stories appear in a chapter from his eponymous book, a chapter entitled "Perfect Happiness."

When Zhuangzi's wife died, Huizi went to convey his condolences. He found the widower sitting on the ground, singing, with his legs spread out at a right angle, and beating time on a bowl.

"To live with your wife," exclaimed Huizi, "and see your eldest son grow up to be a man, and then not to shed a tear over her corpse—this would be bad enough. But to drum on a bowl and sing; surely this is going too far."

"Not at all," replied Zhuangzi. "When she died, I could not help being affected by her death. Soon, however, I remembered that she had already existed in a previous state before birth, without form, or even substance; that while in that unconditioned condition, substance was added to spirit; that this substance then assumed form; and that the next stage was birth. And now, by virtue of a further change, she is dead, passing from one phase to another like the sequence of spring, summer, autumn, and winter. And while she is thus lying asleep in Eternity, for me to go about weeping and wailing would be to proclaim myself ignorant of these natural laws. Therefore I refrain."

———————

A hunchback and a one-legged man were looking at the tombs of departed heroes, on the K'un-lun Mountains, where the Yellow Emperor rests. Suddenly, ulcers broke out upon their left elbows, of a very loathsome description.

"Do you loathe this?" asked the hunchback.

"Not I," replied the other, "why should I? Life is a loan, and the borrower only adds more dust and dirt to the sum total of existence. Life and death are as day and night; and while you and I stand gazing at the evidence of mortality around us, if the same mortality overtakes me, why should I loathe it?"

———————

Certain germs, falling upon water, become duckweed. When they reach the shore they become lichen. Spreading up the bank, they become the dog-tooth violet. Reaching rich soil, they become *wu-tsu*, the root of which becomes grubs, while from the leaves come butterflies. These are changed into insects, born in the chimney corner, which look like skeletons. Their name is *ch'ü-to*. After a thousand days, the *ch'ü-to* becomes a bird, called *Kan-yü-ku*, the spittle of which becomes the *ssŭ-mi*. The *ssŭ*-mi becomes a wine fly, and from that comes an *i-lu*. The *huang-k'uang* produces the *chiu-yu* and the *mou-jui* produces the fire-fly. The *yang-ch'i*, grafted to an old bamboo that has not put out shoots for a long time, produces the *ch'ing-ning*, which produces the leopard, which produces the horse, which produces man.[1]

Then man goes back into the great Scheme, from which all things come and to which all things return.

———

[1] Translator's note: Many of the names in the above paragraph have not been identified even by Chinese commentators.

20

Death

Thomas Nagel

In this much-discussed paper, American philosopher Thomas Nagel (b. 1937) considers the question whether death, conceived as the permanent end of existence, is a bad thing. He answers in the affirmative: death is bad because of what it deprives us of. To make his point, Nagel argues that the good or bad fortune of a person does not depend only on that person's momentary state; it also depends on that person's history and possibilities. With this point in mind, Nagel concludes that misfortune can befall someone even though that person is not around to experience it.

Nagel is perhaps most famous for his article, "What Is It Like to Be a Bat?" (1974), in which he argued against the view that mental processes and conscious experiences can be explained entirely in terms of physical processes in the brain and body. His paper "Death" appeared in its original form in 1970,[1] but our excerpt is a revised version from his book *Mortal Questions*.[2] The revised paper includes a response to Bernard Williams' article in Part IV.

If death is the unequivocal and permanent end of our existence, the question arises whether it is a bad thing to die.

There is conspicuous disagreement about the matter: some people think death is dreadful; others have no objection to death *per se*, though they hope

---

[1] In the philosophy journal *Nous* IV, no. 1: 73 seq.
[2] New York: Cambridge University Press, 1979: 1–10.

their own will be neither premature nor painful. Those in the former category tend to think those in the latter are blind to the obvious, while the latter suppose the former to be prey to some sort of confusion. On the one hand it can be said that life is all we have and the loss of it is the greatest loss we can sustain. On the other hand it may be objected that death deprives this supposed loss of its subject, and that if we realize that death is not an imaginable condition of the persisting person, but a mere blank, we will see that it can have no value whatever, positive or negative.

Since I want to leave aside the question whether we are, or might be, immortal in some form, I shall simply use the word *death* and its cognates in this discussion to mean *permanent* death, unsupplemented by any form of conscious survival. I want to ask whether death is in itself an evil; and how great an evil, and of what kind, it might be. The question should be of interest even to those who believe in some form of immortality, for one's attitude towards immortality must depend in part on one's attitude toward death.

If death is an evil at all, it cannot be because of its positive features, but only because of what it deprives us of. I shall try to deal with the difficulties surrounding the natural view that death is an evil because it brings to an end all the goods that life contains. We need not give an account of these goods here, except to observe that some of them, like perception, desire, activity, and thought, are so general as to be constitutive of human life. They are widely regarded as formidable benefits in themselves, despite the fact that they are conditions of misery as well as of happiness, and that a sufficient quantity of more particular evils can perhaps outweigh them. That is what is meant, I think, by the allegation that it is good simply to be alive, even if one is undergoing terrible experiences. The situation is roughly this: There are elements which, if added to one's experience, make life better; there are other elements which if added to one's experience, make life worse. But what remains when these are set aside is not merely *neutral*: it is emphatically positive. Therefore life is worth living even when the bad elements of experience are plentiful, and the good ones too meager to outweigh the bad ones on their own. The additional positive weight is supplied by experience itself, rather than by any of its consequences.

I shall not discuss the value that one person's life or death may have for others, or its objective value, but only the value that it has for the person who is its subject. That seems to me the primary case, and the case which presents the greatest difficulties. Let me add only two observations. First, the value of life and its contents does not attach to mere organic survival; almost everyone would be indifferent (other things equal) between immediate death and immediate coma followed by death twenty years later without reawakening. And second, like most goods, this can be multiplied by time: more is better than less. The added quantities need not be temporally continuous (though continuity has its social advantages). People are attracted to the possibility of long-term suspended animation or freezing, followed by the resumption of conscious life, because they can regard it from within simply as a *continuation* of their present life. If these techniques are ever perfected, what from outside appeared as a dormant interval of three hundred years could be experienced by the subject as nothing more than a sharp discontinuity in the character of his experiences. I do not deny, of course, that this has its own disadvantages. Family and friends may have died in the meantime; the language may have changed; the comforts of social, geographical, and cultural familiarity would be lacking. Nevertheless those inconveniences would not obliterate the basic advantage of continued, though discontinuous, existence.

If we turn from what is good about life to what is bad about death, the case is completely different. Essentially, though there may be problems about their specification, what we find desirable in life are certain states, conditions, or types of activity. It is *being* alive, *doing* certain things, having certain experiences, that we consider good. But if death is an evil, it is the *loss of life*, rather than the state of being dead, or nonexistent, or unconscious, that is objectionable.[3] This asymmetry is important. If it is good to be alive, that advantage can be attributed to a person at each point of his life. It is good of which Bach had more than Schubert, simply because he lived longer. Death, however, is not an evil of which Shakespeare has so far received a larger portion than Proust. If death is a disadvantage, it is not easy to say when a man suffers it.

There are two other indications that we do not object to death merely because it involves long periods of nonexistence. First, as has been mentioned, most of us would not regard the *temporary* suspension of life, even for substantial intervals, as in itself a misfortune. If it ever happens that people can be frozen without reduction of the conscious lifespan, it will be inappropriate to pity those who are temporarily out of circulation. Second, none of us existed before we were born (or conceived), but few regard that as a misfortune. I shall have more to say about this later.

---

[3] It is sometimes suggested that what we really mind is the process of *dying*. But I should not really object to dying if it were not followed by death.

The point that death is not regarded as an unfortunate *state* enables us to refute a curious but very common suggestion about the origin of the fear of death. It is often said that those who object to death have made the mistake of trying to imagine what it is like to *be* dead. It is alleged that the failure to realize that this task is logically impossible (for the banal reason that there is nothing to imagine) leads to the conviction that death is mysterious and therefore a terrifying prospective state. But this diagnosis is evidently false, for it is just as impossible to imagine being totally unconscious as to imagine being dead (though it is easy enough to imagine oneself, from the outside, in either of those conditions). Yet people who are averse to death are not usually averse to unconsciousness (so long as it does not entail a substantial cut in the total duration of waking life).

If we are to make sense of the view that to die is bad, it must be on the ground that life is a good and death is the corresponding deprivation or loss, bad not because of any positive features but because of the desirability of what it removes. We must now turn to the serious difficulties which this hypothesis raises, difficulties about loss and privation in general, and about death in particular.

Essentially, there are three types of problem. First, doubt may be raised whether *anything* can be bad for a man without being positively unpleasant to him: specifically, it may be doubted that there are any evils which consist merely in the deprivation or absence of possible goods, and which do not depend on someone's *minding* that deprivation. Second, there are special difficulties, in the case of death, about how the supposed misfortune is to be assigned to a subject at all. There is doubt both to *who* its subject is, and as to *when* he undergoes it. So long as a person exists, he has not yet died, and once he has died, he no longer exists; so there seems to be no time when death, if it is a misfortune, can be ascribed to its unfortunate subject. The third type of difficulty concerns the asymmetry, mentioned above, between our attitudes to posthumous and prenatal nonexistence. How can the former be bad if the latter is not?

It should be recognized that if these are valid objections to counting death as an evil, they will apply to many other supposed evils as well. The first type of objection is expressed in general form by the common remark that what you don't know can't hurt you. It means that even if a man is betrayed by his friends, ridiculed behind his back, and despised by people who treat him politely to his face, none of it can be counted as a misfortune for him so long as he does not suffer as a result. It means that a man is not injured if his wishes are ignored by the executor of his will, or if, after his death, the belief becomes current that all the literary works on which his fame rest were really written by his brother, who died in Mexico at the age of twenty-eight. It seems to me worth asking what assumptions about good and evil lead to these drastic restrictions.

All the questions have something to do with time. There certainly are goods and evils of a simple kind (including some pleasures and pains) which a person possesses at a given time simply in virtue of his condition at that time. But this is not true of all the things we regard as good or bad for a man. Often we need to know his history to tell whether something is a misfortune or not; this applies to ills like deterioration, deprivation, and damage. Sometimes his experiential *state* is relatively unimportant—as in the case of a man who wastes his life in the cheerful pursuit of a method of communicating with asparagus plants. Someone who holds that all goods and evils must be temporally assignable states of the person may of course try to bring difficult cases into line by pointing to the pleasure or pain that more complicated goods and evils cause. Loss, betrayal, deception, and ridicule are on this view bad because people suffer when they learn of them. But it should be asked how our ideas of human value would have to be constituted to accommodate these cases directly instead. One advantage of such an account might be that it would enable us to explain *why* the discovery of these misfortunes causes suffering—in a way that makes it reasonable. For the natural view is that the discovery of betrayal makes us unhappy because it is bad to be betrayed— not that betrayal is bad because its discovery makes us unhappy.

It therefore seems to me worth exploring the position that most good and ill fortune has as its subject a person identified by his history and his possibilities, rather than merely by his categorical state of the moment—and that while this subject can be exactly located in a sequence of places and times, the same is not necessarily true of the goods and ills that befall him.[4]

These ideas can be illustrated by an example of deprivation whose severity approaches that of death. Suppose an intelligent person receives a brain injury that reduces him to the mental condition of a contented infant, and that such desires as remain to him can be satisfied by a custodian, so that he is free from care. Such a development would be widely regarded as a severe misfortune, not only for his friends and relations, or for society, but also and primarily, for the person himself. This does not mean that a contented infant

---

[4]It is certainly not true in general of the things that can be said of him. For example, *Abraham Lincoln was taller than Louis XIV*. But when?

is unfortunate. The intelligent adult who has been *reduced* to this condition is the subject of the misfortune. He is the one we pity, though of course he does not mind his condition. It is in fact the same condition he was in at the age of three months, except that he is bigger. If we did not pity him then, why pity him now; in any case, who is there to pity? The intelligent adult has disappeared, and for a creature like the one before us, happiness consists in a full stomach and a dry diaper.

If these objections are invalid, it must be because they rest on a mistaken assumption about the temporal relation between the subject of a misfortune and the circumstances which constitute it. If, instead of concentrating exclusively on the oversized baby before us, we consider the person he was, and the person he *could* be now, then his reduction to this state and the cancellation of his natural adult development constitute a perfectly intelligible catastrophe.

This case should convince us that it is arbitrary to restrict the goods and evils that can befall a man to nonrelational properties ascribable to him at particular times. As it stands, that restriction excludes not only such cases of gross degeneration, but also a good deal of what is important about success and failure, and other features of a life that have the character of processes. I believe we can go further, however. There are goods and evils which are irreducibly relational; they are features of the relations between a person, with spatial and temporal boundaries of the usual sort, and circumstances which may not coincide with him either in space or in time. A man's life includes much that does not take place within the boundaries of his life. These boundaries are commonly crossed by the misfortunes of being deceived, or despised, or betrayed. (If this is correct, there is a simple account of what is wrong with breaking a deathbed promise. It is an injury to the dead man. For certain purposes it is possible to regard time as just another type of distance.) The case of mental degeneration shows us an evil that depends on a contrast between the reality and the possible alternatives. A man is the subject of good and evil as much because he has hopes which may or may not be fulfilled, or possibilities which may or may not be realized, as because of his capacity to suffer and enjoy. If death is an evil, it must be accounted for in these terms, and the impossibility of locating it within life should not trouble us.

When a man dies we are left with his corpse, and while a corpse can suffer the kind of mishap that may occur to an article of furniture, it is not a suitable object for pity. The man, however, is. He has lost his life, and if he had not died, he would have continued to live it, and to possess whatever good there is in living. If we apply to death the account suggested for the case of dementia, we shall say that although the spatial and temporal locations of the individual who suffered the loss are clear enough, the misfortune itself cannot be so easily located. One must be content just to state that his life is over and there will never be anymore of it. That *fact*, rather than his past or present condition, constitutes his misfortune, if it is one. Nevertheless if there is a loss, someone must suffer it, and *he* must have existence and specific spatial and temporal location even if the loss itself does not. The fact that Beethoven had no children may have been a cause of regret to him, or a sad thing for the world, but it cannot be described as a misfortune for the children that he never had. All of us, I believe, are fortunate to have been born. But unless good and ill can be assigned to an embryo, or even to an unconnected pair of gametes, it cannot be said that not to be born is a misfortune. (That is a factor to be considered in deciding whether abortion and contraception are akin to murder.)

This approach also provides a solution to the problem of temporal asymmetry, pointed out by Lucretius. He observed that no one finds it disturbing to contemplate the eternity preceding his own birth, and he took this to show that it must be irrational to fear death, since death is simply the mirror image of the prior abyss. That is not true, however, and the difference between the two explains why it is reasonable to regard them differently. It is true that both the time before a man's birth and the time after his death is time of which his death deprives him. It is time in which, had he not died then, he would be alive. Therefore any death entails the loss of *some* life that its victim would have led had he not died at that or any earlier point. We know perfectly well what it would be for him to have had it instead of losing it, and there is no difficulty in identifying the loser.

But we cannot say that the time prior to a man's birth is time in which he would have lived had he been born not then but earlier. For aside from the brief margin permitted by premature labor, he could not have been born earlier: anyone born substantially earlier than he would have been someone else. Therefore the time prior to his birth prevents him from living. His birth, when it occurs, does not entail the loss to him of any life whatever.

The direction of time is crucial in assigning possibilities to people or other individuals. Distinct possible lives of a single person can diverge from a common beginning, but they cannot converge to a common conclusion from diverse beginnings. (The latter would represent not a set of different possible lives of one individual, but a set of distinct possible individuals, whose lives have identical conclusions.) Given an identifiable individual, countless possibilities for his continued existence are imaginable, and we can clearly conceive of what it would be for him to go on existing indefinitely. However inevitable it is that this will not come about, its possibility is still that of the continuation of a good for him, if life is the good, we take it to be.[5]

We are left, therefore, with the question whether the nonrealization of this possibility is in every case a misfortune, or whether it depends on what can naturally be hoped for. This seems to me the most serious difficulty with the view that death is always an evil. Even if we can dispose of the objections against admitting misfortune that is not experienced, or cannot be assigned to a definite time in the person's life, we still have to set some limits on how possible a possibility must be for its nonrealization to be a misfortune (or good fortune, should the possibility be a bad one). The death of Keats at twenty-four is generally regarded as tragic; that of Tolstoy at eighty-two is not. Although they will both be dead forever, Keats' death deprived him of many years of life which were allowed to Tolstoy; so in a clear sense Keats' loss was greater (though not in the sense standardly employed in mathematical comparison between infinite quantities). However, this does not prove that Tolstoy's loss was insignificant. Perhaps we record an objection only to evils which are gratuitously added to the inevitable; the fact that it is worse to die at twenty-four than at eighty-two does not imply that it is not a terrible thing to die at eighty-two, or even at 806. The question is whether we can regard as a misfortune any limitation, like mortality, that is normal to

---

[5]I confess to being troubled by the above argument, on the ground that it is too sophisticated to explain the simple differences between our attitudes to prenatal and posthumous nonexistence. For this reason I suspect that something essential is omitted from the account of the badness of death by an analysis which treats it as a deprivation of possibilities. My suspicion is supported by the following suggestion of Robert Nozick. We could imagine discovering that people developed from individual spores that had existed indefinitely far in advance of their birth. In this fantasy, birth never occurs naturally more than a hundred years before the permanent end of the spore's existence. But then we discover a way to trigger the premature hatching of these spores, and people are born who have thousands of years of active life before them. Given such a situation, it would be possible to imagine *oneself* having come into existence thousands of years previously. If we put aside the question whether this would really be the same person, even given the identity of the spore, then the consequence appears to be that a person's birth at a given time *could* deprive him of many earlier years of possible life. Now while it would be cause for regret that one had been deprived of all those possible years of life by being born too late, the feeling would differ from that which many people have about death. I conclude that something about the future *prospect* of permanent nothingness is not captured by the analysis in terms of denied possibilities. If so, then Lucretius' argument still awaits as answer. I suspect that it requires a general treatment of the difference between past and future in our attitudes toward our own lives. Our attitudes toward past and future pain are very different, for example. Derek Parfit's unpublished writings on this topic have revealed its difficulty to me.

the species. Blindness or near-blindness is not a misfortune for a mole, nor would it be for a man, if that were the natural condition of the human race.

The trouble is that life familiarizes us with the goods of which death deprives us. We are already able to appreciate them, as a mole is not able to appreciate vision. If we put aside doubts about their status as goods and grant that their quantity is in part a function of their duration, the question remains whether death, no matter when it occurs, can be said to deprive its victim of what is in the relevant sense a possible continuation of life.

The situation is an ambiguous one. Observed from without, human beings obviously have a natural lifespan and cannot live much longer than a hundred years. A man's sense of his own experience, on the other hand, does not embody this idea of a natural limit. His existence defines for him an essentially open-ended possible future, containing the usual mixture of goods and evils that he has found so tolerable in the past. Having been gratuitously introduced to the world by a collection of natural, historical, and social accidents, he finds himself the subject of a *life*, with an indeterminate and not essentially limited future. Viewed in this way, death, no matter how inevitable, is an abrupt cancellation of indefinitely extensive possible goods. Normality seems to have nothing to do with it, for the fact that we will all inevitably die in a few score years cannot by itself imply that it would be good to live longer. Suppose that we were all inevitably going to die in *agony*—physical agony lasting six months. Would inevitability make *that* prospect any less unpleasant? And why should it be different for a deprivation? If the normal lifespan were a thousand years, death at eighty would be a tragedy. As things are, it may just be a more widespread tragedy. If there is no limit to the amount of life that it would be good to have, then it may be that a bad end is in store for us all.

21

The Collective Afterlife

Samuel Scheffler

In his lecture "Death and the Afterlife," Scheffler constructs a "crude and morbid" thought experiment to draw attention to a circumstance that has received surprisingly little attention from philosophers. We take it for granted that other humans will continue to exist long after each of us has died. (The circumstance of other humans continuing to exist after we die is what Scheffler calls "the afterlife." Clearly, his "afterlife" has little to do with the traditional scenarios we have discussed with reference to, say, the doctrines of rebirth and resurrection.) But what if we faced the prospect of imminent extinction? According to Scheffler's "Afterlife Conjecture," "we would regard the extinction of humanity with more horror than we do our own deaths, and [...] we would find it harder, if not impossible, to live meaningful lives under this assumption that we do under the acknowledgment of our personal morality."

Of course, it is likely that, even without Scheffler's doomsday scenarios, our terrestrial species will have a rather brief career, relative to a geological timeframe. *Homo sapiens* will, in rather quick order, either evolve into a different species or manage to make itself extinct in a more abrupt fashion. Either way, there is not much hope of everlasting survival here, even as a species. But as we know by now, Scheffler is not alone in claiming that if there is anything even remotely similar to an "afterlife" in store for humans, then it is a collective afterlife—an "afterlife" tied up not with the survival of individuals but with the continuity of future generations.

———————

[...]

2.

I will begin by asking you to consider a crude and morbid thought experiment. Suppose you knew that, although you yourself would live a normal life span, the earth would be completely destroyed thirty days after your death in a collision with a giant asteroid. How would this knowledge affect your attitudes during the remainder of your life? Now, rather than respond straightaway, you may well protest that I haven't given you enough information to go on. How, in my imagined scenario, are we to suppose that you acquired your doomsday knowledge? Are other people in on the secret, or is this devastating piece of information your solitary burden to bear? I haven't told you, and yet surely the answers to these questions might affect your reactions. I freely concede these points. I also concede that, even if I were to fill in the story in the greatest possible detail, I would still be asking you to make conjectures about your attitudes under what I trust are highly counter-factual circumstances. Such conjectures, you may point out, are of questionable reliability and in any case impossible to verify. All this is true. But indulge me for a few minutes. Perhaps, despite the skimpiness of the description I have provided and the conjectural character of any response you may give, some things will seem relatively clear.

You won't be surprised to learn that, although I have asked you how you would react, I'm not going to let you speak for yourself, at least not just yet. Instead I'm going to make some conjectures of my own, conjectures about the kinds of reactions that you and I and others—that "we"—would be likely to have in the situation I have described. I will begin with a negative suggestion. One reaction that I think few of us would be likely to have, if confronted with my doomsday scenario, is complete indifference. For example, few of us would be likely to say, if told that the earth would be destroyed thirty days after our death: "So what? Since it won't happen until thirty days after my death, and since it won't hasten my death, it isn't of any importance to me. I won't be around to experience it, and so it doesn't matter to me in the slightest." The fact that we would probably not respond this way is already suggestive. It means that, at a minimum, we are not indifferent to everything that happens after our deaths. Something that will not happen until after our deaths can still matter or be important to us. And this in turn implies that things other than our own experiences matter to us. A postmortem event that matters to us would not be one of our experiences.

As against this, someone might object that, although the post-mortem event would not be one of our experiences, our prospective contemplation of that event would be part of our experience, and if such contemplation distressed us, then that distress too would be part of our experience. This is undeniable, but it is also beside the point. It does not show that only our own experiences matter to us. In the case at hand, what would matter to us, in the first instance, would not be our distress—though that might matter to us too—but rather the predicted postmortem event whose contemplation gave rise to that distress. If the postmortem event did not matter to us, there would be nothing for us to be distressed about in the first place. So, as I have said, the fact that we would not react to the doomsday scenario with indifference suggests that things that happen after our deaths sometimes matter to us, and that in turn implies that things other than our own experiences matter to us. In this sense, the fact that we would not react with indifference supports a *nonexperientialist* interpretation of our values. It supports an interpretation according to which it is not only our experiences that we value or that matter to us.[1]

There is another reaction to the doomsday scenario that I think few of us would be likely to have. Few of us, I think, would be likely to deliberate about the good and bad consequences of the destruction of the earth in order to decide whether it would, on balance, be a good or a bad thing. This is not, I think, because the answer is so immediately and overwhelmingly obvious that we don't need to perform the calculations. It is true, of course, that the destruction of the earth would have many horrible consequences. It would, for example, mean the end of all human joy, creativity, love, friendship, virtue, and happiness. So there are, undeniably, some weighty considerations to place in the minus column. On the other hand, it would also mean the end of all human suffering, cruelty, and injustice. No more genocide, no more torture, no more oppression, no more misery, no more pain. Surely these things all go in the plus column. And it's at least not *instantly* obvious that the minuses outweigh the pluses. Yet few of us, I think, would react to the scenario by trying to do the sums, by trying to figure out whether on balance the prospect of the destruction of the earth was welcome or unwelcome. On the face of it, at least, the fact that we would not react this way suggests that there is a *nonconsequentialist* dimension to our attitudes about what we

---

[1]To that extent, it supports the conclusions drawn by Robert Nozick in his discussion of "the experience machine" in *Anarchy, State, and Utopia* (New York: Basic Books, 1974), 42–45.

value or what matters to us. It appears that what we value, or what matters to us, is not simply or solely that the best consequences, whatever they may be, should come to pass.[2]

Let us now move from negative to positive characterizations of our reactions. To begin with, I think it is safe to say that most of us would respond to the doomsday scenario with what I will generically call, with bland understatement, profound dismay. This is meant only as a superficial, placeholder characterization, which undoubtedly subsumes a range of more specific reactions. Many of these reactions have to do with the deaths of the particular people we love and the disappearance or destruction of the particular things that we care most about, where "things" is understood in a broad sense that encompasses not only physical objects but also social forms such as institutions, practices, activities, and ways of life. During our lifetimes, we respond with grief, sadness, and other forms of distress to the sudden death of people we love and the sudden loss or destruction of things that we value deeply. We are bound to have similar reactions to the prospect that every particular person and thing that we treasure will soon be suddenly destroyed at once.

The fact that we would have these reactions highlights a *conservative* dimension in our attitudes toward what we value, which sits alongside the nonexperiential and nonconsequentialist dimensions already mentioned. In general, we want the people and things we care about to flourish; we are not indifferent to the destruction of that which matters most to us. Indeed, there is something approaching a conceptual connection between valuing something and wanting it to be sustained or preserved. During our lifetimes, this translates into a similarly close connection between valuing something and seeing reasons to act so as to preserve or sustain it ourselves. Part of the poignancy of contemplating our own deaths, under ordinary rather than doomsday conditions, is the recognition that we will no longer be able to respond to these reasons; we will not ourselves be able to help preserve or sustain the things that matter to us. We can, of course, take steps while we

---

[2]Of course, someone might argue that, despite the appearances, our reactions do admit of a consequentialist interpretation. Perhaps, in reacting as we do, we simply jump to a possibly erroneous but nevertheless consequentialist conclusion, namely, that the negative consequences I have mentioned would outweigh the positive ones. Or perhaps we accept some axiology according to which the impersonal value of human existence per se is so great that any outcome in which human life continues is better than every outcome in which it does not. I don't find these claims very plausible, but I won't argue against them. One aim of these lectures is to offer a different account of why the continuation of human life matters so much to us.

are alive to try to bring it about that other people will act after our deaths to preserve or sustain those things. For example, the devices of wills and bequests are important to us largely because they offer us—or seem to offer us—an opportunity to extend the reach of our own agency beyond death in an effort to help sustain the people and things that matter to us. In addition, some of the most elaborate and ingenious measures we take to try to ensure the postmortem preservation of our values are those we take as groups rather than as individuals, and I will discuss them at greater length later. But apart from taking steps now to influence the actions of others in the future, all we can really do is hope that the things that matter most to us will somehow be preserved or sustained. The doomsday scenario dashes all such hopes, and the emotional consequences of this, for someone facing this scenario, are likely to be profound.

In addition to the generic conservatism about value just noted, something more specific is involved in our reaction to the prospective destruction of the particular *people* we love and treasure. It is a feature of the scenario that I have described that all of our loved ones who survive thirty days beyond our own death will themselves die suddenly, violently, and prematurely, and this prospect itself is sufficient to fill us with horror and dread. In other words, it would fill us with horror and dread even if it were *only* our own loved ones who would be destroyed, and everything and everyone else would survive. Indeed, this dimension of our reaction is liable to be so powerful that it may make it difficult to notice some of the others. For this reason, I want to postpone discussion of it for a few minutes and to concentrate for a bit longer on our more general reactions to the doomsday scenario.

3.

I have so far said only that the prospect of the earth's imminent destruction would induce in us reactions of grief, sadness, and distress. But we must also consider how, if at all, it would affect our subsequent motivations and our choices about how to live. To what extent would we remain committed to our current projects and plans? To what extent would the activities in which we now engage continue to seem worth pursuing? Offhand, it seems that there are many projects and activities that might become less important to us. By this I mean several things. First, our reasons to engage in them might no longer seem to us as strong. At the limit, we might cease to see any reason to engage in them. Second, our emotional investment in them might weaken. For example, we might no longer feel as eager or excited at the prospect of engaging in them; as frustrated if prevented from engaging in them; as pleased if they seemed to be going well; as disappointed if they seemed not to be going well; and so on. At the limit, we might become emotionally detached from or indifferent to them. Third, our belief that they were worthwhile activities in which to engage might weaken or, at the limit, disappear altogether.

It is difficult to be sure exactly which projects and activities would seem to us diminished in importance in these respects, and no doubt there are interesting differences in the ways that different individuals would react. On the face of it, however, there are several types of projects and activities that would appear fairly obviously to be vulnerable to such changes in our attitudes. Consider, to take one representative example, the project of trying to find a cure for cancer. This project would seem vulnerable for at least two reasons. First, it is a project in which it is understood that ultimate success may be a long way off. Even the very best research that is done today may be but a step on a long road that will lead to a cure only in the indeterminate future, if at all. The doomsday scenario, by cutting the future short, makes it much less likely that such a cure will ever be found. Second, the primary value of the project lies in the prospect of eventually being able to cure the disease and to prevent the death and suffering it causes. But the doomsday scenario means that even immediate success in finding a cure would make available such benefits only for a very short period of time. Under these conditions, scientists' motivations to engage in such research might well weaken substantially. This suggests that projects would be specially vulnerable if either (a) their ultimate success is seen as something that may not be achieved until some time well in the future, or (b) the value of the project derives from the benefits that it will provide to large numbers of people over a long period of time. Cancer research is threatened because it satisfies both of these conditions. But there are many other projects and activities that satisfy at least one of them. This is true, for example, of much research in science, technology, and medicine. It is also true of much social and political activism. It is true of many efforts to build or reform or improve social institutions. It is true of many projects to build new buildings, improve the physical infrastructure of society, or protect the environment. No doubt you will be able to supply many other examples of your own.

The effect of the doomsday scenario on other types of projects is less clear. For example, many creative and scholarly projects have no obvious practical aim, such as finding a cure for cancer, but they are nevertheless undertaken with an actual or imagined audience or readership of some kind in mind. Although the doomsday scenario would not mean that audiences would disappear immediately, it would mean that they would not be around for very long. Would artistic, musical, and literary projects still seem worth undertaking? Would humanistic scholars continue to be motivated to engage in basic research? Would historians and theoretical physicists and anthropologists all carry on as before? Perhaps, but the answer is not obvious.

Nor is it merely projects of the kinds I have been discussing, as opposed to more routine aspects of human life, whose appeal might weaken or disappear. Consider, for example, procreative activity. Would people still be as motivated to have children if they knew that those children would die no later than thirty days after their own death? It seems unlikely that they would. But if they would not, then neither would they be as motivated to engage in the wide, varied, and life-altering array of activities associated with raising and caring for children. By contrast, the projects and activities that would seem least likely to be affected by the doomsday scenario are those focused on personal comfort and pleasure. But it is perhaps not altogether obvious what would be comforting and pleasant under doomsday conditions.

The upshot is that many types of projects and activities would no longer seem worth pursuing, or as worth pursuing, if we were confronted with the doomsday scenario. Now it is noteworthy that the attractions of these same projects and activities are not similarly undercut by the mere prospect of our own deaths. People cheerfully engage in cancer research and similar activities despite their recognition that the primary payoff of these activities is not likely to be achieved before their own deaths. Yet, if my argument is correct, their motivation to engage in these same activities would be weakened or even completely undermined by the prospect that, in consequence of the earth's destruction, there would be no payoff *after* their deaths. In other words, there are many projects and activities whose importance to us is not diminished by the prospect of our own deaths but would be diminished by the prospect that everyone else will soon die. So if by the afterlife we mean the continuation of human life on earth after our own deaths, then it seems difficult to avoid the conclusion that, in some significant respects, the existence of the afterlife matters more to us than our own continued existence. It matters more to us because it is a condition of other things mattering to us. Without confidence in the existence of the afterlife, many of the things in our own lives that now matter to us would cease to do so or would come to matter less.

Of course, there are many things that are causally necessary in order for our pursuits to matter to us now. Without the presence of oxygen in the atmosphere, for example, nothing would matter to us now because we would not be alive. Similarly, we can imagine that some mineral deficiency in our diet might cause us to lose confidence in the value of our pursuits. Yet we would not conclude that the mineral matters more to us than our own future existence because it is a condition of other things mattering to us now. But the point about our confidence in the afterlife is not merely that it is a causal condition of other things mattering to us now. The continuation of life on earth, unlike the mineral, is something that also matters to us in its own right. And unlike a mineral deficiency, the imminent disappearance of human life on earth would strike us as a *reason* why other things no longer mattered as much. Our belief that humanity was about to disappear would not just be a cause of their ceasing to matter to us.

It is easy to underestimate the significance of this point, at least insofar as it concerns goal-oriented projects like trying to find a cure for cancer. It may seem that, although it is true that such projects would become less important to people who were faced with the doomsday scenario, that is simply because it is pointless or irrational to pursue goals that are known to be unachievable. The goal of reducing the suffering and death caused by cancer would be unachievable under doomsday conditions, so engaging in cancer research would be instrumentally irrational under those conditions. This mundane point about instrumental rationality is all that is needed to explain why people would no longer regard such projects as worth pursuing in the doomsday scenario. But this misconstrues the significance of the example. Granted, it is not surprising that people should lose interest in a goal-oriented project once it is known that the goal of the project is unachievable. What may be surprising, however, is the fact that people are often happy to pursue goals that they do not expect to be achieved until after their own deaths. What the doomsday scenario highlights, in other words, is the extent to which we regard projects as worth undertaking even when the successful completion of those projects is not expected to take place during our own lifetimes. What is significant about the example is what it reveals, not about the familiar role of instrumental rationality in our practical deliberations, but rather about our willingness to harness the resources of instrumental rationality to pursue goals whose achievement will occur only after we are gone.

4.

As I have said, I have so far been concentrating on our general reactions to the doomsday scenario and the general attitudes toward the afterlife that they reveal. However, I want now to consider our more specific reactions to one feature of that scenario, namely, that it involves the sudden, simultaneous deaths of everyone that we love or care about. Since the strength of these reactions can blind us to other aspects of our response to the doomsday scenario, I have so far set them aside in the hope of identifying some of our more general attitudes toward the afterlife. But now I want to return to these more specific reactions, and to see what they add to the general picture that has so far emerged. The salient feature of the doomsday scenario, for these purposes, is that everyone we love who is alive thirty days after our own death will then suddenly be killed. What do our powerful reactions to this prospect tell us about ourselves?

Some elements of our reaction seem obvious and straightforward. We don't want the people we love to die prematurely, whether we are alive to witness their deaths or not. We care deeply about them and their well-being, and not merely about the effects on us of setbacks to their well-being. This is just an example of the non-experiential dimension of our values and concerns. So the knowledge that all the people we love who are still alive thirty days after our own deaths will then die suddenly and more or less prematurely is horrible. That much is clear. Still, I think that there is more to our reaction than this. One way to approach the issue is to ask why it matters to us that at least some people we care about should live on after we die. I take it that most people do regard it as a bad thing if everyone they love or care about dies before they do. Few of us hope to outlive all of our friends and loved ones. Why should this be?

There are, I think, a number of answers to this question, and once again, some of them seem straightforward. The considerations about prematurity just mentioned play a large role, though our preference to predecease at least some of the people we care about may persist even if both we and they are old enough that none of our deaths would qualify as significantly premature. A different kind of consideration is that, if we predecease our loved ones, then we will be spared the pain and grief that we would experience if they died first. Similarly, we will be spared the feelings of loneliness and emptiness and loss to which we may be subject after they are gone. Much better for us if we die first, and they are the ones who have to experience all the unpleasantness. Much as we love them, it seems, we would rather that they suffered in these ways than that we did.

Relatedly, there may be something like a principle of loss minimization at work here. It's bad enough that we will lose our own lives, but there's nothing we can do about that. Given the inevitability of that one final loss, it's better for us that we not experience, in addition, the separate losses of each of the people we care about. It's better if the pain of our separation from them is simply "folded into" the one great calamity of our own deaths. This is essentially a matter of the efficient organization of personal disaster.

But I think that there is something else going on as well. If, at the time of our deaths, there are people alive whom we love or about whom we care deeply, and with whom we have valuable personal relationships, then one effect of our deaths will be to disrupt those relationships. Odd as it may sound, I think that there is something that strikes us as desirable or at any rate comforting about having one's death involve this kind of relational disruption. It is not that the disruptions per se are desirable or comforting, but rather that the prospect of having one's death involve such disruptions affects one's perceived relation to the future. If at the time of one's death one will be a participant in a larger or smaller network of valuable personal relationships, and if the effect of one's death will be to wrench one out of that network, then this can affect one's premortem understanding of the afterlife: the future that will unfold after one is gone. In a certain sense, it personalizes one's relation to that future. Rather than looming simply as a blank eternity of nonexistence, the future can be conceptualized with reference to an ongoing social world in which one retains a social identity. One can imagine oneself into that world simply by imagining the resumption of one's premortem relationships with people who will themselves continue to exist and to remember and care for one. One needn't fear, as many people apparently do, that one will simply be forgotten as soon as one is gone. In fact, to a surprising extent, many people seem to feel that not being remembered is what being "gone" really consists in and, correspondingly, those who are bereaved often feel a powerful imperative not to forget the people they have lost. Faced with the fear of being forgotten, the fact that there are other people who value their relations with you and who will continue to live after you have died makes it possible to feel that you have a place in the social world of the future even if, due to the inconvenient fact of your death, you will not actually be able to take advantage of it. The world of the future becomes, as it were, more like a party one had to leave early and less like a gathering of strangers.

There may be a temptation to protest that the attitudes I have just described are silly or irrational. Death is in fact final, and its finality is not increased if one is forgotten or diminished if one is remembered. Dying, not being forgotten, is what being "gone" consists in. In any case, even if one is remembered for a while, the memories will fade and the people who remember will themselves die soon enough, so it's only a matter of time before nobody who remembers any of us personally will survive. But these protests are beside the point. On the one hand, my aim has not been to show that our attitudes are rational, but, on the other hand, the claim that they are irrational appears to depend on just the kind of experientialism that I have tried to discredit. The fact that it does matter to us to have other people we care about live on after we die, and it also matters to us to be remembered, at least for a while. These things matter to us, I have argued, partly because they help to personalize our relation to the future. One reason why we react so strongly to the doomsday scenario is that it seems to render our own relation to the future incurably bleak. We are used to the idea that we ourselves will not be a part of the future after our deaths. In the doomsday scenario, we must reconcile ourselves to the fact that nobody we care about will be a part of the future either, and that fact, I have suggested, makes the future itself seem more alien, forbidding, empty. It is idle to protest that, if we were rational, it would seem just as empty to us even if the doomsday scenario were suspended and we could be assured that the people we care about would live normal life spans. Why, the protester asks, should we take comfort in their survival given that they too will die soon enough? But the vantage point from which these attitudes are judged irrational enjoys no special privilege or authority. If the idea that some of the people we care about will live on is one of the things that enables us to make our peace with the future, and if, in reacting that way, we make no error of reasoning and rely on no false belief, then the basis for criticism is obscure.

I should say something at this point about children. I have been arguing that our participation in valued relationships with people we hope will outlive us transforms our attitudes toward the future after we are gone. It is obvious that, for people who have children, their relationships with their children have a special role to play here. The desire for a personalized relation to the future is one of the many reasons why people attach such importance to those relationships, and why the loss of a child is one of the most devastating things that can happen to a person. But I have deliberately avoided making children central to the argument, because I do not think that the desire for a personalized relation to the future is limited to people with children, nor do I think that relationships with children are the only kinds of personal relationships that can help to satisfy that desire. Those who tend to think about things in the terms of evolutionary biology will point out that it is all too easy to explain in those terms why people should be motivated to have biological descendants who will survive them. For the purposes of my argument, however, these explanations are doubly irrelevant. They are irrelevant, first, because the relationships that can help to satisfy the desire for a personalized relation to the future are not limited to relationships with one's biological descendants. And they are irrelevant, second, because I am interested simply in the fact that we have that desire and in its relations to others of our attitudes. An evolutionary explanation of the desire would not show that we do not have it, or that it is not a genuine desire, any more than an evolutionary explanation of our perceptual abilities would show that we do not really have those abilities or an evolutionary explanation of parental love would show that it is not really love.

At this point, let me pause to summarize the arguments I have presented so far. First, I have argued that our reactions to the doomsday scenario highlight some general features of the phenomenon of human valuing, which I have referred to as its nonexperientialist, nonconsequentialist, and conservative dimensions. We do not care only about our own experiences. We do not care only that the best consequences should come to pass. And we do want the things that we value to be sustained and preserved over time. Second, I have argued that the afterlife matters to us, and in more than one way. What happens after our deaths matters to us in its own right and, in addition, our confidence that there will be an afterlife is a condition of many other things mattering to us here and now. Third, I have argued that the doomsday scenario highlights some of our attitudes toward time, particularly our impulse to personalize our relation to the future.

[…]

7.

[…] I have already noted that one effect of the doomsday scenario is to highlight the importance we attach to the survival of the particular people who matter to us, and we have now seen that the survival of particular groups and traditions may be of comparable importance, at least for some people. In general, the desire to personalize our relation to the future, which is one of the desires whose tacit power is revealed by the doomsday scenario, is a desire that seems to require *particularistic* satisfaction. What enables us to establish a personalized relation to the future, it seems, is our confidence in the survival after our deaths of some particular people we love or particular groups or traditions to which we are committed. And this may tempt us to conclude that the afterlife that matters to us is the afterlife of those people alone.

Yet this conclusion is too hasty. Recall that, when first discussing the doomsday scenario, I deliberately concentrated on our more general reactions to the scenario, and provisionally set aside our more specific responses to the prospect that our own loved ones would die. The aim was to prevent the power of those more particularistic responses from obscuring other, less conspicuous elements of our reaction. So in discussing various projects that might come to matter less to us, I deliberately focused on projects, such as the project of engaging in cancer research, that lacked any obvious dependence on particularistic loyalties or affections. To the extent that pursuing that project would come to seem less important to a researcher confronting the doomsday scenario, it is not because the scenario involves the imminent death of particular people she loves or the destruction of particular groups to which she belongs and is committed. If that is correct, then our concern for the existence of an afterlife is not solely a concern for the survival of particular people or groups.

This conclusion can be strengthened. It is clear that the prospective destruction of the particular people we care about would be sufficient for us to react with horror to an impending global disaster, and that the elimination of human life as a whole would not be necessary. But, surprisingly perhaps, it seems that the reverse is also true. The imminent disappearance of human life would be sufficient for us to react with horror even if it would not involve the premature death of any of our loved ones. This, it seems to me, is one lesson of P.D. James' novel *The Children of Men*,[3] which was published in 1992, and a considerably altered version of which was made into a film in 2006 by the Mexican filmmaker Alfonso Cuarón. The premise of James' novel, which is set in 2021, is that human beings have become infertile, with no recorded birth having occurred in more than twenty-five years.

---

[3]James' novel was first published by Faber and Faber (London, 1992). Page references, which will be given parenthetically in the text, are to the Vintage Books edition published by Random House in 2006.

The human race thus faces the prospect of imminent extinction as the last generation born gradually dies out.⁴ The plot of the book revolves around the unexpected pregnancy of an English woman and the ensuing attempts of a small group of people to ensure the safety and freedom of the woman and her baby. For our purposes, however, what is relevant is not this central plot line, with its overtones of Christian allegory, but rather James' imaginative dystopian portrayal of life on earth prior to the discovery of the redemptive pregnancy. And what is notable is that her asteroid-free variant of the doomsday scenario does not require anyone to die prematurely. It is entirely compatible with every living person having a normal life span. So if we imagine ourselves inhabiting James' infertile world and we try to predict what our reactions would be to the imminent disappearance of human life on earth, it is clear that those reactions would not include any feelings about the premature deaths of our loved ones, for no such deaths would occur (or at any rate, none would occur as an essential feature of James's scenario itself). To the extent that we would nevertheless find the prospect of human extinction disturbing or worse, our imagined reaction lacks the particularistic character of a concern for the survival of our loved ones. Indeed, there would be no identifiable people at all who could serve as the focus of our concern, except, of course, insofar as the elimination of a human afterlife gave us reason to feel concern for ourselves and for others now alive, despite its having no implications whatsoever about our own mortality or theirs.

Of course, the infertility scenario would mean that many groups and traditions would die out sooner than they otherwise would have done, and this would presumably be a source of particularistic distress for those with group-based or traditional allegiances. Still, because the infertility scenario suppresses the influence of any particularistic concern for individuals, it is more effective than the original doomsday scenario in highlighting something that I think is evident despite the persistence of group-based

---

⁴On July 28, 2009, *New York Times* columnist David Brooks, citing a brief item posted by Tyler Cowen a few days earlier on the *Marginal Revolution* blog, http://www.marginalrevolution. com/ marginalrevolution/2009/07/masssterilization.html#comments, wrote an article titled "The Power of Posterity," in which he considered what would happen if *half* the world's population were sterilized as a result of a "freak solar event" (http://www.nytimes.com/2009/07/28/opinion/28brooks.html? scp=l&sq=power%20of%20posterity&st=cse). Although some of Brooks' speculations evoke, albeit rather stridently, some of the themes of James' novel (and of these lectures), the proviso that only half the world's population becomes infertile leads him ultimately in a different direction. Neither Cowen nor Brooks cites *The Children of Men,* although online reader comments responding to Cowen's blog post and to Brooks' column both note the connection.

particularistic responses. What is evident is that, for all the power of the particularistic elements in our reactions to the catastrophe scenarios we have been discussing, there is also another powerful element that is at work, namely, the impact that the imminent end of humanity as such would have on us.

[…]

9.

For my purposes, however, it is not necessary that all the details of James' version of the story should be found convincing, nor is it necessary to arrive at a settled conclusion about the exact range of activities whose perceived value would be eroded in an infertile world. All that is necessary is to suppose that, in such a world, people would lose confidence in the value of many sorts of activities, would cease to see reason to engage in many familiar sorts of pursuits, and would become emotionally detached from many of those activities and pursuits. As I have said, this seems plausible to me, and I hope that it will seem plausible to you too. So let me just stipulate that this assumption—which I will call " the afterlife conjecture"—is true. I take the afterlife conjecture to have implications of a number of different kinds. Perhaps the most striking of these has to do with the nature and limits of our egoism. We are all rightly impressed by the power and extent of our self-concern, and even the most ardent defenders of morality feel the need to argue for what Thomas Nagel called "the possibility of altruism" in the face of the more or less universal assumption that our default motivations are powerfully self-interested.[5] But consider this. Every single person now alive will be dead in the not-too-distant future. This fact is universally accepted and is not seen as remarkable, still less as an impending catastrophe. There are no crisis meetings of world leaders to consider what to do about it, no outbreaks of mass hysteria, no outpourings of grief, no demands for action. This does not mean that individuals do not fear their own deaths. To the contrary, many people are terrified of death and wish desperately to survive for as long as possible. Despite this, neither the recognition of their own mortality nor the prospect that everyone now alive will soon die leads

---

[5]Thomas Nagel, *The Possibility of Altruism* (Oxford: Clarendon Press, 1970).

most people to conclude that few of their worldly activities are important or worth pursuing. Of course, many people do find themselves, through bad luck or lack of opportunity, engaged in activities that do not seem to them worthwhile. Similarly, many individuals do at some point in their lives experience episodes of depression or despair, and the tragedy of suicide remains an all too common occurrence. But relatively little of this, I venture to say, is explained by reference to the impact on people of the recognition that all the earth's current inhabitants will someday die. Not only is that fact not regarded as a catastrophe, it is not even on anybody's list of the major problems facing the world.

You may be tempted to say that it is not seen as a major problem because it is known to be inevitable. People have accepted the fact that everyone now alive will die and that nothing can be done about it. Yet in the infertile world, the disappearance of the human race is also widely understood to be inevitable, but it *is* regarded as a catastrophe. In James' vivid depiction, it is regarded as a catastrophe whose prospect precipitates an unprecedented global crisis and exerts a profoundly depressive effect on many familiar human motivations. And if, as the afterlife conjecture supposes, at least the core of this depiction is accurate, the implication seems clear. In certain concrete functional and motivational respects, the fact that we and everyone we love will cease to exist matters less to us than would the nonexistence of future people whom we do not know and who, indeed, have no determinate identities. Or to put it more positively, the coming into existence of people we do not know and love matters more to us than our own survival and the survival of the people we do know and love. Even allowing for the likelihood that some portion of our concern for these future people is a concern for the survival of particular groups with which we specially identify, this is a remarkable fact which should get more attention than it does in thinking about the nature and limits of our personal egoism.[6]

---

[6]Here it seems worth mentioning Dan Moller's interesting argument to the effect that the participants in loving relationships have much less importance for one another than we normally suppose. Moller bases his argument on empirical findings which suggest that the participants in such relationships are surprisingly resilient in the face of the loss of a partner or spouse. There is a superficial similarity between Moller's claim about the relative unimportance that spouses and partners have for one another and my claim that, in some respects, our own survival and the survival of the people we love matters less to us than does the existence of future people. Yet the two claims are in fact quite different. Moller's concern is with our reactions to actual losses while mine is with our reactions to prospective losses. Since we can have no reactions at all to our own actual deaths, Moller focuses exclusively on our reactions to the deaths of other people one loves, whereas I am concerned with the prospective loss not only of one's loved ones but also of one's own life. And whereas my point is that

It may seem that this is too hasty a conclusion to draw. Although people in the infertility scenario do come to view the disappearance of the human race as inevitable, this involves a change in their expectations. As I have described the scenario, most of these people begin life thinking that humanity will endure and learn only later that it will not. So the infertility scenario involves a drastic change of expectations for them. By contrast, we all grow up understanding that we will someday die, and we have formed our expectations accordingly. Perhaps the differing responses to which I have called attention are evidence not of the limits of our egoism but merely of the power of disappointed expectations. If people had grown up knowing that they were the last generation of humans, perhaps this would have no greater impact on them than the prospect of our own deaths has on us. But I find this difficult to believe. I agree, of course, that the change in expectations might itself have a dramatic effect on people's attitudes. It would surely have a dramatic effect on our attitudes if we grew up thinking that we were immortal and discovered our own mortality only in middle age. But I do not think that those who grew up knowing that they were the last generation of human beings would be exempt from the phenomena that I have described. To me it seems implausible that the effect of this grim piece of knowledge would be to support their confidence in the value of their activities. It seems at least as plausible that, in contrast to those who discovered only later in life that they were the last generation, those who grew up with this understanding would simply lack such confidence from the outset.

It may be objected that there is another, simpler explanation for the differing responses to which I have called attention, and this explanation also does not support any conclusions about the limits of our egoism. The fact that everyone now alive will soon die is not regarded as a catastrophe, and does not precipitate a global crisis, because it poses no threat to society itself. By contrast, the infertility scenario would mean the end of society, and so of course it would be viewed as catastrophic. This fact is unremarkable and shows nothing one way or another about the extent of our egoism. But this objection misses the point. It is true that the infertility scenario would mean the end of society, and it is not wrong to say that that is why it would be regarded as a catastrophe. However, under the terms of that scenario, "the

---

the relevant prospective reactions reveal some limits of our egoism, he takes our reactions to actual losses as evidencing a kind of emotional shallowness—a failure to register the true value of our loved ones and our relationships with them—which we have reason to regret. See Dan Moller, "Love and Death," *Journal of Philosophy* 104 (2007): 301–16.

end of society" would neither cause nor result from any change in the mortality or longevity of anyone now alive. From the perspective of those now living, the only difference between the infertility scenario and the mundane circumstance that everyone now living will soon die is that, in the infertility scenario, it is also true that no as yet unborn people will come into existence. So in finding that scenario but not the mundane prospect of universal death catastrophic, one is evincing a level of concern about the nonexistence of future people that exceeds one's concern about the mortality of existing people. Characterizing this heightened level of concern as a concern about "the end of society" doesn't change this fact. It merely redescribes it. And however one describes it, it continues to suggest some striking limits to our personal egoism.

A different kind of objection would be to concede that our reaction to the infertility scenario evinces concern about the nonexistence of future people, but to argue that this concern can itself be explained as a manifestation of, rather than a departure from, our egoism. For the youngest among us, it may be said, the infertility scenario implies that there would be nobody alive to support or care for them when they became old. In the final years of their lives, there would effectively be no economy; no goods would be produced or services provided. As the last generation of humans on earth, they would have no successors to provide the emotional, material, or medical support that they would require. So the infertility scenario would be, from a purely self-interested point of view, a disaster for them, and it would also alter for the worse their relations with other living generations. It might, for example, make them less willing to provide support for their own elders, and those elders might in turn be less willing to provide support for *their* elders, and so on. The result would be a ripple effect in which the disastrous implications for the youngest people would be passed up the generational ladder and would ultimately include everyone in society. In consequence, the infertility scenario might well be viewed as catastrophic by all of those now living, but only for instrumental, self-interested reasons.

This objection clearly has some merit, but I do not believe that it is the whole story. If it were, it would imply that, provided that the comfort of the youngest generation in their final years could be assured (perhaps by providing with them with thoughtfully preprogrammed caregiver robots),[7]

---

[7]When I first wrote this, I thought that I was describing something purely in the realm of science fiction, but that turns out not to be true. See, for example, Daniel Bartz, "Toyota Sees Robotic Nurses

then they, and by implication the rest of the living, could contemplate the imminent end of human life on earth with equanimity, or at least with no less equanimity than that with which people now contemplate their own deaths. But this strikes me as incredible. To me it seems clear, as I hope it will to you, that the infertility scenario would be viewed as catastrophic even if it were known in advance that it would not have any negative effect on either the physical comfort or the longevity of any living person.[8] That, at any rate, is what the afterlife conjecture supposes.

[…]

---

in Your Lonely Final Years," *Wired*, January 19, 2010, http://www.wired.com/gadgetlab/2010/01/toyota-sees-robotic-nurses-in-your-lonely-final-years/, and, in the same vein, Calum Macleod, "A Glimpse of the Future: Robots Aid Japan's Elderly Residents," *USA Today*, November 5, 2009, http://www.usatoday.com/tech/news/robotics/2009-ll-04-japan-robots_N.htm.

[8] Is it the survival of human beings that matters to us or the survival of people (persons)? In the text I treat the two ideas as equivalent, but many philosophers suppose that, in principle, there might be members of nonhuman species who qualified as persons. Suppose we knew that the disappearance of human beings was imminent but that it would be accompanied by the sudden emergence on earth of a new species of nonhuman persons. Would that be sufficient to restore our confidence in the value of our activities? If so, then perhaps it is the existence of people rather than the existence of human beings that matters to us. If not, then perhaps it is the survival of human beings in particular that we care about. But perhaps it is neither of these things. Perhaps what matters is the survival of people who share our values and seek to perpetuate our traditions and ways of life. If so, then the survival of human beings is neither necessary nor sufficient. Nonhuman persons with our values might do just as well. And human beings without our values would not help.

To the extent that these are questions about how we would react in various highly counterfactual circumstances, they are empirical questions that are extremely difficult to answer. My own view, as should be clear from the text, is that most of us do hope that future generations will share our most important values, but that the survival of humanity also matters to us in a way that is not exhausted by this concern. It is important to us that human beings should survive even though we know that their values and cultures will change in ways that we cannot anticipate and some of which we would not welcome. The future existence of nonhuman persons might provide some consolation if human beings did not survive, though a lot would depend on what exactly this new species was like and how its history was related to ours. In any case, though, I doubt whether the emergence of the new species would seem to us just as good as the survival of our own. That is in part because, despite what the terminology might suggest, I doubt whether we would view the existence of these nonhuman persons as providing us with the basis for what I have called "a personalized relation to the future." In short, what I take the arguments of these lectures to show is that the survival of human persons matters greatly to us, although it is not the only thing that matters to us, and although there are other imaginable things that might provide some consolation if we knew that human persons were about to disappear.

22

The Significance of Doomsday

Susan Wolf

In her review of the preceding reading, American philosopher Susan Wolf agrees that, in certain respects, the survival of humanity, including strangers who will exist long after we have died, is more important to each of us than our own personal survival. However, she doubts that Scheffler's afterlife conjecture can bear the full weight of this claim. In Wolf's alternative afterlife conjecture, our reaction to immanent extinction is less dispiriting than Scheffler makes out: the prospect of immanent extinction might shift our understating of our activities, and it might shake the foundations of their having meaning and value for us; however, once the initial phase of disorientation and depression has passed, rational reflection would bring value and meaning back to many of the activities that Scheffler thinks the doomsday scenarios would undermine by making pointless. Life in the shadow of the doomsday scenario would not count as a happy life, of course; however, it could still be a meaningful life. Wolf concludes that "the very idea that things matter relies on a valuing community (of more than one), but that community need not have a future—that it have a past and a present would be enough."

In his response to Wolf (not included here), Scheffler writes, "The fact that even quintessential egoists would be demoralized or even devastated by the nonexistence of future people means that they are vulnerable to and dependent on others in unexpected ways. And I take these forms of vulnerability and dependence to show something significant not only about the nature but also about the limits of their egoism" (*Death and the Afterlife* 179).

Wolf (b. 1952) is Professor of Philosophy at the University of North Carolina, Chapel Hill. She has made notable contributions to the fields of ethics and the meanings of life.

Virtually all of us take it for granted that human life will go on long after we are gone. How long? Hundreds of years? Thousands of years? Tens of thousands? Hundreds of thousands? The fact that many of us are vague about how many zeroes to tack on to the answer shows how little we are accustomed to considering the matter. Nonetheless, I suspect that virtually all of us are confident that, at any rate, humanity will go on for *a good long time*. In his fascinating and deeply original Tanner Lectures, "The Afterlife," Samuel Scheffler speculates on the role this assumption plays in the formation and sustenance of our values and in the activities that structure our lives, and he explores the significance it would have for our self-understanding if his speculations are right.

With Scheffler, I believe that our confidence in the continuation of the human race plays an *enormous,* if mostly tacit, role in the way we conceive of our activities and understand their value. With Scheffler, I agree that if we were to lose this confidence, our lives would change radically, and much for the worse. Still, my conjectures about how they would change, my interest in the question of how it would be reasonable for them to change, and the conclusions I am inclined to draw from the answers to these questions about the relation of our values to our belief in posterity are somewhat different.

Scheffler begins by asking us to consider a doomsday scenario in which each of us is to imagine learning that although we ourselves will live to the end of our natural lifespans, thirty days after our death the earth will collide with a giant asteroid and be destroyed. Later he offers a variation of this thought experiment, based on a novel by P. D. James and a subsequent film directed by Alfonso Cuarón, in which humans have become infertile.[1]

---

[1] In this variant, the doom is more gradual, as people slowly die out. Furthermore, in this variant the planet survives, even though humanity does not. There are interesting questions to be explored about the differences between these scenarios, and how these differences might affect our responses to them, but these are not Scheffler's focus nor will they be mine.

After taking us through a series of imagined reactions to different types of activities and values, Scheffler suggests, in keeping with James and Cuarón, that a world in which the demise of humanity is known to be imminent would be "characterized by widespread apathy, anomie, and despair; by the erosion of social institutions and social solidarity; by the deterioration of the physical environment; and by a pervasive loss of conviction about the value or point of many activities" (40). Calling this, or something like it, "the afterlife conjecture," Scheffler draws out what he takes this conjecture to imply.

Scheffler is rightly cautious in his conclusions, acknowledging that his predictions are but conjectures. Still, it might be worthwhile to explicitly acknowledge how ill-equipped we are to make reliable judgments about this. The question of how we would react to the prospect of imminent extinction appears to be an empirical question, which philosophers and novelists are not especially well placed to answer. But with respect to this issue, I would not place much credence in the conclusions of psychologists or social scientists either. Although they could conduct surveys and experiments, asking large numbers of people how they *think* they would react or even, perhaps, simulating environments in which the subjects half-believe that the doomsday or infertility scenario is true, they could at best get evidence for predicting people's first and early reactions to this. We are not very good at predicting our reactions to changes in deeply ingrained habits or beliefs, and it seems reasonable to expect that a change in a belief as deeply ingrained and fundamental as the belief in posterity would take considerable time to integrate into a stably revised worldview.[2]

This will not keep me from adding my own conjectures to those of Scheffler and James and Cuarón. I am as comfortable in my armchair as the next philosopher (or philosophical novelist). But my own conjectures about how we *would* react are inextricable from thoughts about how we *should* react—that is, thoughts about how it would be *reasonable* to react. Although Scheffler shies away from this more prescriptive question, I find it irresistible. My conjectures are thus to some extent unavoidably informed

---

[2]When the practice of women's choosing to keep their own surnames after marriage was new, people predicted (quite wrongly, in my experience) that it would be very complicated and confusing for others. Indeed, many still make these mistaken predictions. People also predicted that having to separate out paper and plastic for recycling would be very troublesome, but now it is second nature for many. A more apt comparison to the present case might be the speculations people living in a nearly universal Christian society made about the consequences of losing faith.

by my unreflective intuitions about what would be reasonable. After offering some of these conjectures, I shall also raise some prescriptive questions explicitly.

The nature and limits of egoism

Let me begin, however, with a question that grants Scheffler the likelihood of his afterlife conjecture and asks about his interpretation of what the truth of that conjecture would imply. Noting that we would regard the extinction of humanity with more horror than we do our own deaths, and that we would find it harder, if not impossible, to live meaningful lives under this assumption than we do under the acknowledgment of our personal mortality, Scheffler concludes, "In certain concrete functional and motivational respects, the fact that we and everyone we love will cease to exist matters less to us than would the nonexistence of future people whom we do not know and who, indeed, have no determinate identities. Or to put it more positively, the coming into existence of people we do not know and love matters more to us than our own survival and the survival of the people we do know and love." He takes this to reflect something both striking and surprising about "the nature and limits of our personal egoism" (45).

Although I agree with Scheffler that, in certain respects, the survival of humanity is more important to us than our own survival, and agree, on entirely independent grounds, that people are much less egoistic than some philosophers and economists make us out to be, it is unclear to me how the first point, or the afterlife conjecture from which it derives, provides any particular support for the second.

Though I don't think that most people are (either purely or dominantly) egoistic, I do think that some people are. Donald Trump, perhaps, or Mike Tyson or a contemporary nonfictional Don Juan. In the spirit of the afterlife conjecture, I can easily imagine that upon learning that the end of the world is near, any one of these individuals might lose interest in the activities and pursuits that until then made his life exciting and fun. What's the point, one of them might wonder, of being the richest man in the world, or the heavyweight champ, or the world's most impressive seducer, if the world will come to an end in thirty or fifty years? But would this reaction show these characters to be any less egoistic than they seemed to us before? I don't see how. What it does show rather is, first, that self-concern on any but the most hedonistic conception is not to be identified with a concern for maximizing one's survival or even one's pleasure,[3] and second, that many of the goals and states the realization of which *would* answer to one's self-concern are parasitic on the existence of other people, including, as the afterlife conjecture particularly reflects, of other people who live on after we are gone.[4]

This is clearest in cases in which fame, prestige, and other competitive goals figure into a person's conception of the good—and in which, whether consciously or subconsciously, one's ambitions for such things extend beyond the present generation. But if, as the afterlife conjecture plausibly suggests, even "the appetitive pleasures of food, drink, and sex might be affected" (42), I don't see why this should be taken to imply that the individual's *interest* in food, drink, and sex is any less egoistic than it would have been if the gourmand, the glutton, or the stud were unmoved by the prospect of doomsday and carried on as gleefully as before. According to the afterlife conjecture as I understand it, the prospect of doomsday would, to quote Huckleberry Finn, "take the tuck all out of [us]."[5] It would unsettle us, making many of our goals and values seem shallow, and so less satisfying to achieve. But this wouldn't show that our goals and values are any more, or any less, egoistic, than they seemed before—it would only show that happiness would, on the doomsday scenario, be harder for an egoist to achieve.

Since Scheffler is careful to qualify his claims about the comparative strengths of our interest in ourselves and in others with phrases like "a very specific sense" and "in certain concrete … respects" (73, 45), he and I may not really disagree. Moreover, he takes the afterlife conjecture to show us something about "the nature *and* limits of our egoism" (45, emphasis added)—if we place the stress on "nature" rather than on "limits," my remarks may even be understood to complement his own. For, as I have mentioned, the afterlife conjecture does make clear that even egoists are not solipsists, or, in Scheffler's vocabulary, individualists (about value), and that many of our egoistic concerns are dependent on the existence and attention of others, including, probably more than we realize, the existence of others who exist long after we have died.

---

[3]This is connected to Scheffler's point that our values are nonexperientialist.
[4]This is connected to Scheffler's point that our values are not individualist.
[5]Mark Twain, *The Adventures of Huckleberry Finn* (New York: Charles L. Webster and Co., 1885), chapter XVI.

An alternative afterlife conjecture

Few people, however, are as egoistic as I am imagining Donald Trump and Mike Tyson to be, so let us set them aside and accept Scheffler's invitation to speculate on how the rest of us would react to the doomsday or the infertility scenario. When I engage in these speculations, I find myself wondering whether Scheffler's afterlife conjecture, more specifically, that part of it that predicts "widespread apathy" and "anomie" (40)—is ultimately significantly more plausible than an alternative one, in which our reaction to extinction is less dispiriting.

As Scheffler points out, the prospect of imminent extinction would immediately give us reason to abandon many of our current activities and projects—in some cases, by rendering their goals unattainable, and in others, by undermining the value or point of attaining them. The fact that the prospect of extinction would call for changes of this sort, however, is not in any obvious way philosophically surprising. We always have reason to change our projects when circumstances arise that render them pointless: If the place one had planned to go to for a holiday is flattened by a hurricane, one must find a new destination. If the company one works for goes out of business, one must find a new job. And if the people you were counting on to help you with your projects or whom your projects were aimed at pleasing or helping will be destroyed or aborted by the planet's collision with a giant asteroid—well, you had better find something else to do with your time.[6] But what?

After considering the wide variety of projects that would manifestly be rendered pointless by imminent extinction, Scheffler discusses a range of activities and goals with respect to which the relevance of extinction is less obvious or direct. Regarding creative and scholarly projects, for example, he asks "Would artistic, musical, and literary projects still seem worth undertaking? Would humanistic scholars continue to be motivated to engage

---

[6]Scheffler appears to address this reaction when he writes, against those who would say "this mundane point about instrumental rationality is all that is needed to explain why people would no longer regard such projects as worth pursuing," that "this misconstrues the significance of the example" (27). "What may be surprising," he goes on to say, "is the fact that people are often happy to pursue goals that they do not expect to be achieved until after their own deaths" (27). As it happens, this does not seem particularly surprising to me, but, as I go on to say, the likelihood that some of our other activities and goals may be undermined by the prospect of our imminent extinction does strike me as surprising and deeply philosophically puzzling.

in basic research? Would historians and theoretical physicists and anthropologists all carry on as before? Perhaps, but the answer is not obvious." (25) By the time Scheffler offers the afterlife conjecture, his speculations have grown more pessimistic.

Insofar as the afterlife conjecture is a plausible one—and, with Scheffler, James, and Cuarón, I believe that it is—we have here reached something of great philosophical interest. *Why* would our interest in theoretical research and in artistic expression weaken? One answer that would make this reaction intelligible is that when artists create, scholars write, and scientists do research, they are hoping to produce work that will be enjoyed and esteemed for many generations. But this seems unlikely, and even the less grandiose hope of producing work that will at any rate have a small and possibly unrecognized effect on the direction and character of their fields seems more than most artists and scholars would insist on. If, as I think, for most artists and scholars, at least in the humanities, it would be profoundly gratifying for one's work to be found useful or beautiful or worthwhile by even a small portion of one's own generation, then it is puzzling why the absence of subsequent generations should take the sails out of one's efforts. Even more puzzling, if the afterlife conjecture is right, is why the doomsday scenario would weaken the motivations of practitioners of the performing arts. Would the prospect of human extinction weaken our motivation to play piano, to act, to dance?

Puzzling as it is, I don't deny that the prospect of doomsday might affect us this way. As a *first* reaction to the scenario, indeed, it seems to me quite natural that it would. Having the confidence we do that our species and even our society will continue long after we are gone, we tend implicitly to conceive of our activities as entering or as being parts of one or another ongoing stream—of the history and community of art or of science; of an ethnic or religious culture; of legal, political, industrial, technological developments, and so on. This feature of the way we conceive of activities, unconscious and unarticulated though it may be, may well play a significant role in the meaning and value these activities have for us. Even if we do not think of ourselves as affecting the direction or shape of these streams, the mere fact that we are contributing to them gives us a place in or attachment to a larger and independently valuable whole.[7] Learning that the streams we

---

[7]I argue that engagement in activities that connect us in a positive way to things of independent value are crucial to living meaningful lives in *Meaning in Lives and Why It Matters* (Princeton, NJ: Princeton University Press, 2010).

thought our activities were a part of would be coming abruptly to an end would profoundly shift our understanding of what we have been doing; it would shake the foundations on which the meaningfulness and value of these activities rested.

The idea that the expectation of our imminent extinction would profoundly *shift* our understanding of our activities and *shake* the foundations of their having meaning and value for us seems plausible to me. But would it utterly destroy their meaning and value? It is not obvious to me that it would.

At least twice in the course of his speculations about how many of our ordinary concerns would weaken or disappear under the shadow of imminent extinction, Scheffler acknowledges the likelihood that a few values and interests would remain. In Lecture 1, he mentions that "the projects and activities that would seem least likely to be affected by the doomsday scenario are those focused on personal comfort and pleasure" (though he rightly adds that "it is ... not altogether obvious what would be comforting and pleasant under doomsday conditions"). (25) In Lecture 2, he admits that "Even in an infertile world, it seems plausible to suppose that it would be important to people to be free from severe pain ... Nor, similarly, does it seem likely that friendship and other close personal relations would cease to matter to people." (54) In fact, what seems *to me* the least likely sort of activity to be affected by the doomsday scenario might be thought of as an integration or synthesis of these remarks: The sorts of activities least likely to be affected by the doomsday or infertility scenario are those that are explicitly focused on the care and comfort of others.

It is a striking fact how much time and money and effort we are willing to spend on the care of those who are close to us—not just care for our children, but, when we reach a certain age, care for our parents as well (and, of course, for our spouses, our siblings, and our friends, when they are in need of our care). Our devotion includes and perhaps especially extends to our loved ones who are dying. In cases where it is vivid to us that our loved ones will die soon and that they have little chance of contributing more to the communities and institutions of which they have been a part, it seems least likely that the doomsday scenario will make any difference to us. Even if doomsday threatens to send us into a depression and sap our enthusiasm for everything else, the concern to comfort those in immediate need of care is likely to make us resist giving in. This suggests the possibility of an alternative conjecture to the dystopian one that James, Cuarón, and eventually Scheffler propose. Specifically, it suggests the possibility that once the immediate shock of our immanent extinction has worn off and we have come to accept it, we also come to recognize that we are, so to speak, "all in this together," a single community on this sinking ship of a planet. And as we come to think of our fellow humans in this way, perhaps we will find ourselves moved to provide the same care for each other that we have shown ourselves so ready to lavish on our dying or despairing relatives and friends.

For empirical evidence about the likelihood of this, it would be helpful to know how people behave on literally sinking ships, downed submarines, or space shuttle missions that have gone disastrously wrong so as to isolate their crews, with nothing to look forward to but their collective annihilation. It seems to me at least possible that with the right leadership, such groups would remain motivated to think and act and care for each other right to the end, and that, analogously, with the right leadership, we, too, if faced with imminent extinction, could resist the tendency toward apathy and anomie portrayed in the afterlife conjecture, and think and act and care for each other. Moreover, since we would have time and resources that these other groups lack,[8] we would have a wide range of means for caring and comforting each other at our disposal. We could create and perform music and plays, we could plant gardens, hold discussion groups, write books and commentaries. Being motivated at first to help and comfort each other, we might find ourselves reengaged by the beauty, the challenge, and the interest these projects held for us in our predoomsday lives. In other words, in helping each other, we might help ourselves.

I do not say that we would be happy. Even on this conjecture, much less pessimistic than Scheffler's, I share Scheffler's doubt "that there is something [available in this community on the brink of extinction] that we would be prepared to count as a good life." (43) But even if, under the circumstances, we would not be in a position to live a good life or a happy one, we could, on this conjecture, at least live a meaningful one.

Up to a point, my speculations and alternative afterlife conjecture follow and agree with Scheffler's. My remarks about seeing ourselves as contributors to ongoing "streams," for example, echo his reflections in Lecture 2:

> Our concerns and commitments, our values and judgments of importance, our sense of what matters and what is worth doing—all these things are formed and sustained against a background in which it is taken for granted

---

[8]We would have even more resources than we have now, in fact, since on that scenario we would have no reason to make efforts at conservation.

that human life is itself a thriving, ongoing enterprise. Many of our deepest and most defining values and aspirations and ambitions … depend on our taking this for granted. In fact, we take it so much for granted that we seldom recognize its role … But this does nothing to diminish its significance. Humanity itself as an ongoing, historical project provides the implicit frame of reference for most of our judgments about what matters. Remove that frame of reference, and our sense of importance … is destabilized and begins to erode. (59-60)

Where I suggest, however, that our destabilization might be temporary, and that we might, as a result of a robust concern to mitigate the despair and apathy of others, pull ourselves back from the brink of our own despair, Scheffler voices no such hope. To the contrary, he writes, "We need humanity to have a future if many of our own individual purposes are to matter to us now. Indeed, I believe that something stronger is true: we need humanity to have a future for the very idea that things *matter* to retain a secure place in our conceptual repertoire." (60)[9]

If my alternative afterlife conjecture is plausible—it need not be *more* plausible than Scheffler's, just plausible—and my description of the people imagined in it as living meaningful, even if not happy, lives is coherent, then it seems that Scheffler's final claim about the reliance of the very idea of things mattering on posterity cannot be right. An alternative hypothesis, compatible with Scheffler's anti-individualism about values, but also with my somewhat less pessimistic afterlife scenario, is that the very idea that things matter relies on a valuing community (of more than one), but that community need not have a future—that it have a past and a present would be enough.

What we can learn from Alvy Singer

How are we to decide whether either of these afterlife conjectures is truly plausible, or whether either Scheffler's or my speculations about the conditions or grounds for "the very idea that things matter" are correct? How, in other words, are we to proceed in constructing a theory of value

---

[9]Of course, if humanity does not have a future, neither does our conceptual repertoire. But we may leave this point to one side.

(or a theory of things mattering)? Obviously, these questions are much too large to be addressed in this commentary. But as I mentioned at the beginning of my remarks, my own reflections on how we *would* respond to the doomsday scenario are inextricable from reflection on how we *should* respond. Similarly, my speculations on what the idea of value depends on are inextricable from my thoughts about what it would make rational sense for it to depend on.

In his lectures, Scheffler seems to want to resist any questions of this sort. At its most general, the question, "how would it be rational, or even reasonable, to respond to the doomsday scenario?" might well be greeted with suspicion. In the spirit of P. F. Strawson or Bernard Williams, one might reasonably be skeptical of the power and appropriateness of expecting "rationality" to help us in responding to so enormous a catastrophe as doomsday. Further, we might wonder from what perspective the question is supposed to be addressed. What assumptions about the nature and status of our values—and of their independence from an ongoing form of life—are we making insofar as we take that question to be intelligible, and why should we give those assumptions any authority? Perhaps such thoughts and concerns are behind Scheffler's resistance to talking about how we should or ought to respond to the prospect of extinction, to his determination to stick to conjectures about how we *would* respond instead and considering what these conjectures might reveal about us. Whether or not they are Scheffler's concerns, they are fair enough. Nonetheless, the question of how we should respond and that of how we would respond cannot be kept so separate as to warrant dismissing the first one entirely. For we are rational and rationality-valuing creatures, and our thoughts about what is rational, reasonable, and sensible to do and to feel affect what we ultimately decide to do and feel. If, from within the perspective of our own values, we find our initial reaction to the prospect of imminent extinction rationally unstable or mysterious, it may weaken that reaction, and if we find another reaction to be more rationally appropriate, that might move us some way toward having this other reaction.

Speaking for myself, I am moved by the question, which Scheffler explicitly dismisses, of why if imminent extinction is so catastrophic, more distant extinction is not. We know, after all, that sooner or later, the earth will be destroyed and our species will die out. When we focus on activities and projects that do not in obvious ways appear to depend on posterity for either their attainability or their point, it is hard to see why, if such projects are rendered less meaningful by the prospect of *imminent* extinction, they are not meaningless anyway, for reasons that, though available to us, we typically push from our attention.

This seems essentially to be the viewpoint of Alvy Singer. As Scheffler reminds us in Lecture 2, when the nerdy protagonist in Woody Allen's film *Annie Hall* was in grade school, his mother took him to a doctor because he was refusing to do his homework on the grounds that the universe is expanding and will someday break apart. According to Scheffler's analysis, the scene is funny not only because of Alvy's precocity but also because he takes an event so far distant in the future to be a reason not to do his homework. As Scheffler reminds us, the doctor attempts to reassure Alvy by saying that won't happen for "billions of years." (62)

As an aside, it may be worth mentioning that, even if it's true that the earth's exploding won't occur for billions of years, we can expect that our species' extinction will come much, much earlier than that. According to the biologist Ernst Mayr, the average life of a species is 100,000 years, and we have already existed about that long.[10] So, we should not expect to go on for another billion years or even another 100,000. Not even close.

But let us return to Alvy's concern and Scheffler's response. According to Scheffler, it is simply a datum that in general we do not respond to our recognition that the earth will someday be destroyed with angst or nihilism or ennui. But, he concedes, "if the universe were going to end soon after the end of his own natural life, then … Alvy might have a point." (62) I doubt that the precocious Alvy would be satisfied by this response. The fact that people don't get upset by the prospect of our eventual extinction does not mean that they shouldn't. "If I would have a point in refusing to do my homework under the doomsday scenario," Alvy might insist, "why don't I have a point anyway?" It seems to me that Alvy is within his rights, at least within the seminar room, to ask for more of an answer.

In fact, the more I think about Alvy's question (a question also asked, in essence, by Camus and Tolstoy, among others), the less confident I am that it is answerable. For if Alvy would be justified in not doing his homework if the doomsday scenario were true, this would presumably be because, as Scheffler suggests, humanity must have a future—and indeed a future of more than

---

[10]Mayr's claim is mentioned by Noam Chomsky in, among other places, his "Intelligence and the Environment," *International Socialist Review* 76 (2011), http://www.isreview.org/issues/76/feat-chomsky.shtml.

thirty days—if anything (that could give Alvy a reason to do his homework) is to matter. But why would this be true? If the answer were that in order for anything to matter, it would have to make a *permanent* difference to the world, then Alvy's resistance to homework would be justified by the fact that the earth would explode in a billion years. If it is suggested instead that for anything to matter, it would have to make a long-lasting but not permanent difference (or, perhaps better, a difference to a long-lasting but not permanent community), then one might point out that from a cosmic perspective, even a billion years (much less 100,000) is not really "long-lasting."[11]

Happily, though, we can also run this puzzle the other way: If the fact that humans will eventually die out does not render dancing the tango (or walking in the woods or writing a philosophy lecture) meaningless *today*, why should the fact that we will die out in thirty or fifty or a hundred years render it meaningless either? Though I acknowledge the possibility that wish fulfillment is distorting my reasoning powers, I have to say that I find the rational pull coming from this direction fairly persuasive. That is, since the eventual extinction of humanity does not render our current efforts at creating beauty, gaining wisdom, and helping each other valueless, neither does, or would or should, our more imminent extinction. Probably we would be initially disoriented, unsettled, and depressed by the falsification of so major an assumption that we have until now taken for granted. But just as we are disoriented, unsettled, and depressed by the loss of our life's savings or the unexpected death of a loved one—or to offer a closer analogy, just as we are disoriented, unsettled, and depressed by the loss of faith in a benevolent God and a personal afterlife—we should, at least as a community, eventually, snap out of it and get back to our lives and our world. According to this line of thought, then, if we came to believe that our extinction was imminent, it would be more reasonable to resist the initial tendency to grow detached, apathetic, and depressed than to give in to it. Such reasoning, over time,

---

[11]Scheffler, one may recall, speculates that the scene in the doctor's office is funny because Alvy takes an event so far in the future to be a reason not to do his homework. If, as I am imagining, Alvy's reasoning cannot be dismissed, this explanation is less plausible. Perhaps our laughter at Alvy is rather the nervous laughter of people who are made uncomfortable by being asked to acknowledge what they would prefer not to confront. Alternatively, the humor in the scene may derive from what, in the spirit of Thompson Clarke, we might put in terms of the problematic relation between the philosophical level of thought and the everyday. Woody Allen frequently exploits this relation as a source of humor. Thus, my favorite line in another of Allen's works: "What if everything is an illusion and nothing exists? In that case, I definitely overpaid for my carpet." Woody Allen, *The Complete Prose of Woody Allen* (New York: Wings Books, 1991), 10.

ought to bring back the meaning and value to many of our activities that we initially thought doomsday would undermine.

Moreover, since the doomsday scenario is just a scenario—that is, an imaginary thought experiment—this reasoning should also bring back for us the meaning and value of the activities that would truly have been rendered pointless by imminent extinction. Now, once again, we have a reason to cure cancer, to find more sustainable energy sources, to build buildings, plant trees, repair infrastructures, and so on. Rationality, if I am right about where rationality on this topic leads, has given us our lives back, restoring the meaning and value to most, if not all, of the activities around which we previously fashioned our lives.

This might seem to deflate the point and impact of Scheffler's lectures. For, if I am right about the direction that reflection on doomsday scenarios should eventually take us, such reflection ultimately leaves everything almost where it is.[12] According to Wittgenstein, though, this is precisely what philosophy *should* do, and he at least did not regard this as in any way deflationary. Nor should we. Scheffler has done us an invaluable service by focusing our attention on the role of posterity in our lives and in our values, and by guiding us along one plausible path toward some tentative conclusions. I take it that the jury is still out on whether that path and those conclusions are right, but the rewards of reflection on these issues and arguments seem secure, no matter how long we as a species will last.

---

[12]I say "almost" everything because, even if I am right that the very ideas of meaning and value do not depend on humanity having a future (but only a past and a present), "The Afterlife" brings out the extent to which what is actually valuable to us does depend on humanity continuing for a good long time. As Scheffler notes, our vulnerability to the prospect of human extinction gives us more reasons to work to ensure that humanity survives than we are used to noticing (78–79).

23

Death, Failure, and Neoliberal Ideology

Beverley Clack

In our readings we have encountered arguments for and against various accounts of our posthumous fate. The reader will have judged some of these arguments to be more convincing than others. They could not all be true, of course; indeed, it is possible that none of them are true in all of their details. Reviewing our readings, some students might well have come to agree with the philosopher Mary Mothersill, whom we met in the Introduction to Part One: there is not much to say on the topic of death that is interesting. Perhaps Epicurus has been right all along: perhaps death is indeed nothing to us. But even if Mothersill and Epicurus are right, and even if there is not much to be said on the topic of death proper, it should be clear by now that there is much to consider when it comes to *what people have said about death*.

In our next and final reading, we complete our turn from the metaphysics of death toward considerations of axiology. Beverley Clack, Professor in Philosophy of Religion at Oxford Brookes University in the UK, describes how prevailing attitudes and assumptions about death have shifted from recognizing death as an inevitability and a reminder of the fragility of life, towards a new model of subjectivity and a new common sense rooted in a particular economic and ideological setting. According to the secular and individualistic assumptions that prevail among adults today, the human subject is a rational, self-contained pleasure maximizer, a consumer and a bargain-hunter by nature. Our freedom consists in large part of the ability to live out this nature. "Forget self-knowledge as the aim of life," Clack writes, "now the goal is self-expression," and shopping is the quintessence of self-expression. But shopping, consumption, and self-expression must come to an end for each of us; thus, for each of us the game of life can only end in failure.

The original title of Clack's paper was "Constructing Death as a Form of Failure: Addressing Mortality in a Neoliberal Age." As this title indicates, she believes that attitudes and assumptions about death are not fixed, and that prevailing attitudes and assumptions tell us something about a particular ideology that, in the final years of the last century, appeared to have defeated all contenders for all time. One of the words associated with this ideology is *neoliberalism*. The word *neoliberalism* has been attached to various and sometimes-inconsistent meanings. Drawing from partisan debates in the UK over the past several decades, and policy developments, including education and healthcare policy, Clack sorts through the various meanings of *neoliberalism*, taking up such ideas as privatization, deregulation, austerity, free trade, the priority of the price mechanism and the system of competition, "small government," and opposition to labor union influence as a market distortion. We have been told that the private sphere is primordial, that citizens are consumers, that public policy consists of compromises among pre-given private interests, and that the common good is an illusion. All of these are assumptions and policy prescriptions associated with nineteenth-century laissez-faire economic liberalism, and also with neoliberal ideology today.

Clack argues that neoliberalism holds up a clear picture of success in life, and carries with it an equally clear picture of failure. "Death," Clack writes, "reveals the ultimate failure of all neoliberal success." After all, if those who are dying are the ultimate losers, then it turns out that we are all ultimate losers. If Clack is right, then death, that proverbial inevitability, is everything that neoliberal success is not—and life itself is a losing game, not just for the have-not majority, but for all mere mortals.

To reject neoliberal ideology, of course, is easier said than done: in a profound way, perhaps, we are all products of that ideology. Clack envisions "different ways of thinking about what makes for a meaningful life," and part of that involves "accepting the inevitability of death." But this is no easy matter, she says, "for it necessitates rejecting the habitual construction of human beings as fundamentally different from the rest of the natural world." Toward the end of her paper, in the section entitled "Living well with death and loss," she describes a way of "acknowledging mortality." Her view here, as she notes, endorses the advice of the ancient school of Stoicism: "In the face of death, the right response is not petulant refusal but acceptance." But to accept death, according to the Stoics, "requires reflective practice."[1] This emphasis, it should be noted, is a far cry from the equally ancient school of Epicurus, and his view that "death is nothing to us."

For nearly forty years, Western politics has been dominated by a particular account of what it is to be a human subject. This model of subjectivity owes much to the Enlightenment vision of the self as rational, autonomous, and capable of choice. In its contemporary iteration, this "neoliberal" construction of the human subject places subjectivity in a specific economic setting where one's individual destiny is shaped through exercising one's ability to make rational choices in a marketplace; choices which are invariably shaped in terms of the ability to purchase and consume the material goods deemed necessary for a meaningful life.[2]

In this chapter I explore the model of success which arises from thinking of the human subject in this way. My focus is on the problems this model of the successful life encounters when confronted with the inevitability and inescapability of death. This necessitates, firstly, addressing the model of failure that arises from the neoliberal account of success; and secondly, resisting the neoliberal construction of death as the ultimate failure, in order to reassert the fact that to be human *is* to be mortal. My contention is that recognizing the inevitability of death for the human subject enables a set of values to emerge which are more conducive to human flourishing than those currently offered by dominant neoliberal philosophies.

---

[1]Refer to the Epictetus entry, in the Further Readings on Living with Mortality section at the end of Part V, below.

[2]For an excellent account of the forces that shaped the emergence of neoliberal thinking on economics, society and politics, see David Harvey, *A Brief History of Neoliberalism* (Oxford: Oxford University Press, 2005).

Success, failure, and the neoliberal subject

It is worth spending a little time identifying what precisely makes the neoliberal account of subjectivity distinctive from other accounts which similarly prioritize rationality and autonomy.[3] Starting in this way illuminates what success and failure mean for the individual conceived thus. David Harvey provides the clearest definition of neoliberalism which highlights its relation to classic liberal accounts of the self, while also recognizing its distinctiveness:

> Neoliberalism is in the first instance a theory of political economic practices that proposes human well-being can best be advanced by liberating individual entrepreneurial freedoms and skills within an institutional framework characterized by strong private property rights, free markets, and free trade.[4]

In order to free the entrepreneurial spirit of the individual, neoliberal societies embark on policies of deregulation and privatization. As the state withdraws from most areas of social provision,[5] the focus falls on the responsible self, whose freedom to pursue their own goals is framed through a corresponding commitment to the freedom of the market. It is in the marketplace that this self is to be actualized, the neoliberal subject being a

---

[3]The identification of the key attributes that make an economic theory or a view of the human subject "neoliberal" is something of a complex task. Philip Mirowski aligns neoliberalism with a suite of attitudes regarding economics, subjectivity, and society, and he emphasizes that these ideas and attitudes must always be understood as "a movable feast" (Philip Mirowski, *Never Let a Serious Crisis Go To Waste: How Neoliberalism Survived the Financial Meltdown* (London: Verso, 2014), 50), a "Russian doll" (Philip Mirowski and Dieter Plehwe, *The Road from Mont Pelerin: The Making of the Neoliberal Thought Collective* (Cambridge, MA: Harvard University Press, 2009), 43), rather than a clear statement of an ideological perspective. He, and others, direct attention to the role of the Mont Pelerin Society, which gathered around the political philosopher Friedrich von Hayek in 1947 as a group committed to rejecting the postwar Keynesian consensus. In contrast to the active role of the enabling state, their focus was on advancing "general issues such as liberty and private initiative" (Jamie Peck, *Constructions of Neoliberal Reason* (Oxford: Oxford University Press, 2010), 47). Harvey (in *A Brief History*) notes the different forms these values have subsequently taken in different cultural contexts, a variety that makes it difficult to name only one form taken by neoliberalism. Jamie Peck, likewise, details the "mongrel, shape-shifting forms" (Peck, *Constructions of Neoliberal Reason*, 276) of neoliberal theory and practice.
[4]Harvey, *A Brief History*, 2.
[5]Ibid., 3.

consumer rather than a *producer* of goods.[6] Through exercising the ability to choose, the individual is expected to be able to construct a successful life: success being measured in financial terms. This involves not just being able to choose from the marketplace the goods that are desired, but also attaining the material resources necessary to create, more broadly, the kind of life one wants. Drawing upon Foucault's insight, to be human in a neoliberal society is no longer to be *Homo sapiens* (the wise animal) but *Homo oeconomicus*, an economic unit with the power to shape its own (economic, social, and political) destiny.[7]

Subjectivity, then, is shaped by faith in free market economics. Given this economic framing it is not surprising that work should take on a particular role in the shaping of the human subject. If past generations assumed a life separate from the labor which they traded in the workplace, now it is *in* the workplace that one is expected to find meaning for one's life: through acquiring the money necessary for the good life, but also through the opportunity it provides for creating the kind of lifestyle that one desires.[8] To use Thomas Lemke's telling phrase, individuals are now understood as "entrepreneurs of themselves," "human resources" who must monopolize and market their talents, strengths and achievements, for it is only in this way that one is able to be deemed a success.[9]

The skills for success can—indeed, should—be taught. To be successful, attention must be paid to improving the self, acquiring the kind of skills that will enable you to become a successful individual. Just as a business would invest to improve itself, so the individual should be prepared to invest in the self, learning to cultivate the image of the winner through "the management of the interpersonal relations upon which winning depends."[10]

Cultivating success involves being prepared to take risks. The risk-taking subject is at the heart of neoliberalism, defined through "the story of an

---

[6]Nikolas Rose, *Governing the Soul: The Shaping of the Private Self* (London: Free Association, 1999), 102.
[7]See Thomas Lemke's 2001 article ("'The Birth of Bio-Politics': Michel Foucault's Lecture at the College de France on Neo-Liberal Governmentality," *Economy and Society* 30 (2): 190–207), in which this phrase is used. Lemke draws upon a lecture given by Foucault in 1979, which is only available as a recording. Lemke's article is both a reconstruction of the lecture material and a commentary upon it.
[8]Rose, *Governing the Soul*, 104.
[9]Lemke, "The Birth of Bio-Politics," 199.
[10]Rose, *Governing the Soul*, 117.

entrepreneurial self."[11] The ideal human subject is the one prepared to "take up any challenge, transcend any limitation, and embody any quality."[12] If you are bold enough and willing enough to challenge yourself you can become anything that you want to be. Forget self-knowledge as the aim of life: now the goal is self-expression. Aspiration becomes the guiding principle for how to live. Note that neoliberal ambition is framed by the rejection of the social self: to achieve self-actualization you must be willing to embrace competition (the neoliberal's "primary virtue"), rejecting solidarity with others as "a sign of weakness."[13] No class consciousness or group identity can shape your experience. You alone must create yourself and your destiny.

The goal of this aspiring subject? Ansgar Allen claims that it is difficult to identify any aim beyond "the narcotic of constant activity."[14] There is some truth in this: define the self as entrepreneurial, and work will necessarily appear as an end in itself. At its most lofty, the goal of the neoliberal subject seems to be acquiring the resources necessary for constructing a lifestyle that allows for self-expression. At its most prosaic, in a precarious world where the state provides limited protection from the ills of life, acquiring material goods acts as a buffer against the swings and arrows of outrageous fortune. In order to be secure, you need monetary resources capable of providing that security.[15]

Here we start to get a glimpse of the shadow that haunts neoliberal success: failure. That not all can be successful under such a model, that economic or educational success will have to be weighed against others failing, that success can just as easily give way to failure, is rarely acknowledged. Following Judith Butler, we might note the significance of this unacknowledged experience, for as Butler says, attending to those things which are absent from discourse is just as important as considering those things which are present. Those things which are excluded "haunt signification as its abject borders or as that which is strictly foreclosed: the

[11]Mirowski, Serious Crisis, 92.
[12]Ibid., 117.
[13]Ibid., 92.
[14]Ansgar Allen, "The Cynical Educator," Other Education: The Journal of Educational Alternatives 4(1) (2015): 4–15.
[15]While Guy Standing (The Precariat, London: Bloomsbury, 2011) identifies the "precariat" with a specific strata dependent on zero hours contracts and low pay or benefits, it could be argued that with the exception of the top 10 percent, most who depend on work for their income fall into this category.

unlivable, the nonnarrativizable, the traumatic."[16] Exploring neoliberal attitudes to failure makes possible the illumination of neoliberal fears and desires; it also opens up the possibility of thinking differently about what makes for a meaningful life.

So how is failure conceived in neoliberal discourse? Crucially, failure is viewed as something which reflects flaws in the self rather than something resulting from problems in the socioeconomic system that one inhabits. If one does not become successful in the way outlined above, blame lies squarely with the self, the assumption being that one's failure results from either failing to "work hard enough" or from a failure of character. Failure to achieve ends with the belief that if you fail, you *are* a failure.[17]

That failure is never something that happens to you, but that it always arises from a flaw in your character informs the way those deemed failures are treated in societies that refuse to accept that individual achievement might be constrained by economic or social conditions way beyond the scope of the individual's control. Attitudes to the poor are most telling, for they reveal not just the desire to separate the successful subject from those deemed to have failed, but also suggest something of the ethics supporting neoliberal subjectivity that makes it extremely difficult to establish a sense of the common life we share.

At one point in his analysis of "Everyday Neoliberalism," Philip Mirowski homes in on what he calls "the theatre of cruelty" attending to the treatment of the poor. No longer understood to exist as a class, "it is easier to hate them as individuals." Rather than seek to protect those rendered vulnerable by market forces or social inequality, the relatively better-off are "galvanised to find within themselves a kind of guilty pleasure in the thousand unkind cuts administered by the enforcers of trickle-down austerity."[18]

Here's an example. Since the global financial crisis of 2008 which heralded in the UK's new "age of austerity," British TV has been saturated with what commentators have taken to calling "poverty porn." These reality TV shows claim to reveal the feckless lifestyles of the "undeserving poor" and glory in titles such as "Benefits Street" and "Benefits Britain." At the time of writing, the BBC (world renowned public service broadcaster) has commissioned a

---

[16]Judith Butler, *Bodies That Matter* (London: Routledge, 1993).
[17]The toxicity of this notion that hard work is central to what it is to succeed is being identified and increasingly challenged (see George Monbiot, "Aspirational Parents Condemn Their Children to a Desperate, Joyless Life," *Guardian*, June 9, 2015 (http://gu.com/p/49jk9/sbl)).
[18]Mirowski, *Serious Crisis*, 130.

show that it is gleefully describing as akin to *The Hunger Games*, where the unemployed will be pitted against the low paid in order to find "Britain's Hardest Grafter."[19] Crucial to such "entertainments" is the erosion of empathy: in order to be entertained, you, the viewer, must not see yourself in *their* plight. It is hard not to concur with Mirowski's conclusion that such programs are there to direct attention away from those who benefit from an unjust socioeconomic system to those who suffer from it. The poor are to blame for their situation and thus are worthy of contempt. As Mirowski puts it, "In the neoliberal theatre of cruelty, one torments the poor or indigent precisely *because* they are prostrate."[20]

I want to pick up on this response to perceived failure, because I believe it reveals the problem at the heart of the neoliberal subject. To shape the subject as an entrepreneur whose meaning resides in the extent to which they are a success in the marketplace has a pernicious effect on how we shape supportive and inclusive societies. For neoliberal societies, economic theory is not simply restricted to the realm of economics: it comes to shape our ethics, our understanding of ourselves, and our place in the world. Free market exchange is not "just" an economic theory: it is "an ethic in itself, *capable of acting as a guide to all human action, and substituting for all previously held ethical beliefs.*"[21] To fail in the marketplace is to *be* a failure: worthy of contempt and ill-treatment. It is my contention that not only does this way of thinking cultivate cruelty, it does so by misrepresenting the facts of what it is to be human. By failing to engage with the social aspect of our humanity, we end up with disconnected communities incapable of supporting the flourishing of more than a few. In what follows, I suggest that one way of challenging the problems that attend to neoliberal accounts of success and failure is to turn to that feature of life which is inescapable and to which philosophers have repeatedly directed their gaze when considering the nature of human subjectivity: death. Through reconsidering what it means to be mortal we can form better ways of understanding subjectivity, as well as, crucially, returning to the importance of community for living well.

---

[19]Bradley Allsop, "The BBC's 'Britain's Hardest Grafter' Show Should be Britain's Greatest Shame," *Huffington Post* (June 3, 2015, http://www.huffington-post.co.uk/bradley-allsop/britains-hardest-grafter_b_7499800.html).

[20]Mirowski, *Serious Crisis*, 131.

[21]Paul Treanor, quoted in Harvey, *A Brief History*, 3, emphasis added.

Death and the limits of neoliberal subjectivity

Death stands at the limits of human existence. It denotes the ultimate boundary, the end point, for all human striving. In existentialist philosophy, death is that which defines life.[22] While it is possible to discern in the neoliberal call to self-expression the ghostly presence of the existentialist call to self-creation,[23] the attention paid to death is not similarly present. For Jean-Paul Sartre, death reveals the ultimate absurdity of human striving.[24] Its unpredictability means we cannot assume our goals will be attained or our projects completed. Life is tragic, the possibility and projects of human life rarely being achieved.

To accept that there might be limits of human endeavor, to grapple with the reality of "being-towards-death,"[25] challenges the relentless optimism of neoliberal aspiration. Acknowledge the skeleton beneath the skin, and the idea that we are always "in control" of our lives seems a peculiar conclusion to draw from the facts of existent being. Yet, the success of neoliberalism as an ideology stems from the way it appeals to what *we like to think* about our lives. As David Harvey notes, for any ideology to be successful, "a conceptual apparatus has to be advanced that appeals to our intuitions and instincts, our values and desires, as well as the possibilities inherent in the social world we inhabit."[26] The central tenets of neoliberalism are appealing as they map onto how we like to think of ourselves: as responsible, creative, and free.

Not surprising, then, that the neoliberal strategy for dealing with death is not dissimilar to that advanced for dealing with poverty. Rather than accept that there might be things outside our control (be they socioeconomic forces or death itself), facing the feelings of vulnerability that such an acceptance engenders, we prefer to believe that we are in control of our own destinies. The consequence of this overweening faith in our own capacity lends itself to

---

[22]For a commentary on this aspect of existentialist thought, see David Cooper, *Existentialism* (Oxford: Blackwell, 1990), 127–46.
[23]See for example Jean-Paul Sartre, *Being and Nothingness* (London: Methuen, 1969 [first published in 1943]), 26–28.
[24]Ibid., 533.
[25]See Martin Heidegger, *Being and Time* (Oxford: Blackwell, 1962), 264; also Cooper, *Existentialism*, 136–39, for discussion of the broader application of this concept.
[26]Harvey, *A Brief History*, 5.

a view of death where it is just another variety of failure, best explained by reference to the capacities—or lack of them—of those who are dying.

The language commonly used in accounts of terminal illness reveals something of the power of this construction. Philip Gould, one of the architects of the neoliberal political project in the UK which was New Labor, illustrates this with his initial framing of his treatment as not dissimilar to a political campaign that will test his resolve and his personal resources: "Everything I thought about the battle with cancer was strategic, as if I was fighting an election campaign. I saw the elimination of the cancer as victory, and the test results as opinion polls."[27] If the elimination of the cancer is victory, if the test results highlight whether he is winning the battle, it is not surprising that negative results are experienced as failure. Telling, perhaps, that Gould should structure his experience of cancer in this way, given his political commitment to the values of autonomy and choice. Later, as he realizes he cannot win this battle, he is forced to shift his focus away from such notions to acceptance, developing a sense that what really matters is less this individual battle and more his relationship with his family and nature,[28] a move to which we will return later in this chapter.

Gould is not alone in recognizing the failure of neoliberal values in the face of death. Kate Gross' account of terminal illness gives understandable expression to her anger at the unfairness of her diagnosis. Like Gould, Gross was an advisor to the UK's New Labor government. In the face of advanced colon cancer, she finds the values by which she has structured her life no longer make sense: "I am not used to this uncertain terrain. In every other aspect of my life, diligence and hard work have been rewarded with getting what I want."[29] Now she finds that dying has "freed me from convention and from ambition."[30] It takes struggle to get to this point: a struggle not helped by the prevailing culture that has little place for loss, dying, or, indeed, anything which suggests limits might be placed on the kind of achievements that have shaped Gross' life.

Reading death through the lens of failure is not a move peculiar to neoliberalism—though, I shall argue, it takes on a particular form shaped by the neoliberal application of economics to all areas of life. Early Christian theological reflection on death reflects a similar pull toward thinking of

---

[27]Philip Gould, *When I Die: Lessons from the Death Zone* (London: Little, Brown, 2012), 20.
[28]Ibid., 110, 134, 141.
[29]Kate Gross, *Late Fragments* (London: William Collins, 2015), 153.
[30]Ibid., 179.

death as aberrant rather than natural. While Pelagius (390-418) and Julian of Eclanum (386-455) saw death as very much a natural part of life,[31] Saint Augustine (354-430), their opponent and victor in the battle for Christian orthodoxy, understood death as far from natural: it was an aberration humans "brought upon ourselves" through our failure to obey God's command.[32] Had there been no sin there would be no death, for, as St Paul pithily puts it, "the wages of sin is death" (Romans 6:23).

Elaine Pagels suggests that before we dismiss Saint Augustine's claims as "anti-natural and even preposterous,"[33] we should look a little more closely, for the view that death is an aberration is all-too-familiar. Death strikes us as obscene because it throws into stark relief our insignificance in the face of cosmic forces. In the face of death, neoliberal aspiration is rendered as absurd as existentialist self-creation. While Sartre makes absurdity a cornerstone of his philosophy, aspiring neoliberals turn to the market for an answer to the problem of mortality. And why not? After all, "neoliberalisation has meant . . . the financialization of everything."[34] If all areas of life—including education, health, and the utilities deemed necessary for sustaining human life—can be bought and sold, monetarized in order to create profit for companies and shareholders, why can a similar method not be applied to confronting death itself?[35] Indeed, large sums of money are being put into making the dream of conquering death a reality.[36] In the most well-known of these, cryonics, the body is frozen immediately after death in the hope that future medical advances will enable the deceased to be returned to life. With cryonic procedures costing anywhere between $28,000 and $200,000, the implication is that the advantages of wealth extend even to the most basic fact of our humanity. If you are rich enough, even death need not apply.[37]

---

[31]See Elaine Pagels, *Adam, Eve and the Serpent* (Harmondsworth: Penguin, 1988), chapter 6, for details of this debate.

[32]Ibid., 128.

[33]Ibid., xxvi.

[34]Harvey, *A Brief History*, 33.

[35]This viewpoint has not gone unchallenged in the years following the global financial crisis of 2008. See Michael Sandel's critique in *What Money Can't Buy: The Moral Limits of Markets* (New York: Farrar, Strauss, and Giroux, 2012).

[36]In September 2014, the online blog *Techcrunch* reported that scientists in Palo Alto were offering a $1 million prize to anyone who could end aging.

[37]It is probably no accident that Robert Ettinger created the Cryonics Institute at a time when neoliberalism was being consolidated as the new economic orthodoxy (1976). In 1979, Margaret Thatcher became UK prime minister, while Paul Volcker became chair of the US Federal Reserve. In 1980, Ronald Reagan became US president. All were committed to rejecting Keynesian economics

It is too early to say whether such procedures will succeed. Regardless, what they do reveal is something crucial about how *homo oeconomicus* approaches death. Those who commit to spending their money on such hopes pay little attention to how the success of such strategies would affect future generations: what happens to the already-stretched resources of the planet if the yet-to-be-born are also faced with the demands of the should-be dead? That we are part of an ecosystem, that from the perspective of the natural world we are not the isolated economic units of neoliberal theory, is refuted by the cryonicist as they push against the notion that death might reveal the limits to human striving. But this is about more than the individual cryonicist pursuing a radical solution to dying. What is revealed here is the more general problem of the neoliberal construction of subjectivity. Conceived in isolation from community and others, it is not surprising that some should take this notion into the battle with death. Neoliberal subjectivity is conceived as transcending family, friends, culture, and history. In cryonics this disconnect from the elements that ground subjectivity is simply taken a step further, the individual now focusing on life in a future world without these relational ties. Death is approached as a problem *for the individual,* the proffered solution being found in having the financial resources to combat it. Little discussion is had about whether death might be more than something to fear: that perhaps it might be read as a feature of life which reveals something significant about our humanity, and, crucially, about our need the one for the other.[38]

Vulnerability, mortality, and the sick body

How might consideration of death lead us to an understanding of what it means to live well *together*? Perhaps the best way into this theme is through consideration of vulnerability. There are different ways of understanding this feature of life, and I want to suggest that if we read it through the discussion

---

in favor of a free-market economics that was the method, but, as Thatcher noted, "the object [was] to change the soul" (Harvey, *A Brief History*, 22–23).
[38]Recently, Atul Gawande, an oncologist, has argued for this kind of discussion to be at the heart of medical practice (*Being Mortal: Illness, Medicine, and What Matters in the End* (London: Profile Books, 2014)).

of mortality we might be able to construct better ways of living than those currently offered by societies dominated by neoliberal paradigms.

What it means to be vulnerable takes on a particular shape under neoliberalism. We have noted the attraction of the claim that economic, social, or political factors need have little impact upon the extent to which anyone can be successful. If you utilize your talents and skills effectively enough, it is possible to rise above forces apparently outside your control. If you have shaped a sufficiently entrepreneurial self, adaptive to circumstance, you will not need an interventionist government to address inequalities arising from the economic system. This confident imaging of the self may be attractive, but it is not without its anxieties. Accepting responsibility for one's lot, not surprisingly, leaves many feeling vulnerable in the face of the expectation that they should be able to be the self-actualizing individual peddled by neoliberal politics and culture. Recent studies suggest something of the strain felt in societies basing social policy on this model, governments since the 1990s attempting to find ways of explaining the puzzling lack of correlation between increased affluence and a greater sense of well-being in the general population.[39]

Governments have struggled to cope with what might be called "the well-being deficit." That well-being is now measured alongside things like Gross Domestic Product says much about the importance successive governments have given to this. Social policy has been directed at addressing the fact that many struggle with the feelings of vulnerability that come with accepting the responsibilities necessary for being a successful neoliberal citizen. Governmental interventions in this area do not, however, include recognizing the limits to the responsibility one can reasonably be expected to bear for one's life. In practice, quite the reverse is true: in accepting the idea of the vulnerable self, state-sponsored interventions in schools and workplaces focus on cultivating resilience through teaching strategies which enable the individual to overcome their feelings of vulnerability in order that they *can*, indeed, become successful members of society.[40]

---

[39]See Richard Layard, economist and advisor to the New Labor government, for strategies promoting greater individual happiness (*Happiness: Lessons from a New Science* (Harmondsworth: Penguin, 2005)). That the source of much unhappiness might be found in the practices of neoliberalism Layard advocates is suggested by Ted Shrecker and Clare Bambra's *How Politics Makes Us Sick: Neoliberal Epidemics* (London: Palgrave Macmillan, 2015).

[40]Ecclestone and Hayes (Kathryn Ecclestone and Dennis Hayes, *The Dangerous Rise of Therapeutic Education*, London: Routledge, 2009) describe a number of interventions supported by New Labor policy makers for dealing with feelings of vulnerability, ranging from circle time in primary schools

Such strategies have not been without their critics. Kathryn Ecclestone and Dennis Hayes have challenged the promotion of the vulnerable self which, they claim, lies behind "therapeutic" forms of education focused on cultivating emotional well-being in students at the expense of cultivating knowledge. Much depends in their argument on identifying a trend toward "therapeutic education,"[41] and they draw upon accounts of the "diminished self," formulated by Christopher Lasch and Frank Furedi,[42] to support their thesis. In refuting the idea of the vulnerable individual, they aim to assert the cultivation of "aspiring, optimistic and resilient learners who want to know everything about the world."[43]

In rejecting the legitimacy of addressing vulnerability as an educational concern, Ecclestone and Hayes inadvertently reveal the connection between the values shaping the classical liberal construction of subjectivity that they reassert, and the values shaping the neoliberal self which they do not examine. By grounding the meaning of vulnerability in therapeutic practices, they underplay, crucially, its formation through an economic model which requires governments to address citizens' feelings of inadequacy and low self-esteem in order to create the resilient and adaptive subjects required by the contemporary workplace.[44] While noting that "political interest in people's emotional 'skills' and well-being is, of course, integral to the demands of the labor market,"[45] Ecclestone and Hayes do not pursue this theme, preferring to direct attention at what they consider to be the creeping influence of psychotherapeutic practices over the last forty years. As a result, they identify a crucial issue—vulnerability—but fail to explore its relationship to the stresses and strains of a world defined by a particular economic and social model that makes work the principal arena in which the successful life is to be constructed. Moreover, they neglect the effect of making the individual primarily responsible for cultivating the attributes necessary for success in that workplace. Far from being the fictional burden that Ecclestone

---

(28–31), peer mentoring schemes in secondary schools (55–57), through to staff development activities in the workplace designed to deal with stress and bullying (110–20). That many of these strategies survive in the Age of Austerity instigated by the Conservative-Liberal Democrat Government of 2010–15 says much about the strength of this cultural narrative.

[41]Ibid., viii–xv.

[42]Christopher Lasch, *The Culture of Narcissism* (New York: W. W. Norton, 1979), and Frank Furedi, *The Therapy Culture: Cultivating Vulnerability in an Uncertain* Age (London: Routledge, 2004).

[43]Ecclestone and Hayes, *Therapeutic Education*, back cover.

[44]Lisa Adkins, *Revisions: Gender and Sexuality in Late Modernity* (Buckingham: Open University Press, 2002), chapter 3.

[45]Ecclestone and Hayes, *Therapeutic Education*, 18.

and Hayes claim, the diagnosis of the vulnerable self tells us much about an economic paradigm that is not capable of supporting human flourishing.

Absent from governmental interventions designed to address feelings of vulnerability is the discussion of death and the lessons that might be drawn from its reality. Rather than attempt ways of overcoming "debilitating" vulnerability, an alternative approach might be to think of vulnerability as an appropriate response to acknowledging the *limits* of overcoming. In facing death we are forced to confront the ultimate vulnerability of every human subject. Tracing vulnerability back to death requires envisioning it less as an emotional response made by (some) individuals in isolation, and more as the ontological reality of human animals. Making this move necessitates thinking again about the kind of connections that might be made between self and other.

A useful way into this alternative way of thinking about the vulnerable self is found in Arthur Frank's work on chronic illness. Frank rejects medical interventions that tend to fragment the patient into a set of body parts in need of fixing. Instead, he wants to start *from* the perspective of the one who is ill, using their experience to transcend the "facts" of medical science that all-too-easily turn them into another case of a particular illness, rather than allowing them to be seen as a person in their own right.[46]

Frank's approach is not concerned with developing the kind of healthcare provision that focuses on the individual as "responsible" for their health and recovery. Instead, he connects the individual's suffering with an acknowledgment of relationship: "the disease that sets the body apart from others becomes, in the story [told by the sick person], *the common bond of suffering* that *joins bodies in their shared vulnerability.*"[47] Rather than pathologize sickness and chronic illness, Frank suggests allowing the stories told by the sick to shape understandings of our common life together. His account is particularly convincing as he is himself a person in remission from cancer.[48] The sick person is not an aberration set apart from the broad mass of healthy humanity; neither are they the passive recipient of care. Rather, they are someone with a story to tell about the human condition. Their story links to the stories we *all* might tell—indeed, most likely, *will* eventually tell—for it highlights the experience of being vulnerable beings

[46]Arthur Frank, *The Wounded Storyteller* (Chicago: University of Chicago Press, 1995), 7.
[47]Ibid., xi, emphasis added.
[48]Arthur Frank, *At the Will of the Body: Reflections on* Illness (Boston: Houghton Mifflin Harcourt, 2002).

in a mutable world. Therefore "any sickness is an intimation of mortality,"[49] for the suffering of the ill is "a common condition of humanity."[50]

If sickness is seen as a fundamental part of the experience of being human, Frank directs our attention to stories that we might not like to hear. If "restoration stories" can too easily be adapted to tales of "winning" and "losing" the battle with death, Frank's interest is with stories that do not lend themselves to such a neat story arc. In "chaos stories" we are confronted with experiences that defy the desire for happy endings. Told by the terminally and chronically ill, such tales reveal the "bulwark of remedy, progress and professionalism [cracking] to reveal vulnerability, frailty, and impotence."[51] As language breaks down in the chaos wrought by such illnesses, the assumption that death can be overcome is challenged, laying bare the fact that "in the midst of life we are in death." Human interventions can only do so much when faced with the reality of being mortal beings in a mutable world.

The sick body, then, acts as a reminder of mortality, a fleshier version of the traditional, skeletal *memento mori*.[52] In illness, we live with the reality of "lost control"; we live with the knowledge that responsibility for our life extends only so far. To be human is to be limited, subject to the constraints facing all animals. Chronic illness challenges the claim that the natural human state is to be capable and resilient; a view easily lending itself to the fantasy that death is an aberration, that we are—or should be—"immortal." When Pagels attempts to understand that perplexing victory of Saint Augustine's view that death is unnatural over the eminently more reasonable claims of his critics, she hits on the difficulty of accepting the limits accompanying mortality. With Saint Augustine, we prefer to "feel guilty [rather] than helpless."[53] Filtered through the optimism of the entrepreneurial self, this claim resonates even more strongly. To take responsibility for one's death sits comfortably with the narrative that tells us our destiny is shaped by our own endeavors. To accept that notion seems far preferable to the alternative, which is revealed in illness; namely, the reality of our dependence on a mutable, physical world.

---

[49]Frank, *The Wounded Storyteller*, 6.
[50]Ibid., 30.
[51]Ibid., 97.
[52]*Memento mori* ("remember you must die") was the medieval Christian practice of reflecting on mortality, as a way to convince oneself of the vanity of earthly life. —MM
[53]Pagels, *Adam, Eve*, 147.

Refusing to accept that there are limits to human existence is not without an impact on our relationships. In particular, it is felt by those who stand in close proximity to death. As Martha Nussbaum notes, to be sick or ill or dying carries with it the "sense of failure to achieve some ideal state."[54] That feeling of shame is met in the common response made by healthy others to the bodies of the sick, used as receptacles for displaced fears of their own failure, their own terror of death. Rather than face up to our own vulnerabilities, we project them onto the bodies of the ill, making it possible to ignore our fears by marginalizing the people who embody them. All of this comes at a price: in the desire to maintain the illusion of control, even over death, connection is lost with those who are suffering and dying. The tragedy of this lost connection is that one day, almost inevitability, our own illnesses, aging and dying will be similarly marginalized.[55]

Living well with death and loss

What happens if we begin, not with ideals of control, but with the experience of vulnerability that comes through acknowledging mortality? In what remains, I offer an approach that proceeds from that recognition of the inevitability of death. Foregrounding death enables a set of values to emerge that challenge neoliberal constructions of success, resulting in a different understanding of what it means to flourish as a human being.

Revisiting the history of philosophical engagements with death is useful for considering alternatives to the neoliberal avoidance of accepting mortality. If the practices of Stoic philosophy have been used to shore up the vulnerable self in order to create resilient subjects,[56] other aspects of its creed have not proven so acceptable to the neoliberal gaze. Central to Stoic

---

[54]Martha Nussbaum, *Hiding from Humanity: Disgust, Shame, and the Law* (Princeton: Princeton University Press, 2004), 184.

[55]Leo Tolstoy's *The Death of Ivan Ilyich* (1880) offers a powerful insight into this process at work. Ivan's friends see Ivan's illness and death as an *accident* that has befallen him, but that they will avoid through showing the requisite care that Ivan lacked. Where Ivan failed, they will be more successful. The result of this disaggregating of Ivan's experience from the possibility that they will one day be similarly afflicted is a false attitude towards Ivan that makes his experience incapable of genuine expression, contributing to the isolation he feels.

[56]Beverley Clack, "What Difference Does It Make? Philosophical Perspectives on the Nature of Wellbeing and the Role of Educational Practice," *Research Papers in Education* 27 (4) (2012): 497–512.

philosophy was the importance of facing death, a crucial part of the process by which one learned what it meant to live well. The right response to recognizing one's mortality was not petulant refusal but acceptance.[57] Coming to accept death is no easy matter: it requires reflective practice, [as in] the Stoic practice of "the spiritual exercise," an imaginative exercise where one contemplates death and comes to terms with its reality.[58]

To accept death's reality is to accept *limits*. Nothing lasts forever. In the face of death, all is, to echo Marcus Aurelius, "smoke and nothingness."[59] Marcus' words are bleak, a suitably dismissive rejection of the idea that fame or status or wealth could ever provide a secure basis for the good life. Yet the very bleakness of his words holds out the necessity of challenging models of subjectivity which evade grappling with the reality of mortality. To ground our hopes in material possessions or the garnering of glittering prizes is to lose the deeper possibilities of being human which emerge from recognizing that all is vulnerable to chance and change. When we recognize this fundamental vulnerability, we are confronted with that which neoliberalism is least comfortable with: dependence on world and others.

When the Stoic is confronted by dependence, their solution is to cultivate detachment from anything that might disturb one's tranquility in the face of death. To live well, one should not value too highly the things most vulnerable to loss in a mutable universe. The unfortunate consequence of such a viewpoint is that it suggests the individual is best advised to seek detachment from those among whom they live, for after all, all existent beings are subject to loss and death. This is not, however, the lesson we need draw from acknowledging the vulnerability of our status as existent beings. The things

---

[57]Seneca [Lucius Annaeus Seneca (c. 4 BC–65 AD), Roman statesman and Stoic philosopher—MM] berates those who would have life otherwise: "There's no ground for resentment in all this. We've entered into a world in which these are the terms life is lived on—if you're satisfied with that, submit to them; if you're not, get out, whatever way you please" (Seneca, Letter XCI in *Letters from a Stoic* (Harmondsworth: Penguin, 1969), 181–82).

[58]Again from Seneca: "Without anxiety, then, I'm making ready for the day when the tricks and disguises will be put away and I shall come to a verdict on myself, determining whether the courageous attitudes I adopt are really felt or just so many words ... Away with the world's opinion of you—it's always unsettled and divided. Away with the pursuits that have occupied the whole of your life—death is going to deliver the verdict in your case ... It's only when you're breathing your last that the way you've spent your life will become apparent. I accept the terms, and feel no dread of the coming judgment" (Seneca, *Letters*, 71). [Seneca himself obeyed an order from Emperor Nero to commit suicide.—MM]

[59]Marcus Aurelius, *Meditations* (Oxford: Oxford University Press, 1998), 97.

that are most vulnerable are precisely those things which are most valuable: our loved ones, children, friends.[60]

To accept the vulnerability of the things that make life worth living—to recognize that to love is also to be open to loss—necessitates developing a different solution to death than that offered by the Stoics. Thinking about the subject's vulnerability in the face of death directs the gaze toward the other with whom we are in relationship. If the neoliberal vision of subjectivity forces us to face death alone,[61] an alternative vision makes our shared vulnerability the basis for stronger relationships. As Frank says, "sooner or later everyone is a wounded storyteller . . . [T]hat identity is our promise and responsibility, our calamity and our dignity."[62] In accepting our vulnerability toward death, we recognize the need each has for the other.

In accepting the need we have for each other, a different focus emerges about how we might live together than that offered under neoliberalism. Rather than start from the belief in the resilient, responsible self fundamental to neoliberalism, we might start, instead, with the shared experience of being vulnerable, mortal subjects. Frank suggests such a starting point might lead us to reclaim the value of generosity toward the others.[63] Under the neoliberal paradigm, generosity has become indelibly attached to philanthropic giving.[64] In a world where resources are spread unequally, being philanthropic is undoubtedly better than being miserly or misanthropic. Yet to identify generosity exclusively with philanthropy is not unproblematic, as aspects of Nietzsche's critique of pity reveal. Rejecting Christian "slave-morality" in favor of cultivating strength and nobility, he notes that, "pity on the whole thwarts the law of evolution, which is the law of selection. It preserves what is ripe for destruction."[65] Such a view does not seem particularly helpful for the attempt to build an ethic based on shared vulnerability in the face of death. Where he is more useful for my purposes is when he turns his

---

[60]Nussbaum, *Hiding from Humanity*, 374.

[61]Zygmunt Bauman, *Mortality, Immortality, and Other Life Strategies* (Cambridge: Polity, 1992), 48–50.

[62]Frank, *The Wounded Storyteller*, xiii.

[63]Frank, *The Renewal of Generosity: Illness, Medicine and How to* Live (Chicago: University of Chicago Press. 2004).

[64]An example of this marketized view of generosity can be found in a comment of Margaret Thatcher's from 1980: "Nobody would remember the Good Samaritan if he had only good intentions. He had money as well." We might think of the billionaire philanthropists Bill Gates and Warren Buffet as examples of what Thatcher was getting at.

[65]Friedrich Nietzsche, *Twilight of the Idols/Anti-Christ* (Harmondsworth: Penguin, 1990).

attention to the complex motivations and emotions that attend to the expression of pity and the experience of being pitied.

For the one pitying another, "the thirst for pity is . . . a thirst for self-enjoyment, and that at the expense of one's fellow men."[66] Far from enabling a sense of solidarity with the one who is suffering, pity depends upon condescension. In the movement from the one above to the one perceived as below, Nietzsche spies "the pleasure of gratification in the exercise of power." He goes further: if the person we pity is "very close to us, we remove from ourselves the suffering we ourselves feel by performing an act of pity."[67] In pity Nietzsche identifies the attempt to distance self from other. The emphasis is on assuaging one's own feelings. There is, as a result, nothing noble about the act of pitying.

And the one who is pitied? Nietzsche suggests that the effect is to be rendered invisible to the other. To be pitied is to experience contempt for one's humanity: "pity is felt as a sign of contempt because one has clearly ceased to be an object of *fear* as soon as one is pitied. One has sunk below *the level of equilibrium.* "[68] This brings us to the heart of the matter: what happens to parity of relationship between the one suffering and the one who is not? Is it possible to create reciprocal relationships, the basis for the good society, if we enshrine pity in our version of generosity? To equate generosity with philanthropy is to accept the unequal starting point between the one who gives and the one who receives. Instead of *seeing* the sufferer, instead of hearing their story and recognizing in it our shared struggles, the bestower of pity overrides that story and "gaily sets about quack-doctoring at the health and reputation of its patient."[69] Pity becomes a means of asserting inequality rather than *assuming* equality of humanity.

Nietzsche's careful unraveling of the psychology of pity is persuasive. An alternative account of generosity is possible, if one begins with the shared experience of being vulnerable human beings standing in the face of death. Such an approach can be found in the writings of Nietzsche's erstwhile mentor, Schopenhauer.

In seeking the basis for morality, Schopenhauer rejects Kant's view that it is found in rational recognition of the dignity of the other. While Kant

---

[66]Friedrich Nietzsche, *Human, All Too Human* (Cambridge: Cambridge University Press, 1996), 39 (HAH I §50).
[67]Ibid., 56 (HAH I §103).
[68]Ibid., 322 (HAH: WS §50); emphasis added.
[69]Ibid., 229 (HAH 2: WS §68).

depends on an abstract construction of the individual, Schopenhauer bases his morality in the emotions, specifically in *experiencing* another's suffering as one's own. The basis for morality is in compassion for the other; in the *felt recognition* of a common humanity.[70]

Nietzsche denies Schopenhauer's compassion to be immune from the criticisms he directs at pity.[71] David Cartwright dismisses this claim, arguing that Nietzsche's pity and Schopenhauer's compassion are not one and the same. Cartwright draws attention to the relationship Nietzsche identifies between pity and contempt: there is no parity of esteem in pity. In Schopenhauer's account of compassion (or "fellow-feeling") "the other's misery assumes the same status as my own by moving me to relieve it."[72] When faced with the one who is suffering, "I feel his woe just as I ordinarily feel only my own."[73] I identify myself with the other. In making this identification, "the barrier between the ego and the non-ego is for the moment abolished."[74] In that first moment of looking in the other's face, I realize "an intuitive and immediate truth":[75] that the other's suffering matters as much as my own. There is nothing unusual about this experience: "it is the everyday phenomenon of compassion," of "participation . . . in the suffering of another."[76] Crucially, this fellow-feeling acts as a call to action. Generosity is called forth by recognizing the other's suffering to be *just as* important as my own.

Schopenhauer's account of compassion rests upon a far-reaching critique of the pretensions surrounding the process of individuation by which we come to believe ourselves separate from others and nature. Human life is miserable because we misrepresent our place in the world. Salvation from such misery lies for Schopenhauer in identifying and overcoming "the Will,"

---

[70]Schopenhauer extends this argument to animals, arguing that this compassionate feeling for a fellow being in pain should affect their treatment (Arthur Schopenhauer, *The Basis of Morality* (Indianapolis: Hackett, 1995), 179).
[71]See Robert Solomon, *Living with Nietzsche* (Oxford: Oxford University Press, 2003), 98, who accepts Nietzsche's claim that Schopenhauer's *Mitleid* ["pity"] does not convey the parity of esteem between sufferer and subject, represented by his own use of *Mitgefühl* ["compassion"] as a basic virtue.
[72]David Cartwright, "Schopenhauer's Compassion and Nietzsche 's Pity," *Schopenhauer Jahrbuch* 69 (1988): 557–67, 561.
[73]Schopenhauer, *The Basis of Morality*, 143.
[74]Ibid., 166.
[75]Gerard Mannion, *Schopenhauer, Religion and Morality* (Farnham: Ashgate, 2003), 19.
[76]Schopenhauer, *The Basis of Morality*, 144.

that "constant yearning simply to be."[77] In order to extirpate desiring, Schopenhauer advocates asceticism; but this does not mean the removal of our obligations to the other. If anything, our obligations become more pressing when we recognize that there is no difference between self and other:

> Every good or kind action that is done with a pure and genuine intention proclaims that, whoever practices it, stands forth in absolute contradiction to the world phenomenon in which other individuals exist entirely separate from himself, and that he recognizes himself *as being identical with them*.[78]

Seeing the nature of the world correctly means we will not see living well as something to be achieved apart from our relationships with others. The promotion of self-reliant neoliberal subjectivity makes it difficult to cultivate the sense of fellow-feeling at the heart of Schopenhauer's ethics. Where the successful life is understood to be cultivated through one's own endeavors, it is difficult to acknowledge the limits imposed on all subjects by the fact of mortality. As a result, the suffering of the other, a fellow traveler on the path to death, cannot easily be recognized.

A different model of subjectivity, grounded in the recognition of the dependence each has on the other is necessary to cultivate the fellow-feeling Schopenhauer places at the heart of his ethics. To recognize that we are all subject to death challenges the claim that humans are best understood as isolated economic units in control of their lives and destiny. We are, as Aristotle set down so many centuries ago, "social animals," and no more is that sense of solidarity more obvious than in the need to support each other in the face of death.

Conclusion

When neoliberalism aligns death with failure, it renders impossible discussion about what it means to be a mortal subject, standing as we all do in the shadow of death. Ignoring death's inevitability marginalizes the vulnerable and limits the ability to reflect on the fragility of life. By way of contrast, thinking about mortality has the capacity to restore a sense of

---

[77]Mannion, *Schopenhauer*, 3.
[78]Arthur Schopenhauer, *Parerga and Paralipomena*, Vol. 2 (Oxford: Oxford University Press, 1974), 219.

shared experience, allowing acceptance of death's reality to forge the basis for a new life together. When we look death in the face we are reminded of the things that emerge from our shared life—love, relationship, friendship, laughter—all vulnerable in a mutable world. Recognizing our shared vulnerability enables us to prioritize the things which help build connection and relationship, the things that are called forth as we look in the face of the other and see a fellow being whose suffering demands a response. In building again that social principle for understanding humanity we might go some way to addressing the anxiety that all too often emerges from the impossible models defining success which proliferate in neoliberal society. In thinking again about death, we might come to a better sense of what makes for the well-lived life.

For Discussion or Essays

- In the Introduction to our reading from Walpola Rahula in Part II, we encountered the First Noble Truth of Buddhism: life is *dukkha*. What bearing, if any, might the First Noble Truth have on Thomas Nagel's contention that death is always a misfortune?

- A related question: Nagel asserts (without much in the way of a supporting argument) that "experience itself," stripped of whatever might make life better or worse, is "positive." What are we to make of this term *experience itself*?

- In the quote from Giacomo Leopardi that appears at the beginning of the Introduction to Part V, we read that, "Death is not an evil, because it frees us from all evils, and while it takes away good things, it takes away also the desire for them." How might Thomas Nagel respond to Leopardi? With whom do you agree more? Explain.

- Nagel has argued that the symmetry argument should not dispel dread of death, because the question of my non-existence cannot be posed with reference to a period of time before I could exist. Moreover, he argues, the dread of death is justifiable because *we can imagine never more being aware of anything* for eternity. Are you convinced by either of these arguments? Why or why not?

- Samuel Scheffler's *collective afterlife* and Thomas W. Clark's *generic subjective continuity* both seem clearly to entail the end of a first-person consciousness, subjectivity, or experiencer. Clark and Scheffler add the compensatory consideration that *other* subjectivities or experiencers will continue to exist, to experience their lives as continuous, and to die while still others are conceived. Compare and contrast these two views.

- If a person faced with Scheffler's doomsday scenario were convinced of the Eternal Return, would this permit him or her to continue to live a "value-laden" life? Why or why not? What about a person faced with the infertility scenario?

- How might Epicurus respond to Clack's advice to "look death in the face," "prioritize the things which help build connection and relationship," and recognize our vulnerability, in order to "come to a better sense of what makes for a meaningful life"?

Further Readings on Living with Mortality

Anonymous. *The Epic of Gilgamesh*, in various translations and editions. Refer to the discussion in the Introduction to Part V.

Anonymous. *Satipatthana Sutta: The Foundations of Mindfulness*. In various translations, including a translation from the Pali by Thanissaro Bhikkhu. http://www.accesstoinsight.org/tipitaka/mn/mn.010.than.html (accessed September 1, 2013). Section II of this well-known Buddhist scripture recommends that a practitioner meditate on a corpse through the nine phases of its decomposition.

Dreyfus, Hubert L. *Being-in-the-World: A Commentary on Heidegger's Being and Time, Division I*. Cambridge, MA: MIT Press, 1991. In Division II of Part One of *Being and Time*, the German philosopher Martin Heidegger (1889–1976) presented his much-discussed notion of *Dasein* as "Being-towards-Death." This is not casual reading. In order to tackle Division II, it would be helpful to get a handle on Division I, and as far as I am aware so far, Dreyfus has produced the most accessible exposition of this part of *Being and Time*. For a very different evaluation of Heidegger on death, see Paul Edwards, "Heidegger and Death as 'Possibility'," *Mind* 84, no. 336 (October 1975): 548–66.

Epictetus. From *The Manual* or *The Handbook* (*The Enchiridion*), in various translations. Written around AD 60. The reader might compare what the stoic philosopher Epictetus has to say about anticipating death to what Lucretius has to say about it.

Khayyam, Omar. *Rubaiyat*, in various translations and editions. Some scholars describe Omar Kayyam (1048–1131) as a Sufi mystic, and others describe the Persian poet, mathematician, and astronomer as a follower of Epicurus. "One thing is certain, and the rest is lies," the poet wrote, "The Flower that once has blown forever dies" (Edward Fitzgerald trans).

Lu Hsun (Lu Xun). "Death," (trans. Yang Xianyi and Gladys Yang), reprinted in Phillip Lopate, ed., *The Art of the Personal Essay: An Anthology from the Classical Era to the Present*, 329–33. New York: Anchor Books, 1995. Lu Hsun (1881–1936), one of the greatest modern Chinese writers, wrote this essay in 1936, during his final illness with tuberculosis and bronchitic asthma. A month before he died, he wrote: "Hold the funeral quickly … do not stage any memorial services. Forget about me, and care about your own life—you're a fool if you don't."

Timpanaro, Sebastiano. *On Materialism*. London: Verso, 1980. The Marxist philosopher takes inspiration from Giacomo Leopardi, to present a naturalistic and materialist case for making peace with our mortality.

List of Readings that Appear in this Book

Acharya, Madhava. "The World Outlook of the People." In *Sarvadarsana Samgraha*, translated by E. B. Cowell and A. E. Gough, 1882. Available online: http://www.gutenberg.org/files/34125/34125-h/34125-h. htm#CHAPTER_I (accessed January 6, 2018).

Aquinas, Thomas. *Summa Theologiae*, translated by Fathers of the English Dominican Province, second and rev. ed., 1920. Available online: http://www.sacred-texts.com/chr/aquinas/summa/sum615.htm (accessed January 6, 2018). Our reading is from the First Part, Question lxxv, Articles 1–6.

Baker, Lynne Rudder. "Persons and the Metaphysics of Resurrection." *Religious Studies* 43, no. 3 (September 2007): 333–48.

Bergström, Lars. "Death and Eternal Recurrence." In *The Oxford Handbook of Philosophy of Death*, edited by Ben Bradley, Fred Feldman, and Jens Johansson, 167–85. Oxford: Oxford University Press, 2013.

Bortolotti, Lisa, and Yujin Nagasawa. "Immortality without Boredom." *Ratio: An International Journal of Analytic Philosophy* 22, no. 3 (September 2009): 261–77.

Chuang Tzŭ (Zhuangzi). *Chuang Tzŭ*, Chapter XVIII, "Perfect Happiness." Translated by Herbert A. Giles, 1889. Available online: https://en.wikisource.org/wiki/Chuang_Tzŭ_(Giles)/Chapter_18 (accessed January 6, 2018).

Clack, Beverley. "Constructing Death as a Form of Failure: Addressing Mortality in a Neoliberal Age." In *Immortality and the Philosophy of Death*, edited by Michael Cholbi, 115–34. London and New York: Rowman & Littlefield, 2016.

Clark, Thomas W. "Death, Nothingness, and Subjectivity." In *Humanist: A Magazine of Critical Inquiry and Social Concern* 54, no. 6 (November–December 1994): 15–20. Reprinted with kind permission of the author.

Darrow, Clarence. "The Myth of the Soul." In *The Forum* (October 1928): 524–33. The article appears here under the title "Next Stop Goofville."

Epicurus. *Letter to Menoeceus*, in Diogenes Laertius's *Lives of Eminent Philosophers*, translated by Peter Sainte-Andre, 2011. Available online: http://monadnock.net/epicurus/letter.html (accessed January 6, 2018).

Holmes, John Haynes. "Ten Reasons for Believing in Immortality." In
*A Modern Introduction to Philosophy: Readings from Classical and
Contemporary Sources*, edited by Paul Edwards and Arthur Pap, 3rd ed. 250–
60. New York: The Free Press, 1973. First delivered as a sermon in 1929 and
published as a book in 1929–30. Permissions granted by The Community
Church of New York, 2017.

Hume, David. "Of a Particular Providence and of a Future State." In *An Inquiry
Concerning Human Understanding*, edited by Charles W. Hendel, 142–57.
Indianapolis: The Bobbs-Merrill Company, 1955. The work was completed
in 1739–40.

Lucretius (Titus Lucretius Carus). *De rerum natura* [On the Nature of
Things], translated by Anthony M. Esolen, 91–121. Baltimore: Johns
Hopkins University Press, 1995. Our selection consists of Book III, entitled
"Mortality and the Soul."

Nagel, Thomas. "Death." In *Mortal Questions*, 1–10. Cambridge: Cambridge
University Press, 1979.

Plato. *Phaedo*, translated by Hugh Tredennick. In *The Last Days of Socrates*,
Harmondsworth, Middlesex: Penguin Classics, 1954. Reprinted in Edith
Hamilton and Huntington Cairns, *Plato: Collected Dialogues* (Princeton:
Princeton University Press, 1961), 40–98. Our selection consists of five
excerpted passages, from Stephanus numbers 64c–68c; 70a–72d; 72e–75e;
78d–80b, and 104e–105e.

Price, H. H. "The Soul Survives and Functions after Death." In *Immortality*,
edited by Terence Penelhum Belmont. Berkeley: Wadsworth Publishing Co.,
1973. Reprinted in Michael Peterson, William Hasker, Bruce Reichenbach,
and David Basinger, *Philosophy of Religion: Selected Readings*, 5th ed.
(Oxford: Oxford University Press, 2014), 489–96.

Rahula, Walpola. "The Third Noble Truth: *Nirodha*: 'The Cessation of *Dukkha*'."
In *What the Buddha Taught*, revised and expanded edition, 35–44. New
York: Grove Press, 1974 [1959].

Scheffler, Samuel. *Death & the Afterlife*, edited by Niko Kolodny. Oxford:
Oxford University Press, 2013. Our selection is from the first of Scheffler's
three Tanner Lectures, this one delivered at the University of California,
Berkeley, on March 13, 2012. The selection consists of the following sections
from Lecture 1, Part I: Sections 2, 3, and 4 (pp. 18–32), and Sections 7, 8,
and 9 (pp. 18–32 and 37–49). Reprinted courtesy of the University of Utah
Press and the Trustees of the Tanner Lectures on Human Values.

Unamuno, Miguel de. *The Tragic Sense of Life for Men and Nations*, translated
by J. E. Crawford Flitch, 38–57. New York: Dover Publications, Inc., 2005.
First published as *Del Sentimiento Trágico de la Vida* (1913).

Unknown. *Katha Upanishad*, translated by Eknath Easwaran. Copyright 1987,
2007; reprinted by permission of Nilgiri Press, P. O. Box 256, Tomales,

CA 94971, www.bmcm.org. The translator, Eknath Easwaran (1910–99), is the founder of Passage Meditation and of the Blue Mountain Center of Meditation in Tomales, California.

Unknown. *The Milinda Pañha* [*The Questions of King Milinda*], translated by T.W. Rhys Davids, Part I of II, Volume XXXV of *The Sacred Books of the East*, 1890. Available online: http://www.sacred-texts.com/bud/sbe35/sbe3504.htm (accessed January 6, 2018).

Williams, Bernard. "The Makropulos Case: Reflections on the Tedium of Immortality." In *Problems of the Self*, 82–100. Cambridge: Cambridge University Press, 1973.

Wolf, Susan. "The Significance of Doomsday." In *Death & the Afterlife*, edited by Niko Kolodny, 113–29. Oxford: Oxford University Press, 2013.

Index